Hope Lives

When Faith Meets Cancer

By Faye Mildred Dewhurst
With chapters by Dawn Ure
and preface by Wayne Dewhurst

xulon PRESS

There is never a time in life when one can be prepared to hear that ones' life itself is a matter of time.

PREFACE

There may be one of two reasons you have been inspired to pick up this book and then to flip open the front cover and begin reading. Either you are a friend or family member of the author, or you are someone who is in search of hope. Either way, the desire of the author is that you will find it—hope.

Faye 'Mildred' Dewhurst was a mom, grandmother, friend, mentor, wife and woman who found hope. Though the vehicle that she drove to find it was not the Rolls Royce we all wish would lead us there. It was the road travelled that led her to Hope; a twisted, rocky, pot-hole filled road.

Let me set the stage for what you are about to read over the next many days; and what you will discover if you truly experience the blogs written by my mother during her journey with cancer.

There are a few things that we all share in common in life, one of which is trouble. It is something we all find ourselves in at times in life. Faye knew trouble was all around her—in her family, business, morals, thoughts, emotions and financial life. At our worst moment we look for trouble for the pure adrenaline thrill that satisfies some superficial need. I know Faye experienced this satisfying of the sinful nature at times in her life as well. But most of the time you do not need to seek trouble; it finds you! Some of us seem to have trouble follow us closer than the newest electronic device. It is as if trouble is a best friend, and not by choice!

It is likely that the larger majority of the readers of this book are experiencing some trouble in life right now. Whether you stole your friend's parents' car and smashed it, or you have disregarded the advice of your parent, trouble has found you. Perhaps financially broken, emotionally distraught or even physically sick. We all experience trouble and we definitely feel the effects of loved ones' trouble! However, amidst the trouble that invades this life there is another thing that we all share in common—life itself.

The complexity of how life begins is astonishingly mind blowing. Whether it is the beginning of time at creation or at the time of conception the multitude of variables that need to be just right for life to exist is staggering. Yet life begins. Because of the supreme complexity of it, many scientists have commented that life itself is but an accident. An accident is something not planned and therefore you were not involved in. You had nothing to do with your birth, but your parents played a significant part.

Another shared experience we will have is death. It is for certain. Though I'm also sure that you are not planning to have anything to do with your death, in which your parents, at times, may have wanted to play a part. Perhaps, you know of some siblings who caused your parents to feel this way? Like life's beginning, death too is something in which you are not involved. If we are to think that life is an accident and death is as well, we could easily come to a quick conclusion that each of us is an accident suspended between two accidents—life and death.

More important than either of these two 'accidents,' is the road that attaches life and death. My mother travelled this road. It contained trouble on every turn. But the vehicle she drove was Hope. If ever we can allow ourselves to understand the purpose in trouble, hope is that vehicle. And further, this hope leads us to a faith in something greater than ourselves.

My mom's news of cancer in 2012 brought us all—family and friends—down a road of trouble to the discovery of hope and faith. In this life some will only ever experience trouble. They will journey the wretched road without purpose. Some may find hope in medicine, healing, or temporary satisfactions. But those who find hope and faith, in the midst of trouble, find what makes any person whole, and that is God.

You may ask and wrestle with similar difficult questions: "Why do bad things happen to good people?" Or "How does a loving, all powerful God allow suffering and trouble to percolate among us?" Let me leave you with this question, in which the answer is my mother's road travelled, "What happens when cancer meets faith?" My mother proved to me that in the end hope and faith can prevail, but only when that hope and faith is in God. When you face the most devastating news of your life or during a time of great trouble, it is a time for hope to live.

Listen to my mother's words. In an excerpt from her blog entitled "Hope Lives."

Hope is "to look forward with confidence or expectation" and believe me my friend, apart from God there is nothing but a dreadful and disheartened future. Finding hope requires that we take action, read, believe and have faith. We will not find hope by relying on our feelings but by solely depending on God for strength and believing Him to be not only faithful and loving but also in total control. Hope lives in Jesus Christ. Hope lives in His Word:

But now, Lord, what do I look for? My hope is in you. – Psalms 39:7, NIV

No one whose hope is in you will ever be put to shame. – Psalms 25:3, NIV

Remember your promise to me, for it is my only hope. – Psalms 119:49, NLT

Be strong and let your heart take courage, all you who wait for and hope for and expect the Lord! – Psalms 31:24, AMP

Be joyful in hope, patient in affliction, and faithful in prayer. My hope is in the Lord! I will be strong and wait on the Lord. – Romans 12:12, NIV

The following pages of this book are a true story of a mom who found a hope that drove her to faith—a faith in God. At first, a faith in God for healing and then a faith in God during hurting; a faith in the God who carried her home.

—Wayne Dewhurst

DEDICATION

To my children: Dawn, Mark, Wesley, Wayne and my husband John. God's abundant blessings have been immeasurable. I have every reason to be proud of each and every one of you for your distinct characteristics which God has created in each of you, and the ways you serve Him as you grow in Him as well.

The greatest blessing was having a committed husband, both to aid my spiritual walk and allow me to cultivate a family by being a stay-at-home mom. Praise the Lord.

My prayer is that you will honour God and model Christ in that you too will have a legacy of grandchildren being raised to know Him. May the light you shine before your own create an over-glow that carries others on the sidelines to the golden banks of heaven just because you love Him more than anything in this world. See you soon. I'll be waiting for you while I sing praises above the clouds.

To my grand-children: Jesse, Dalton, Brooke, Jordan, McKenna, Adam, Kaden, Lauryn, Tanner, Sarah, Austin, Brynn, and any more that may follow.

You brought me more joy than you can ever know. I love you bigger than the moon.

CONTENTS

❧

Contents

GOD, MY ROCK

❧

"The LORD is my rock, my fortress and my deliverer; my God is my rock, in whom I take refuge, my shield and the horn of my salvation, my stronghold." – Psalm 18:2, NIV

I have to admit that when I envision a 'rock,' it is not small. I would describe a rock as being bigger than a skipping stone, or a decorative stone you place in your garden. Though when you marvel at God's creation of the Rocky Mountains, Mount Rushmore or other infamous ranges, they are far beyond what I would call a rock. There is a very large rock in the middle of a nearby pasture, and the owner of the land attempted to remove it with dynamite, quite unsuccessfully. That's what I would call a rock. It measures approximately the magnitude of a mid-sized automobile, and that references only the portion that is visible above the ground. But when the scriptures refer to God as a rock, they are not denoting God's size but rather His stability or steadfastness. He cannot be moved.

There are several instances throughout scripture where the 'rock' was of great significance. God hid Moses in the cleft of the rock for his protection. During the wilderness wandering, God used a rock to provide water for the Israelites. Hannah used the rock to figuratively refer to God. "There is none holy as Jehovah: For there is none besides Thee, neither is there any rock like our God" (1 Samuel 2:2, ASV). David, in Psalms, mentions 'God as a Rock' roughly twenty four times. In reading Old Testament references, we can conclude that: God is our provider; God is our refuge; God is our fortress; God is our source of strength; God is our deliverer; God is solid, unchangeable and so much more.

Let's consider another verse recorded by David: "From the ends of the earth I call to you. I call as my heart grows faint; lead me to the rock that is higher than I" (Psalms 61:2, NIV). In desperation David expressed his great need for God when he prays, "from the ends of the earth." His fearful prayer indicates that he feels unsafe, uncomfortable, and far away from God. When we are overwhelmed, we often desire to run and hide hoping that ignoring the trial will help it go away. Perhaps we are weary and incapable of facing misfortune and find our human reserves totally empty, and we have doubts we will survive. This is not the time to flee, but rather do as David did, cry out for God's mercy. Petition that He would lead you to the "towering rock of safety," where the enemies will not find you and the floods will not drown you. Ask that He would place you in the cleft of the rock for protection. Don't' flee, don't fear, but trust and know there is a "rock that is higher." Amazingly, I don't remember the exact emotions experienced when I was first diagnosed with cancer, but I do recall the feeling of desperation. I was acutely hungry for accurate information, anxious for time to fly so treatments could begin, and fearful that the slight delay would allow the cancer to overtake my body. Like David, in my desperation I screamed for God's presence and begged for clear direction. He met me in my despair and was faithful to meet my needs. He is my provider and can be yours also.

If you find yourself overwhelmed by your trials and the challenges of life that stand before you, or if you are in a lonely place because you have strayed away from God, cry out to the 'Rock of Ages' and let Him lead you to 'the Rock that is higher.'

> Rock of Ages, cleft for me, let me hide myself in thee;
> Let the water and the blood, from thy wounded side which flowed,
> Be of sin the double cure; save from wrath and make me pure.

Prayer: Lord, help me not to be overwhelmed by my unwanted trials. Thank you for being faithful to meet me in my time of need. Give me the strength and wisdom to continually fall at your feet in weariness, knowing you are able to lift me up to the 'Rock that is higher' and find your comfort and your peace. Amen.

Tidbits:

> "My God is my rock, in whom I find protection. He is my shield, the power that saves me, and my place of safety. He is my refuge, my Saviour, the one who saves me from violence." – 2 Samuel 22:3, NIV

> "Prayer is a strong wall and fortress of the church. . ." – Martin Luther

> "The person who looks up to God rarely looks down on people." – Unknown

> "Refuse to be fearful about what will happen to you. God is faithful and He will take care of you if you trust Him." – Unknown

Song Selection: God, My Rock – written by Brenton Brown, Paul Baloche

GOD OF ALL COMFORT

"Praise be to the God and Father of our Lord Jesus Christ, the Father of compassion and the God of all comfort, who comforts us in all our troubles, so that we can comfort those in any trouble with the comfort we ourselves receive from God." – 2 Corinthians 1:3-4, NIV

The world seldom thinks that those of faith live a life of comfort, for they feel religion is full of uncomfortable demands, rules and regulations. They don't want to worry about their every move coming under judgment by community or world superiors, let alone a Holy God. However, for the Christian, the words 'comfort' and 'Jesus' are distinctly linked, and the love we receive from Him inspires feelings far beyond a mere expression of comfort. The believer, as he walks the pilgrim pathway, gets to know Christ deeper and uses prayer and the studying of his words to learn of His comforting Holy Spirit.

For arguments sake, let me demonstrate the wide difference of opinion between the world's and Christian's view of comfort. The world considers success or financial wealth the greatest of all blessings, yet to a believer the 'love' of money is the root of all evil. Their greatest treasure is the forgiveness of sins in relation to their salvation experience. The world believes bodily pleasure and physical comfort to be a great achievement, and while an intimate relationship is of prime importance to a Christian marriage, the actual bond of love between two people, whether it be spousal or simple friendships, is of higher priority. The world considers happiness, laughter and celebrating to be venues of comfort. On this point we probably don't totally disagree, yet there is a balance, as God commands us to do all things in moderation. We would be mindful to meet the needs of the afflicted, sorrowful and depressed by not immersing ourselves in selfish comfort but by helping them in whatever way we can to find 'comfort' and also peace by showing them they are loved by God. As Paul states in Corinthians, God is the God of all comfort, so what better comfort can we offer others or experience ourselves than the comfort of the Almighty and majestic God of the universe.

We know that being a Christian does not eliminate us from experiencing trials and troubles, but we should grow stronger through them, for it is during the storms that God supplies His greatest measure of comfort. "God is our refuge and strength, an ever-present help in trouble" (Psalm 46:1, NIV).

God is comfort in pain, weakness and hardship. "God of all comfort, who comforts us in all our troubles. . ." (2 Corinthians 1:3b). As Christians, being linked to Christ and God through the Spirit, we experience a comfort that can be matched by no other. God knows exactly the comforting relief that is needed to meet our distress. Whether our trials are trivial or severe, God always has compassion for us. Just like the attributes of God, His comfort is exceptional: boundless, eternal, unchangeable, and enduring.

Until my recent diagnosis of esophageal cancer, I didn't realize how immeasurable the comfort of God could be. I have daily relied on scriptural promises in the Word to remind myself and to reinforce decades of pastoral teachings of the comfort and peace that God has supplied. It has been totally amazing! As Christ was a comfort to His disciples in times of distress, He has met my needs as well. His mercies overflow and are new every morning! Through the Spirit, the divine Comforter, I have experienced many 'God moments' that leave me with no doubt of God's controlling hand and loving care. His love knows no end! So as I experience this season of life 'outside of my comfort zone,' I am lavishly comforted by my Lord and Saviour, Jesus Christ.

Prayer: Lord, you have promised that your Word would bring joy, comfort, and that in you my joy would be complete and your Word has been proven true. Thank you for endless comfort during this current trial and help me to share your love and comfort with others in their season of need. Amen.

Tidbits:

> "Even though I walk through the darkest valley, I will fear no evil, for you are with me; your rod and your staff, they comfort me." – Psalm 23:4, NIV

> "It was a huge comfort to have a person who'd keep you honest with yourself and who also gave you safe harbor." – Lauren Dane

> "For as we share abundantly in Christ's sufferings, so through Christ we share abundantly in comfort too." – 2 Corinthians 1:5, ESV

> "If you look for truth, you may find comfort in the end; if you look for comfort you will not get either comfort or truth. . . ." – C. S. Lewis

> "Sometimes, the best way to help someone is just to be near them." – Veronica Roth

Song Selection: Closer – written by Braden Lang, Jason Ingram, Joel Davies, Reuben Morgan; performed by Hillsong Worship

HE KNOWS MY NAME

"Now this is what the LORD says—he who created you, Jacob, he who formed you, Israel: "Do not fear, for I have redeemed you; I have summoned you by name; you are mind. When you pass through the waters, I will be with you; and when you pass through the rivers, they will not sweep over you. When you walk through the fire, you will not be burned; the flames will not set you ablaze." – Isaiah 43: 1-2, NIV

When I was first diagnosed with cancer, a close personal friend shared this passage from Isaiah, and by inserting my name within, it jumped off the page. It read, "Faye, I am the Lord who created you and who formed you. Do not fear, Faye, for I have redeemed you... etc." Personalizing scripture penetrates the heart deeper and underscores its importance.

Using a person's name immediately gets their attention. No doubt you have been in a crowd of people where there are various conversations and you hear your name mentioned. Are they talking about you, or trying to get your attention? Whatever the reason, the mere mention of your name causes you to stop whatever is occupying your mind at that moment. Your mind is swirling with curiosity and you find yourself cautiously eavesdropping on the other.

Studies have shown that you are most likely to remember comments when your name is mentioned. When we use formality in addressing people as Mr., Mrs., or Sir, etc., a behaviour of obedience and respect is understood just as using an informal style of a first name welcome communicates a more casual and friendly atmosphere. Personally, I have always had difficulty in addressing our pastors by their first names without prefacing it with their designation of 'Pastor,' and when I am introducing or referring them to others I usually address them with their full name.

My husband was a regular visitor to the local café assembly with other early bird caffeine 'cuppers' to shoot the breeze. Most of them knew each other by name; it wasn't unusual to greet each other with, "Hey, you," or "How are you, bud?" In fact, many nicknames were used, but there was one dude whose visits were sporadic as well as his memory, and he would greet my husband with, "Hey, You!" To this day he still addresses him with the same salutation, despite knowing His first name.

Nameless greetings are depersonalizing, for there is quite a difference in saying, "I love you," and "I love you, John." Try addressing the next store clerk, receptionist, or teller by their first name and see the favourable response. Even those with embarrassing names like Barker, Galahad, Vanslow, Flick, etc., are attentive when you take the time to acknowledge their individuality.

Jesus knows your name. Psalm 139 tells us: "God drafted the blueprint for my life before I was ever conceived; He knows me so intimately that before a word is formed on my tongue He knows it completely; He knows when I sit down and when I rise up; He knows every thought and the very numbers of hairs on my head (or at the moment the ones that were once there); He knows me and loves me beyond all measure. He keeps me from drowning in the waters of despair and the flames of fire will not consume me." What joy and security that Jesus knows me by name and I am not just a number or a dusty file in His filing cabinet. I am ransomed and redeemed; the Good Shepherd has my very name inscribed on the palm of His hands and in His book of life.

Prayer: Lord, thank you for calling and knowing me by name. May I show respect by addressing others properly and encourage them by speaking with them by name. Most importantly, help me to raise awareness that there is nothing more important than having their name written in the palms of your hands. Amen.

Tidbits:

> "The LORD called me from the womb; while I was still in my mother's body, He pronounced my name." – Isaiah 49:1, ISV

> "Don't tell your friends about your indigestion.' How are you' is a greeting, not a question." – Arthur Guiterman

> "I am the good shepherd; and I know those that are mine, and am known of those that are mine." – John 10:14, DBT

> "The one who is victorious will, like them, be dressed in white. I will never blot out the name of that person from the book of life, but will acknowledge that name before my Father and his angels." – Revelation 3:5, NIV

Song Selection: He Knows My Name – written by Tommy Walker

JESUS, TAKE THE WHEEL

"Direct my footsteps according to your word; let no sin rule over me." – Psalm 119:133, NIV

The song choice for today's devotion is about a young woman, who with her young child, was travelling to spend Christmas with her parents. She had made some earlier poor life choices and now found herself spinning out of control on a patch of ice, and in fear cried, "Jesus take the wheel."

I was immediately drawn to the message of the song for I knew it had a common denominator not only for me, but also for many members of my immediate family. Besides my children and grandchildren being 'hit in the stomach' by my declaration of having esophageal cancer, they all had various major hurdles they were facing in their own lives. One's parent-in-law was already battling bladder cancer. Two family businesses were facing closure due to the current economic recession. A third family business had two of three productive employees abandon them for higher wages. There was indescribable heartbreak as godly parents disappointedly watched a precious foster child's behaviour result in his transferal to another home. One adult was amid nine months of medical tests with hopes of revealing the 'whys' of multiple physical complications. A lifetime elementary school closure was requiring several children to be introduced, after eight years, to a new school several miles away. You can be sure that several of us were ready to shout the same chorus: "Jesus, take the wheel."

There is always a time in each of our lives when we feel we are hanging on by a thread. Our happiness seems to fade, the clouds crowd out the sun's warming rays, and we are waiting for the final axe to fall. Whatever is on your list to bring you to a point of desperation, I can guarantee you that God has an answer to your pleas and He already has control of the wheel.

Jairus was a Jewish leader, unlike the other leaders who did not follow Jesus, chose to put his trust in Him. He was frantic in his search for a physician to heal his dying child. His search was futile until He heard about Jesus, the Son of God, who was rumoured to have healed many others. He managed to convince Jesus to follow him home in order to heal his daughter only to be greeted with the devastating news that she had already died. Instantly, Jairus chose not to abandon his hope in Jesus and approached Him to heal her, and Jesus did. Jairus stepped out in faith despite putting his reputation as a Jewish leader at risk.

Despite the emotional, physical or spiritual frustrations listed, we cannot allow distress to prevent us from exercising our faith. Fears cause us to freeze up and focus erroneously on our own abilities instead of trusting by faith in the unmatchable abilities of God. We are encouraged to move forward in faith—which may involve some personal risk—and just believe. Believe that our life's challenges are not too big for Jesus to overcome. Believe that there is no sickness that He is unable to conquer. And know that we are never too sinful that we are not redeemable. Whatever has you stressed? Know that Jesus has always had the wheel and He will steer you straight to a path of safety.

Prayer: Lord, I trust you, and you alone to steer me in the right path. You will not allow my trials to overcome me, but you will provide me with the wisdom and strength to endure. I know that I can lay all my burdens at your feet and entrust my future into your hands. Thank you, for taking my wheel. Amen.

Tidbits:

> "And we know that all things work together for good to those that love God and are called according to His purpose." – Romans 8:28, NIV

> "Let us give thanks to the God and Father of our Lord Jesus Christ, the merciful Father, and the God from whom all help comes!" – Unknown

> "I am your God and will take care of you until you are old and your hair is gray. I made you and will care for you; I will give you help and rescue you." – Isaiah 46:4, GNT

> "Jesus, the only chauffeur to our mansion divine."
> – Unknown

> "When fear knocks on your door, answer it with faith." – Unknown

Song Selection: Jesus, Take the Wheel – written by James Brett, Hillary Lindsey, Gordy Sampson; performed by Carrie Underwood

PEACE OR PANIC

"I have said these things to you, that in me you may have peace. In the world you will have tribulation. But take heart; I have overcome the world." – John 16:33, ESV

As I reflect back on my life and try to think of a time when I felt sheer panic, the first recollection is a time in my teens when my boyfriend, John, now my husband, was trying to teach me how to try a stick shift. We were jerking along a peaceful country road while I attempted to get the hang of the balance of releasing the clutch and accelerating on the gas. It was obvious within minutes that there would be much to learn as we approached a railroad crossing. In those days we were required to stop at all rail crossings. I stopped and then proceeded only to stall out on the tracks, and before I could advance, I heard the train whistle. Panic! Despite having lived within 50 feet of a railroad for over eight years, that specific whistle frightened me to the core. Thankfully, John remained calm and patiently coached me forward in plenty of time to proceed off the tracks before the train crossed. Needless to say, I didn't spend much more time on clutch training that day.

At the beginning of this cancer journey, weeks before it was confirmed, an upper gastrointestinal exam revealed that there was a growth. In two weeks medical staff would reveal the biopsy results. The first three days following that exam compared to railroad track experience. Panic! A jittery phone call to my general physician didn't bring the peace that I was looking for, yet his advice to eat something calmed my physical shaking and a short-term mild sedative helped my nerves. On the fourth day I came to my senses and turned to the problem solver, Jesus! You could find me praying, reading the scriptures and spending endless hours listening to gospel music. I know I am not alone in being derailed, I was just searching in the wrong place for the peace I needed.

The Israelites panicked when the Egyptian army was angrily approaching, as there appeared to be no way to escape. Moses remained calm and said "Do not be afraid. Stand still, and see the salvation of the LORD, which He will accomplish for you today." (Exodus 14:13a, NKJV).

In Jesus' time, people reacted the same way as we do. Peter panicked when a servant girl approached him twice and a group of people accused him of being one of Jesus' followers. He remained in a state of denial until the rooster crowed for the third time and then he realized what he had done. The disciples were terrified when their fishing boat was threatened by the angry waves of a hostile storm. They awoke Jesus saying, "Lord, save us!" Jesus replied, "You of little faith, why are you so afraid?"

We all have times in our lives when are weak in our faith and we panic. Bereavement, financial worries, unemployment, failed health, divorce, the situations are endless. We can identify with the disciples in their plea, "Lord, save (help) me!"

Our human nature pushes us to panic instead of seeking peace. When you feel your anxiety intensifying and sheer panic approaching, do you cling onto God's promises? He watches over us always and He will not be found sleeping. "I lift up my eyes to the mountains; where does my help come from? My help comes from the Lord, the maker of heaven and earth. He will not let your foot slip; he who watches over you will not slumber; indeed, he who watches over Israel will neither slumber nor sleep" (Psalm 121: 1-4, NIV).

I thank God for His love for us and that He faithfully provides. He replaces: our panic with His peace; our anxiety with His calm; our weakness with His strength; our fear with His hope; and our loneliness with His presence. He promises to always be with us. Don't panic but choose His peace. Peace knowing that whatever comes our way, God has promised to never forget us, to always be our helper and strength and He always keeps His promises.

Prayer: Heavenly Father, thank you for your peace. Thank you that you have left us with the Holy Spirit who brings us comfort during times of fear, anxiety, and panic. Thank you for the promise that you will watch over me while I sleep. I praise your for your faithfulness to me. Amen.

Tidbits:

> "For the mountains may depart and the hills be removed, but my steadfast love shall not depart from you, and my covenant of peace shall not be removed," says the Lord, who has compassion on you." – Isaiah 54:10, ESV

> "Constant pressure and anxiety leads to fear and depression. Have faith in God. He will come to your rescue. – Unknown

> "May the God of hope fill you with all joy and peace in believing, so that by the power of the Holy Spirit you many abound in hope." – Romans 15:13, ESV

Song Selection: Praise You in this Storm – by Bernie Herms, Mark Hall; performed by Casting Crowns

PRAYER IS NOT A FEELING

"Do not be anxious about anything, but in every situation, by prayer and petition, with thanksgiving, present your requests to God." – Philippians 4:6, NIV

Prayer is supposed to be a distinguishing characteristic that marks us out as followers of Christ, but all too often, because of sin in our lives, we do not feel like praying. However, we should not trust our feelings when it comes to prayer, because our feelings can often betray us. Over the years I have known several people who would occasionally choose to miss church services because they didn't feel like going. Without pause, the devil accepted the invitation and stepped in to capitalize on those inaccurately assessed 'feelings.' Consequently, their attendance soon became sporadic, and shortly there afterwards they completely discarded their Christian life and any resemblance to it. Sadly, the devil entraps many Christians with 'feeling' excuses, and while God never will abandons us, we stray away from His Spirit and the result is a damaged testimony for ourselves as well as God.

Prayer should be a part of everyday life, and it can take on a variety of forms: adoration, requests, praise, confession, mediation, intercession, and thanksgiving. Prayer is a time to listen, to be quiet, to sing, to dance, and worship. It is not to be a grocery list where we confuse our needs with our greed but a time where we regain perspective on our relationship with Christ and to help it deepen. We pray to remind ourselves that God is God and we are not. There are countless reasons and ways to pray but, primarily, our motive should be one of obedience. God commands us to pray. "Pray without ceasing" (1 Thessalonians 5:17, KJV). Since God commands us to pray, then if prayer is not present in our lives we are living in sin and in disobedience.

Picture this: You have spent several years providing for your child, teaching him to grow to be responsible, and intelligent. There is absolutely nothing you have withheld or would withhold to help them in their time of need or to pave a way for a mature and profitable life, but that child opted to completely ignore your existence. You are basically dead to them.

Many of us parallel this story in that we claim to know God but don't ever talk to Him. Statistics show that even within the context of evangelical churches, there are more people who fail to pray than those who are fervent in prayer. There will be times you don't feel like praying, as well as times you will find yourself struggling with what to say, but if you wait until you feel like praying, you will probably never pray! Set aside time to pray if only to express your appreciation and thanks to God for His many blessings. Prayer is not intended to produce a change in God, but in us. Prayer is for our spiritual benefit and, after all is said and done, you will have no regrets for you will become more like Christ and you will have learned how to love.

Prayer: Heavenly Father, I come in an attitude of grief for I have caused you great pain in my lack of connecting with you. I may have an attitude of prayer throughout most of my day but I seldom come to you in quietness and 'be still' so that I can hear the whisper of your voice. Forgive me Lord, for my disrespect and absence. Continue to convict me of my deficiency in prayer and thank you for those times when the Holy Spirit has uttered petitions on my behalf. Thank you for not giving up on me despite my unfaithfulness. Amen.

Tidbits:

> "And without faith it is impossible to please God, because anyone who comes to him must believe that he exists and that he rewards those who earnestly seek him." – Hebrews 11:6, NIV

> "No man is greater than his prayer life. The pastor who is not praying is playing; the people who are not praying are straying." – Leonard Ravenhill

> "One day Jesus told his disciples a story to show that they should always pray and never give up." – Luke 18:1, NLT

> "The more you pray, the less you'll panic. The more you worship, the less you worry. You'll feel more patient and less pressured." – Rick Warren

> "The LORD is close to all who call on him, yes, to all who call on him in truth." – Psalm 145:18, NLT

> "Prayer is like water – something you can't imagine has the strength or power to do any good, and yet give it time and it can change the lay of the land." – Jodi Picoult

Song Selection: Make My Life a Prayer to You – written by Keith Green

BABY THAT CHANGED THE WORLD

"But when the time arrived that was set by God the Father, God sent his Son, born among us of a woman, born under the conditions of the law so that He might redeem those of us who have been kidnapped by the law. Thus we have been set free to experience our rightful heritage." – Galatians 4:4-5, MSG

Every now and then something happens, or someone initiates an idea that changes the whole world around it. I'll mention a few: Alexander the Great, the King of Macedon undefeated in battle and considered one of history's most successful commanders. Thomas Jefferson, primary author in drafting the American Declaration of Independence. Martin Luther King Jr., a most influential civil rights activist. Abraham Lincoln, civil war President, saved the union and brought an end to slavery. Adolf Hitler, a personification of human evil, responsible for the Holocaust and extermination of Jews.

In terms of events that changed the world, the Chernobyl disaster was the most alarming nuclear power plant catastrophe in history. The 1201 Mediterranean earthquake disaster killed over 1.1 million people in Egypt and Syria. The 1588 succession of storms that sank the Spanish Armada destroyed their attempt to invade England. The atomic bombings of the cities of Hiroshima and Nagasaki in Japan were conducted in the final stages of World War II in 1945. We cannot begin to exhaust the events that changed the world, but I can declare that more eventful than any is the birth of the baby that changed the world. Jesus Christ, son of God, born of Mary.

Christmas is a constant reminder of God's gift to us, teaching us that it doesn't take influential and dominant men to change the world for He provided an infant Son who changed the world. Christmas signifies the miracle of birth so unexpected that no one could imagine it happening. The Jews were awaiting a Messiah but did not expect Him to come as an infant but as a mighty ruler. Like the Jews, we should live life with a sense of expectancy because it is prophesied that Jesus will come again to redeem His own. Christmas shows us not to expect big things but that the best things of life can often be delivered in small packages. Don't wait for big answers from God, but search for God even in the smallest blessings He lovingly gives us. Know that whether you serve God in big ways or small, He will reward those who diligently seek Him, and we are all important in the spread of the gospel.

Christmas represents the greatest of miracles and, shamefully, even we as Christians have been caught up in the commercialism and worldly celebrations to such a degree that Jesus is just a tag-on to the events. Instead of worrying about the political correctness of "Merry Christmas" or "Happy Holidays" focus on placing Jesus in the front of your celebrations. "Has he changed your life? If He has, then why not share that fact during this time of year when the world is more sensitive and tolerant of a Christian presence. There is absolutely no worldly event, of an idea conceived by man or natural disaster that will ever have the magnitude of change that this baby, Jesus Christ, did. His changes are eternal.

Prayer: Loving and merciful God, I open my heart to your Spirit. May Christ's light and love flood my soul. Thank you for your gift of life and faith provided through your Son. I'm grateful that the Christmas story is personal to me, to celebrate your birth and help me openly share the wonder of your love. Amen.

Tidbits:

> "But miracles still happen, even if we don't think they do."
> – Diet Eman

> "For to us a child is born, to us a son is given, and the government will be on his shoulders. And he will be called Wonderful Counselor, Mighty God, Everlasting Father, Prince of Peace."
> – Isaiah 9:6, NIV

> "We should live our lives as though Christ was coming this afternoon." – Jimmy Carter

> "Therefore the Lord himself will give you a sign: The virgin will conceive and give birth to a son, and will call him Immanuel."
> – Isaiah 7:14, NIV

> "In Christ, for the first time, we see that in God himself there exists—within his inseparable unity-the distinction between the Father who gives and the Gift which is given (the Son), but only in the unity of the Holy Spirit." – Hans Urs von Balthasar

> "This will be a sign to you: You will find a baby wrapped in cloths and lying in a manger." – Luke 2:12, NIV

Song Selection: This Baby – written by Steven Curtis Chapman

AUDIENCE OF ONE

"Work willingly at whatever you do, as though you were working
for the Lord rather than for people." – Colossians 3:23, NLT

Are you a people pleaser or a God pleaser? People pleasers do these things: avoid conflict; worry about hurting other's feelings; do more than their share; rarely make decisions; attract people needing rescue; feel insecure about their abilities; easily volunteer and seldom decline; overly apologetic; bend over backward for others; feel guilty about being inactive; and seldom express their own opinion for fear of rejection. People pleasers live life disappointed because pleasing everyone just isn't humanly possible. They are often taken advantage of or taken for granted.

Many characteristics of a people pleaser should parallel with that of being a God pleaser with the difference being revealed in the motive. The deeds of kindness should be expressed with a servant's heart in love and not in an attempt to gain the approval of mankind. Personally, during the years that I led worship, it was a challenge to have upright motives in pleasing an audience of one (God) instead of looking for the praises of man. It was necessary to remind myself regularly that we are not here to entertain or to impress the congregation but to worship God. We always need to be evaluating our attitudes, motives, thoughts and actions against scripture. In order to be a God-pleaser, one needs to walk in obedience and serve with a sincere heart so that the love of God is evident and the unconditional, divine love He has for others shines through.

What exactly pleases God? Put simply it is discerning between good and evil and walking obediently in worship of Him. We need to realize when we live our life for the "Audience of One," our upright conduct will not be readily accepted by the world; in fact you may face rejection and persecution, but God is pleased when we set ourselves apart from the world. "Do not conform to the pattern of this world, but be transformed by the renewing of your mind" (Romans 12:2a, NIV).

When you come before God in prayer, He is pleased when you ask Him for the right things, requests that align with His will for you. "If you remain in me, and my words remain in you, ask whatever you wish, and it will be done for you" (John 15:7, NIV).

God sees and knows everything about us and He is pleased when we do not attempt to hide from Him or deceive Him but to live honestly and focus on doing everything for His glory. "So, whether you eat or drink, or whatever you do, do all to the glory of God" (1 Corinthians 10:31, NIV)

In Matthew we are warned about performing acts of kindness and our walk of obedience in vagueness. We are not to be dramatic or theatrical in our service, or to boast about our gifts to God, and when we pray, to avoid public display. "Be careful not to practice your righteousness in front of others to be seen by them" (Matthew 6:1, NIV) "Give your gifts in private, and your Father, who sees everything, will reward you. (Matthew 6: 4) "And when you pray, you must not be like the hypocrites. For they love to stand and pray in the synagogues and at the street corners, that they may be seen by others" (Matthew 6:5)

As for me, I opt to perform to an Audience of One, and be a God-pleaser.

Prayer: Heavenly Father, may the praise of my mouth and the actions from my heart be found in obedience with your will and find my motives honest and just so that your name is glorified. Amen.

Tidbits:

"Do not neglect to do good and to share what you have, for such sacrifices are pleasing to God." – Hebrews 13:16, ESV

"Ultimately, we live our lives before an audience of one. It is what He thinks that counts the most." – Dr. James L. Wilson

"And whatever we ask we receive from Him, because we keep His commandments and do what pleases Him." – 1 John 3:22, ESV

"Today Lord I am going to do my best with Your help and for Your glory. . . I will concentrate on being a God-pleaser and not a self-pleaser or man-pleaser." – Joyce Meyer

Song Selection: Audience of One – written by Michael Weaver; performed by Big Daddy Weave

BEAUTY BEYOND SKIN DEEP

"Do not look on his appearance or on the height of his stature, because I have rejected him. For the LORD sees not as man sees: man looks on the outward appearance, but the LORD looks on the heart." – 1 Samuel 16:7, ESV

Without realizing it, the value of outward beauty is stimulated as soon as we are born. Infants or toddlers are wheeled about in designer strollers, and passersby are quick to say, "What an adorable little girl," or "What beautiful baby blues your son has." Even the storybooks we read to our children, such as *Beauty and the Beast* and *The Ugly Duckling* will unintentionally communicate that we should be 'pleasing to the eye.' The pressure to be beautiful is compounded as we age, and with each season of life, different beauty expectations are suggested by 'Hollywood type' media. The world's view of beauty is based entirely on one's external appearance.

Particularly, as women, we quickly fall prey to the beauty snare and are alert to observe fresh hairstyles, new designer fashions to wear, and often we are quite willing to go to extreme lengths to achieve them. Even if prancing from salon to salon and from boutique to boutique makes us outwardly beautiful, the effect wears off in a few days. Beyond the adorning of a 'quick fix' to our outward appearance, thousands seek to change physical characteristics and, consequently, plastic surgery is an ever growing business not just only for the rich and famous anymore. A problem with placing our personal values in alignment with the world is that often Hollywood images are false and are digitally enhanced, portraying a beauty criterion that is nearly impossible. At the end of the day, everyone wants to look better; however, looking beautiful from God's point of view begins on the inside, not the outside.

While God has designed us to appreciate beauty, design and order, we are repeatedly instructed in scripture not to place our emphasis on 'the braiding of our hair,' so to speak. During my battle with cancer, I was quick to recognize that any outward beauty that I believed myself to have was not only vain and hopeless, but extremely temporary. The chemotherapy treatments resulted in hair loss and the surgeon's strict instructions not to lose any weight at all thwarted any hopes I had of slimming down the pounds I'd gathered over the years. After almost a lifetime of obsessing with my body's exterior, and in particular my weight, being a couple of sizes larger than my slim sister, I now needed to transform my thinking.

"Don't become like the people of this world. Instead, change the way you think. Then you will always be able to determine what God really wants-what is good, pleasing, and perfect" (Romans 12:2, GW).

The Bible does not say that the outer appearance doesn't matter, but we should not let it become an obsession. Don't let a concern for beautification substitute the heavenly importance of matchless inner beauty which is an honest and durable impression that far outshines what is physically seen. When you feel inadequate, unlovely and rejected for how others see you, remember that you should be focusing on your God-worth, not your self-worth. You are His treasure, His creation!

Prayer: Heavenly Father, I am amazed to think that you know how many hairs are on my head, and that you love me just how you made me. You work on my inner beauty by exchanging my ashes for a crown, turn my sorrow into praise, and deliver victory over setbacks. Might I continually cultivate a quiet and gentle spirit representative of treasured inner beauty that will forever outweigh any attempts to attain outward beauty? As your Spirit works within my heart peel away the deposits of vanity and pride and mold me into a woman 'who fears the Lord." Amen.

Tidbits:

> "Charm is deceptive, and beauty is fleeting; but a woman who fears the LORD is to be praised" – Proverbs 31:30, NIV

> Some people, no matter how old they get, never lose their beauty—they merely move it from their faces into their hearts. – Martin Buxbaum

> "No matter how plain a woman may be, if truth and honesty are written across her face, she will be beautiful." – Eleanor Roosevelt

> "Therefore we do not lose heart. Though outwardly we are wasting away, yet inwardly we are being renewed day by day." – 2 Corinthians 4:16, NIV

Song Selection: Beautiful – written by Barry Graul, Bart Millard, Brown Bannister, Dan Muckala, Jim Bryson, Mike Schuechzer, Nathan Cochran, Robby Shaffer; performed by MercyMe

BLOOM WHERE
YOU ARE PLANTED

"The wilderness and the dry land shall be glad; and the desert shall rejoice, and blossom as the rose. It shall blossom abundantly, and rejoice even with joy and singing." – Isaiah 35:1-2, ASV

"**B**loom where you are planted!" Here's a popular phrase used in sermons today. It never ceases to amaze me how weeds manage to flourish in the weirdest of places. From minute cracks in pavement to the seams of eaves troughs and yet we can plant, fertilize and water a particular seed or bulb in fertile soil to no avail.

In Luke 8, in the parable of the sower and the seed, Jesus spoke about the types of the soil and the outcome of each. The first was hardened soil where the seed fails to penetrate deep enough to produce any root and lies unchanged and easily snatched up by the birds of the air. The second is rocky soil where the seed take takes root quickly, but lacking soil depth and sufficient moisture, it terminates just as quickly as it began. The third soil is thorny and while the seed has found sufficient depth, nutrition and moisture, it is soon choked to death by the surrounding thorns that are flourishing. The final soil is fruitful and the seed has found all the necessary ingredients to produce a bountiful crop.

Hardened soil represents people who peddle through the Christian life in their own strength without taking root in Christ. They may be impressed with moral living and feel good about themselves for doing so, but they are quickly snatched away by the devil's next trap. Rocky soil represents those who have attempted to grow, even possibly finding momentary root and minimal moisture for temporary sustenance, but are spindly and spineless and wither under heat and pressure. Thirdly, we have thorny soil where people have attended church, perhaps for years, but have listened with their ears but not their heart. They lack understanding of the Word, conviction in their heart, and are present in body but absent in spirit. They are simply choked out of existence by the wiles of the devil. Lastly, there's the fruitful and fertile soil where a true believer has taken root and with a responsive mind, a hearing ear and a willing attitude, they tend to the seed faithfully and flourish with fruit for Christ.

We are not responsible to grow the branches, leaves or flowering buds for our spiritual tree; the root system and the core structure of our tree is the work of Christ. But the production of fruit is our responsibility. Producing fruit is a life-time procedure, but with transformed lives and maturing behaviour, each year of growth will bear more fruit such as joy, peace, kindness, goodness, generosity, gentleness, faithfulness, modesty, self-control—the fruit of the Spirit. Many Christians fail miserably where they are planted. Forget about blooming, sometimes they choose to be planted where they can't even survive. A good root system requires being rooted in God's Word. Properly measured with faith, it will produce in good time. If you are not rooted in Christ the best time to plant is now and begin to "Bloom Where You Are Planted!"

Prayer: Lord, when the roots of my life are not spreading throughout the world as you have planned, send your moisture and help me to flourish right where I am. Help me to find the exact spot in the garden where my buds will bloom consistently and change the landscape for your glory. May my blossoms produce a fragrance and sweet aroma that is pleasing to you. May I always be found on the sunny side of the garden. Amen.

Tidbits:

"Bloom Where You Are Planted." – Mary Engelbreit

"My people will again live under my shade. They will flourish like grain and blossom like grapevines." – Hosea 14:7, NLT

"In his days may the righteous flourish and prosperity abound till the moon is no more." – Psalm 72:7, NIV

"Trying to do the Lord's work in your own strength is the most confusing, exhausting, and tedious of all work. But when you are filled with the Holy Spirit, then the ministry of Jesus just flows out of you." – Corrie ten Boom

"The righteous will flourish like a palm tree." – Psalm 92:12, NIV

"For evil to flourish, it only requires good men to do nothing." – Wiesenthal

"The flower that blooms in adversity is the rarest and most beautiful of all." – Walt Disney Company

"All the flowers of tomorrow are in the seeds of yesterday" – Proverb

Song Selection: For Your Splendour – written by Christy & Nathan Nockles

DON'T WORRY, BE HAPPY

"Consider the ravens: They do not sow or reap, they have no storeroom or barn; yet God feeds them. And how much more valuable you are than birds! Who of you by worrying can add a single hour to your life?" – Luke 12:24-25, NIV

"Why me... why this... why now?" These are very common questions each one of us asks when we are facing difficulties and trials. Depending on the severity of the challenge you are facing, your questions may be more detailed. "How do I ever stand to find gainful employment during this recession?" or "Why am I left to suffer with infertility while mothers give birth to children they don't love?" and even "What in the world am I going to do now that my husband has left me with all these bills?"

One can spend countless hours worrying about their challenges and at the end of the day there are still no solutions. Worry is like running on a treadmill; you walk, run, sprint, and after exerting all that energy, you are no further than when you first started. Worry is a waste of time for it is said that more than forty percent of what we worry about never happens. Rick Warren says, "Worry is the warning light that God is really not first in my life at this particular moment." Because worry says that God is not big enough to handle my troubles.

Trouble and difficulty come to everybody and being a Christian does not exempt us from trials. Troubles are inevitable and are not something we can opt out of. Disease, loneliness, suffering, bankruptcy, sickness, unemployment, and trials of every kind afflict the confident and the humble, the rich and the poor, the just and the unjust, people at every level of society face troubles and worry. Worry is damaging to your physical health because it adds stress, raises your blood pressure, and causes ulcers and lack of sleep. James 1:2, NIV challenges us to "Consider it pure joy, my brothers, when you meet trials of various kinds." This is quite contrary to the way the majority reacts to their troubles. To James, faith is a commitment to the will of God. We may not want to acknowledge this truth, but troubles are purposeful. "For our light and momentary troubles are achieving for us an eternal glory that far outweighs them all."

As we grow in our faith, while we don't seek to find trouble, nor do we choose to suffer, we realize that the dividends of enduring the trial are greater than the discomforts we endure, so we choose to rejoice. We may not know exactly what God's long term plan is for allowing our current trials, but we do know that "the testing of our faith develops perseverance," and will shape and mould us to mature faith. (James 1:2, ESV, 2 Corinthians 4:17, NIV)

God has been faithful to care for the ravens of the air and the lilies of the field, they do not toil nor do they worry about their survival, so we, who are far more important than they are, need to trust Him. Jesus wants us to take our eyes off of our problems and put them on Him for He who created life in you can be trusted with the details of that life. Trusting God to provide eliminates the need for worrying. So don't worry, be happy because:

"For I know the plans I have for you," says the Lord. "They are plans for good and not for disaster, to give you a future and a hope." Jeremiah 29:11, NLT

Prayer: Heavenly Father, I thank you for your faithfulness in caring for me. I am grateful for the promise that you are taking care of all things. I need not worry. Help me to consider each new day with whatever happens in complete joy for all things are from your hand. Amen.

Tidbits:

> "Now to him who is able to do far more abundantly than all that we ask or think, according to the power at work within us." – Ephesians 3:20, ESV

> "The more you pray, the less you'll panic. The more you worship, the less you worry. You'll feel more patient and less pressured." – Rick Warren

> "The Lord hears his people when they call to him for help. He rescues them from all their troubles." – Psalm 34:17, NLT

> "Whatever is going to happen will happen, whether we worry or not." – Ana Monnar

> "And this same God who takes care of me will supply all your needs from His glorious riches, which have been given to us in Christ Jesus." – Philippians 4:19, NLT

> "If the problem can be solved why worry? If the problem cannot be solved worrying will do you no good." – ntideva

Song Selection: God Is Able – written by Ben Fielding, Reuben Morgan; performed by Hillsong

FACING DISAPPOINTMENT

"We can rejoice, too, when we run into problems, (disappointments) and trials for we know that they help us develop endurance. And endurance develops strength of character, and character strengthens our confident hope of salvation. And this hope will not lead to disappointment. For we know how dearly God loves us, because He has given us the Holy Spirit to fill our hearts with His love." – Romans 5:3-5, NLT

Disenchantment, dissatisfaction, disillusionment, and displeasure can be wrapped up in one word, Disappointment. When facing disappointment, one often feels their life is falling to pieces and the frustration and pain they are feeling is almost unbearable. Our flattened dreams could be a result of an unrealistic expectation of another, a business deal crumbling, or perhaps a special promise made that was broken. Sometimes our disappointment is of our own hands, but for the believer, disappointment does not have to be a tragic event. Even when we are centered in God's will, we can face disappointments, but the key to facing disappointments is having a proper focus. Where is your focus?

The key in facing disappointment is to keep our focus on God. If we maintain a godly focus and place our desire in alliance with God's will, whatever comes, good or bad, we know it comes from God. He always has our best interest in mind and answers our prayers. The answer may be no, but only because He knows our desire may lead to loss and He has something better for us. God may allow disappointments so that we will strive to rise above them and accept them with grace, or to force us to realize that He is more than sufficient to help us through them. Every disappointment has a purpose. "Count it all joy when you fall into various trials knowing that the testing of your faith produces patience. . . That you may be perfect and complete, lacking nothing" (James 1:2-4, NKJV).

There were many heroes in the Bible who met with disappointment, some of whom were even Christ's chosen disciples. They had followed Jesus for years and participated closely in His ministry and they witnessed many miracles, and yet as the veil was torn and Christ was crucified, they fled in fear and believed their purpose of ministry had ended. However, their disappointment met with elation when they realized that Jesus had been raised from the dead.

The resurrection had provided them abiding hope, for death had not conquered their Saviour and it would not conquer them. Their life's purpose wasn't over, it was just beginning. They realized that neither the years they had spent with Jesus in ministry, nor what would continue in His name was in vain, but was actually an investment in their eternal future. Put your faith in the Almighty and expect Him to open closed doors, and He will strengthen you through your disappointments and to lead you to victory.

Prayer: Lord there have been many disappointments in this battle against cancer. Delays, changed appointments and derailed medical plans, but the daily assurance of you being in total control of my journey and the outcome makes all these disappointments bearable. You are faithful and I thank you for carrying me, comforting me and for holding me close to you as I continue my journey. Amen.

Tidbits:

> "Blessed is the man who perseveres under trial; for once he has been approved, he will receive the crown of life which the Lord has promised to those who love Him." – James 1:12, NASB

> "If you're betrayed, release disappointment at once. By that way, the bitterness has no time to take root." – Toba Beta

> "Help me God, as you promised, so that I may live. Do not turn my hope into disappointment." – Psalm 119:116, GW

> "We must accept finite disappointment, but never lose infinite hope." – Martin Luther King, Jr.

> "The disappointment has come - not because God desires to hurt you or make you miserable or to demoralize you or ruin your life or keep you from ever knowing happiness. He wants you to be perfect and complete in every aspect, lacking nothing. It's not the easy times that make you more like Jesus, but the hard times." – Kay Arthur

> "Our best successes often come after our greatest disappointments." – Henry Ward Beecher

Song Selection: I'm Standing on the Rock – written by Harold Lane

FORGETFULNESS

"Be careful that you do not forget the LORD your God . . ."
– Deuteronomy 8:11, NIV

I f you have a family member who is 'over the hill' or you are blessed to be living in your gray and silver years, you have probably heard the phrase "having a senior moment." This phrase is often used when a person has forgotten to follow through on something and is offered as a humorous excuse. Many times busy people are juggling too many balls or have too much going on and their brain is so overloaded with details that some of them slip though their brain waves. Those of us who are dealing with cancer often forget things and echo "Chemo Brain."

Recently I missed two very important dates on my calendar even though I had also entered them into my cell phone calendar, and I humbly had to apologize for the oversight. My excuse couldn't be blamed on having a senior moment, chemo brain, or that I was too busy, for my days were mostly uneventful and my chemo treatments were over three months before. This forgetfulness so bothered me that I researched some recent health ailments and discovered that an inactive thyroid was the guilty party. Besides my findings, it served as a 'light bulb' moment to remind myself to post dates in plain sight.

We all make commitments and promises with good intentions, but we often fail. Such was the case of Joseph, a member of the Israelites. Joseph went from being comfortable with his family to being thrown in a pit and rescued by traders. Then he found favour with the Pharaoh but rejected advances from the Pharaoh's wife who then falsely accused him of making sexual advances. He was jailed and while there befriended the butler and interpreted his dream. Joseph reassured the man that he would be found innocent of the alleged crime. In return, Joseph asked, "But when all goes well with you, remember me and show me kindness; mention me to Pharaoh and get me out of this prison" (Genesis 40:14, NIV). Yet he forgot all about Joseph and it was two long years that he waited for his release from prison. I guess you might call this an "out of sight, out of mind" situation. Being the recipient of a dismissed commitment, a broken promise, or to be plain forgotten is painful and causes us to mistrust the pledger. It puts a strain on relationships. Though forgetfulness is not all bad, it has the ability to help us put to temporary rest the past pain and failures in our life. If we had constant recollection of those things, we would find life almost unbearable. It is also beneficial to us to forget the times we have been offended and offer forgiveness to them. "Brothers, I do not consider that I have made it my own. But one thing I do: forgetting what lies behind and straining forward to what lies ahead" (Philippians 3:13, ESV).

Forgetfulness is a problem that we all experience and, regretfully, many people today have forgotten God. Even when they do remember Him, they offer empty devotions and traditional practices. Even as Christians we forget to include Him in day-to-day decisions, seek Him for solutions to our problems. or many our fervent love for Him has dwindled as we slowly allow the world's values to invade our conscience. God desires our love, our attention and our company. He is ever faithful to tend to our personal concerns and needs, and will refresh and restore those who seek him with repentant and loving hearts. God will never need an excuse such as being too busy, having a senior moment and or saying, "out of sight, out of mind" for thankfully, God does not ever forget us.

Prayer: I praise you, Lord, for your forgiveness to me and that your love is not dependent on my behaviour. Your faithfulness during my cancer journey has been more than amazing and prayerfully as I recover the instances of forgetfulness will decrease and my love and trust will be increased. Amen.

Tidbits:

> "My son, do not forget my teaching, but keep my commands in your heart, for they will prolong your life many years and bring you peace and prosperity." – Proverbs 3:1-2, NIV

> "Praise the LORD, my soul, and forget not all his benefits, who forgives all your sins and heals all your diseases, who redeems your life from the pit and crowns you with love and compassion, who satisfies your desires with good things so that your youth is renewed like the eagle's." – Psalm 103:2-5, NIV

> "Don't treat people with disrespect and hope that one day they will still respect you back. It does follow how you treat another becomes a memory to them. They may forgive you but they will never forget." – Rubyanne

> "God is not unjust; he will not forget your work and the love you have shown him as you have helped his people and continue to help them." – Hebrews 6:10, NIV

Song Selection: I'll Not Forget You – written by Charles Barth, Bryan Duncan

GIVE THANKS

"Giving thanks is a sacrifice that truly honours me." – Psalm 50:23, NLT

"Be thankful in all circumstances, for this is God's will for you who belong to Christ Jesus." – 1 Thessalonians 5:18, NLT

Giving thanks to God in all situations is not an easy task. When our bodies are writhing in pain, our hearts overcome with grief, or our minds overwhelmed with worry, our first reaction is not to fall on our knees and give thanks. We may fall to our knees, but it is usually in despair, not with a heart full of praise. God understands our humanness and we are not condemned because we fail in uttering 'thanks' as our first response, but I do believe that we have to come to a place in our tragic circumstances where we acknowledge God's love and control and offer thanks. We are not ever totally thankful that we must suffer but, in acknowledgement of God's unfailing love and in an act of obedience, we should offer sincere thanks to God for His love and eternal protection. We may not feel like it, but an authentic walk with Christ is not always based on feelings but with our heart, soul and mind. Most of the time, when we step out in obedience and offer thanks in all circumstances, our feelings eventually catch up with our obedience and only then we truly experience a thankful spirit in spite of our situation.

One of the most amazing stories to me of absolute trust in God is that of Abraham. "Then God said, "Take your son, your only son, whom you love—Isaac—and go to the region of Moriah. Sacrifice him there as a burnt offering on a mountain I will show you" (Genesis 22:2, NIV). I am sure that as Abraham went to the mountain with his son, he didn't feel like offering Isaac as a sacrifice to God. I have no doubt that his heart was racing and tears streamed down his face, but he went forward in incomprehensible obedience and trusted God. He had no idea what God's purpose was in commanding this sacrifice only that God had originally promised an innumerable nation of descendants. Abraham was probably questioning in his mind how that would be possible if he was being asked to kill his son. Questions aside, Abraham stepped out in obedient faith with an immeasurable trust in God, which I cannot comprehend, and showed willingness to sacrifice his own child. God intervened in his own timing. "Do not lay a hand on the boy," He said. "Do not do anything to him. Now I know that you fear God, because you have not withheld from me your son, your only son" (Genesis 22:12, NIV). Abraham looked up and in the bushes God had provided a ram as a sacrifice, and Isaac was spared.

Abraham, no doubt, had a heart full of thanksgiving after God had provided the ram instead of requiring Isaac's life. But knowing the level of obedience and faith he displayed, I know Abraham's heart would have been just as full of praise to God even if Isaac had been required as a sacrifice to the Almighty. When I review this story of extreme faith it brings me to contemplate two things. "Would I be willing to offer any of my children's lives, if asked?" As a mother, I would more likely be willing to exchange my own life for theirs, but not willing to take theirs. Secondly, it makes me realize in some small measure, the pain and anguish that God must have felt when He offered His only son to be the sacrifice for our sins. God actually did what Abraham was exempt from doing, and presented Christ as the lamb of choice in our stead. It was our slaughter that was deserved, not His. I don't believe in our finite minds that we can ever begin to comprehend the breadth of emotions in God's loving sacrificial gift, in Christ's devoted obedience, or the measure of thanks that we should be giving to God. He simply says, "But giving thanks is a sacrifice that truly honors me. If you keep to my path, I will reveal to you the salvation of God" (Psalm 50:23, NLT).

Prayer: Lord, the first words I can think to say are, "How can I say thanks for the things you have done for me?" So many things undeserved and yet you give them to prove your love for me. Thank you for the gift of cancer, for its journey has produced perseverance, character, and hope. Thank you for the gift of your Son, an eternal gift that is unbelievable, immeasurable and just totally amazing. You are an awesome God. I give you thanks! Amen.

Tidbits:

> "To speak gratitude is courteous and pleasant, to enact gratitude is generous and noble, but to live gratitude is to touch Heaven." – J A. Gaertner

> "Always thanking the Father. He has enabled you to share in the inheritance that belongs to His people, who live in the light." – Colossians 1:12, NLT

> "If the only Prayer you ever say in your entire life is Thank You, it will be enough." – Johannes Eckhart

> "...Thank the Lord! Praise His name! Tell the nations what He has done. Let them know how mighty He is!" – Isaiah 12:4, NLT

Song Selection: Thanks – by Scot Golley, Daniel Yemin, David Palaitis, AriZev Katz, Peter Martin

HE'S IN THE MIDST

"The Lord your God is in your midst, a mighty one who will save;
He will rejoice over you with gladness; He will quiet you
   by His love;
He will exult over you with loud singing."
– Zephaniah 3:17, ESV

If you pay attention to daily news, you probably find yourself adversely overwhelmed with all hatred, destruction and natural disasters. We are currently witnessing earthquakes in unexpected places, the invasion of unexplained plagues, oversized hurricanes as well as countless tornadoes flattening complete towns in their path. There is a threat of nuclear war, economically the recession is not recovering, unemployment rates are growing and entire countries and major cities are declaring bankruptcy. These are very uncertain times and the future appears unstable. Who can be trusted when we continually witness greed and corruption in our corporate and political world leaders.

Perhaps, the world's moral and economic decline is not your priority focus for maybe you are struggling with something more personal. You are unemployed, have insurmountable financial struggles, or maybe like me you are facing the life-threatening health condition. Focusing on these earthly events produces a state of fear and depression. We fail miserably in where we place our trust. Can I encourage you today with the absolute fact that no matter how bleak the outlook for you that "The God of angel armies is always by (your) side?"

Take comfort that He is not just a bystander of our misery but He actually desires to participate in our distress. When we are fragmented, slighted, anxious and hopeless, He instructs us to "come unto me" for all who are "heavy burdened." He adds, "And I will give you rest." Be encouraged for God is always in the midst no matter what the storm. He has unlimited love and continual comfort to give you and will carry your burdens if you surrender then to Him. We need to realize there is very little, if anything, that we can do to rectify the economy, to stop the wars or change immorality and crime, but we make a choice on what or 'whom' we focus.

Satan uses the world's philosophy, values and miserable situations to bring us down and he seeks to avert our attention and destroy our hope. The ultimate war is a spiritual battle for our minds and souls, and by distracting our heavenly focus, he causes us to plummet spiritually, and thus we find it difficult to believe that God still cares.

Fellow believers, the things of this earth will pass away:

"And this world is fading away, along with everything that people crave. But anyone who does what pleases God will live forever" (1 John 2:17, NLT).

Anxious friends, God is in total control.

"God is our shelter and strength, always ready to help in times of trouble. So we will not be afraid, even if the earth is shaken and mountains fall into the ocean depths; even if the seas roar and rage, and the hills are shaken by the violence. There is a river that brings joy to the city of God, to the sacred house of the Most High. God is in that city, and it will never be destroyed; at early dawn He will come to its aid" (Psalm 46:1-6, GNT).

Troubled colleagues, if God is for us, who can be against us?

"God knew what He was doing from the very beginning. He decided from the outset to shape the lives of those who love Him along the same lines as the life of His Son. . . . . After God made that decision of what His children should be like, He followed it up by calling people by name. . . . He set them on a solid basis with Himself. . . . After getting them established, He stayed with them to the end, gloriously completing what He had begun. So, what do you think? With God on our side like this, how can we lose?" (Romans 8:29-31, MSG).

Tidbits:

"Sir, my concern is not whether God is on our side; my greatest concern is to be on God's side, for God is always right." – Abraham Lincoln

"Unless God has raised you up for this very thing, you will be worn out by the opposition of men and devils. But if God be for you, who can be against you? Are all of them together stronger than God? O be not weary of well doing!" – John Wesley

"Our "safe place" is not where we live, it is in whom we live." – Tom White

Song Selection: Whom Shall I Fear (God Of Angels Armies) – written by Scott Cash, Ed Cash, Chris Tomlin

GREAT IS THY FAITHFULNESS

"The steadfast love of the Lord never ceases, His mercies never come to an end; they are new every morning; great is your faithfulness." – Lamentations 3:22-23, ESV

"Great is Thy Faithfulness," a beloved hymn penned by Thomas Obadiah Chisholm, spoke of his astonishing gratefulness to God's unfailing faithfulness in blessing him with provisional displays of His care throughout years of impaired health. Most often this song is used at reminiscing occasions such as weddings and graduations; times we are reflecting on the past and the record of God's goodness to us. However, when he wrote the hymn, Chisholm was reflecting on the lamenting of Jeremiah when he was angry and grieving the destruction of Jerusalem. We respectfully sing this hymn when our hearts are full of gratitude to God, but it is more of a challenge to be spiritually moved by the hymn when our current situation is not pleasant. No matter how bad things seem, it is only because of God's 'mercies that never end' that they don't get worse. "Because of the Lord's great love we are not consumed." (Lamentations 3:22, NIV)

Recently I had a discussion with a friend who had relocated from our country to a region in the United States. Please understand as I share his tidbit of revelation that I don't consider it to be limited geographically but something noticeable in the different cultures regardless of where you live. He mentioned that many of the people he met during this move all seemed to have a 'sense of entitlement' and that was quite apparent that people at large have lost a sense of gratitude for the many blessings we enjoy in our North American countries, especially when compared to others. Unfortunately, in today's society, we tend to look for grand, grander and grandiose ways we can be happy instead of being grateful for the small but richest blessings of all. Such as having coffee with a friend, quietly reading a book while relaxing in a hammock, and biking a manicured trail while enjoying nature, etc. "His mercies never come to an end." When one is diagnosed with cancer, one envisions life to be shortened, no longer having decades to get ready to meet God. There are unsaved loved ones needing to be led to the Lord, some bad habits to get rid of, maybe even broken relationships to be mended, and definitely a need to become most Christ-like, yet because of the anticipation of death one fears there is not enough time to accomplish these goals.

Perhaps you are not focused on preparing for death, but in your day-to-day sufferings you're having trouble focusing with optimism on anything. This is where you need to realize that because of God's grace, His faithfulness and the mercies that He promises us with each new morning you can lean on Him and be thankful for blessings no matter how small. I have found His divine blessings in the compassionate hands of nurses and doctors, the faithful prayers of countless friends, the provision of meals through others and even thankful to Him for simple nights of peaceful sleep. I choose to count the blessings He bestows because the 'steadfast love of the Lord never ceases." How about you? Consider the words of C.S. Lewis, "He who has God and many other things has not more than he who has God alone."

Prayer: Almighty God, how can I possibly express adequate words of thanks for unlimited mercies, steadfast love and unfailing faithfulness? Thank you, that your faithfulness does not depend on our performance or heavenly preparation to meet you. Thank you for the countless people you have surrounded me with to show love and pray for my battle against cancer. You alone know the outcome and my life is in your loving hands. Amen.

Tidbits:

> "Success certainly isn't achievement of popularity. Success in God's kingdom is loving God, loving one another, and being faithful to what He's called us to do." – Gabriel Wilson

> "He is the Rock, His works are perfect, and all His ways are just. A faithful God who does no wrong, upright and just is He." – Deuteronomy 32:4, NIV

> "There have been times of late when I have had to hold on to one text with all my might: "It is required in stewards that a man may be found faithful." Praise God, it does not say "successful." – Amy Carmichael

> "No dependence can be placed upon our natural qualities, or our spiritual attainments; but God abideth faithful. He is faithful in His love; He knows no variableness, neither shadow of turning. He is faithful to His purpose; He doth not begin a work and then leave it undone. He is faithful to His relation-ships; as a Father He will not renounce His children, as a friend He will not deny His people, as a Creator He will not forsake the work of His own hands." – Charles H. Spurgeon

Song Selection: Great Is Thy Faithfulness – by Thomas O Chisholm, William M. Runyan

I CAN TRUST JESUS

"I will say of the Lord, "He is my refuge and my fortress, my God, in whom I trust." – Psalm 91:2, NIV

Today's song suggestion, "I Can Trust Jesus," conveys the tender care of our Heavenly Father for one of His simplest of creation, a sparrow. It speaks of a sparrow that could no longer fly and Jesus lovingly picked it up, brushed off its wounds and released it to soar into the sky. God seeks to find us when we are in a lonely, isolated place and desires to brush off our wounds and to teach us how to fly above the clouds, but we often choose to doubt His love and remain in our 'city of pity.' We allow haunting words of a peer to penetrate our very soul and cast shadows over the worth we have in Jesus. Perhaps it is a dismal diagnosis of cancer or another incurable disease that crowds out the faith that you once had of God being in total control. Some will view their awful situation as an unloving disciplinary measure of their sin and cultivate a spirit of bitterness towards God and turn their backs on Him completely. Others will allow their grief over the loss of a loved one to paralyze them and they voluntarily chain themselves in a dungeon of darkness where they believe His love, mercy and grace would dare not enter. No matter what traumatic circumstance has brought you to the depths of despair you can trust Jesus.

In Luke 12:24, NASB we read "Consider the ravens, they do not sow or reap, they have no storeroom or barn; yet God feeds them. And how much more valuable you are than the birds." Jesus has such love for us that we are instructed not to worry about our daily needs or for our future. Do you believe that you are more valuable to Him than the birds? Jesus cares about your todays, your tomorrows and your eternity.

There is no where you can hide that He will not find you, not a dungeon too dark or an ocean too deep. (Psalm 139:7-11) There is no sin from the east to the west, north or to the south that that His grace does not cover. (Psalm 103:12) There is no sickness or disease beyond His control that He as the Great Physician cannot heal. (Psalm 103:3) Each day God precious thoughts of you outnumbered the grains of sand on a beach. (Psalm 139:17)

Remaining in a state of desperation or depression is a waste of precious time that not only robs time from our friends, family and God, but it wastes away our quality of life. Worry dissolves the energy we need to heal from our disease. We can thrive despite our wounded spirit, soar with eagles beyond the clouds of despair and forgive ourselves of past sins.

Rise up from your darkened pit, open your heart to His love, see with your eyes His sacrifice and hear with your ears the truth. Jesus can be trusted.

Trusting Jesus is a growth process and it involves the transforming of your mind. Reach for your Bible and weed out the anxiety by meditating and digesting His word. Jesus will lovingly provide for your daily needs that shower you with the right moisture and help your faith grow. Trusting Jesus encompasses more than feelings, it is an active choice of faith cultivated by prayer. Worrying has never produced speedy answers but casting all your cares on Him will enable you to find divine peacefulness in the waiting and strength for the journey. A worldly trial or weary journey is 'a walk in the park' when we trust Jesus and lean not unto our own understanding.

Prayer: Jesus, I come with a heart full of thanksgiving for your unconditional love for me. Your word tells me that I can trust you no matter what challenges will fall into my path. You have never once failed to meet my needs. As I release control of my life and lean on your will, knowing what's best for me, my faith will blossom, blessings will abound and you will be glorified. Conquer my darkness of despair with your perfect light. Be my strong tower in times of weakness. Help me to hold tight to your hand and keep trusting you. Amen.

Tidbits:

> "Don't be afraid; just believe." – Luke 8:50, NIV

> "God is God. Because He is God, He is worthy of my trust and obedience. I will find rest nowhere but in His holy will, a will that is unspeakably beyond my largest notions of what He is up to." – Elisabeth Elliot

> "I will trust Him. Whatever, wherever I am, I can never be thrown away. If I am in sickness, my sickness may serve Him; in perplexity, my perplexity may serve Him; if I am in sorrow, my sorrow may serve Him. My sickness, or perplexity, or sorrow may be necessary causes of some great end, which is quite beyond us. He does nothing in vain." – John Henry Newman

Song Selection: I Can Trust Jesus – written by Gerald Crabb; performed by The Collingsworth Family

QUIETNESS, BLESSED QUIETNESS

"The LORD your God in your midst, The Mighty One, will save; He will rejoice over you with gladness, He will quiet you with His love, He will rejoice over you with singing." – Zephaniah 3:17, NKJV

Blessed quietness, holy quietness,
What assurance in my soul!
On the stormy sea, He speaks peace to me,
How the billows cease to roll!
What a wonderful salvation,
Where we always see His face!
What perfect habitation,
What a quiet resting place!
(Written by: J. Jefferson Cleveland, Manie Payne Ferguson, Verolga Nix, W.S. Marshall)

Ponder quietness and the great effect it has on calming one's soul. The Bible tells us much about quietness: A soft answer turns away wrath; the shepherd leads His sheep by quiet still waters; a quiet spirit in a woman is an ornament of great price. God also uses His creation to convey quietness: soft ripples of flowing water at river banks; warming quiet rays of sunshine caressing our body; gentle refreshing dew drops glistening on morning flora; tender snowflakes drifting and brightening gray skies; bright stars twinkling in the stark silence of night, and in the words of The Four Seasons, "Silence is golden."

Quietness is not just the absence of sound but a state of tranquility or calmness that can be found during a season of stress. A depressing diagnosis of cancer or any other life threatening health complication may manufacture stress like you have never known before. Maintaining a quiet spirit offers physical benefits that positively affect your overall health. Meditation and quiet sessions are known to reduce risk for heart attacks, strokes, high blood pressure and diabetes. Periods of peace automatically relax muscles and help lower anxiety and pain levels. Beyond the health rewards spending quiet time with God will also bring eternal benefits.

When you flood your mind with the truths of the Most High God, His divine virtues transfer to you. They will trickle at first, but before too long they will flow in and eventually become second nature; what goes in is what comes out.

The more quiet time spent in His word the more you acquire wisdom, increase knowledge, conquer fear with enlarged faith, attain better understanding, and gather more confidence. The love of Christ in the heart makes one like Christ.

Christ was quiet natured. Anxiety and worry were not characteristic of Him. He didn't waste time fretting about things. There was quietness in His soul that showed itself whenever He spoke. I believe people are drawn to those with a quiet, calm spirit. We will do well to learn this lesson of calmness. Then we would be less likely to use harsh or hasty words that cause pain to another and would be more apt to convey a cheerful attitude despite the depressions of life. This is not a state of mind we humans necessarily display but is a quietness that God will produce in our soul. We cannot change the people or situations around us, but we can choose to react to them honourably. We can have the peace of God and strength to endure if we will simply rely on Him!

Prayer: Thank you, Jesus for being our perfect example of quietness. As I grow in your likeness may my words be complimentary and edifying so that you are glorified. Continue to teach me this spirit of quietness, teach me to rest beside your still waters so that I can restore my soul. Let me be to others an example of how having a quiet peace can help us endure our current situations with assurance of your plan and control over everything. I will wait eagerly in quietness for your peace and direction in my life. Amen.

Tidbits:

> "Do not conform to the pattern of this world, but be trans-formed by the renewing of your mind. Then you will be able to test and approve what God's will is—his good, pleasing and perfect will." – Romans 12:2, NIV

> "True silence is the rest of the mind; it is to the spirit what sleep is to the body, nourishment and refreshment." – William Penn

> "Better one handful with tranquility than two handfuls with toil and chasing after the wind." – Ecclesiastes 4:6, NIV

> "Prayer is commission. Out of the quietness with God, power is generated that turns the spiritual machinery of the world. When you pray, you begin to feel the sense of being sent, that the divine compulsion is upon you." – E. Stanley Jones

> "The quiet words of the wise are more to be heeded than the shouts of a ruler of fools." – Ecclesiastes 9:17, NIV

Song Selection: Be Still and Know– written by Steven Curtis Chapman

REDEEMING THE TIME

"For if you keep silent at this time, relief and deliverance will rise for the Jews from another place, but you and your father's house will perish. And who knows whether you have not come to the kingdom for such a time as this?" – Esther 4:14, ESV

Are you using your most valuable asset wisely? Time should be the most cherished commodity that God has given us, and yet when life is just breezing along and our river of life is flowing without interruptive dams, we toss many hours down the stream that we will never see again. Almost any other commodity such as money, crude oil, natural minerals and agricultural products can be redeemed, but time is something that when it has 'passed by' can never be retrieved or be used productively again. It's literally gone. Most of us waste it as if we had more time than we can ever spend and expect that our tomorrows will continue to come. But when it appears that our days are soon to be numbered, because we are exposed to disaster, held hostage, defending a war-torn country or have been diagnosed with a life-threatening illness, we ache for more time to spend with family, to complete something on our bucket list, or more time to witness to an unsaved friend or family member. We find there is not nearly enough time to settle our accounts. Why does it take threatening dangers for us to realize the irreplaceable value of time?

Fortunately, for the Jews in the reign of King Xerxes, a Jewish woman named Esther finally responded to the leading of the Lord and redeemed the time. Esther's beauty had caught the eye of the King so much so that it wasn't long before she was made queen, however, because the Jews were not favoured in Persia, she hid her nationality from the King until she heard of the King's plans for the Jews to be annihilated. Her cousin Mordecai, knowing her place of prominence, realized she would be the ideal choice to approach the King and said to her, "Who knows whether you have come to the kingdom for such a time as this?" Despite the obvious conflict between her potential death and the slaughter of her people, she seized the opportunity, redeemed the time, and appealed to King Xerxes to spare her people. Her request was eventually honoured by the King, who conversely turned the tables and ordered the death of his evil chieftain, Haman, who had headed up the plot to destroy the Jews.

Just as God used Esther for a specific purpose, each of us has a divine purpose in His plan. Finding our purpose or heeding His call requires that we are fine-tuned to His channel. We may also be faced with inner conflict as to which direction to take, but we are expected to redeem the time. Every day God blesses us with comes with responsibility to live our days focused, happy, positively and ready to claim victory. So if you are like me, newly aware that your days are numbered, or maybe you expect thousands of tomorrows to still be yours, look beyond the distractions, shake off the discouragement and pity parties and redeem the time. There is "Only One Life," as Avis Marguerite Burgeson Christiansen, Merrill Dunlop write.

Prayer: Heavenly Father, I again come before you confessing that I am not redeeming the time or budgeting it properly so that you are always first. Forgive me and help me to take progressive steps towards being more accountable for the precious time you have blessed me with. Amen.

Tidbits:

> "The time is always right to do what is right." – Martin Luther King, Jr

> "There is a time for everything, and a season for every activity under the heavens: a time to be born and a time to die, a time to plant and a time to uproot, . . . a time to weep and a time to laugh, a time to mourn and a time to dance . . . a time to embrace and a time to refrain from embracing, a time to search and a time to give up . . . a time to tear and a time to mend, a time to be silent and a time to speak . . . a time for war and a time for peace." – Ecclesiastics 3:1-8, NIV

> "Take care in your minutes, and the hours will take care of themselves. – Lord Chesterfield

> "At just the right time, I heard you. On the day of salvation, I helped you." Indeed, the "right time" is now . . . the day of salvation." – 2 Corinthians 6:2, NLT

Song Selection: Only One Life – written by Avis Marguerite Burgeson Christiansen, Merrill Dunlop

SOVEREIGN OVER US

"Remember the former things of old; for I am God, and there is no other; I am God, and there is none like me, declaring the end from the beginning and from ancient times things not yet done, saying, 'My counsel shall stand, and I will accomplish all my purpose." – Isaiah 46:9-10, ESV

"There is strength within the sorrow." No one really knows just how they will handle suffering until it happens to them, whether it's on account of the death of a loved one, health crisis or a community tragedy. The Apostle Paul encourages us to stay true to the Lord during times of suffering, and when you are ready to quit, remember Him and His multiple sufferings. There is a mystery to it, but we know God understands since He sacrificed His one and only Son on the cross for our sins. Every time we suffer for the cause of Christ, we are becoming more like Jesus, and divine strength is provided for our journey.

As the song states, "There is beauty in our tears." When we journey through difficult trials, physical challenges or critical finances, tears are a common expression of emotion. King David said, "You keep track of all my sorrows. You have collected all my tears in your bottle. You have recorded each one in your book" (Psalm 56:8, NLT). What a comfort it is to know that God understands the tears we shed and He grieves right along with us. Tears are a language that God understands and what beauty to know that our collected tears fall onto His hands and He, in return, comforts us.

God will meet us in our mourning. Despite having a heart that will be obliterated by death, hurt by searing words, or devastated by a physical crisis, God is prepared to meet us in our mourning. There will be times that our pain will make us question everything we believe in, but instead of clinging to pain, we must grasp onto the unfailing love that God has for us. When our hearts are broken and we feel that God isn't near, the truth tells us that He is. "The LORD is near the brokenhearted; He delivers those who are discouraged" (Psalm 34:8, NB). He knows all the places where the pieces of your heart are scattered and is prepared to mend them.

God is faithful in supplying us with an unending love, peace that casts out fear, and He is working while we are waiting for answers. Through our suffering He is sanctifying us and when all that is happening around us is beyond our understanding, He is simply teaching us to trust. Many persons of the world race to fortunetellers, soothsayers, crystal balls or horoscopes in hopes of being prepared for the future. But the only one who knows the future is the Almighty one who planned it before the beginning of time. When we are faced with overwhelming circumstances will we turn and praise God for His power and grace and bow in submission to His sovereignty, or resist Him and remain in pain and agony? Our only hope in all of life, good or bad, is God! For God, and God alone is sovereign over us!

Prayer: Oh Sovereign God, how I praise you for your wondrous works in my life and for your continued loving presence. During this cancer crisis, please give me the strength to be everything you have planned for me and show me the way to demonstrate your love despite my pain. Help me to stand when I am weak and to lean on you for all my needs, physical, emotional and, in particular, spiritual. And if it be your will, please heal me.

Tidbits:

> "Our God is in the heavens; He does all that He pleases." – Psalm 115:3, ESV

> "God is unchanging in His love. He loves you. He has a plan for your life. Don't let the newspaper headlines frighten you. God is still sovereign; He's still on the throne." – Billy Graham

> "Yours, O Lord, is the greatness and the power and the glory and the victory and the majesty, for all that is in the heavens and in the earth is yours. Yours is the kingdom, O Lord, and you are exalted as head above all. Both riches and honour come from you, and you rule over all. In your hand are power and might, and in your hand it is to make great and to give strength to all." – 1 Chronicles 29:11-12, ESV

> "Many are the plans in the mind of a man, but it is the purpose of the Lord that will stand." – Proverbs 19:21 ESV

> "Cheer up, Christian! Things are not left to chance: no blind fate rules the world. God hath purposes, and those purposes are fulfilled. God hath plans, and those plans are wise, and never can be dislocated." – Charles Spurgeon

Song Selection: Sovereign Over Us – written by Aaron Keyes, Jack Mooring, Bryan Brown

STUCK LIKE GLUE

"And I am convinced that nothing can ever separate us from God's love. . ." – Romans 8:38a, NIV

Think back, way back. Did you have a time in your life that you can recall being 'stuck like glue' to someone? It may have been a special friendship in grade school, high school or even college, when you spent nearly every waking moment with your sibling or a friend. Or maybe it was the budding love relationship that you shared with your first sweetheart whom perhaps has since become your spouse. Others looking on may have described your relationship as 'being stuck like glue,' but not all glues stick as well as they promise. I have attempted to use 'super glue' to mend broken items only to have my fingers covered with glue and yet the item is still broken. Far too many relationships are like that today. They have come unglued and they are fragmented. It is tough enough to lose the love of another person, a spouse, a friend, a parent or a child but even more difficult when they are able to turn around and say, "I hate you." Fortunately, there is one relationship that is rock solid, and it does stick like glue, better than super glue, and that is the relationship we have with Christ.

God designed us to have a permanent intimate relationship with Him. God is love, and no matter what we do, the Lord will not stop loving us. Consider the cost of this eternal relationship. Christ, God's only Son, died an agonizing death for the penalty of our sins, not His, for He was sinless. None of us as sinners deserve this perfect love, but it has been freely given to us anyway. We will never in a million years be worthy of His love and it is our choice whether or not we accept that love. When we do, we become co-heirs with Christ (Romans 8:17), we are adopted children of God (8:15). He is a friend who stays closer than a brother (Proverbs 18:24) and He loves us passionately. In Ephesians 5, the description of a passionate love relationship between a husband and wife is compared to that which exists between Christ and the church. A relationship so deep that they would do anything for each other and their love is so strong that nothing can keep them apart. That is how powerful and deep our relationship with God is supposed to be. The affection we experience with our family or our spouse is just a glimpse of the great compassion and care that God has for us. God has a perfect purpose and plan for every person's life and wants to be actively involved in every aspect of it.

But then when the tough times come, we find it easy to say, "I don't think God loves me anymore, why else would He make me suffer." Tribulation makes us wonder. Paul mentions, distress, persecution, famine, nakedness, peril and sword as methods used by the devil in an attempt to separate us from the love of God. We will face numerous oppositions throughout our lives, but we are told not to worry because God has a perfect plan for each of our lives and He promises to be actively involved. "And we know that in all things God works for the good of those who love Him, who have been called according to His purpose" (Romans 8:28, NIV).

"Christ loves us!" Just think of that. He who loves you is God Himself. The divine Almighty loves us and there is nothing at all that can separate us from the love of Christ. "And I am convinced that nothing can ever separate us from God's love. Neither death nor life, neither angels nor demons, neither our fears for today nor our worries about tomorrow—not even the powers of hell can separate us from God's love. No power in the sky above or in the earth below—indeed, nothing in all creation will ever be able to separate us from the love of God that is revealed in Christ Jesus our Lord." (Romans 8:38, 39, NIV) This verse clearly explains that nothing, not demons, not fears, not earthly powers, indeed nothing can separate us from the love of God. We are stuck like glue. Thank you Jesus!

Tidbits:

"The Son is the image of the invisible God, the firstborn over all creation. He is before all things, and in him all things hold together." – Colossians 1:15, 17, NIV

"And as Christ, our Head, prays, so also must we who cleave to Him pray that He may be glorified in us." – Martin Luther

"Never will I leave you; never will I forsake you," – Hebrews 13:5b, NIV

"Christ Jesus is God's super glue that holds our lives together even when things seem to be broken or falling apart." – Gaither Bailey

"In Him you also, when you heard the word of truth, the gospel of your salvation, and believed in Him, were sealed with the promised Holy Spirit." – Ephesians 1:13, ESV

"The grace glue of your God can hold you together, no matter what hits you!" – Ron Hutchcraft

Song Selection: Blest Be the Tie that Binds – by John Fawcett, Lowell Mason

THE BEST PRESCRIPTION OF ALL

"A joyful heart is good medicine, but a broken spirit drains one's strength." – Proverbs 17:22, ISV

Feeling rundown? Try laughing more. Cheerfulness of spirit has a great influence upon the health and welfare of the body. Especially Christians, whose minds and hearts are focused on God, for they have a heart full of spiritual joy and peace of conscience. Medical researchers have concluded that laughter just might be the best medicine to putting gas in your tank and helping you feel better. While their studies are not conclusive to whether it is the act of laughter or the good sense of humour and a positive attitude that is the greater influence the Bible says a joyful heart is beneficial and that enough for me. God said it and I believe it.

Let's look at the health benefits that are simple laughter can produce: An increased heart rate increases the blood flow and supplies more oxygen to the lungs. Laughter raises the level of infection-fighting antibodies, thus boosting the level of immune cells.

Several diabetics, after watching a comedy movie, had markedly lower blood sugar levels. Another participant said that ten minutes of laughter allowed him two hours of pain-free sleep.

With a good bout of laughter, we stretch face and body muscles alike, as well as improve physiologically. One pioneer researcher says that fifteen minutes of consistent belly-jiggling laughter actually burns fifty calories, but don't go eating that yummy chocolate bar unless you want to spend a full twelve hours laughing.

One doctor was quoted as saying, "You know what's wrong with this world? People expect me to solve their problems and all I can do for the most part is relieve the symptoms. If they would just live right they would feel better." This is where "A merry heart does good like medicine" (Proverbs 17:22, NKJV) makes sense.

You probably know some people who have a constant pessimistic outlook on life? This does not sync with being a Christian, where upon being born again, we are gifted with a new nature and should be conveying a positive outlook on life.

I have a very close friend whose company I totally enjoy. She is a contagious giggler and even when there is nothing to laugh about, I am guaranteed to depart totally refreshed and feeling better for having been with her.

As Christians we are cautioned to be sober minded, but that is a big difference from being somber. Jesus condemned the Pharisees for having long faces, displaying somber attitudes, so others would think they were spiritual. He compared them to white washed tombs. God doesn't want us to be miserable, gloomy or falsely communicating that the Christian life is depressing, but rather quite the opposite. When the prodigal son came home there was rejoicing and cheerfulness. There is joy in heaven when even one sinner repents. God wants a glad heart displaying a cheerful face. When we are filled with the Holy Spirit, we radiate love, joy and peace, but a merry heart is not something to keep to ourselves; we must share it. Like any medicine to be effective it must be applied. Are you a person who shares this kind of medicine?

Prayer: Lord, I am so thankful for the many positive, encouraging people that you have surrounded me with during this battle against cancer. And I also stand in awe at the measure of peace you have provided in my own heart. I owe my cheerful attitude to and your divine answer to tons of prayers. Amen.

Tidbits:

> "For the despondent, every day brings trouble; for the happy heart, life is a continual feast." – Proverbs 15:15, NLT

> "I am determined to be cheerful and happy in whatever situation I may find myself. For I have learned that the greater part of our misery or unhappiness is determined not by our circumstance but by our disposition." – Martha Washington

> "A glad heart makes a cheerful face, but by sorrow of heart the spirit is crushed." – Proverbs 15:13, ESV

> "A cheerful frame of mind, reinforced by relaxation. . . is the medicine that puts all ghosts of fear on the run." – George Matthew Adams

Song Selection: You Are My All in All – written by Dennis Jernigan

TRANSFORMATION

"Therefore, since we have such a hope, we are very bold." – 2 Corinthians 3:12, NIV

In reading, *Praying Through Cancer*, by Susan Sorensen and Laura Geist, a 'God sent' gift for my walk through cancer, a contributor spoke of how she never thought boldness would come with her becoming bald. She feared would become a hermit to avoid being named with the "Bald and the Breastless." She didn't. I don't face the trauma of breast cancer, but baldness did happen and fortunately that was not devastating to me. If you ask someone who knows me, they would not describe me as being meek or mild, but perhaps a bit bold. I don't consider myself to be bold or overly confident, but due to a hearing disability I do come across very loud. There is one thing that I am certainly bold about and will boldly state, "Via, Veritas, Vita!" There is 'One Way' to heaven and that is through the Lord, Jesus Christ. "Jesus answered, "I am the way and the truth and the life. No one comes to the Father except through me" (John 14:6, NIV). That's bold. That's from Christ Himself.

The Apostle Paul explained in Corinthians that Jesus had reason for being bold. He brought a simple message of the redeeming gospel in plain and intelligible words and, because of hope, spoke boldly.

Still, many people—even God's chosen—choose to live under the old conditional covenant which could never be upheld by sinful men instead of choosing the new unconditional covenant, guaranteed by God and finalized by Christ. Paul spoke boldly, desiring them to understand their need for Christ despite being threatened with imprisonment and death. Even today some believers think by keeping the Ten Commandments they are good enough to enter heaven. Only when one is converted to God, by accepting Christ's sacrifice, is the veil removed, they are guaranteed eternity and the Holy Spirit becomes a resident translator and comforter. This is the ultimate transformation.

The metamorphosis of a caterpillar into a butterfly is a miraculous transformation. It is astonishing to watch a slow, crawling, worm-like creature be transformed into a beautiful colourful winged insect that takes flight. The actual conversion process is somewhat tedious for it all happens inside a cocoon hidden from our view, but we marvel at the results.

Once we realize our sinful condition, repent, and accept Christ we, too, begin a lifetime of metamorphosis. Our change is subtle and tedious like that of the butterfly and not easy since we live in a society that is 'wearing a veil to biblical truths' and rely on our own sense of right and wrong. Scores of Christians still attempt to live their lives under the old covenant by keeping laws or traditions instead of living under grace. Genuine transformation comes with staying in tune with the Holy Spirit through prayer, devotions and communion, thus the Lord brings about change. Transformation develops with your realization of what God has provided and how He desires you to develop. When change is not fast enough, we become frustrated, but remember the caterpillar. Change happens slowly. As you are being made over by God, speak boldly and encourage others to remove their veil and accept Christ. With the great moral divide of today's society, only Christ will make a difference. It is guaranteed to be a bold difference.

Prayer: Heavenly Father, thank you for my spiritual transformation through the completed work of Christ, for the ongoing soul transformation with each day of growing closer to you, and for the bodily transformation yet to come on the day you claim me for eternity. Amen.

Tidbits:

> "We are not saved by good deeds; we are saved for good deeds. Jesus transforms us to transform others." – Dillon Burroughs

> "Though I think and speak of greater becoming, I, too, am an infinite work in progress." – T.F. Hodge

> "Do not be conformed to this world, but be transformed by the renewal of your mind, that by testing you may discern what is the will of God, what is good and acceptable and perfect." – Romans 12:2, ESV

> "Did you ever stop to consider that God made us to remake us? He created us so we would seek Him and be transformed by Him." – Dillon Burroughs

> "And we all, with unveiled face, beholding the glory of the Lord, are being transformed into the same image from one degree of glory to another." – 2 Corinthians 3:18, ESV

Song Selection: For All You've Done – written by Reuben Morgan; performed by Hillsong

ANGELS WATCHING OVER ME

"For He (God) will command his angels to protect you in all your ways." – Psalm 91:9-13, ISV

Angels are mentioned in 34 books of the Bible for a total of 273 times. For the most part, angels are God's unseen source of help when we are facing a physical or spiritual crisis. Though primarily unseen, we are cautioned to exercise the gift of hospitality as we might be entertaining angels in human formation. "Do not neglect to show hospitality to strangers, for thereby some have entertained angels unawares." There are good and bad angels and both are mentioned in the Bible. The good angels did not participate in rebellion against God, and the bad angels sided with Lucifer, the devil, and were cast out of heaven (Isaiah 11). For the sake of remaining positive, we will focus on the heavenly hosts, angels sometime called "ministering spirits." (Hebrews 13:2, ESV)

Angels serve God in different ways. They are responsible to praise God, exclaiming His magnificence, majesty and wonder. John, the revelator speaks of thousands upon thousands of angels encircling God's throne and singing. Angels also made special announcements such as Jesus' impending birth, His divine presence in the manger of Bethlehem, and declaring the resurrection at the tomb. They were ministering spirits meeting Jesus in the wilderness and at His highest point of unbearable grief as He suffered crucifixion.

Unfortunately we live in a culture that worships materialism, and secular minds think of the universe as being complete and absent of spiritual life. While there is an intense revival in a belief in angels, they are not always viewed as being the ministry of God but associated with mystery and false religion, but 'ministering spirits' of their own accord. While we cannot see angels with our eyes, it should be enough to know that God speaks of them throughout the Bible and sends them. They are performing the duties of protection in quietness, so our focus should be on Jesus, and not on them or their works. Knowing that God's angels are on our side provides comfort and strengthens our trust in God.

Prayer: Lord, I believe that you not only send unseen guardian angels to watch over us but that you provide ministering spirits among us such as nurses. Thank you for comforting angels, unseen and seen, and I plead for their continued presence through my journey. Amen.

Tidbits:

"Likewise, I say to you, there is joy in the presence of the angels of God over one sinner who repents." – Luke 15:10, KJB

"Be an angel to someone else whenever you can, as a way of thanking God for the help your angel has given you." – Eileen Elias Freeman

"See, I am sending an angel before you, to guard you on the way and bring you to the place I have prepared." – Exodus 23:20-23, NIV

"Raindrops resplendent with angels patter my head and drizzle God's love over me. Wet rejoicing abounds!" – Terri Guillemets

"The angel of the Lord encamps around those who fear him, and he delivers them." – Psalm 34:7, NIV

"Angels descending, bring from above, Echoes of mercy, whispers of love." – Fanny J. Crosby

Song Selection: Angels Watching over Me – written by Amy Grant, Gary Winthur Chapman, Michael W. Smith, Brown Bannister

BETTER IS ONE DAY

"Better is one day in your courts than a thousand elsewhere;
I would rather be a doorkeeper in the house of my God than
dwell in the tents of the wicked." – Psalm 84:10, NIV

We have heard every excuse people make for not coming to church, but have you ever really stopped to think about why you do come? In a church survey you would probably get as many reasons for attendance as you would excuses from the non-goers. Ashamedly, when I first accepted Christ in the 1970s my attendance was due to feeling that I owed God. Not a guilt response, but demonstration of my gratitude for forgiveness of my sins. Shortly thereafter, I gained understanding that forgiveness is a debt that cannot be recompensed and then I began to attended church to learn and to serve. Other possible positives for faithful attendance may include: Being with likeminded individuals who sincerely love the Lord; finding inspiration from the message and encouragement from fellow believers; a closeness and feeling of oneness with the Spirit when immersed in worship; amazing awe when unveiled truths capture the mind as the sermon 'turns on the light.' Each one of these reasons was mine for attending, but seldom all at the same time.

Unfortunately, I was victim of the 'guilt trap' for years and performed in nearly every service in the church that I was possible, with the exception of preaching. Some may even say I preached indirectly as my expectations of others were too high and I would occasionally admonish them. My 'ministry' started as a Sunday school teacher, a huge benefit that provided knowledge of the basic Bible stories and the level of accountability was mere grade school. As years passed, other ministries included Sunday School Superintendent, Adult Fellowship Head, Junior Church Coordinator, Nursery Attendant, Pianist, Treasurer, Secretary, Worship Coordinator, Choir Director, Drama Coach, and so on. I don't list these to 'toot my own horn' but to warn you of the dangers of becoming 'service enchained' to the point that your personal relationship with Christ suffers. Mine did. Thankfully, He is faithful and never failed to put bumps in the road to get my attention.

There were plenty of bumps but none enormous enough to derail my train for long periods of time. At one point as a young mother of four children, who were all beneath the age of six, I came close to a physical breakdown that left me coasting for a few miles. Once I regained momentum, it wasn't long before I followed the same pattern. Another pause came when our entire family was under verbal attack from leadership and gossip mongers to the point that 3 out of 4 of our children opted to find a different church. And still a few years later, I found myself being coaxed out of my leadership position in worship. I failed to stop and take notice of God's deliberate detours. Don't get me wrong, with each deviation in ministry I prayed, asked the Lord to search my heart. Minor transformations occurred, yet never was there an unbelievable treasured personal relationship with Christ until now.

God knew my life was too fast paced and that I was neglecting Him. In love, mercy and wisdom, He designed a big detour totally forcing a roadblock and opening my eyes. He allowed my body to form cancer cells and I knew this was a battle that I could not do alone. What a blessing it has been to reassess my relationship with Him. His plan for me has been unfolding since the beginning. Each detour had purpose, and each moment with Him is an eternal gift. These days of slowness, quiet and, yes, sometimes boredom, are divinely designed for me. Just as Mary took the time to sit at Jesus feet, basking in His presence, instead of being a busy Martha, I am relishing His nearness. Now, when physically able, I faithfully attend church, and each of the aforementioned reasons are encompassed together to make each Sunday a "Better is One Day in Your House" day. And with each day spent with Christ, enriching our relationship. . . Better is each day with Jesus.

Prayer: Heavenly Father, I thank you for not allowing my train to derail and for staying right by my side through the detours. Unfailing is your love and I treasure the relationship that we are now nurturing together. Amen.

Tidbits:

> "Let us not give up the habit of meeting together, as some are doing. Instead, let us encourage one another all the more, since you see the Day of the Lord is coming nearer." – Hebrews 10:25, GNT

> "My home is in Heaven. I'm just traveling through this world." – Billy Graham

> "No eye has ever seen or no ear has ever heard or no mind has ever thought of the wonderful things God has made ready for those who love Him." – 1 Corinthians 2:9, NLV

> "Ah, but a man's reach should grasp, or what's heaven for?" – Robert Browning

Song Selection: Better is One Day – by Matt Redman

RED TAPE

"It is for freedom that Christ has set us free. Stand firm, then, and do not let yourselves be burdened again by a yoke of slavery." – Galatians 5:1, NIV

Red tape is regulation or rigid conformity to rules that are considered a hindrance to an action or decision-making, and it is usually applied when speaking of governments and other large organizations. We have experienced walls of red tape a couple of times in our lives, once when we were enlarging our own small business to accommodate new governmental 'clean air' laws and another when we added a large three-season room to our home in order to entertain our growing family. Red tape that required duplicated paper work, fees, permits and inspections, which we understood were necessary, but made the 'wheels' move along very slowly. However, our experience with constructional red tape is not limited to worldly involvement, for we have encountered much red tape or legalism in our forty years of faith. Red tape in the Christian realm is known as legalism.

Legalism is the practice of placing an over-emphasis on our conduct all the while neglecting the provision of mercy and grace. There is often misguided pride with one who emphasizes and practices the letter of the law over the application of God's grace. A legalist is usually self-righteous and one who serves out of motivation by guilt and sacrifice. I don't intend to be critical of those who are convicted to keep biblical standards to a higher degree than others, but I do want to emphasize Romans 14:5, NLT: "In the same way, some think one day is more holy than another day, while others think every day is alike. You should each be fully convinced that whichever day you choose is acceptable."

I believe that this principle can be applied beyond the concept of choosing which day should be honoured as the Lord's day. One can use the same principal to test their own religious observances, and choose to obey the Lord according to what they are convicted of by scripture. We are cautioned in James 2:8, NIV, to be mindful of the royal law over all. If you keep the law found in Scripture—"Love your neighbour as yourself"—you are doing right.

Just as the Pharisees unfairly cast judgment on others, based on their own religious standards, we are often guilty of the same. We minimize our sins while gossiping about the outrageous sins of our brother and show little or no tolerance for fellow Christians who behave differently than we do. I know from experience that legalism can take an energetic faith and cause it to become subdued and lacking joy because of the extensive and often fleshly effort required to keep the rules. Instead of being lost in a maze of do's and don'ts or a jungle of regulations, I opted to live under the grace of God and weigh every decision or deed against scripture, allowing God to convict me. All the while I do not behave with such freedom that I become a stumbling block to others who may be weaker in their faith. God created human as an individual, to be diverse, not narrow-mindedly focusing on laws, but on grace, love and mercy. There is nothing that discourages a spiritual seeker from accepting Christ more than a list of rules and regulations. Grasp the amazing grace that Christ has given to us and live in the freedom of being His forgiven child. Jesus said, "So if the Son sets you free, you will be free indeed" (John 8:36, NIV).

Prayer: Heavenly Father, help me to recognize when I am being judgmental and holding others to a standard that is not evident in the Word of God. Help me to live in the path of freedom, yet keep me from abusing your gift of grace and mercy which you have so lovingly given to me. Thank you for the gift of freedom through your eternal grace. Amen.

Tidbits:

> "In Him [Christ] and through faith in Him we may approach God with freedom and confidence." – Ephesians 3:12, NIV

> "The lost enjoy forever the horrible freedom they have demanded." – C. S. Lewis

> "If you abide in my word, you are truly my disciples and you will know the truth, and the truth will set you free." – John 8:31-32, ESV

> "May we think of freedom, not as the right to do as we please, but as the opportunity to do what is right." – Peter Marshall

> "Because Christ offered himself to God, he is able to bring a new promise from God. Through his death he paid the price to set people free from the sins they committed under the first promise. He did this so that those who are called can be guaranteed an inheritance that will last forever." – Hebrews 9:15, GW

> "Our freedom is tied to our individual souls, a gift from God, not from government." – Mike Huckabee

Song Selection: In Your Freedom – written by Marty Sampson, Raymond Badham; performed by Hillsong

HIS EYE IS ON THE SPARROW

"Look at the birds of the air; they neither sow nor reap nor gather into barns, and yet your heavenly Father feeds them. Are you not of more value than they?" – Matthew 6:26, ESV

This title "His Eye is On the Sparrow" is a popular Christian song, written in 1905, that my operatic mother-in-law often sang as a solo in church. It brings me such comfort not only because of the truth that is written within the song but that the memories of a wonderful individual who herself survived three bouts of cancer. God blessed her for an abundant ninety-two years.

The author, Civilla D. Martin, and her husband had been staying in New York state where they met a couple named Mr. and Mrs. Doolittle. Civilla said this about her inspiration in writing the song.

Mrs. Doolittle had been bedridden for nigh twenty years. Her husband was an incurable cripple who had to propel himself to and from his business in a wheel chair. Despite their afflictions, they lived happy Christian lives, bringing inspiration and comfort to all who knew them. One day while we were visiting with the Doolittles, my husband commented on their bright hopefulness and asked them for the secret of it. Mrs. Doolittle's reply was simple: "His eye is on the sparrow, and I know He watches me." (Wikipedia)

The writer of the song was so gripped by this metaphor of God's grace that she wrote this hymn "His Eye Is on the Sparrow."

Despite the hundreds of chairs and beds that line walls of the chemo clinic, I often felt extremely alone and empty as if I were just a number among the masses. I needed to feel loved and that my life really mattered. God was faithful and reminded me of this song. If Jesus kept his eye on the smallest of the birds of the air, the sparrow, then I knew He would keep His eye on me. Sparrows are dirty, worthless birds without colour or song yet not one of them would fall to the ground apart from the Father's will.

How many times have you felt like a lonely sparrow? Like the sparrow, my righteousness is as filthy rags, and many times in my cancer battle, I felt I was without song, but I knew Jesus cared. None of the things of this world can ever fill my heart like Jesus!

Prayer: Heavenly Father, you care for the birds of the air and provide for them daily so I know you care for me. You tell me not to worry because you know exactly what I need from day to day. Keep me safe, keep me company and satisfy my longings when I feel so alone. Praise you for your daily care. Amen.

Tidbits:

"Happy is the person who not only sings, but feels God's eye is on the sparrow, and knows He watches over me. To be simply ensconced in God is true joy." – Alfred A Montapert

"Why, even the hairs of your head are all numbered. Fear not; you are of more value than many sparrows." – Luke 12:7, ESV

"Birds sing after a storm; why shouldn't people feel as free to delight in whatever sunlight remains to them?" – Rose Kennedy

"He who dwells in the shelter of the Most High will abide in the shadow of the Almighty. . . For He will deliver you from the snare of the fowler and from the deadly pestilence. He will cover you with his pinions, and under his wings you will find refuge. – Psalm 91:1, 3-4, ESV

"The problem is not the problem. The problem is your attitude about the problem." – Captain Jack Sparrow

Song Selection: His Eye is on the Sparrow – written by Civilla D Martin, Charles H. Gabriel

COUNT IT ALL JOY

"Consider it a sheer gift, (count it all joy) friends, when tests and challenges come at you from all sides. You know that under pressure, your faith-life is forced into the open and shows its true colours. So don't try to get out of anything prematurely. Let it do its work so you become mature and well-developed, not deficient in any way." – James 1:2-4, MSG

This passage of scripture was taught in depth during a study in the book of James, and has been my stronghold for several years since. It was specifically placed on my heart by God, though I didn't fully understand its meaning until I accepted it as sheer truth and the divine purpose that God intended.

When we get bad news, a health scare, someone dies, or when facing financial destruction, all of our pronounced words about faith are worthless. What matters is how we react and what we do in the midst of troubling circumstances. I know what we are supposed to do. We are to count it all joy! Really? Joy? You've got to be kidding. God tells us trials are going to happen and they purposely come to test our faith and refine us. No matter how faithful we claim to be, how much service we have performed, how many encouraging platitudes we share or how much we feel we have sacrificed for the Lord, trials will still come our way.

Counting it all joy is not about pretending there is no pain or questions; it is about recognizing in the end all things work for good to those who love the Lord. "And we know that in all things God works for the good of those who love Him, who have been called according to His purpose" (Romans 8:28, NIV). Temptations, trials, and tribulations will test our faith and have purpose to develop patience and perseverance. As a young mother and dealing with daily frustrations of consistently spilled milk at the table (before the invention of 'sippy cups'), I shared at Bible study, "I'm asking the Lord for patience in this matter." In humour, but with all sincerity, the leader said, "Honey, you don't want to pray for patience, for the Lord will just allow the spilling of milk to continue." She wasn't totally serious, but I paid much more attention to the content of my prayers after her comment. The spilling of milk is a normal consequence of raising a young child and maybe just filling the cup too full. There were different way to find joy in this frustration and I chose to count it all joy instead of distressing over spilled milk.

As humans we dislike the testing process because it often involves pain, sorrow, stress, and upheaval, but James tells us not to try and wiggle out of the hard times too soon, for we short-circuit the process and remain immature, like little babies.

This raises the subject of Sippy cups again. Oh yes, decades have passed, I'm a grandmother and the sippy cup is popular. To lessen the spill disasters this time around, the sippy was in constant use. Sadly, this did not allow for the training of the children to set their cups in a safe position or on a solid surface. Without the training, they would remain as babies, so to speak, untrained, spoiled and untested for too long. Spilled milk provides a teaching opportunity.

With each testing the Lord brings, my way I am learning to count it all joy." Even cancer! The blessings from this test have been numerous and I look forward to the path that God already has mapped out because I know that He loves me and has plans to bless me. Do I look forward to the process and the potential pain or suffering? No! But I do look forward to moving towards the person that Christ desires me to become through it. Come what may, I'll sing for joy at the work of His hands.

Prayer: Thank you Lord for providing joy in the most unlikely of places and how earlier lessons have taught me to count it all joy, even cancer. You promise good for those who love you, and I look forward to the daily blessings that are mine in Christ. Help me to share joy and a gift of laughter with another who is suffering and may not know your ultimate joy. There is none like you and I praise the wonders of Your mighty love. Amen.

Tidbits:

> "Joy does not simply happen to us. We have to choose joy and keep choosing it every day." – Henri Nouwen

> "Clap your hands, all you peoples! Shout to God with a loud cry of joy!" – Psalms 47:1, ISV

> "Joy is not in things; it is in us." – Richard Wagner

> "May the God of hope fill you with all joy and peace in believing, so that by the power of the Holy Spirit you may abound in hope!" – Romans 15:13, ESV

> "Happiness is not the absence of problems but the ability to deal with them." – Anonymous

Song Selection: Shout to the Lord – written by Darlene Zscheck

INNER BEAUTY

"Don't be concerned about the outward beauty of fancy hairstyles, expensive jewelry, or beautiful clothes. You should clothe yourselves instead with the beauty that comes from within, the unfading beauty of a gentle and quiet spirit, which is so precious to God." – 1 Peter 3:3-4, NLT

God created a world full of majestic beauty and there is nothing wrong with a desire to be beautiful, for God designed women to be creatures of beauty; however, that is a very small part of what makes a woman truly beautiful. We can apply layers of makeup, spend countless hours with our hair-stylist, purchase mountains of moisturizer and wrinkle creams, relish manicure and pedicure treatments, and even cross the line, so to speak, and try Botox injections or plastic surgery, but these will not make the Christian woman totally beautiful. Unfortunately, we place so much importance on our body's features and flaws that we lose sight of the uniqueness in which God created us. If we all pursued the same perfect beauty, we would all just be clones of each other and what uniqueness is there in being a clone?

There have been several instances when we have been watching a movie where keeping track of the individual female characters is difficult because they all look alike. Let's change our focus on the outward appearance by: maintaining a reasonably fit body that radiates with healthy energy; dressing modestly so as to not to attract the wrong kind of attention; and displaying a degree of femininity so that our gender is not in question.

A truly beautiful woman radiates inner beauty that brings honour and glory to God. If you truly are interested in knowing the characteristics of an "inner beautiful" woman of God, then take note of the qualities listed in Proverbs 31:10-31: A woman to be treasured is noble (10), trustworthy (11), honours her husband (12), is hardworking (13), and exercises good judgment (14). She has laid out a plan (15), is thrifty (16), works willingly (17), and is productive (18) through hard work (19). She is generous (20), a visionary (21), also creative (22) and talented (24). Her behaviour is an honour to her husband (23) and she wisely prepares for the future (25). She is found to be busy as well as attentive (27) and never fails to speak kindly (26).

Any fleshly attempt to manifest these godly attributes is impossible and the feat thereof is overwhelming, but by the grace of God we should seek to develop an inner self that not only ingratiates our personality to others but also displays the importance of God in our lives and our worthiness to Him.

Jesus was not a creation of loveliness, nor did He come to display beauty, but he makes us beautiful and our inner radiance is an indication of our relationship with Him. I am so thankful that God looks on the heart and our inner beauty is more important to Him than any other quality we can possess. We should daily strive to develop the potential that God intended for us. A woman who is overly conscientious about her outward beauty and neglects to cultivate her inner beautification is nothing but a vacant physique lacking spiritual impact.

Prayer: Heavenly Father, You have fearfully and wonderfully created me just as I am, and for that I am thankful. All my cells, even the cancerous ones, are under your control and you find beauty in every sinew of my being. Help me to develop inner beauty as I rely on the Holy Spirit for divine guidance. Amen.

Tidbits:

> "Do not look on his appearance . . . For the Lord sees not as man sees: man looks on the outward appearance, but the Lord looks on the heart." – 1 Samuel 16:7, ESV

> "The beauty of a woman is not in a facial mode but the true beauty in a woman is reflected in her soul. It is the caring that she lovingly gives the passion that she shows. The beauty of a woman grows with the passing years." – Audrey Hepburn

> "Those who look to Him are radiant, and their faces shall never be ashamed." – Psalm 34:5, ESV

> "What's the whole point of being pretty on the outside when you're so ugly on the inside?" – Jess C. Scott

Song Selection: Beautiful One – written by Tim Hughes

JESUS, OUR THIRST QUENCHER

"As a deer pants for the flowing streams, so my soul pants for
You, O God. My soul thirsts for God, for the living God." –
Psalm 42:1-2, ESV

Thirst is an amazing sense, although it is not mentioned with the other more common senses, sight, smell, touch and hearing. It is important because it signals our brain to pay attention that our body needs water. In fact, doctors say that if we have waited until we feel thirsty we have waited too long to drink. One of the most important recommendations given to me during my weeks of chemotherapy was to make sure to drink more water than usual. Chemo treatments may cause swallowing problems, nausea, diarrhea, constipation and there is also potential danger to the kidneys. In order to try and avoid these possible evils or even dehydration, I made a concentrated effort to drink more water, which I have never really liked, and other liquids which thankfully counted towards the suggested total of nine cups per day.

Your body knows when it is becoming dehydrated for the following symptoms appear: fatigue, headache, lightheadedness, dry mouth and skin, decreased urination, constipation and, of course, extreme thirstiness. With every drink of cool water, I envisioned my healthy cells being refreshed while the chemo zapped my cancer cells. Just as the liquid water was recommended for better health, the Bible has recommends 'living water' to refresh our souls.

Very few of us have ever been thirsty to the point that our lips are chapped, the tongue is thick, or we have extreme headaches and body weakness. But do you know how to recognize a thirsty soul? In the very beginning, there is uneasiness in our soul and we attempt to fill our emptiness with entertainment or possessions. We may have a nagging conscience and try to mask it with earthly thrills or numerous friendships. This condition is a dehydrated heart—the absence of God—which can only be quenched by accepting Christ. If you do not know Him personally take time to revitalize your heart right now.

After becoming a Christian, there is still much danger in starving our soul and becoming dehydrated spiritually. Max Lucado in his book, *Come Thirsty*, tells us just a few of the ways to recognize a thirsty soul: "Snarling tempers, waves of worry, growling mastodons of guilt and fear, hopelessness, sleeplessness, loneliness, resentment, irritability, insecurity are the warnings of a dryness deep within." Christians often resort to the same vices the world uses to quench this deep dryness, such as alcohol, drugs, pornography, gambling, habits, hobbies, or a full schedule, just usually not to the same degree or as openly for they are more likely to hide their behaviour and deny their thirst.

God knows that it is He alone whom can quench our thirst and He tells us to forsake all other routes where we think we can find joy. "Seek ye first the kingdom of God." (Matthew 6:33, NIV) We are to rely on Him alone for complete success of quenched thirst, a strong faith and deeper fellowship. We need to bury self-centredness and focus on Christ and His Word. Become totally dependent on Jesus and He guarantees we will never thirst again. "Whoever drinks of the water that I will give him will never be thirsty again" (John 4:14, ESV).

Prayer: Lord, help me to be aware of my spiritual thirstiness before I become parched and dry. I am grateful that the refreshing water you offer quenches our thirst, today and for the eternal tomorrows. You alone are the fountain of water that springs up into everlasting life. Amen.

Tidbits:

> "Blessed are those who hunger and thirst for righteousness, for they shall be satisfied." – Matthew 5:6, ESV

> "As clouds are blown away by the wind, the thirst for material pleasures will be driven away by the utterance of the Lord's name." – Sri Sarada Devi

> "They will never again be hungry or thirsty; they will never be scorched by the heat of the sun. For the Lamb on the throne will be their Shepherd. He will lead them to springs of life-giving water. And God will wipe every tear from their eyes." – Revelation 7:16-17, NLT

> "Spiritual hunger and spiritual thirst, but you got to change it on the inside first to be satisfied" – Van Morrison

> "You, God, are my God, earnestly I seek you; I thirst for you, my whole being longs for you, in a dry and parched land where there is no water" – Psalm 63:1, NIV

Song Selection: Beneath the Waters (I Will Rise) – written by Scott Ligertwood, Brooke Ligertwood

JOY OF THE LORD

"The joy of the Lord is my strength." – Nehemiah 8:10, NIV

What brings you joy? Is it the kind gesture of a grandchild when she hands you a bouquet of dandelions she picked for you? How about watching the beautiful wedding ceremony of a childhood friend? Maybe it's the long sought after graduation ceremony of a wayward child. Situations that can bring us joy during our journey here on earth are probably endless, but this is not the joy that Nehemiah is referring to. He found his strength from delighting in the Lord and having joy despite adverse circumstances.

I would dare to say that when our circumstances are challenging and our trials monstrous that joy is not our first response. Every Christian should have "the joy of the Lord" for is part of our inheritance. Our heart should be filled with it. But is there really true joy in the hearts of those of us who call ourselves Christians?

The Old Testament is full of festivals that were full of joy, one of which was the Feast of Tabernacles. However in Nehemiah, after the return of the captives and the rebuilding of Jerusalem, "All the people wept, when they heard the words of the law! (v.9) It was painful reading, for it reminded them of their sins and exposed the holiness of God. They were ashamed and wept. Nehemiah stilled their weeping and called them to enter into the joy of the occasion. "This day is holy to the Lord your God. Do not mourn or weep. Go and enjoy choice foods and sweet drinks, and send to those who have nothing prepared. This is a holy day to our Lord. Do not grieve, for the joy of the Lord is your strength!" (Nehemiah 8:9-10, NIV)

Despite adverse circumstances we are commanded in James to "Count it all joy when we fall into various trials and temptations knowing that the testing of our faith produces patience." Joy is a deeper experience than happiness, for happiness is dependent on favourable conditions, yet true joy defies environment and adverse situations. We misrepresent Christ and the joyful life we have in Him when we are facing challenges and behaving with somber and depressed attitudes.

Cancer is possibly a journey where we fail in communicating 'the joy of the Lord' for the passage is long and it involves months of harsh treatments. Yet if we propose to grow toward Christ-likeness and become more filled with Him, our joy will grow. I can testify that if it were not for the 'joy of the Lord' providing daily strength during my cancer journey, I would be overwhelmed, but I have the "joy. . . down in my heart."

So I ask you again, what brings you joy? The joy of the Lord is not earth's joy, which comes from earthly pleasures and possessions, but the joy that comes from knowing God and from being His child. True joy comes only when we are focused on walking with the Lord. This is not a joy the world can give nor can it take away. When you are facing the deepest and fiercest of storms, remember "The joy of the Lord is your strength."

Prayer: May I be found prostrate at your feet in worship and appreciation for supplying me with joy through this journey. My life with success and failures can be filled with the joy of the Lord because of you alone. Amen.

Tidbits:

"Joy is the serious business of Heaven." – C. S. Lewis

"Clap your hands, all peoples! Shout to God with loud songs of joy!" – Psalms 47:1, ESV

"What I am anxious to see in Christian believers is a beautiful paradox. I want to see in them the joy of finding God while at the same time they are blessedly pursuing Him. I want to see in them the great joy of having God yet always wanting Him." – A. W. Tozer

"The hope of the righteous brings joy, but the expectation of the wicked will perish." – Proverbs 10:28, ESV

"The out-and-out Christian is a joyful Christian. The half-and-half Christian is the kind of Christian that a great many of you are little acquainted with the Lord. Why should we live halfway up the hill and swathed in the mists, when we might have an unclouded sky and a radiant sun over our heads if we would climb higher and walk in the light of His face?" – Alexander Maclaren

"May the God of hope fill you with all joy and peace in believing, so that by the power of the Holy Spirit you may abound in hope." – Romans 15:13, ESV

Song Selection: The Joy of the Lord – written by Twila Paris

MY EBENEZER?

"Then Samuel took a stone and set it up between Mizpah and
Shen. He named it Ebenezer, saying, 'Thus far the Lord has
helped us.'" – 1 Samuel 7:12, NIV

What is an Ebenezer?" Most people, along with my husband a *Christmas
Carol* fanatic, would first think of Ebenezer Scrooge, the crotchety
old man that totally despised Christmas. However, the term actually come
from the Bible and is derived from a Hebrew word meaning 'help' and in the
case of Samuel's usage, "Stone of Help." Ebenezer also names a geographical
location where the Israelites were defeated by the Philistines and the Ark of
the Covenant was stolen. After a later Israelite victory, Samuel placed a stone to
signify that God had miraculously changed Israel's outcome and delivered the
Philistines into their hands. After a long period of waywardness, the Israelites,
under the leadership of Samuel, recommitted their hearts and minds to the
Lord. The Ebenezer stone was a representation of a fresh beginning for them.

I am sure you can identify with Israel, as we have all experienced periods
of disobedience and consequently needed rededication, refreshing, and a new
beginning in which to refocus on God, to love, serve and live for Him again.
Unfortunately, I certainly also identify and shamefully confess my failures. While
there are many 'little sins' in need of continual confession and forgiveness, there
are a couple of 'biggies' that resulted in two seasons of backsliding, followed
with a period of weeping over my sin and humble requests for forgiveness from
God. I had volunteered and positioned myself in too many areas of service
and ended up crashing under the weight of too many responsibilities. While it
is honourable to serve God, is it a sin to replace the priority of a relationship
with Christ with a surplus of service. Years later I sought God's mercy when
I was a young mother to two children under three. My infant son's stomach
complications produced projectile 'spit-ups" and confined me to the house. Out
of my feelings of utter seclusion, I created my own 'pity party' and, as a result,
made some very selfish decisions that nearly cost me my marriage. Thankfully,
God, in all His love, restored me and I have "Ebenezers" to remind me I am
totally and marvelously forgiven. Thanks to Paul's reminder in Philippians there
is no need to 'kick myself around the block' for my past failures, but I am much
more cautious about being tripped up by the devil's snares. "Forgetting the past
and looking forward to what lies ahead, I strain to reach the end of the race and
receive the prize for which God, through Christ Jesus, is calling us." (Philippians
3:13b, 14, NLT).

I have had an amazing period of rededication, refreshing and spiritual revival with the Lord throughout my cancer journey and personally look forward to the 'fresh beginning' that comes after surgery and a period of healing. What will I raise for an Ebenezer? I am not sure, but you can count on my thinking of something to be a significant reminder of God's faithfulness to me.

Prayer: Heavenly Father, I thank you for your never ending mercy and forgiveness of my sins and waywardness. Your great love overwhelms me and I am grateful for your constant presence throughout my battle with cancer. You will provide victory and I will once again be able to raise an Ebenezer. Amen.

Tidbits:

> "Help us, O God of our salvation, for the glory of your name; deliver us, and atone for our sins, for your name's sake!" – Psalm 79:9, ESV

> "The Christian life is not a constant high. I have moments of deep discouragement. I have to go to God in prayer with tears in my eyes, and say, 'O God, forgive me,' or 'Help me.'" – Billy Graham

> "Let us then with confidence draw near to the throne of grace, that we may receive mercy and find grace to help in time of need." – Hebrews 4:16, ESV

> "We can't help everyone, but everyone can help someone." – Dr. L Scott

> "It is necessary to help others, not only in our prayers, but in our daily lives. If we find we cannot help others, the least we can do is to desist from harming them." – Dalai Lama

Song Suggestion: Come Thou Font of Every Blessing – written by John Wyeth, Robert Robinson

OPEN HANDS, OPEN HEART

"And I will give you a new heart, and I will put a new spirit in you. I will take out your stony, stubborn heart and give you a tender, responsive heart." – Ezekiel 36:26, NLT

I have just finished reading the *People* magazine's special edition celebrating 25 seasons of the Bachelor & Bachelorette. Yes, I admit, I am a 'reality show junkie.' I love watching how different personalities mesh and clash, and how the actions and reactions of normal everyday people affect others. Unfortunately, very few reality shows can boast success measured by the 'goodness factor' but more from poor to bad behaviour of the villains. With only three couples currently able to boast 'love being a reality' for them, it did cause me to ponder my own spousal relationship and what makes it work. Foremost, our commitment to God bears the highest praise for its success, but on a more personal level it has been that of having open hearts and open hands. Our hearts are open to receive and give love. Regardless of occasional frustrations, we have vulnerable hearts always willing to extend forgiveness so love continues to grow. Secondly, we nurture the relationship by sharing open hands, hands willing to help, comfort and commend one another, and encouraging one another with deeds of kindness, especially those not expected or requested.

Our personal relationship with Christ is somewhat the same as we come to Him with an open heart and open hands. We first come with an open heart to receive Him as a personal Saviour, and a willingness to be changed to become more like Him. God invites us to open our heart to the leading of the Holy Spirit, responding with a readiness to be obedient. Instead of hardening our heart in times of difficulty and blaming God, we should have a heart increasing in tenderness. Demonstrating a tender compassionate heart towards God benefits you and the people around you. Your example of being reachable, teachable and correctable by the Holy Spirit helps others to be more receptive to Him as well, for they witness the benefits of obedience. A truly open heart accepts whatever it takes to be shaped into a beautiful useful vessel for Christ.

Open hands turned towards the heavens are a symbol of willingness to receive whatever God gives and a readiness to give back. Open hands signify a preparedness to release our own premeditated plans and openness to God's plan. A cancer path may bring upsetting losses of physical abilities, clear thinking, hair loss and normal ways of life that we may be inclined to thrust a bitterly clenched fist towards God, resenting the path He has chosen for us. Oh, may the shame be on us if we open our hands only when the circumstances are in our favour. When examining my own hands, I want them to be always open, ready to receive whatever God has planned, and ready to give whatever He asks of me. My future holds much uncertainty, but His promises are forever certain. He has promised peace to those who trust Him, and assurance that whatever He has planned for my life is far better than anything that I could ever plan for myself. My heart is open to receive His love and my hands are open to receive and perform His will. God desires every part of me, not just the parts I feel comfortable turning over to Him. He will provide the strength to move forward.

Prayer: Heavenly Father, thank you for opening my heart to your unfailing love and encouraging me to respond with open hands, willing to follow whatever path you have planned. I do not trust in my own abilities but depend totally upon you to provide whatever it takes to be used of you. Continue to transform me into the person you want me to be and thank you for never giving up on me. Amen.

Tidbits:

> "For I know the plans I have for you," declares the LORD, "plans to prosper you and not to harm you, plans to give you hope and a future." – Jeremiah 29:11, NIV

> "We turn, and give ourselves body, soul, and spirit back to God, asking him to cleanse our hearts and make them new. And he does. He gives us a new heart. And he comes to dwell there, in our hearts." – John Eldredge

> "Therefore, if anyone is in Christ, the new creation has come: The old has gone, the new is here!" – 2 Corinthians 5:17, NIV

> "The thing that ought to make the heart beat is a new way of manifesting the Son of God." – Oswald Chambers

> "God's love has been poured out into our hearts through the Holy Spirit, who has been given to us." – Romans 5:5, NIV

Song Selection: The Heart of Worship – written by Matt Redman

THERE IS A BALM IN GILEAD

"Is there no balm in Gilead? Is there no physician there? Why then is there no healing for the wound of my people?" – Jeremiah 8:22, NIV

The hymn, "There is a Balm in Gilead," an African-American spiritual, speaks of something so wonderful that it healed whatever was wrong with people. It's also referred to as healing spiritual ills.

There is a balm in Gilead to make the wounded whole;
There is a balm in Gilead to heal the sin sick soul.
Sometimes I feel discouraged and think my work's in vain,
But then the Holy Spirit revives my soul again.

This particular balm was made from the resin of a flowering plant in the Middle East, and was similar to honey and very pleasant smelling. It was sometimes mixed with olive oil and swallowed or put on wounds for healing. The 'balm of Gilead" was a high-quality balm with medicinal properties and a cherished, sought after ointment.

The Bible uses the term "balm of Gilead" symbolically as an example of something with restorative or comforting powers. The song also relates its ability to heal the sin-sick soul. Not only are there many walking around who are "sin-sick," but there are many believers walking around with various kinds of baggage that need to be unburdened. The Lord does not want us to carry this baggage alone. Whether it emotional or physical baggage, He wants to set us all free so we can realize our full potential for Him.

Jeremiah was called by the Lord to deliver depressing news to the Israelites after centuries of warnings that they would be destroyed. He cries out in anger and in grief, all coming from a deep love for his people and for which he gave his entire life to stop the pending destruction. Israel simply forgot who they were. Jeremiah understood that the time for Judah to repent and change her ways had passed. Their demise was certain, but that didn't stop him from pleading with God. The promised chaos did come, as many prophets had warned, but thankfully, this key upset produced transparency for Israel. They were never totally abandoned by God and future prophets declared God's love to them, "Since you are precious in my sight, since you are honored and I love you, I will give other men in your place and other peoples in exchange for your life" (Isaiah 43:4, NASB).

We are no different than Israel when it comes to our foolish independence; we often reject the one who can apply the healing balm. No matter what it is that we have suffered in our past, the only answer is still God's Word, Jesus, the Word who became flesh. We, sometimes, simply live like Israel did, forgetting who we are and manage just fine independently, but then severe circumstances arise and we are faced with our baggage once again. We have failed to be obedient in yielding it to Christ. Why do we attempt to protect or mend ourselves instead of trusting the one our lives are supposed to be entrusted to? We do a great disservice to God and others when we refuse to face reality and acknowledge our weakness. Because it is through our weakness that God shows His strength and power. No one else can provide the comfort, peace and strength that we need to face our difficulties and our pains. He truly understands so let Him apply the Balm of Gilead.

Prayer: I praise you, Heavenly Father, for despite our stupidity and selfish ways you never fail to express your unending love for us. You have provided a balm that heals all wounds and soothes all grief. Help me to face uncertain days expecting a fulfillment of promise of perfecting your work in me. Amen.

Tidbits:

> "LORD my God, I called to you for help, and you healed me." – Psalm 30:2, NIV

> "The good physician treats the disease; the great physician treats the patient who has the disease." – Sir William Osler

> "Praise be to the God and Father of our Lord Jesus Christ! In His great mercy He has given us new birth into a living hope through the resurrection of Jesus Christ from the dead, and into an inheritance that can never perish, spoil or fade." – 1 Peter 1:3-4, NIV

> "The Great Physician makes house calls." – Unknown

> "Come to me, all you who are weary and burdened, and I will give you rest." – Matthew 11:28, NIV

> A wise physician said to me: "I've been practicing medicine for 30years and I have prescribed many things. But in the long run I have learned that for most of what ails the human creature, the best medicine is love."
> "What if it doesn't work?" I asked.
> "Double the dose." He replied. – Unknown

> "He sent out his word and healed them, and delivered them from their destruction." – Psalms 107:20, ESV

Song Selection: There is a Balm in Gilead – Traditional Spiritual

GRUMBLING

"Don't grumble about each other, brothers and sisters, or you
will be judged. For look—the Judge is standing at the door!"
– James 5:9, NLT

The definition of grumble is to groan, murmur, complain, and protest.
Grumbling is as old as creation, in fact, we could accuse Eve of complaining about being unable to eat of the tree of good and evil. Cain, who
murdered his own brother, complained about the level of punishment he
received from God. The Israelites were constant complainers about anything
that went amiss in their wilderness journey, even though the Lord continued to
supernaturally and powerfully provide for them. Biblical heroes such as Jacob,
Elijah, Gideon, Job and Jeremiah all found things to grumble about.

You would think that after reading about the destruction of the Israelites
and Paul's stiff warning against the Corinthians about grumbling, we would
know enough to be cautious with our tongue. Unfortunately, grumbling could
probably be declared an epidemic in our society that holds many blessings.
When we are discontented and choose to complain about the government, our
employer, our wages, our teachers, our pastor, or fellow Christians, do we even
realize that we are grumbling against God? He is Sovereign and in control of
all things so when we choose to grumble we are complaining against God and
His plan. He who promised to be a friend forever, and knows exactly what
He has planned for our lives, is grieved when we grumble about troubling
circumstances for we are complaining against Him. We know, as Christians,
that when we murmur against a brother that we are wrong and actually judging
them despite the instruction of Jesus, "Do not judge, or you too will be judged."
(Matthew 7:1, NIV) Grumbling is a sin and does not bring glory to God. Many
fellow believers have been hurt and left the church or fallen away from Christ
entirely, simply because of the grumbling of others. Unfortunately, we, too,
have experienced malicious murmuring, leaving our family of twelve to suffer
seasons of much pain, but we are thankful to God that He kept each of us near
to Himself and restored us to areas of service for His glory.

Regrettably, the arrows of criticism are often aimed at the pastors or leadership of our churches. Several have been discouraged, suffer burn-out and many
abandon the call because of unleashed tongues.

Shame on us who do not heed Jesus words, "Why do you look at the speck
that is in your brother's eye, but do not notice the log that is in your own eye? Or
how can you say to your brother, "Let me take the speck out of your eye" and
behold, the log is in your own eye? You hypocrite, first take the log out of your
own eye, and then you will see clearly to take the speck out of your brother's
eye." (Matthew 7:3-5, NASB)

None of us are immune to this sin either as a victim or an aggressor, but we can strive purposefully each day to grumble less and guard our tongue before casting judgment on others. We need to continually be reminded of our own divine but undeserved heritage in Christ. "Therefore, if anyone is in Christ, the new creation has come: The old has gone, the new is here!" (2 Corinthians 5:17, NIV)

Prayer: Heavenly Father, my desire is to honour you in everything I do, including taming my tongue. Forgive me for my unguarded speech and keep me from speaking deceit and to turn my ears away from evil murmurings. Help me to remain focused on things that are lovely and of good report. May my words be only those that are for the building up or encouraging of others, so that my life will be a testimony of your love. Amen.

Tidbits:

> "Nor grumble, as some of them did and were destroyed by the Destroyer." – 1 Corinthians 10:10, ESV
>
> "It is no use to grumble and complain; it's just as cheap and easy to rejoice." – James Riley
>
> "Do all things without grumbling or disputing." – Philippians 2:14, ESV
>
> "Remember, if you are criticizing, you are not being grateful. If you are blaming, you are not being grateful. If you are complaining, you are not being grateful." – Rhonda Byrne
>
> "How long shall this wicked congregation grumble against me? I have heard the grumblings of the people of Israel. . ." – Number 14:27, ESV
>
> "Don't find fault, find a remedy; anybody can complain." – Henry Ford
>
> "The tendency to whining and complaining may be taken as the surest sign symptom of little souls and inferior intellects." – Lord Jeffrey
>
> "Do not grumble among yourselves." – John 6:41-43, ESV

Song Selection: Grumbler Song – by Thoro Harris

> In country, town or city some people can be found
>
> Who spend their lives in grumbling at everything around
>
> Oh yes, they always grumble, no matter what we say
>
> For these are chronic grumblers and they grumble night and day.
>
> Oh, they grumble on Monday, Tuesday, Wednesday
>
> Grumble on Thursday too.
>
> Grumble on Friday, Saturday, Sunday
>
> Grumble the whole week through.

YOUR GRACE IS ENOUGH

"My flesh and my heart may fail, but God is the strength of my heart and my portion forever." – Psalm 73:26, NIV

This is such a short verse, yet it manages to pronounce within it how inadequate I am, and how much I need God! An ultimate sense of failure conjures feelings of frustration and abandonment, and while I know that I am not alone there are moments, that verify this verse is absolutely accurate. My flesh and heart fail, producing fear. Thankfully, due to the grace of God, fear is a temporary visit. As I was searching to find answers on how to become better prepared to face upcoming radiation treatment, one of those fleeting fearful moments surfaced. Unfortunately, the simple search produced too much information; in particular, the grim statistics of esophageal cancer survival and, voila, fear appeared.

I tend to be far too analytical of my feelings and sought to try and understand why I can have God's peace that passes understanding one minute and then minutes later I am flip-flopping to a spirit of fear. As this battle period lengthens, it is only in my times of peace that I can completely accept God's will. But that peace is often disrupted by a growing desire to remain here on earth. Is that disruption because I don't want the battle against cancer to be in vain? Or am I more prepared to face my own mortality, because with completely devastating news, I am more inclined to lean on God? One thing that I know for sure is that our 'feelings' are not a foundation on which to base anything and I also know that fear is not from God.

So if fear is not from God, the only other source is the devil. And to battle the devil, we are encouraged to use God's Word. So each and every time that the devil succeeds to cast a temporary spirit of fear into my path, I draw on the promises in God's Word, and gospel music to shield me from evil influences. I count on God's grace: God's riches at Christ's expense. The work of Jesus Christ on the cross makes this precious gift of grace available to me. Grace is unmerited, undeserved and unearned favour. "For it is by grace you have been saved, through faith—and this is not from yourselves, it is the gift of God—not by works, so that no one can boast" (Ephesians 2:8-9, NIV).

God is a God of grace. Grace is not simply a part of God's redemption plan but is an element woven into every fibre of our Christian life, salvation, maturing, ministry and stability. Saving grace covers my sinful past and sanctifying grace aids in maturing my faith, through reliance on the Holy Spirit. Serving grace helps me to recognize and use God-given gifts in ministry, while sustaining grace is provided by God to help me face adversity, suffering and 'rid a spirit of fear.' So in the face of anything the devil wants to throw my way, His grace is enough! "My grace is enough; it's all you need. My strength comes into its own in your weakness" (2 Corinthians 12:9, MSG).

Prayer: Heavenly Father, thank you for unmerited favour and unfailing love! Your daily measures of grace are enough to see me through every trial, danger and moments of fear. When I am weak, you can make me strong with your all-exceeding power. Thank you for grace. Amen.

Tidbits:

> "Let us then approach God's throne of grace with confidence, so that we may receive mercy and find grace to help us in our time of need." – Hebrews 4: 16, NIV

> "Grace does not grant permission to live in the flesh; it supplies power to live in the Spirit." – John MacArthur

> "But He gives graced generously. As Scripture says, 'God opposes the proud but favours the humble." – James 4: 6, NLT

> "I am not what I ought to be. I am not what I want to be. I am not what I hope to be in another world; but still I am not what I once used to be, and by the grace of God I am what I am." – John Newton

> "For the LORD God is our sun and our shield. He gives us grace and glory. The LORD will withhold no good thing from those who do what is right." – Psalm 84: 11, NLT

> "Where the will of God leads you, the grace of God will keep you." – Unknown

Song Suggestion: Your Grace Is Enough – written by Matt Maher

NO BARGAIN ALLOWED?

"Don't bargain with God. Be direct. Ask for what you need. This is not a cat-and-mouse, hide-and-seek game we're in. If your little boy asks for a serving of fish, do you scare him with a live snake on his plate? If your little girl asks for an egg, do you trick her with a spider? As bad as you are, you wouldn't think of such a thing—you're at least decent to your own children. And don't you think the Father who conceived you in love will give the Holy Spirit when you ask him?" – Luke 11:10-13, MSG

Have you ever found yourself in a difficult situation and made a bargain with God? Many people, as if attending a yard sale, have tried to bargain with God and wished for an advantage in return for a commitment. I'm not talking about the typical prayers where we petition God for answers but a direct plea for an exchange of favours. First of all, it is not scriptural. A deal or bargain begins with our setting the restrictions and not the Almighty. From the get go, that is wrong. There is nothing, absolutely nothing, we can do that will merit God's favour. He may choose to bless us as He had intended to do from the very beginning, but that doesn't mean the bargain was consummated, it just appears that way.

In an example from Genesis 28:20-21, NLT, "Then Jacob made a vow, saying, "If God will be with me and will provide me with food to eat and clothing and if I return safely to my father's home, then the LORD will certainly be my God."

Jacob appears to be striking a bargain with God, but we know better and realized that God intended to bless Jacob anyway. God designed several difficult lessons along Jacob's faith journey to show that He couldn't be bargained with, but still provided grace and mercy for the journey. Do you think you are better than Jacob and know better than to bargain with God? Consider the following. Do they sound familiar?

"Lord, if you'll just give me a promotion, I'll be able to tithe more."

"Lord, if you just change my husband, I'll make this marriage work."

"Lord, if you provide me a much-needed vacation, I'll serve you faithfully."

"Lord, if you bless me with another child, I promise to stop shouting."

Now you probably are annoyed that you wouldn't be so foolish to attempt bargaining with God, but let me show a more subtle 'let's make a deal." I served the Lord in several capacities, thinking that a project or program would not survive without me and I would be doing God a favour by doing so, and silently expecting blessings for my service. We often walk in obedience with a false thinking, that by being compliant we are staying in God's good graces. Let me reiterate that there is nothing, absolutely nothing, that we can do or offer that merits the love of God. God simply loves us. He wants a relationship with us and He creates needs in our lives so that we will build a relationship and not treat Him like Santa Claus. He desires to be first in our lives and longs for us to "seek first the kingdom of God." God doesn't want anything to steal our hearts away from Him.

Prayer: Father, thank you for making it clear that when my heart is in sync with you, I need to simply ask and receive, and no bargaining is required. I desire to be convicted, to repent and to be restored each time I have strayed, so that my fellowship with you is authentic. Cleanse me of my selfishness and prod me continually to seek first your kingdom and your righteousness. Amen.

Tidbits:

> "Life is an intangible gift from GOD. We can neither see it, feel it, nor bargain with it. Life is an unsubstantial flimsy thing. It is here today and gone tomorrow." – Justice Cabral

> "Ask, and it will be given to you; seek, and you will find; knock, and it will be opened to you." – Matthew 7:7, ESV

> "The bargain that yields mutual satisfaction is the only one that is apt to be repeated." – B. C. Forbes

> "Therefore I tell you, whatever you ask in prayer, believe that you have received it, and it will be yours." – Mark 11:24, NIV

> "Life is the greatest bargain - we get it for nothing." – Yiddish Proverb

> "To sell something, tell a woman it's a bargain; tell a man it's a deductible." – Earl Wilson

> "Necessity never made a good bargain." – Benjamin Franklin

Song Suggestion: The More I Seek You – written by Zach Neese

ABOVE ALL

"Now to Him who is able to do immeasurably more than all we
ask or imagine, according to his power that is at work within
us." – Ephesians 3:20, NIV

Have you ever had a family member or close friend who went the extra
mile and sacrificed much of their success or comfort for your benefit?
As I ponder my life, I am totally stretching my memory to think of an example
of whether I have been the recipient of such blessing, or if I have shown a
servant's heart and ministered to another at the cost of my own comfort. I
can't recall the reason that warranted bringing our friends to lend us a hand,
nor why my husband wasn't capable of completing the tasks at hand, but I do
remember that despite their own domestic needs, they spent the afternoon and
fixed our kitchen drain, vacuumed and dusted the entire house, hoed the garden
and harvested the garden's bounty. These were simple mundane tasks, but they
went the extra mile to minister to our needs. Amazingly I have vivid images of
each of them performing their acts of kindness, but the personal trial we were
suffering at the time has drifted away. It is wonderful how God has created our
minds to forget the undesirable and remember the blessings. I hope that my life
is testimony that I was willing to go the extra mile to bring comfort to others
and to serve them with the love of Christ. I do know for certain God always
goes the extra mile, blessing me above all I could ever expect.

God desires to pour out blessings on us, exceeding abundantly above all
that we ask or think. He wants to fill us with His indescribable presence and to
experience life to the fullest. But the blessings do not always come all at once;
sometimes the 'abundant' is a process. The process may be challenging; there may
be thorns along with the roses; but you can depend on God to go the extra mile.

An example of God's abundant blessing being part of a process is demonstrated in the story of Joseph. He was betrayed by his brothers and cast into a pit
and then sold to a travelling caravan. He found favour with Potiphar, wife of the
King, only then to be falsely accused of attempting to seduce her and, as a result,
suffered imprisonment. Joseph experienced years of dismal complication before
God provided the 'above all' blessing when he was promoted to a position of
supreme leadership of Egypt.

Our expectations of God should not be confined to human boundaries
or be limited to what we think is possible. God is prepared and able to do the
impossible for you. He who created the Rocky Mountains, Great Barrier Reef,
Grand Canyon, Niagara Falls, Sahara Desert and other majestic wonders is more
than interested in going above all to bless you. "What no eye has seen, what no

ear has heard, and what no mind has conceived – the things God has prepared for those who love Him" (1 Corinthians 2:9, NIV).

If we limit God's power by praying for things that can be solved by our own intervention or that of others, then people don't witness God providing the impossible. However, pray and expect the impossible, ask God to go above and beyond, and then when He answers your prayers, the hand of God will be evident to all. God wants to demonstrate His power, mercy, and ability to provide kindness and love so that the world will come to know Him. When we let God use us to do things we can't possibly do ourselves, He gets the glory. So when you need the impossible, ask God! When you desire to go the extra mile for someone else, ask God! For anything small and anything large, and for the impossible, ask God!

Prayer: Heavenly Father, I pray that my faith in you would be the mustard seed that can move the mountain of physical complications I currently endure as result of cancer. I ask that you would do what the medical profession deems impossible and heal me completely of this cancer. As you continue to provide my soul with your peace for the journey, may my healing and recovery be such that there is no doubt that you have been in total control of my life and the blessings have been from your loving hand. Amen.

Tidbits:

> "From His abundance we have all received one gracious blessing after another." – John 1: 16, NLT

> "However many blessings we expect from God, His infinite liberality will always exceed all our wishes and our thoughts." – John Calvin

> "And God is able to bless you abundantly, so that in all things at all times, having all that you need, you will abound in every good work." – 2 Corinthians 9:8, NIV

> "God denies a Christian nothing but with a design to give him something better." – Richard Cecil

Song Suggestion: Above All – written by Paul J Baloche, Lenny LeBlanc

ABUNDANT LIVING

"And God is able to bless you abundantly, so that in all things
at all times, having all that you need, you will abound in every
good work." – 2 Corinthians 9:8, NIV

'Abundance' is defined as 'plentiful' or 'abounding with' and from the world's point of view 'abundant living' is one that is 'affluent' or 'rich.' The abundance of God's blessing does not necessarily refer to our prosperity or success but to the 'quality of life' we should experience. Christ came to bring the same, "I am come that they might have life, and that they might have it more abundantly!" (John 10:10, KJV)

God does not expect us to simply withstand life but to see it as a precursor of what eternal life is intended to be. Everyone desires a life full of love, joy, peace, longsuffering, gentleness, goodness, faith, meekness, soberness and contentment but unsure of how to achieve it. There is no way anyone can experience the fullness of 'abundant living' if they do not personally know the Lord and understand His love for us. It is said, "But whoever is united with the Lord is one with him in spirit." (1 Corinthians 6:17, NIV)

Attainment of 'abundant life' does not happen overnight but it is a step-by-step learning process where we modify our values and beliefs by bringing them into alignment with the teaching of the scriptures. With repentance, prayer, meditation and studying God's Word, our views of wrong or right are slowly transformed, and we begin to view sin differently. Sometimes these revisions are achieved through challenges and obstacles that God determines are necessary for our reconstruction. When I was diagnosed with cancer and compelled to reexamine my past and search for my purpose, I realized how much was lacking in the spiritual characteristics necessary for me to face this battle (with Christ) and how that was hindering my ability to live a life full of abundance. Most of us think of our trials as an inconvenience or an unwanted interruption, but I chose to view cancer as God's purpose to fortify and strengthen my character. It was my desire that this unexpected journey would have explicit purpose. . . His purpose.

It is very depressing that so many people in this world are filled with a dark emptiness and severely lack understanding of the wonderful life God intended for them. They pursue happiness in perverted entertainment, fulfillment in selfish careers, and satisfaction in immoral lifestyles, revenge in committing crimes and, despite their attempts to live what they may conceive as a plentiful lifestyle, they unknowingly sprint towards their own earthly demise.

Nothing can bring more satisfaction then to know 'why' we are born and the direction in which we are advancing. Everything in this mortal life is secondary to salvation, and the countless blessings such as confidence, assurance, peace, patience, long suffering and more that are found in Christ are invaluable. Understanding this is the very first step to beginning a life that is extra wonderful and much more abundant than one can ever imagine. I humbly testify that I stand in awe of the gift of new life in Christ.

Prayer: Lord, help me to reflect on the abundant blessings you so mercifully bestow on me each day for they are plentiful. I plead with you to keep me faithfully walking the narrow road you have mapped out for me. May my life be a yielded "jar of clay" to be fashioned by you, the divine potter, and might this vessel glow and bring glory to your name. My cancer journey is a temporary trial that has resulted in amazing spiritual growth and the outcome of this medical battle and the future beyond rests entirely in your divine hands. Thank you for awakening my wavering spirit and setting it afire once again. Help me to not let the flames expire but to share and live the gospel message so others can experience abundant living as well. Amen.

Tidbits:

"Gratitude is the open door to abundance." – Unknown

"Whoever pursues righteousness and love finds life, prosperity and honour." – Proverbs 21:21, NIV

"Abundance is not something we acquire. It is something we tune into." – Wayne Dyer

"Riches are not from abundance of worldly goods, but from a contented mind." – Unknown

"The one who blesses others is abundantly blessed; those who help others are helped." – Proverbs 11:25, MSG

Song Suggestion: Abundantly – written by Janna Long, Sam Mizell, Brian White, Joe Beck

ALPHA & OMEGA

"Therefore, since we are surrounded by such a great cloud of witnesses, let us throw off everything that hinders and the sin that so easily entangles. And let us run with perseverance the race marked out for us, fixing our eyes on Jesus, the pioneer and perfecter of faith. For the joy set before Him He endured the cross, scorning its shame, and sat down at the right hand of the throne of God." – Hebrews 12:1-2, NIV

No narrative story is much good if the author starts it but does not finish. No composition of music can be played without a final stanza. No race is successful if the runner quits before he reaches the finish line. In Hebrews, Paul is encouraging us to throw off any hindrances (sin) that slow us down in running the race and focus our eyes on Jesus, the forerunner and faultless nurturer of our faith.

The disastrous news of the bombing during the Boston Marathon dominated the headlines for days and, sadly, spectators and runners alike were severely injured, with three suffering death, having nearly reached the end of their own race. At the beginning, thousands of runners were entirely focused on reaching the finish line, despite only one being a winner. Providentially, many had crossed the finish line, accomplishing their goal or exceeding it, but many had their dream derailed by fellow humans propelled by evil. Fortunately for us, our race as Christians, in this rat race we call life, will not encounter a derailment to steal our victory, because it is guaranteed by God.

Athletes in all sports train vigorously and work energetically to achieve their goals, striving for a reward that is temporary, but we do it for a crown that will last forever. Some people are motivated by power or supremacy, and that objective of success is also temporary. When a runner is training for a race, he is repeatedly instructed not to look to the right or to the left for even the slightest side glance will slow his race. This is a great concept for us to adopt, reminding us not be focused on the past or our mistakes. We are instructed to look ahead, looking to Jesus, who is our spotless example of persevering through trials and temptation. He is the Alpha and Omega of our faith. Our faith should grow and be the result of depending on Him and His promises.

As I begin to struggle with the difficulty of swallowing due to the inflammation of my radiated esophagus, I zeroed in on the potential result ahead of me, a life without cancer. Knowing full well that even that reward is temporary, I will stay intently and accurately focused on things that are of heavenly gain, those that yield an incorruptible crown.

Jesus is an author who promises to finish his work. In Psalm 138:8 (NIV), we are assured that "the Lord will work out the plans for my life." Jesus is the composer who never fails to produce harmony. He is the beginner and finisher of my race. With His help, I will withstand the race of life—through every struggle, even cancer. Every day He is helping me, step by step, stride by stride, and mile by mile to reach the finish line. My life may be filled with trials and challenges, but Jesus will inspire, encourage, push me and most definitely carry me at times so I am able, with Him, to reach the end of my earthly journey. He is the Alpha and Omega of my life and with my last breath, I will begin eternity with Him.

Prayer: Heavenly Father you mapped out my race from the very beginning and you know where you have placed my finish line. Help me to run faithfully, fixing my eyes on Jesus, and to share His love along my route. I depend on you to help me over whatever bumps lie ahead and may my victory by your glory. Amen.

Tidbits:

> "I am the Alpha and the Omega," says the Lord God, "who is, and who was, and who is to come, the Almighty." – Revelation 1:8, NASB

> "I believe God is managing affairs and that He doesn't need any advice from me. With God in charge, I believe everything will work out for the best in the end. So what is there to worry about?" – Henry Ford

> "A new morning means a new beginning, a new struggle, a new endeavor, but with the Lord by our side we can overcome any challenges and turn obstacles into stepping stones." – Unknown

> "When you are born, the only guarantee is that life will end one day. Every beginning has an end. But every end also contains the seeds of a new and better beginning. – Unknown

Song Suggestion: Alpha and Omega – performed by Gaither Vocal Band

ENGRAVED ON HIS HANDS

"Can a mother forget her nursing child? Can she feel no love for the child she has borne? But even if that were possible, I would not forget you! See, I have written your name on the palm of my hands." – Isaiah 49:15-16, NLT

I t's been nearly 2,000 years since Jesus ascended to the Father, and the world is becoming more evil and immoral with each passing day. Factoring in man's moral decline, along with the increased geographical disasters such as hurricanes, earthquakes and floods, we might be asking things like: Where is God? Why would a loving God permit such carnage? Why does God allow so much suffering and evil in the world? Has God forgotten us?

Questions about God and His love are as old as the creation of man. Adam and Eve indirectly questioned God's wisdom when they ate of the tree of knowledge (good and evil). The Israelites remained enslaved by the Egyptians for over 400 years, and with each new generation they were promised deliverance. They were certain that God had forgotten about them. After the death of her brother Lazarus, Martha didn't waste time in blaming Jesus for his death because He had tarried in coming. Fortunately to ease her grief, Jesus commanded Lazarus to come forth from the grave. Despite the long wait of the Israelites, the presence of evil and immorality, the carnage caused by earthly disasters or our longing for the Saviour's second coming, we can be assured that we are not forgotten. God has always and will always be with us and for us.

In Isaiah the Lord explains that as much as a mother has compassion on the child in her womb, He has even more for us. While it is hard for us to fathom how a mother would forget about her child, it happens, but God will not forget us. He has inscribed us in the palm of His hands. The sacrifice of God's own son, Jesus Christ, at Calvary was in payment for our sins, not His. His hands bear the marks of the lengths He has gone to show us His love.

When we consider the entire world that God has made and marvel at all its glory, this one thing I know, He still chose to love us more. When we consider His sacrifice for our many ugly sins, we can still stand sure on the promise of his love for us. When we face uncertainty or are overcome by dark circumstances, we can cling to the truth that Jesus is a friend who sticks closer than a brother. He will never ignore us in our time of need, and nothing can separate us from His love. We should have no reasons to cry out, "Lord, have you forsaken me?" The permanent marks of His love for me are "inscribed on the palms of His hands."

Think about your palm for a second. When you have a tiny treasure in your hand, you don't simply hold it loosely and allow it to tumble to the ground. No, you clasp your fingers tight around it. Think of your name. How precious it is. How someone took great care in choosing it for you. That name is a treasure to God and he stakes claim to it. He places your name, the name of his treasured child, safely in the palm of his hand. The same hand, by the way, that holds the universe in motion. "My Father, who has given them to me, is greater than all; no one can snatch them out of my Father's hand" (John 10:29, NIV)

Prayer: Heavenly Father, thank you for your meticulous handiwork in creation that reminds me of your intimate loving care. Thank you for your nailed scarred hands that remind me of the eternal measure of that love you gave. When I walk through valleys of anxiety or discontent, please remind me that you are always right beside me. I am grateful for your promises to love me despite my doubts and infirmities. Thank you for using this difficult time to reassure me of our faithfulness and everlasting love. Amen.

Tidbits:

> "Our deeds will not cause God to love us more; our sins will not cause God to love us less." – Dillon Burroughs

> "For God so loved the world that He gave His only begotten Son, that whosoever believeth in Him should not perish, but have everlasting life." – John 3:16, KJV

> "Genuine self-acceptance is not derived from the power of positive thinking, mind games or pop psychology. It is an act of faith in the God of grace." – Brennan Manning

Song Suggestion: He's Got the Whole World in His Hands – written by Glen Campbell

FREE TRADE

"Even when we were God's enemies, He made peace with us, because His Son died (free trade) for us. Yet something even greater than friendship is ours. Now that we are at peace with God, we will be saved by His Son's life." – Romans 5:10-11, CEV

In the sporting arena whether it be football, hockey, basketball or baseball there is always a draft or trading process that is used to allocate certain players to specific teams. After having raised three physically active sports enthusiasts you would expect me to have an understanding of the trading process. Not! I was quite content in watching them and had no longing to understand the "Trade." At baseball tournaments someone would always have to explain the 'round robin' charts, when, where, why and how.

Recently the Pittsburg Penguins acquired Jarome Iginla; sports headlines were ablaze, and while it didn't tickle my fancy, I knew that it was exhilarating news to my Penguin fanatic son, now a middle-aged adult; I sent a 'text' to inform him I taken notice of the trade. Depending on the sport, the traded or drafted players may come from college, high school or junior teams or from sport teams of other countries. All scouts and coaches hope to acquire the star athlete of the season but not all squads experience a 'trade up' situation but find themselves tolerating a 'trade down' one. Consequently, they spend the season training their draftee and hope the future will produce a draftee that will be beneficial to their team.

As Christians, our day-to-day lives parallel the trading process and involve decisions that are both 'trade up' and 'trade down' results. We can make a decision to resist temptation and 'trade up' or we can fall prey to the devil's enticement and find ourselves reaping consequences that may keep us in a 'trade down' situation for some time. No players desire to be on the losing team and I can guarantee that there is one 'trade up' experience where you will always be on winning team. When you come to the realization of how much Christ loves you and that He 'traded down' from the wonders of heavens, died a horrible death on the cross for the payment of your sins and then accept Him as your Saviour, then you have been officially drafted. This 'free trade' is a 'trade up' process that is unequivocally complete and for all of eternity you are a permanent player on the winning team. The victory has been secured by Christ.

There is another parallel. No matter what qualifications a draftee has he is required to train and strive towards improving his skills with each season for the advancement of the entire team. We are to "desire the pure milk of the word, that ye may grow thereby" 1 Peter 2:2 WB Paul is encouraging us to grow in our understanding of God's word and be 'trained' so that we are more like Christ. The world needs to see us living a "trade up" experience, living out the joy of being redeemed. We are on the winning team for eternity, so rejoice and share your excitement. I am sure there is someone you know that needs to be drafted to 'The Team' declaring eternal victory.

Prayer: Thank you Jesus for being willing to leave the glories of heaven and to sacrifice your life for me. I desire to live my life so that others can see that being 'drafted' to the winning team is an exchange that cannot be beat. Amen.

Tidbits:

> "You see, at just the right time, when we were still powerless, Christ died for the ungodly." – Romans 5:6, NIV

> "God made him who had no sin to be sin for us, so that in him we might become the righteousness of God." – 2 Corinthians 5:21, NIV

Song Suggestion: If That Isn't Love – written by Dottie Rambo

HE WHO BEGAN A GOOD WORK

"Being confident of this very thing, that He who has begun a
good work in you will perfect it until the day of Jesus Christ."
– Philippians 1:6, KJV

I am a creative fanatic and craft-aholic, and I'm prone to dabbling in several different crafts: ceramics, knitting, crocheting, macramé, cross-stitching, sewing, quilting, scrapbooking and tole painting. I am no different from many other crafters who have several projects started yet unfinished. Do you have incomplete works of art? I am a chronic organizer so unfinished crafts haunt me. I try to prioritize them for completion, but every day responsibilities and other things often distract me. Even now there are still incomplete projects buried in closets, but in contrast to that, I know that God is never distracted; we are a high priority to Him. He had plans for a specifically created design for each of us before we took breath. God's creativity didn't end there, because: "He who began a good work in you will perfect it until the day of Jesus Christ." (Philippians 1:6, NASB) We need to yield ourselves to the Master's hand and allow His ongoing creative process to craft His masterpiece. God adjusts the hues and contrasts of our lives, endlessly dabbing and stroking the canvas to enhance our character for His glory. Even this cancer path that I consider undesirable is all part of His cleansing process to encourage maturity and to a closer relationship with Him.

Allow me to embellish Philippians 1:6 so it is understood that we are a divine work in progress. I am confident, convinced, firmly persuaded and absolutely sure that God began a good work in me. I did not come to be His child by chance but because His work of grace that He began in my soul was intentional. He continues to perform a good work by transforming and regenerating my character. It is a work of grace that will not achieve perfection until eternity when He transforms me into a heavenly body perfect in Christ. I will not be abandoned in tribulation and He will keep me safe in His care for He is faithful and promises never to leave. When He comes to receive me as His own, on the Day of Jesus Christ, my renewed soul will rejoice for eternity in His presence.

Regardless of the trials and challenging situations you are facing right now, with God as your designer, your days ahead will improve. There is no disappointment that God cannot turn into a divine appointment. He will change things and disappointments will flee. We don't have to organize, be creative or orchestrate our tomorrows for happiness and success but trust that the Christ-placed appointments will have eternal benefits. I may be an incomplete work, but I know that God is not distracted. He is absolutely focused and His creativity will be fashioned in me because of His promise that "He who began a good work will be faithful to complete it."

Prayer: Heavenly Father, thank you for your creative hand that continues to craft my life. While the transforming is sometimes difficult, I am confident that your masterpiece in me will be completed. As you design changes in my life may your grace be in full measure and give me strength to regenerate those areas that need new development. Thank you that I am a priority to you. Amen.

Tidbits:

> "For we are his workmanship, created in Christ Jesus for good works, which God prepared beforehand, that we should walk in them." – Ephesians 2:10, ESV

> "While I know myself as a creation of God, I am also obligated to realize and remember that everyone else and everything else are also God's creation." – Maya Angelou

> "Now to Him who is able to do far more abundantly than all that we ask or think, according to the power at work within us," – Ephesians 3:20, ESV

> "Man is a creation of desire, not a creation of need." – Gaston Bachelard

> "O Lord, how manifold are your works! In wisdom have you made them all; the earth is full of your creatures." – Psalm 104:24, ESV

> "There is no doubt that creativity is the most important human resource of all. Without creativity, there would be no progress, and we would be forever repeating the same patterns." – Edward de Bono

Song Suggestion: He Who Began a Good Work in You – written by Jon Mohr

PRAYING BIG

"Jabez cried out to the God of Israel, 'Oh, that you would bless me and enlarge my territory! Let your hand be with me, and keep me from harm so that I will be free from pain.' And God granted his request." – 1 Chronicles 4:10, NIV

Let me introduce you to a somewhat unfamiliar biblical character called Jabez, an individual only mentioned three times and whose name is the same of a small town in Judah near Bethlehem. Chronicles notes, "Jabez was more honourable than his brothers. . ." and he is also mentioned in the genealogical list of the tribe of Judah. His name meaning is "pain" and is how his mother described his birth which leaves us to speculate whether his life continued to be filled with pain since his prayer contained a specific request to be kept from harm and free from pain. There is very little information to shed light on his life or what he had done to deserve more respect than his brothers, all we have is this prayer that he uttered: "Jabez prayed to the God of Israel, Oh that you would bless me and expand my territory. Please be with me in all that I do, and keep me from all trouble and pain. And God granted him his request."

Jabez lived when paganism was rampant. Each country believed in many gods and yet he directed his prayer to 'the God of Israel.' We are commanded: "You shall have no other gods before me." Jabez also indicates having a personal relationship with the "God of Israel." The next portion of his prayer appears to be selfish as he requested more land which was a very important and rich commodity to own in those days. This presents controversy as to Jabez's motives for wanting more land, yet we can be sure that God's will regarding a blessing of "enlarged territory" would be a means to bring honour and glory to Himself and not Jabez. The final portion of his prayer is the one that I can most identify with today: ". . . keep me from harm so that I will be free from pain." Other than being safeguarded from his enemies, we are not told in detail of what pain Jabez suffered. I don't believe that any one person from the beginning of creation desires to live a life of pain, yet Charles Spurgeon said the following: "I have oftentimes looked gratefully back to my sick chamber. I am certain that I never did grow in grace one half so much anywhere as I have upon the bed of pain."

While I desire God to bless me with spiritual blessings and He does—that He would enlarge my heart to the things of Christ and He does; that He would lead me, protect me and strengthen me and He does—I am not sure I want to volunteer myself to a life of pain so that I can experience His grace as Spurgeon mentioned. I would much rather state with the Apostle Paul, "For our light and momentary troubles are achieving for us an eternal glory that far outweighs them all" (2 Corinthians 4:17, NIV) with a strong emphasis on the "light and momentary." I do know for certain that Jabez knew how to pray big! We have a tendency to pray for our own little corner of the world and yet many places in the Bible we are challenged to pray for a bigger purpose. Pray with expectation and pray believing in God's magnificent power to not only change our life, but to change the world, one person at a time. A god who can move mountains and destroy nations can do very big things!

Prayer: Heavenly Father, I praise you, Lord, for your eyes are on those who fear you and there is hope in your unfailing love. I pray big, bigger, and biggest that you would heal me from cancer and keep me free from the pain it encompasses. Enlarge my peace and hope in these difficult times. I am thankful for this cancer journey because it has forced me into a deeper relationship with you and I want to not only pray big, but also to live big for you. Amen.

Tidbits:

> "Prayer does not equip us for the greater works, Prayer is the greater work." – Oswald Chambers

> "Now to him who is able to do immeasurably more than all we ask or imagine, according to his power that is at work within us." – Ephesians 3:20, NIV

> "It is better for your Prayer to be without words than your words to be without heart." – John Bunyan

> "Call to me and I will answer you and tell you great and unsearchable things you do not know." – Jeremiah 33:3, NIV

> "If God is your partner, make your plans BIG!" – D.L. Moody

Song Suggestion: Song of Jabez – written by Paul Baloche

SAFE IN THE SHEPHERD'S ARMS

"I am the Good Shepherd. I know my own sheep and my own sheep know me. . . . I put the sheep before myself, sacrificing myself if necessary. . . . They'll also recognize my voice." – John 10:14, MSG

U nbelievably the subject of trust keeps surfacing in my daily Bible studies. Probably because Jesus knows just how easily we, as His sheep, are led astray. All of us desire to trust in something that makes us feel secure about our future. Some of us place our trust in stocks, bonds, insurance and possessions in hopes of providing a secure financial future or retirement. With heightened crime rates, we attempt to keep ourselves and our homes safe by trusting in alarms, firearms or security systems. These things only provide a false sense of security for there is nothing that will provide complete physical safety or a secure financial future. Only when we entrust our souls in the arms of our Great Shepherd will we find the unshakable trust where our future will find a safe haven and confident hope.

You may have seen before, the familiar picture of the Lord cradling a sheep in His arms, but perhaps you may have not given much thought to what it represents. Have you ever wondered why we have been referred to as sheep? Do you know that it is because they are stupid? Sheep are the only domesticated animals that do not have either offensive or defensive reflexes. They have very poor eyesight and hearing which enables an attacker to sneak up on them without notice, and when their life is threatened, they simply panic and run until they tire, usually in a flock which enables the predator to easily overtake them and have them for lunch.

What is the shepherd's responsibility to his flock of sheep? He is required to provide the essentials of life, green pastures for nutrition, quiet waters for safe drinking, and areas of rest to avoid exhaustion or potential death. An experienced shepherd learns to recognize the difference between a bleating of pain from one of pleasure, and if any of his sheep mingled with another flock, he uses a special call and His sheep will respond to His voice. Being a shepherd is a dangerous job and despite all the safety a shepherd provides for the benefit of his flock, they still wander and get lost, drown or experience death. We, too, were once like foolish sheep behaving stupidly, stubbornly and selfishly.

Our God, in His marvelous love for us, provided a Good Shepherd, the Lord Jesus Christ, to restore our soul and carry us in paths of righteousness. More than just offering comfort in our difficult challenges, He carries us through the thorns and briars, lifts us high on His shoulders to find victory in the heights of heaven. We will face trials, suffering and uncertain times, and it is in those times that we most need to draw near to God and rest safe in the Shepherd's arms.

Tidbits:

> "The LORD is my shepherd, I lack nothing. He makes me lie down in green pastures, he leads me beside quiet waters, he refreshes my soul. He guides me along the right paths for his name's sake. Even though I walk through the darkest valley, I will fear no evil, for you are with me; your rod and your staff they comfort me." – Psalm 23:1-4, NIV

> "If ever you find it hard to sleep at night, don't count sheep. Instead, talk to the Shepherd. . . lay all your burdens into GOD and nothing will disturb you. . . – Nishan Panwar

> "All of us like sheep have wandered, each to his own way we have turned, and Jehovah hath caused to meet on Him, the punishment of us all." – Isaiah 53:6, YLT

> "He tends his flock like a shepherd: He gathers the lambs in his arms and carries them close to his heart; he gently leads those that have young." – Isaiah 40:11, NIV

Song Suggestion: Saviour like a Shepherd – written by Dorothy Ann Thrupp, William Bradbury

VALLEY OF WEEPING

"What joy for those whose strength comes from the LORD, who have set their minds on a pilgrimage to Jerusalem. When they walk through the Valley of Weeping, it will become a place of refreshing springs. . . They will continue to grow stronger, and each of them will appear before God in Jerusalem." – Psalm 84:5-7, NLT

Several years ago, we were vacationing with another couple in the Bruce Peninsula of Ontario when our adventurous friend coaxed us into hiking in search of a cabin in the wilderness that he had once visited. It was said to be approximately a half-day hike on a well-worn trail. Decked in regular summer duds and sneakers, we started out and, thankfully, in our limited wisdom we knew enough to pack a lunch and water. We hiked for over four hours, jumping and bellying up to rocks to cross small crevices, slipping often on dewy surfaces, crossing a large rocky beach where occasional snakes would wriggle to safety, yet scaring me half to death. After enduring several hours, I reached my emotional limit and began to weep. Exhausted and desiring to turn back, I heard our friend say said the cabin was 'not much' further, so sunburnt, parched and weary, we trekked on. It happened to be a lot further, in fact, another four hours further, and when we finally arrived at the cabin, we found that it was occupied. Thankfully, the occupants seeing that we were without hiking or camping gear graciously pitched their tent and allowed us to sleep in the cabin for the night. Needless to say, the next day we trekked a short distance to the nearest road and hitch-hiked back to our vacation home. It was an experience never to be repeated, although it is a great story to share.

In biblical times, as many still practice today, Jews were required to travel great distances three times a year to worship at the temple of Jerusalem. This discouraging journey known as the Valley of Baca or the Valley of Tears was a risky trip through a desert filled with many dangers, such as wild animals, snakes, thorny vegetation and scarcity of water. The valley was also known as a garbage dump, which today can parallel our journey through this despicable, grimy and dirty place we call the world. We face a 'valley of tears' when we encounter sickness that ravages the body, divorce that fractures a union, financial stress that topples a business, depression that drowns a mind, and ultimately even death. But we don't have to be stranded in a pool of tears for just as the Jewish people found relief from their sorrow as they neared their temple and worshipped God, we, too, can draw near to God and find reprieve. In fact, the nearer we draw to God and grow in Christ, the more we gain insight into just how vile this world has become. Our close proximity to Christ does not eliminate hardships but it gives us strength to endure. Our momentary afflictions achieve for us an eternal weight of glory, an applauded entrance, an adorned crown, a whiter robe and a sweet eternal rest. Yahoo, no more hiking!

God's eye is forever watching over this travelling pilgrim and He levels out the rocky snake-filled trail. My earthy pilgrimage, or valley of tears, is but a blink of the eye compared to my eternal life. So I obediently hike onward in faith, trusting God to clear my path, with a heart full of gratitude for His presence, daily provisions, and keeping my eyes focused on my destination. There may be several valleys of tears yet to trek through, but my tears are a language that He understands and "weeping may stay for the night but rejoicing comes in the morning" (Psalm 30:5b, NIV).

Prayer: Lord, I thank you for the valleys of tears and for your presence through each and every one. Fill my well with your refreshing water and help me to trek onward to experience the joy that comes with every new dawn. Amen.

Tidbits:

> "He will wipe away every tear from their eyes. There will be no more death, or mourning, nor crying or pain, for the old order of things has passed away." – Revelation 21:4, NIV

> "For godly grief produces a repentance that leads to salvation without regret, whereas worldly grief produces death." – 2 Corinthians 7:10, ESV

> Heaven knows we need never be ashamed of our tears, for they are rain upon the blinding dust of earth, overlying our hard hearts. I was better after I had cried, than before - more sorry, more aware of my own ingratitude, more gentle." – Charles Dickens

> "For everything there is a season, and a time for every matter under heaven. . . a time to weep and a time to laugh, a time to mourn and a time to dance. . ." – Ecclesiastics 3:1-4, ESV

Song Suggestion: Tears are a Language – written by Gordon Jensen

A RAINBOW OF PROMISE

"I have set my bow in the cloud, and it shall be a sign of the covenant between me and the earth." – Genesis 9:13, ESV

In order for us to witness the creation of a rainbow, there must be falling rain (trials) and rays of sunshine (blessings) piercing through the showers forming a prism of majestic colour. Adults and children alike experience awe and wonder with the appearance of God's handiwork whether they associate it with Him or not. The rainbow is not just a wonder of nature but is a colourful representation of God's promise proclaiming that He would never again flood the entire earth. It is a spiritual reminder that even after the roughest of life's storms, things will improve. When things look their worst, just when the sky is at its darkest, our loving heavenly Father will produce a rainbow to shine in our lives.

Many people in society today have forgotten the divine importance of the rainbow and have tarnished this precious symbol by using it for objectionable and sinful illustrations, but as Christians let us not forget its significance. The rainbow can also represent the glory, majesty and honour of the Lord Jesus Christ and His sacrifice to become the mediator between God and man by providing redemption.

In love and with purpose, God permits upsetting storms into everyone's lives so He will have the opportunity to produce a 'rainbow.' Nowhere in the Bible are we told that as Christians we are exempt from experiencing tribulation. All of our challenges are God's tests to see if we will rely on Him or attempt to overcome difficult situations in our own strength. Only when we come to the 'end of our rope' will we realize that our own solutions are not enough to produce favourable results. Only when we 'cast our burdens on Him' will we see a 'rainbow' amidst our storm.

The next time you look to the sky and admire the beauty of a rainbow, remember that it is not just majestic in colour but a royal representation of the divine promise made by God to mankind. It also symbolizes God's covenant of grace in providing redemption through the sacrifice of His Son. In the darkest of storms and unsettling circumstances, let Christ be your guide, keep holding His hand, let Him solve your problems and let Him have complete control and you will truly understand how much of the rainbows peaceful beauty can be yours.

Prayer: Lord, when I am feeling battered by life's storms and my heart is filled with doubt and dismay, help me to lean on you. Might I eradicate my anxiety by casting my burdens on you and realizing that you are only a whisper away. Thank you for your gift of the rainbow, our promise in the midst of every storm. Amen.

Tidbits:

> "The soul would have no rainbow had the eyes no tears." – John V Cheney

> And God said, "This is the sign of the covenant that I make between me and you and every living creature that is with you, for all future generations: I have set my bow in the cloud, and it shall be a sign of the covenant between me and the earth." – Genesis 9:12-13, ESV

> "It's a good thing that when God created the rainbow he didn't consult a decorator or he would still be picking colours." – Sam Levenson

> "May God give you. . .For every storm a rainbow, for every tear a smile, for every care a promise and a blessing in each trial? For every problem life sends, a faithful friend to share, for every sigh a sweet song and an answer for each prayer." – Irish Blessing

Song Suggestion: Blessings – written by Laura Story

A WAY IN THE WILDERNESS

"This is what God says, the God who builds a road right through the ocean, and who carves a path through pounding waves. The God who summons horses and chariots and armies - they lie down and then can't get up; they're snuffed out like so many candles. . . Be alert, be present. I'm about to do something brand-new. It's bursting out! Don't you see it? There it is! I'm making a road through the desert, rivers in the badlands." – Isaiah 43:16-19, MSG

Isaiah gives us a record of the past, present and future deliverance of God's people of Israel. He reminds them of how He delivered them from over 400 years of bondage in Egypt. The passage tells of how He tossed the horse, their chariots and riders into the sea. If you have watched Cecil B. Demille's 1956 movie masterpiece, *The Ten Commandments*, you are familiar with the scene where the Israelites are trapped by the Egyptians at the banks of the Red Sea, and there appears to be no escape. Despite their unbelief and wandering hearts, the Lord provides deliverance by parting the waters of the Red Sea, allowing them to pass through on dry land, while close behind, the walls of water were falling in and drowning the pursuing Egyptian army. "God will make a way," simply because of His boundless love for His people.

Numerous times in the Bible, as in our own lives, there are hopeless circumstances where one is fenced in with no way to escape. What we need to consider is that sometimes they are self-created. Jonah disobeyed God's commands and found himself in the belly of a whale. David sinned and created a dysfunctional family that used murder to solve their problems. Yet in contrast, Abraham—in complete obedience—prepared to sacrifice his only son, Isaac, but then God lovingly provided a lamb instead. No matter what the predicament is—financial, physical, emotional or social—whatever difficulty we are facing, even the prospect of death, God will make a way.

Being attuned to God's method of liberation requires that we know who He is and recognize His voice. When we fail to train ourselves to become more like Christ in our thoughts, words and deeds, our ears are not trained to listen nor our hearts willing to trust, and thus we behave as spiritual infants. We tend to rely on the well-meaning advice of others instead of relying on God. The sovereign will of God is far beyond our human reasoning, yet despite our limited capacity to understand, we can be prepared and refuse to be influenced by our perplexing circumstances and believe that Lord loves us and is completely capable to work in ways we cannot see.

As I walk in this temporary desert called 'cancer,' I know that God is doing a new thing in me and He is making a way in the wilderness and providing streams in the wasteland. One of those streams is the hundreds of prayer warriors that are petitioning the throne for me and with a lovingly answer to that prayer, God has supplied unexplainable belief in my heart, a trust that He is in complete control and this transitory wasteland will one day flourish in beauty. No matter how dry the desert or dark the tunnel, He is lighting my way. This cancerous badland is not the end for me, because God will make a way where there seems to be no way.

If you are struggling to keep your head above the water and feel all alone, be assured that God sees exactly what you are going through and that He loves and care for you.

Prayer: God, you are my sovereign Lord who knows all, sees all, and controls all things. I walk through this dry desert land and praise you for the amazing way you have increased my faith, and I look forward to the growth yet to be revealed as I depend on your guiding hand all the way through this journey. Thank you for using this hard time to demonstrate your steadfast love and faithfulness towards me. In advance, I thank you for making a way for me. Amen.

Tidbits:

> "No temptation has overtaken you except what is common to mankind. And God is faithful; he will not let you be tempted beyond what you can bear. But when you are tempted, he will also provide a way out so that you can endure it." – 1 Corinthians 10:13, NIV

> "One thorn of experience is worth a whole wilderness of warning." – J. Lowell

> "My ancestors wandered lost in the wilderness for forty years because even in biblical times, men would not stop to ask for directions." – Elayne Boosler

> "The promised land always lies on the other side of a wilderness." – Havelock Ellis

> "God is our refuge and strength, a very present help in trouble." – Psalms 46:1, NASB

Song Suggestion: God Will Make a Way – written by Don Moen

WORTHINESS

"Walk in a manner worthy of the Lord, fully pleasing to Him, bearing fruit in every good work and increasing in the knowledge of God." – Colossians 1:10, ESV

Unworthy or worthy, which of these best describe how you feel about yourself? Not necessarily focusing on how you measure in the eyes of God, but how you measure in the eyes of your teachers, parents, co-workers or peers. Almost from the cradle, personality comparisons begin as you are described as cute, beautiful, unique or perhaps they will ask, "Who does he resemble?" in an effort to avoid negative assessment. Then comes the competition of crawling, walking, potty-training, learning ABCs, talking, politeness, scholastics, and within a short span we are facing an onslaught of degrading comments and being told we are failures no matter what the task, or appearance.

Bart Millard, from Mercy Me, commented on the reasons behind the writing of the song, "Beautiful," saying that as a father he already noticed with his young children that his girls faced much more pressure to live up to certain standards than his sons. He wrote the song in hopes of influencing not only his own children, but also people of all ages to realize their worthiness, in particular, the beauty they have in Christ.

I recall thinking I was not of much worth because not only was our family poor, but we also were being raised in a single parent home which was not a sign of respect in the early 60s. My mother worked hard to provide for our basic needs, and it was obvious to our peers through our inability to be fashionable that we didn't "make the grade." Fortunately, my athleticism and a hearing disability that forced me to diligently study provided areas that were praise-worthy accomplishments, but there was always a level of insecurity and unworthiness that hindered me from connecting socially with what was considered to be upper class. Despite achieving an honour roll standing all four years of high school I have never understood why the guidance counselor said I wouldn't amount to anything, stating that I might as well just go and get married. Apparently it was still male dominated scholastic approach even then. Who has told you that you are unworthy? Are you reminded that you are weak, helpless or a total failure? Perhaps you have been led to believe that you are even unworthy to be used of God. These are all lies! Satan loves to drive lies right down to the core of your very being so that we are ineffective tools for Christ.

In our own flesh, we are unworthy but after accepting Christ as a personal Saviour we are never unworthy again. Never! Will you fail? You certainly will. Will you be judged? You certainly will. But we need to quit listening to the lies of the devil otherwise all Christian ministries would shut down completely if we did not believe that we are worthy in Christ. The Lord says of His people, "To the saints that are in the earth, and to the excellent, in whom is all my delight." God loved us even when we were still in sin, and He loves us still regardless of our weaknesses, struggles and failures. We are worthy because of Christ's sacrifice on the cross, which provides us the privilege to worship and serve Him. We cannot obtain this worthiness by doing good deeds or cleaning up our act, it is simply a gift from God by repenting, believing and accepting the sacrifice that Christ made for your sins on the cross. I praise God, that I know that I am worthy and beautiful, He has bought me by the price of the precious blood of Christ and nothing changes my position as a child of the King, nothing! (Psalms 16:3, KJV)

Prayer: Heavenly Father, there is nothing so precious or fulfilling as knowing that I am loved by you and that I am beautiful, treasured and sacred. Thank you for the sacrifice of your Son that provided my worthiness in your sight. Amen.

Tidbits:

"Now to Him who is able to do far more abundantly than all that we ask or think, according to the power at work within us," – Ephesians 3:20, ESV

"Moses spent forty years in the king's palace thinking that he was somebody; then he lived forty years in the wilderness finding out that without God he was a nobody; finally he spent forty more years discovering how a nobody with God can be a somebody." – Dwight L Moody

"For by grace you have been saved through faith. And this is not your own doing; it is the gift of God," – Ephesians 2:8 ESV

"You aren't loved because you're valuable. You're valuable because God loves you." – Anonymous

"But to all who did receive Him, who believed in His name, He gave the right to become children of God," – John 1:12 ESV

"No matter how unloved you have felt in the past, no matter how lost you feel in your sin, God knew all that when He chose you - and He wants you anyway." – Wayne Jacobsenan

Song Suggestion: Beautiful – by Amanda Falk

BLESSED BEYOND
MY WILDEST DREAMS

"What no eye has seen, what no ear has heard, and what no
human mind has conceived"—the things God has prepared
for those who love Him." – 1 Corinthians 2:9, NIV

What did you dream for yourself in life's journey? Were your dreams
focused on a particular occupation, a perfect spouse, a certain number
of children, financial success, or could it be to find simple happiness and to be
a productive citizen? Funny thing is, as I ask you that question, I can't answer it
myself, because I don't recall having any specific dreams, just nonsensical ones.
Dreams that I could recall and would often awake thinking that I needed to write
them into a novel but upon review, I would realize that they made absolutely
no sense at all.

Now as a senior, I reflect back on my life and see how profoundly I have
been blessed. I have been blessed with a faithful husband who has provided
financial stability, four amazing children who love Christ and serve Him, as
well as adding to my 'Nana" quiver, a grandmother's finest blessings—several
beautiful grandchildren. By the world's standards, I am not financially rich, but
I consider myself to be wealthy beyond measure. But believe it or not, even
these marvelous earthly blessings will not compare with those that God has
reserved for me in heaven.

I don't want to lead you astray in thinking that I have had a perfect life
without spot or wrinkle. There were countless choices I made that caused others
to frown in dismay or created a worried brow on my mother, such as staying out
all night and not being considerate enough to call. There were also minor regrets
for things I wished I had done, such as widening my love for photography
and becoming a professional in that field. Too often, even as Christians, we
identify ourselves by who we know, obtaining advanced education, professional
accomplishments or how many worldly possessions we may have accumulated,
but all our earthly gain is wood, hay and stubble and will perish with time.

During this cancer battle and potentially facing an early demise, I have
come to realize that relationships are the most important aspect of a fulfilled
life. Foremost the personal relationship that I have with the Lord Jesus Christ,
but also those precious friendship bonds that He has provided to be my prayer
warriors, optimistic exhorters, caring comforters and domestic helpmates.

These divinely appointed friendships (that includes my family) are and have
been blessings beyond my wildest dreams. With every single chapter of my

life, God has been faithful to provide and lead me through the good times and the troublesome times—there have been plenty of both. Life may be full of disappointments, setbacks, tedious details and even a life-threatening illness like cancer, yet I believe that as I remain faithful to God and completely trust Him, blessings will continue. Salvation is a blessing, forgiveness is a blessing, grace is a blessing, and mercy is a blessing, and so on, and so on. To have God's blessing on my life is a treasure that no man can put a price on. Being blessed beyond my wildest dreams is absolutely priceless!

Prayer: Lord, none of my dreams can ever compare with the plans that you have for me. You have told me that your plans are to prosper me and not to harm me, to give me hope and a future. I find great comfort in knowing you are in control of the smallest details of my life and grateful that I can trust you with my life and my dreams. Thank you for blessing me beyond earthly measure. Amen.

Tidbits:

"The unthankful heart discovers no mercies; but the thankful heart will find, in every hour, some heavenly blessings." – Henry Ward Beecher

"Blessings sometimes show up in unrecognizable disguises." – Janette Oke

"Blessed is the man who remains steadfast under trial, for when he has stood the test he will receive the crown of life, which God has promised to those who love Him." – James 1:12, ESV

"May we be strengthened with the understanding that being blessed does not mean that we shall always be spared all the disappointments and difficulties of life." – Heber J. Grant

"When we quit playing Hokey Pokey with God and keep our whole self in, His blessings pursue us!" – Evinda Lepins

Song Suggestion: God's Been Good – written by Tim Parton

A CHEERFUL COUNTENANCE

"A cheerful disposition is good for your health; gloom and doom leave you bone-tired." – Proverbs 17:22, MSG

When one comes face to face with the diagnosis of cancer, whether it is personal, a family member, or a close friend, there is no humour to be found. There is a period of tears and anxiety while overactive minds race to the absolute worst scenarios. John Diamond said, "Cancer is a WORD, not a (death) sentence." With today's medical advances in cancer treatments, the survival rate is daily increasing.

In my case the diagnosis was my own, and the prognosis for my esophageal cancer is around 40 percent. While I do not consider myself to be an optimist, I firmly stated, "I am going to be in that 40 percent!" That brings me to question, "Are you an optimist or a pessimist?" Is the glass of water half full or half empty? Do you see the doughnut or do you see the hole? It is said that the optimist invented the airplane, but the pessimist invented the parachute. Now there's little bit of humour.

I appreciated all the positive accolades that my friends and family were careful to encourage me with, but I couldn't find myself being totally optimistic, because I was not going to presume that I knew God's will for my life. He is the Mighty Physician and while I have witnessed miraculous healings, I have also witnessed loved ones being promoted to glory before their life had hardly begun. Would God heal me and promote me? That is a question that only He can answer, for it is Him who has numbered my days, not cancer.

During those first weeks of unanswered medical questions and while waiting for an army of doctors to determine my course of treatment, I found myself identifying with the Apostle Paul when he stated in Philippians 1:22, 23, ISV, "Now if I continue living, fruitful labour is the result, so I do not know which I would prefer. Indeed, I cannot decide between the two. I have the desire to leave this life and be with the Messiah, for that is far better."

As a mother, I questioned, "Who in the world would take care of my family?" Yet with the Holy Spirit's confirmation, I knew that it is "far better to be with the Lord." God was faithful to repeatedly assure me in the most intimate of moments that He would be the caretaker of my family. He loves all of my family to a far greater degree than I ever could, and He will watch over them and take care of them abundantly and with sacrificial love! (Philippians 1:23-24, ISV)

Let us now progress from the somewhat morbid to the positive. I am grateful to God for the spirit of peace and irreplaceable humour that God has given me throughout this journey. Believe me, there is humour in having cancer, and I have learned to appreciate that while 'our heart may ache, and our bones are weak' that laughter and a spirit of joy can make all the difference in coping with the disease and promoting healing. Consider a few of the proverbs that suggest there is a direct connection between the state of mind and the ongoing condition of our body.

> "An anxious heart weighs a man down, but a kind word cheers him up." (Proverbs 12:25, NIV)

> "A heart at peace gives life to the body, but envy rots the bones." (Proverbs 14:30, NIV)

> "A happy heart makes the face cheerful, but heartache kills the spirit." (Proverbs 15:13, NIV)

It should not surprise us that medical doctors encourage us to have a positive outlook, because it makes a big difference in our healing process. They also claim to see a big difference between those who know Jesus Christ and those who don't. This is no surprise to me for Jesus Christ has been my hope in this temporary darkness, the peace that conquers all anxiety and pours loving comfort on me without measure. God has been faithful to bring other Christians that have cancer across my path, and the most common statement shared is, "I don't know how those without Christ walk this cancer journey without Him."

Let me share some helpful tips that were my resources for maintaining a cheerful heart: Spend daily time with God in meditation and prayer. Surround yourself with cheerful people. Focus on heavenly things and God's promises. Keep on the sunny side and be an encourager. Fill the empty quietness with gospel music. Share God's love with others.

Prayer: Oh precious Lord, I thank you for empowering me with a positive attitude through this journey, please help me share joy with those put in my path. Amen.

Tidbits:

> "You can be a victim of cancer, or a survivor of cancer. It's a mindset." – Dave Pelzer

> "Hope is living in with confidence and courage, not fear." – Penny Boldrey

> "I look at my cancer journey as a gift; It made me slow down and realize the important things in life and taught me how not to sweat the small stuff." – Olivia Newton John

Song Suggestion: Keep on the Sunny Side – written by A. P. Carter

CRUCIFIED WITH CHRIST

"I am crucified with Christ: nevertheless I live; yet not I, but Christ lives in me: and the life which I now live in the flesh I live by the faith of the Son of God, who loved me, and gave himself for me." – Galatians 2:20, KJV

As I walked through my cancer journey and prayed that God would be faithful in not giving me more than I could handle, I knew there was nothing in this unwanted journey that would ever compare with what He suffered on my behalf. Despite my desires to identify with Christ and to be a testimony of His grace and love, I must admit that 'physical pain' was what I feared most. I was quite willing to endure whatever lay ahead in my treatments and even be willing to be physically promoted to glory but, please, oh, please, eliminate the pain aspect.

In Galatians, Paul was not referring actual physical pain in order to identify with Christ, but that we need to suffer a spiritual death—a death to our old corrupt nature that desired absolute control. By faith in Christ, our repentance and acceptance of His sacrifice made us a new and fresh creation. This is not any easy transition but a lifetime conflict. The greatest obstruction for us to overcome is to surrender our selfish desires, ambitions and yearnings and be willing to submit entirely to God's plan for our lives. If I had been given the option to choose cancer or not to choose cancer, my choice would have most definitely been a selfish one. Even though I was not afforded that decision, and despite the fact that God has allowed this disease to grow in my body, my selfishness still ruled because I constantly prayed that whatever I faced, could it be pain free.

It was not, and no one is capable of eliminating our immoral and wicked nature even for a brief moment, except for the assistance and control of the Holy Spirit. Surrendering my will to God's will was and is a moment-by-moment yielding to the Spirit and a continual leaning on God's promises in His Word. While as a Christian, I continually desire to be obedient and submissive, I will forever struggle with my old sinful and selfish nature until the day Christ returns and replaces this decaying body with my heavenly one.

It is by the gift of grace that we are born again, and through that gift of grace we are given the power of the Holy Spirit to resist yielding to our sinful nature. While we will continue to sin, we are not to let sin dominate and enslave, neither should we continue repeating the same old evil ways. Our old corruptible desires can be replaced and slowly extinguished when we continue to relinquish our will to the will of God. He, and He alone, with bring victory over each dreadful trial and unwelcomed encounter we face and allow us to experience the indisputable peace of God.

Prayer: Father, forgive me for my selfish requests and create in me a new heart that is fully yielded to your plan for my life. You have promised to work out all things, even those undesirable encounters, for my good. Even though my old sinful ways had separated me from you, you reached out in love and redeemed my soul. As I continue to walk down this unknown path, help me to completely trust you. Might I never forget, even for a moment, that I am eternally and immeasurably loved by you and find everlasting comfort in surrendering myself to your reassuring arms. Amen.

Tidbits:

> "Therefore if any person is engrafted in Christ, the Messiah, he is a new creation, a new creature altogether; the old previous moral and spiritual condition has passed away. Behold the fresh and new has come!" – 2 Corinthians 5:17, AMP

> "You aren't loved because you're valuable. You're valuable because God loves you." – Anonymous

> "No matter how unloved you have felt in the past, no matter how lost you feel in your sin, God knew all that when he chose you - and he wants you anyway." – Wayne Jacobsenan

> "Our "safe place" is not where we live; it is in whom we live." – Tom White (Voice of the Martyrs)

> "For the message of the cross is foolishness to those who are perishing, but to us who are being saved it is the power of God." – 1 Corinthians 1:18, NIV

> "It is to the Cross that the Christian is challenged to follow his Master: no path of redemption can make a detour around it." – Hans Urs von Balthasar

Song Suggestion: Crucified with Christ – written by Randy & Denise Phillips, Dave Clark, Don Koch

DANIEL'S BIG GOD

"I issue a decree that in every part of my kingdom people must fear and reverence the God of Daniel. For He is the living God and He endures forever; His kingdom will not be destroyed, His dominion will never end. He rescues and He saves; He performs signs and wonders in the heavens and on the earth. He has rescued Daniel from the power of the lions." – Daniel 6:26-27, NIV

Daniel, a long time administrator for previous kings, was now serving King Darius who recognized his exceptional dream interpretations and proposed to authorize him as sole overseer of his kingdom. Needless to say, this promotion caused other administrators to become very jealous, and so they devised a scheme that would bring about Daniel's demise. They cunningly targeted King Darius' pride, persuading him to pass a new law that would result in the execution of anyone that bowed to another authority outside of the king. Consequently, Daniel, being a faithful prayer soldier, and one who fervently worshipped God, now found himself in a predicament that would challenge his faith. Despite the law forbidding prayer to anyone but the king, he demonstrated faithfulness and continued to pray to God, and God alone.

Daniel is one of the few biblical examples of people who did not have personal failure or sin recorded in the scriptures. He is one of the most courageous and faithful men mentioned, but his courage was not that of facing the lions' den, but was represented in the faultless life he lived in the presence of his peers and enemies. King Darius may have shown some reluctance in carrying out the thoughtless degree when he said to Daniel, "May your God, whom you serve continually, rescue you." Daniel did not know what the outcome would be when he faced the mouths of hungry lions, but he did know that he had a 'Big God' who was capable of providing a miracle, and that is just what happened.

At some point in our lives, the authenticity of our faith will be challenged. We will face a personal trial or crisis, and no matter what direction we look, there appears to be no way out. We will want to give up and then hopelessness takes root. While we may not face the lions' den, we do desire to see God do big things in our life, but many of us may not see God do big things, because we have failed to trust Him in the little things because our faith is small. (Luke 16:10) Daniel's faith was cultivated over decades of cherishing and refining His relationship with God. We often only come to God in prayer when we face a crisis and come to the end of our own resources.

One of the ways God helps us to expand our faith is by designing specific challenges, like cancer, that make us aware of our human limitations. Desperate situations force us to rely on God, and when we realize how big our God is, our faith is intensified. Faith matures when we have the courage to serve God relentlessly in every facet of our life, no matter what the cost. Whether in public or in private, we need to live a life of integrity and be willing to be a 'pot of clay' in which God may choose to show His majesty and greatness.

Prayer: Lord, some days I am weary of the battle both physically and spiritually, and I thank you for rescuing me and graciously lifting me up out of the 'lions' den' and giving me strength to face each day. There is never a time where you do not display your love and faithfulness and help me to abandon my fears to you. I thank you for the provision of compassionate friends, family and medical professionals that have made my cancer journey not only pleasant but also an amazing experience. Like Daniel, I do not know the outcome of this 'cancer den' but I do know that you are a big God who can perform the impossible and I stand in awe of your majesty and unfailing love. Amen.

Tidbits:

> "Be great believers! Little faith will bring your soul to heaven. But great faith will bring heaven down into your soul." – Charles Spurgeon

> "When you affirm big, believe big and pray big, putting faith into action, big things happen." – Norman Vincent Peale

> "Faith is the strength by which a shattered world shall emerge into the light." – Helen Keller

> "One who is faithful in a very little is also faithful in much, and one who is dishonest in a very little is also dishonest in much." – Luke 16:10, ESV

Song Suggestion: Bigger than any Mountain – written by Gordon Jensen

DO NOT WORRY

"Praise the Lord! Hallelujah! Blessed, happy, and fortunate is the man who reveres and worships the Lord . . . He shall not be afraid of evil tidings; his heart is firmly fixed, trusting, leaning on and being confident in the Lord." – Psalm 112:1, 7, AMP

Christian author William R. Inge defined worry as "interest paid on trouble before it becomes due." It relentlessly drains the energy God gives us to face daily problems. Who of us wants to pay interest on a mortgage before we even purchase a house, or pay interest on borrowed funds before we enjoy the benefit of the tangible? Yet we often choose to worry before calamity enters our life. Fear, anxiety, and worry all leave an open door to defeat. It is debilitating! While it is human to worry, we do have a choice on whether to allow it to dominate and dictate how we live our lives.

No matter how your trial is shattering your peace, God has already decided that you are going to win. You just need to work on believing it!

"Here is the bottom line: Do not worry about your life. Do not worry about what you will eat or what you will drink. Don't worry about how you clothe your body. . . .Look at the birds in the sky. They do not store food for winter. They don't plant gardens. They do not sow or reap—and yet, they are always fed because your heavenly Father feeds them. And you are even more precious to Him than a beautiful bird. If He looks after them, of course He will look after you. Worrying does not do any good; who here can claim to add even an hour to his life by worrying? . . .Consider the lilies of the field and how they grow. They do not work or weave or sew, and yet their garments are stunning. So do not worry about tomorrow, let tomorrow worry about itself. Living faithfully is a large enough task for today" (Matthew 6:25-28, 34, Voice).

Jesus defeated the enemy (Satan) and has taken away the power Satan claims to have over us. Despite God's defeat over Satan, a Christian life does not protect us from distresses and frustrations. David lived in caves before he became king, Moses was in exile before he delivered his people from Pharaoh, Joseph experienced bondage before rising to power, Job lost everything, and so on. In the New Testament, the apostles faced persecution.

We may find ourselves encircled by tragedy but we have a God who is the ultimate victor and loves us more than our minds can comprehend. Give your worries to God for He has plenty of tomorrows to handle them.

Prayer: Lord Jesus, forgive me for allowing worry to take root and help me to surrender my anxieties and bring them to you in prayer. Worrisome thoughts diminish my faith and I desire to fix my thoughts on you. Guard my heart and deliver the peace that surpasses all understanding. You are in complete control and are greater, far greater, than any fear I can conceive. When I am overwhelmed lead me to the rock. Transform me. Amen.

Tidbits:

> "Worry weighs us down; a cheerful word picks us up." – Proverbs 12:25, MSG

> "Worry is faith in the negative, trust in the unpleasant, assurance of disaster and belief in defeat. . .worry is wasting today's time to clutter up tomorrow's opportunities with yesterday's troubles." – Walter Kelly.

> "Trust in the LORD with all your heart, and do not lean on your own understanding. In all your ways acknowledge him, and he will make straight your paths." – Proverbs 3:5-6, ESV

> "Every evening I turn worries over to God. He's going to be up all night anyway." – Mary C. Crowley

> "Worry pulls tomorrow's cloud over today's sunshine." – C. Swindoll

> "Pile your troubles on God's shoulders – He'll carry your load, He'll help you out. He'll never let good people topple into ruin." – Psalm 55:22, MSG

> "I am afraid that the schools will prove the very gates of hell, unless they diligently labour in explaining the Holy Scriptures and engraving them in the heart of the youth." – Martin Luther

> "Worry is to deny the very power you claim to believe in." – Justin Miller

Song Suggestion: Nothing's Worrying Me – written by Jerry Kelso, Marty Funderburk

FAITHFUL FRAGRANCE

"But thank God! He has made us his captives and continues to lead us along in Christ's triumphal procession. Now He uses us to spread the knowledge of Christ everywhere, like a sweet perfume. Our lives are a Christ-like fragrance rising up to God. But this fragrance is perceived differently by those who are being saved and by those who are perishing." – 2 Corinthians 2:14-15, NLT

The definition of 'fragrance' is a sweet or pleasant scent or the state of having a pleasing odour. There is hardly anything more unsettling at a social gathering than to have a person that emanates foul body odour or who has splashed on a surplus of perfume. No matter how exquisitely adorned they may be, their disregard for cleanliness or a feeble attempt to possibly hide foul-smelling odour is a quick deterrent to socializing or befriending them.

I remember well the days when we were in the middle of raising three teenage boys who participated in sports of every kind. Soccer, baseball, and hockey, in particular, were their activities of choice. After any rowdy game, you could always count on an opportunity to see just how long you could hold you're your breath while travelling home. Following the gas-mask car ride came trying to convince them to shower and constant reminders to air out their gear. Our backyard was often littered with strongly wreaking equipment, which amazingly enough managed not to kill the grass. After a couple weeks of this routine, it became very apparent that 'fresh air laundering' would no longer provide any relief from the stink and water laundering would be required.

Our lives as Christians can have a 'sweet fragrance' or a 'foul-smelling' effect on our close or new acquaintances, and the odour we exude depends entirely on the ongoing state of our personal relationship with Christ. When we nurture that relationship by digesting and meditating on His word, spending time in prayer and worshiping Him, the 'fragrance' of Christ becomes evident and our words and actions will be represented with the fruit of the Spirit. The fruit of the Spirit is love, joy, peace, patience, kindness, goodness, faithfulness, gentleness and self-control. The Message puts it very clearly. "But what happens when we live God's way? He brings gifts into our lives, much the same way that fruit appears in an orchard—things like affection for others, exuberance about life, serenity." (Galatians 5:22a) "Among those who belong to Christ, everything connected with getting our own way and mindlessly responding to what everyone else calls necessities is killed off for good—crucified." (v.24)

Much as a sweet fragrance makes for an enjoyable physical atmosphere, we are to be the sweet fragrance of Christ. We should not convey a spirit of condemnation and non-acceptance but the forgiving fragrance of God's grace. By communing with Him daily, we begin to see that we are a pleasure to God and a lovely perfume that brings a smile to His face. Christ is the provider of the sweet aroma of life, grace and unfailing love and we are responsible to radiate the same.

Prayer: Lord, let my prayer be like a sweet fragrance to you and my requests be selfish only to the measure that I seek to have you change me into a 'sweet fragrance' of Christ for others to see. I want it to be noticeable that I have spent time with you and despite my current cancer path and its many challenges, physically, emotionally and spiritually, all I desire ultimately is to be more like Jesus. It is your unmistakable grace that upholds me and leads me in a celebrated journey with Christ. I give you thanks. Amen.

Tidbits:

> "And walk in the way of love, just as Christ loved us and gave himself up for us a fragrant offering and sacrifice to God." – Ephesians 5:2, NIV

> "Forgiveness is the fragrance that the flower leaves on the heel of the one that crushed it." – Mark Twain

> ". . .a woman not yet seen, but whose perfume accumulates on the horizon like a storm cloud." – Fernand Dumont

> "Live each day as a fragrance as unto the Lord, make God proud." – Unknown

Song Suggestion: Daystar – written by Steve Richardson

GOD WILL TAKE CARE OF YOU

"Don't be afraid, for I am with you. Don't be discouraged, for
I am your God. I will strengthen you and help you. I will hold
you up with my victorious right hand." – Isaiah 41:10, NLT

During my cancer journey, I came to understand that chemotherapy and
radiation treatments affect every individual differently but initially my
expectations included fear. Needless to say, I borrowed distress where it wasn't
necessary and had mistakenly based my expectations on other people's experiences. God was faithful to reveal my esophageal cancer early and in determining
the course of treatment, a scan revealed thyroid cancer. At the time of this
writing, I have finished both chemo and radiation and surgical consultations
with the thyroid and esophageal surgeons. While neither treatment eradicated
the cancers, I am hopeful and trusting that the surgery to come will be guided
by God's hands and produce success. The waiting game proves to be the most
difficult part of the process as yet another ultrasound is necessary before surgery, and the task of coordinating two surgeons and an anesthesiologist at the
same time, to review the results, will be another miracle for God to perform.

I can testify to the miracles of God and the answered prayers of hundreds
of friends, family and unknowns, for His grace was multiplied to me beyond
measure through this whole journey. There has never been a brief moment where
I didn't feel His comfort and protection, and I believe that it was a miraculous
blessing that the side effects were far less incapacitating than I anticipated. I will
forever stand in awe of the unbelievable peace and ease of the journey thus far.

In order to possess all that God had intended for me, it was required that
I release my fears and anxiety on a moment-by-moment, day-by-day basis and
yield to whatever He willed. We cannot carry the burdens ourselves and expect
God to shoulder the 'backpack' of worries unless we release them.

God will take care of you, and that is an all-powerful truth that requires that
you rehearse, repeat and reapply His promises to your heart and mind over and
over again. Even when you hit an emotional wall and feel spiritually empty, God
does not abandon nor does He leave you helpless or hopeless.

I am sure that Mary and Martha had much anxiety and disappointment when
their brother Lazarus died and while they buried him, all the while knowing
that Jesus could have healed him. They were quick to blame the Lord for His
tardiness and missing a chance to save their brother from death. But Lazarus
was dead, and even when all seemed impossible, Jesus called Lazarus forth and
proved that He overcomes the impossible. Even today He is still the God of
the impossible. His solution may not be what you are looking for, but remember

God does not fail and He will take care of you in ways that will bring glory to His name. Find comfort in your stressful and lonely moments by releasing and relying on an omnipotent God who will take care of you.

Prayer: Thank you, Jesus for answering the hundreds of prayers and making my cancer journey thus far painless and almost symptom free. You are indeed blessing me in the middle of my trial. I will wait on you for yet another miracle as I face the upcoming surgery, recovery and hopefully the total eradication of both cancers. I treasure your presence moment by moment and know that I am not alone no matter what may come. I anticipate abundant blessings because you love me. Amen.

Tidbits:

> "The LORD is my light and my salvation—whom shall I fear? The LORD is the stronghold of my life—of whom shall I be afraid?" – Psalm 27:1, NIV

> "Life is hard but God provides. Life is unpredictable but God guides. Life is unfair but God cares. Life is a challenge but God watches." – Ritu Ghatourey

> "If you want to change something in your life, focus on the inner, and God will take care of the outer." – Unknown

> "God cares about every area of our lives, and God wants us to ask for help." – Ben Carson

> "God is more interested in your future and your relationship than you are." – Billy Graham

> "The LORD himself goes before you and will be with you; he will never leave you nor forsake you. Do not be afraid; do not be discouraged." – Deuteronomy 31:8, NIV

Song Suggestion: God Will Take Care of You – by Civilla D. Martin, W. Stillman

GOD'S GOT MY BACK

"You won't be fighting in this battle. Take your stand, but stand still, and watch the LORD's salvation on your behalf. . . . Never fear and never be discouraged. Go out to face them tomorrow, since the LORD is with you." – 2 Chronicles 20:17, ISV

Music has always had an extraordinary place in my life, but I never knew how important it was until I faced my cancer diagnosis. I have fond childhood memories of my mother's family occasionally gathering in what I now know as a 'jam session.' No proficiency was necessary for they played and sang from their hearts and radiated their love of music. My uncle would pound out some honkey-tonk piano melody resembling an Elvis number while my mother kept rhythm on a bass washtub with an attached broom. You know the kind, the one that you see hillbillies use. Adding an accordion or two, 'squeezed' in along with several vocalists, not necessarily singing on key, would delight the dancing children for hours. Though to my dismay, seldom was anything played that represented the 'rock and roll' tunes of the 60s which would have been my era. A brief season of piano lessons stirred in me and this music legacy began, ultimately to be used by God for His glory in years to come.

I came to know the Lord in my early 20s, shortly after marrying into a 'churchy' family. For many years to follow, I participated in the choir and led Sunday School choruses in the children's department. To my surprise and concern, God orchestrated a situation within our church where I was the only one who could read music and 'tickle the ivories,' and believe me, it was only a 'tickle.' The only song I was truly polished in playing was "chopsticks," which comically enough required two people. I struggled along through mostly unfamiliar songs with my right hand while attempting a chording pattern with my left. Fortunately, my musical skills blossomed and I was privileged to not only play piano, but direct a choir, children's programs, coordinate worship, and sing, sing, sing. Now retired, I sing in a choir at our 'winter snowbird' church in Florida and direct a community chorus where proficiency is not necessary, just a love for music.

Throughout my cancer battle, music has been the demonstration of love from friends and family that "I've got your back." Knowing my love of music, they have 'tagged me' with hundreds of gospel selections that have ministered to the very core of my being. Times when I felt myself being pulled into a dark funk, I would fill the air with music and fire up the boob tube with Gaither Homecoming videos. God used this ministry of music to spark my spiritual journalling and Facebook blogging that has resulting in compiling the book you are currently reading. Between the lines of all the music tags, my blog followers were saying: "I've got your back"," I'm with you", "You've got a friend" and "I've got you covered, (in prayer)." Messages also included: "You're in good hands", "I'm right behind you because I care" and all could be paraphrased as "God's got your back." They were His words being spoken through His people.

Cancer has a way of producing fear and anxiety that can engulf ones spirit but "God's got your back." In Deuteronomy 31:6 (NIV), it says, "Be strong and courageous! Do not be afraid or terrified because of them, for the LORD your God goes with you; he will never leave you or forsake you."

The enemy will seek and attempt to steal your peace but "God's got your back." In James 1:2 (AKJV), we read that, "Blessed is the man that endures temptation: for when he is tried, he shall receive the crown of life, which the Lord has promised to them that love him. . ." A mind that is focused on Christ and a soul that is flooded with His music will not fall prey to shadowy snares of the enemy. God is our comforter, our defense, our guardian, our deliverer, our protector; He is our all in all. We belong to Him and "God has our Back."

Prayer: My soul was overwhelmed and you fill me with the melody of God's love. I express my gratitude and praise you for using music to minister to my soul. Nothing quite comforts the core of my very being but your music. Amen.

Tidbits:

> "Music was my refuge. I could crawl into the space between the notes and curl my back to loneliness." – Maya Angelou

> "Many people will walk in and out of your life, but only true friends will leave footprints in your heart." – Unknown

> "Walking with a friend in the dark is better than walking alone in the light." – Helen Keller

Song Suggestion: I'm Gonna Love You Through It – written by Sonya Isaacs, Jimmy Yeary, Ben Hayslip

GOD'S TAPESTRY

"For you created my inmost being; You knit me together in my mother's womb. I praise You because I am fearfully and wonderfully made; Your works are wonderful, I know that full well." – Psalm 139:13-14, NIV

I have enjoyed many years of crafting in the different artistries of sewing, knitting, crocheting, cross-stitch, quilting, and I currently have a fever for scrapbooking. Despite over 40 years of crafting various projects, I don't believe that I have even one of the completed creations in my home, and as it is with most domestic crafters, I still have many projects that remain untouched or incomplete. Almost all of these handicrafts were given as mementoes or gifts with exception of my paper craft of 'scrapping.' I selfishly hold unto those that I fashioned for my own children so they can be shared with my grandchildren when they visit. The laughter that erupts when they see their own parents in their younger days is priceless.

Even if you have never been crafty, surely you have admired the work of other crafters. Quilting requires an ability to choose fabrics that complement one another, so that when one has been cut apart, pieced and sewn, all the intricate pieces together form a treasured masterpiece.

In Cross-stitching, while it usually has a printed pattern, one still requires a knowledge of the different stitches, as well as keeping appropriate tension to bring the handiwork to a spectacular success. The finished product is a beauty to behold when gazing at the front, but the reverse side is usually an array of crisscrossing threads that bear no resemblance to the completed picture, nor does it reflect anything beautiful. Our lives are much like that tangled back side of the canvas when the working of our life's threads is an attempt by our own hands to create something.

Often we only focus on the mess of threads beneath that cause us to worry and question why, and anxiously contemplate how God can possibly use this for His glory or my good. Yet time and again, God in His infinite wisdom takes the most challenging circumstances, redeems the broken and brings healing, taking what Satan has meant for harm, and makes it good.

God had a unique plan for each one of us even before the beginning of time. He weaves and spins all the pieces of our lives, even those that don't quite match. He can take cancer with its dark threads and undesirable consequences and divinely weave them so they become a perfect tapestry. He is the Master Creator and is supremely aware of what He intends the finished product to be. He masterfully intertwines originality and exquisiteness within each one of us for we are "fearfully and wonderfully made." We will be a complete astronomical work of divine art when He is finished, and I know that God is not finished with me yet.

Prayer: Thank you, Lord, for creating me and knitting me together in my mother's womb. You saw my unformed body and ordained all my days. I praise you for countless blessings and unexpected trials that have been a part of your weaving and purposed to mould and shape me into your divine creation. I give thanks to you that I was marvelously set apart. Your works are wonderful—I know that full well. I don't have to understand your ways but know you have promised to love me, protect me, and give me hope even in the darkest of days. I securely rest under the protective quilt of your unfailing love. Amen.

Tidbits:

> "He who began a good work in you will bring it to completion at the day of Jesus Christ." – Philippians 1:6, ESV

> "Far from what I once was but not yet what I'm going to be." – Unknown

> "Broken things can become blessed things if you let God do the mending." – Unknown

Song Suggestion: He's Still Workin' On Me – written by Joel Hemphill

HOPE LIVES

"I wait in hope for the Lord. He helps me. He is like a shield that keeps me safe. Our hearts are full of joy because of Him. We trust in Him because He is holy. Lord, may Your faithful love rest on us. We put our hope in You." – Psalm 33:20-22, NIR

One of the most depressing aspects of day to day life is to witness the hopelessness that people carry around with them which manifests itself in their countenance and behaviours. The world is filled with difficulty, sickness, pain, disappointment, financial woe, marriage breakdown, political failure, continuing war, and the future for many of them appears very depressing. A person who is overcome by hopelessness feels alone, abandoned and bears an insufferable weight of helplessness. They cannot see even a glimmer of light at the end of the tunnel, and for them hope does not live.

Sometimes, it is so extremely dark in the tunnel that even when we think we see a light at the end, it turns out to be a train coming right at us. Those of us battling cancer can identify with their despair for the slight mention of the "C" word diminishes one's hope for a future.

We can be encouraged for we are not alone; in fact, the Bible is full of examples of God's servants who were encompassed by a spirit of despair. Reflect on Jeremiah whom God had called to be a prophet to the nations. It was a very difficult task, and he never doubted that God was real, but his cries of desperation reveal that he seemed to doubt the sovereignty of God. He often felt alone. How about Elijah's state of mind when Queen Jezebel was plotting revenge and sought to take his life? He was in such despair that he sat under a juniper tree and pleaded with God to kill him on the spot. He felt alone. The Psalms are teeming with David's despair and desperate pleas to God as he spent months and years avoiding capture by King Saul who was determined to eliminate him and his notoriety from the minds of God's people. He felt so alone. But God never fails, then or now. He delivered His people from despair thousands of years ago and continues to deliver today. God always brings a ray of hope to conquer our clouds of despair.

Hope is 'to look forward with confidence or expectation" and believe me, my friend, apart from God, there is nothing but a dreadful and disheartened future. Finding hope requires that we take action, read, believe and have faith. We will not find hope by relying on our feelings but by solely depending on God for strength and believing Him to be not only faithful and loving but also in total control. Hope lives in Jesus Christ. Hope lives in His Word:

"But now, Lord, what do I look for? My hope is in you."
Psalms 39:7, NIV

"No one whose hope is in you will ever be put to shame."
Psalms 25:3, NIV

"Remember your promise to me; it is my only hope." Psalms 119:49, NLT

"Be strong and let your heart take courage, all you who wait for and hope for and expect the Lord!" Psalms 31:24, AMP

"Be joyful in hope, patient in affliction, and faithful in prayer." Romans 12:12, NIV

My hope is in the Lord! I will be strong and wait on the Lord.

Prayer: Heavenly Father, you are the only source of authentic hope and you fill me with joy and peace as I trust in you. The Holy Spirit comforts me and crushes the moments of fear that arise. Help me to be strong and have courage, depending on you throughout this physical battle with cancer and the emotional and spiritual battle that occasionally rage alongside. I do not doubt your sovereignty and put my full trust in the plans that you have for me, "plans to prosper me and not to harm me." Thank you for the promise and blessings of hope. Amen.

Tidbits:

"Hope is the thing with feathers that perches in the soul and sings the tune without the words and

"When you have lost hope, you have lost everything. And when you think all is lost, when all is dire and bleak, there is always hope." – Pittacus Lore

"They say a person needs just three things to be truly happy in this world: someone to love, something to do, and something to hope for." – T Bodett

"Now, faith is confidence in what we hope for and assurance about what we do not see." – Hebrews 11:1, NIV

"Hope itself is like a star- not to be seen in the sunshine of prosperity, and only to be discovered in the night of adversity." – Charles H. Spurgeon

"Everything that is done in the world is done by hope." – Martin Luther

Song Suggestion: All My Hope – written by Jason Ingram, Reuben Morgan; performed by Hillsong

KNOWING HIM

"And by this we know that we have come to know Him, if we keep His commandments. Whoever says "I know Him" but does not keep His commandments is a liar, and the truth is not in him, but whoever keeps His word, in him truly the love of God is perfected. By this we may know that we are in Him" – 1 John 2:3-5, ESV

Do you know God today? Do you know that the Creator of the universe knows you intimately in fine detail and yearns to have a relationship with you? Do you know that there is only one way to know God the Father personally? That is through His son: "I am the way and the truth and the life! No one comes to the Father except through me" (John 14:6, NIV).

If we are to even begin to know Him, we must first acknowledge our sins, repent, and humbly come to Him. If we are to progress in knowing Him, we must spend time with Him, be taught by Him, and not rely on the knowledge and experience of others. God reveals Himself to each of us in His own way, and as we mature in Him, there are frequent modifications to grow and know Him on a deeper level. "Come near to God and He will come near to you" (James 4:8, NIV) The most wonderful blessing of this lifetime is to become more deeply and intimately acquainted with Christ. The Apostle Paul wrote, "I consider everything else worthless because I'm much better off knowing Christ Jesus my Lord. It's because of Him that I think of everything as worthless" (Philippians 3:8, GW).

I count it a privilege to know Christ personally and to grow in Him more with each passing day, month and year. Jesus has been an anchor that is sure and steadfast, and with death potentially knocking at my door, He has been the sole provision of comfort and peace.

When I received my cancer diagnosis, I was not "hit by a ton of bricks" as most are but had already experienced symptoms in the months prior that produced nagging suspicions that cancer may be poisoning my body. Despite having a morsel of mental preparedness, there was temporary heaviness to my soul when it was confirmed. My first question was not "why me" but "for what purpose," for I know God well enough after having spent a few decades as a Christian, that everything in life has a purpose. His purpose! God will choose to reveal His purpose in His time and it may take a lifetime or a promotion to eternity to find out, but I know that He loves me and desires nothing for me but good.

Long before I took my very first breath, my life's blueprint was drafted. Long before I met the man of my dreams, he had been chosen. Long before I conceived my first child, my quiver had already been measured. Long before I received the dismal 50 percent prognosis of cancer survival, my days had already been numbered. God is in control and I can rest on that.

Knowing Him brings hope in darkness, clarity in confusion, comfort for grief, shelter in a storm and a solid rock of stability. I know Him and I know the outcome of this medical battle is totally in His hands, and I thank Him for the peace He has brought to my heart and soul during these challenging days.

Tidbits:

"And by this we know that we have come to know him, if we keep his commandments." – 1 John 2:3, ESV

"While I know myself as a creation of God, I am also obligated to realize and remember that everyone else and everything else are also God's creation." – Maya Angelou

"God grant me the serenity to accept the things I cannot change, the courage to change the things I can, and the wisdom to know the difference." – Reinhold Niebuhr

"I want to know the Messiah – what his resurrection power is like and what it means to share in his sufferings by becoming like him in his death. . ." – Philippians 3:10, ISV

Song Suggestion: I Know Who Holds Tomorrow – written by Ira Stanphill

OUR INTERCESSOR

"In the same way, the Spirit helps us in our weakness; for
we do not know how to pray as we should, but the Spirit
Himself intercedes for us with groanings too deep for words."
– Romans 8:26, NASB

Prayer can sometimes be an unsettling aspect in the life of a Christian. There are countless books on the subject, and as I am not a theologian, pastor, or well-read scholar on the matter, I will not attempt to unravel all of its mysteries. Though I think that over centuries of traditions and liturgical principles, man has made prayer more complex than it needs to be. Prayer can be simple as "the faith of a little child" mentioned Matthew, "I tell you the truth, unless you turn from your sins and become like little children, you will never get into the Kingdom of Heaven." We simply need to be a redeemed child of the King, and with the Holy Spirit residing in our body, we have the necessary Intercessor who can translate all our prayers.

It matters not whether we are standing, sitting, kneeling, bowing down, or sitting at a stop light. Whether we close our eyes or fold our hands. Nor do we have to be in a church or kneeling at an altar. While you may find one way more comfortable than another, there is no physical position or location that completes our prayer s. Some people pray in the morning, some in the evenings, others are more comfortable in a secret closet, while others have no difficulty in verbalizing prayers audibly. Honestly, most of my praying is done with my eyes wide open during daylight hours and are merely unspoken concerns that have momentarily been brought to the forefront of my mind by the Holy Spirit.

Prayer is not a magic formula, and prayers are not answered based on how, when, or where we pray. In fact, prayer is more for our benefit than God's, for it compels us to draw close to Him and to seek His will. God already knows our anxieties and our deepest concerns before we articulate them, and He will answer them in His time. Yet regardless of His foreknowledge, He stills instructs us to "Pray continually" (1 Thessalonians 5:17, NIV).

We are to express our love and gratitude while honestly pouring out our hearts to God, keeping in mind that He knows what is best and is more interested in the motivation of our hearts than the articulation of our words. God delights in prayer that is genuine, real, and honest. He wants our prayer to be our connection to Him.

Even in those times when we are so overcome with our debilitating infirmities or paralyzing trials, we can simply groan before the Father, and the Spirit within us will be our intercessor. This is probably the most comforting verse to me, because I know, despite my failures and occasional inability to verbalize confused thoughts or even find a desire to pray, the Holy Spirit knows the deepest desires of my heart and He will mediate on my behalf.

Prayer: Father, I am completely humbled that you have instructed us to pray without ceasing, and yet we let the busyness of our world get in the way. I confess that I am not always bringing concerns to you in prayer but attempt to find my own solutions, and I ask that you would continue to convict me to place prayer as a high priority in my life. Thank you for your gift of the Holy Spirit received through your Son's sacrifice and that even when we are unable to utter petition and thanks to you, that He intercedes. You are an awesome God and I appreciate your daily provisions.b

Tidbits:

"The function of prayer is not to influence God, but rather to change the nature of the one who prays." – Søren Kierkegaard

"We have to pray with our eyes on God, not on the difficulties." – Oswald Chambers

"Prayer is not asking. It is a longing of the soul. It is daily admission of one's weakness. It is better in prayer to have a heart without words than words without a heart." – Mahatma Gandhi

"To be a Christian without prayer is no more possible than to be alive without breathing." – Martin Luther King, Jr.

"We know not the matter of the things for which we should pray, neither the object to whom we pray, nor the medium by or through whom we pray; none of these things know we, but by the help and assistance of the Spirit." – John Bunyan

Song Suggestion: Down to the River to Pray – written by Alison Kraus

SHELTERED SAFE

"Let the beloved of the Lord rest secure in him, for he shields him all day long, and the one the Lord loves rests between his shoulders. . . .The eternal God is your refuge, and underneath are the everlasting arms." – Deuteronomy 33:12, 27b, NIV

The world we live in is becoming increasingly more dangerous and everyone has some kind of fear they are dealing with. That fear increases the more we spend our time watching the daily news reports or reading the Internet updates and newspapers. Many of the dangers are as close as next door, such as, drug abuse, domestic violence, divorce, kidnappings, abductions, incest, gun slayings, mass murders. We live in false comfort of the more violent crimes happening to someone else. That is far from the truth. Then we have the wider threats that aim for the obliteration of certain factions such as the Kurds (Iran, Syria, Turkey, Iraq), Shiite Muslims, (Lebanon, Yemen, Iraq, Saudi Arabia, Kuwait,) Palestinians (Palestine, Israel, Saudi Arabia, Chile). The list is endless. Even today day the regime of North Korea is threatening nuclear war against South Korea and US allies which will undoubtedly affect the Western Hemisphere if the young dictator makes good on his threat. If immeasurable threats of war are not overwhelming enough, many live in fear of death from health problems.

While life may seem more violent today, the world has not been a safe place since Adam and Eve. After making a sinful choice their lives were filled with shame, embarrassment and even murder as their son, Cain took Abel's life. Since the introduction of sin there has not been an era without moral decline or hatred. There are innumerable periods where Christians were the target of savagery and hostility and that appears to be growing in popularity as media exploits Christian failures and censors honourable testimonies. Yet we have no need to be afraid for God is our safe shelter.

Just how does one obtain the assurance of God's protection? There is a story about two skydivers prepared with functioning parachutes and both jump from the plane. The first dives with his arms folded and ignores the ripcord for he is confident that his parachute will save him. Not! The second skydiver knows that his safety is in need of him doing something, so he pulls the cord and lands safely. Many people are rapidly approaching hell with a padlocked mind and are refusing to pull the ripcord to safety. Jesus is our ripcord: "I am the way, the truth, and the life. No one comes to the Father except through me" (John 14:6, NIV).

After acknowledging that truth, our spiritual protection is absolute, but the peace or assurance of protection is reliant on our building a relationship with God through meditating on His Word and communicating with an open heart. We cannot know what we don't experience. To be sheltered by God is the best security one can sense, a feeling of authentic comfort and care with every breath we take.

Prayer: Father, you are my sovereign Lord and you know every 'bump in the road' that will come along my way. I am so grateful that I can feel the touch of your kind and tender hands, and that they have the power to protect me from evil. You do lead me in paths that I should take, and I can unburden any uncertainties that try to intimidate my peace, for you are faithful to carry my load. Thank you for comforting me through unfamiliar circumstances and for teaching me to trust and to rest sheltered in your loving arms. Amen.

Tidbits:

> "There's no safety outside of God." – Beth Nimmo

> "God walks with us. He scoops us up in His arms or simply sits with us in silent strength until we cannot avoid the awesome recognition that yes, even now, He is there." – Gloria Gaither

> "It is a precious thing beyond all words—especially in the hour of death—that we have a God whose nature is such that what pleases Him is not our work for Him but our need for Him." – John Piper

> "Whoever dwells in the shelter of the Most High will rest in the shadow of the Almighty. I will say of the LORD, "He is my refuge and my fortress, my God, in whom I trust." – Psalm 91:1-2, NIV

Song Suggestion: Sheltered in the Arms of God – written by Dottie Rambo, Jimmy Davis

SMILE, SMILE, SMILE

"The LORD bless you and keep you; the LORD make his face shine on you and be gracious to you; the LORD turn his face toward you and give you peace." – Numbers 6:24-26, NIV

Who of us does not understand the impact that a simple smile can have? It can be an affirmation of acceptance, a reflection of love, an expression of pride in an accomplishment, a confirmation of understanding and more. Sharing your own smiling face may be a representation of contentment, peace, delight, happiness, satisfaction, gratification. The inspiring message it conveys can be endless.

God knew that the wandering Israelites needed encouragement and instructed this Aaronic priestly blessing to be shared with them.

God may not be pleased with all that we are or all we do, but He is delighted in calling us His children. Just knowing that His 'face is turned toward' me and that He makes His face to shine upon me helps to drive out past condemnation or accusations that have brought me shame or disgrace. His loving acceptance heals my brokenness, drives away fear, and erases pain from maltreatment. Despite my humanness and sinful struggles, I can find peace in any situation, because He sees me as being uniquely valuable. God's smiling face is turned in my direction and is a blessing of God's grace. Mother Teresa said, "Peace begins with a smile" and "Every time you smile at someone, it is an action of love, a gift to that person, a beautiful thing."

A simple and genuine smile shared with another can have an impact that is immeasurable. I don't know about you, but I desire to share a smile that not only conveys positive affirmation of recognition, but the ultimate acceptance that God has for all who believe. I aspire to be a sparkling radiance of God's love and grace and not a foreboding image of doom and gloom.

May my yearnings duplicate the same desires that David expressed in the Psalms, to know that I can smile with cheerfulness and never be found with a countenance of shame as I seek first His kingdom and His ways. I believe His word and I am assured that God has pleasure showing on His holy face for me.

Rick Warren, in The Purpose Driven Life, writes "God smiles when we love him supremely."

Prayer: Father, I thank you for smiling upon me and reaching down in love to restore me unto yourself and to set me free. I am extremely grateful that I can fail miserably yet still feel accepted because of your forgiveness, love and grace. Your countless blessings motivate me to radiate your love and smile, smile, smile.

May each day find me thankful for the prayer warriors you have provided and for answered prayers yet to come. I tremble with awe and delight in knowing your face shines on me and is turned in my direction. Amen.

Tidbits:

>"Let your smile change the world, don't let the world change your smile." – Unknown

>"I'm smiling not because I'm stronger than my problems. I'm smiling because my God is stronger than my problems." – Unknown

>"Surely you have granted him unending blessings and made him glad with the joy of your presence." – Psalm 21:6, MKJV

>"Sometimes your joy is the source of your Smile, but sometimes your smile can be the source of your joy." – Ven. Thich Nhat Hanh

>"Those who look to him are radiant; their faces are never covered with shame." – Psalm 34:5, NIV

>"Smile it's the key that unlocks everyone's heart." – A.J. D'Angelo

Song Suggestion: God Has Smiled on Me – written by Isaiah Jones, Jr.

UNDER HIS WINGS

"He will cover you with his feathers his faithfulness will be your shield. . ." – Psalm 91:4, NIV

This morning a friend and I were sharing our personal cancer journeys and we stand in wonder every day at the immeasurable peace we have both found in facing the potential termination of our earthly life. She is battling breast cancer for a second time, and this is my first encounter with cancer. Breast cancer and esophageal cancer are both are very different, yet the medical methods are similar and the benefits of knowing Christ are exactly the same. During what could and should be the darkest time in our lives, God has provided amazing comfort, and just as a mother bird shields her young from treacherous weather elements with the spread of her wings, so is God sheltering us 'under His wings.'

In agreement, we determined that we have made a deliberate choice to yield ourselves to God during these difficult circumstances, instead of wallowing in self-pity. Coming in under the shelter of God's wings is a choice that Ruth also made. There was a famine in Judah, and the death of Naomi's husband and son as well as having two sons depart taking foreign wives, Naomi found herself deeply bitter at God. Providentially, God had positioned a devoted loving daughter-in-law in Ruth who came forward and vowed to care for her. Evidently Ruth saw a need in Naomi's life and sensed God calling her to meet that need, so she left the refuge of her father and mother in Moab and chose refuge under the wings of God. They left their homes and found themselves gleaning the fields of a relative named Boaz. Within a short time Ruth found favour, and she asks, 'Why have I found favour in your eyes. . . When I am a foreigner?" Boaz expressed that he knew of the extraordinary kindness she had shown to her mother-in-law and said, "May the LORD repay you for what you have done. May you be richly rewarded by the LORD, the God of Israel, under whose wings you have come to take refuge?" (Ruth 2:12, NIV). Ruth knew that God's protection was better than all others and she relied on God not only to shelter her, but also to provide hope and joy in her circumstances.

Like Ruth, we, too, need to make the choice to put all of our disconcerting state of affairs in His hands and trust Him for the outcome. God's wings are always available for a shielded covering, protection from the tempting evil elements that seek to lure us away such as grief, pain, suffering, depression and more. When we choose to reach for Christ in times of temptation and trials, we are released from the devil's choking grip. My friend and I know we are extremely blessed for this undeniable and unexplainable rest we find under His wings and know that He is always willing and ready to tuck us securely under His feathers in whatever storms may come.

Prayer: Jesus, you are my resting place and my shelter in the time of storms. You are my refuge and my fortress, and I will not fear the terror of night, or the arrow that flies by day, or the plague that destroys at midday. I will not fear cancer. Though I do not know what lies ahead, I am forever comforted by your sheltering wings. You know me, every intricate part, and you knew that this season of illness would come, so I commit this disease into your hands and wait on you for deliverance. Thank you, for your protective covering and always for drawing me close under its shadow. Amen.

Tidbits:

> "Have mercy on me, God, have mercy, for in you I have placed my trust. Even in the shadow of your wings will I find my refuge until this calamity passes?" – Psalm 57:1, ISV

> "Being under His wings means being close to His heart - You are not only sheltered, you are loved; you are not only secure, you are cared for; you are not only covered, you are reassured." – Roy Lessin

> "God, Your faithful love is so valuable that people take refuge in the shadow of Your wings." – Psalm 36:7, HCSB

Song Suggestion: Under His Wings – written by William Orcutt Cushing, Liz Wagley, Dan Hendrican

UNFAILING LOVE

"But the LORD watches over those who fear him, those who
rely on His unfailing love." – Psalm 33:18, NLT

What is love? Love is something we all hope to experience in our lifetime, at different times and at variable levels. My youngest grandson claims to be in love with Marley, a peer in his junior kindergarten class, and before you are quick to sweep that impossibility under a rug. You can probably recall when you had your first crush in grade school. By high school you're declaring love, which other people often claim to be 'puppy love,' and you manage to sustain a relationship that may last months or more. Usually, not long after college, you might pronounce spousal vows and seal what is believed as an undying love with high expectations of having arrived at the ultimate love. Sometimes it works out that way, but sadly, often that has proven erroneous, according to today's high divorce rate.

Personally, even the love I have for my husband was surpassed by the love for each of my children and grandchildren. From the very day they were born, I would claim it was unfailing love. A love that grew leaps and bounds as the years passed. I had sincere intentions of unconditionally loving them, but there were times when they were not so loveable. Unfortunately, more times than I wish to count, I have witnessed the withholding of parental love that resulted in feelings of abandonment, personal failure, drug use, crime and more. My children and grandchildren know just how much I love them, but even that is not even comparable to the unconditional and 'unfailing love' that God has for them, me or you.

Thankfully, we can all experience God's unfailing love that restores, upholds, redeems and values even the vilest of sinners. God's love for us is not based on performance, perfection, merit, or success. He is not counting how many times we pray each day, how much money we give to charity, how often we attend church or the time we spend volunteering. He doesn't keep score. God loves all of his children, and despite the sinfulness, He sees saints. Because of Christ, He accepts us with open arms, sees beyond our human frailties, problems and erratic emotions. Even at our worst, God loves us unconditionally, with a sacrificial love demonstrated to us in His plan of redemption through His only begotten Son, Jesus Christ.

Following my repentance and acceptance of His sacrifice, Jesus came into my life and changed forever not only my insights, but my eternity. There was a new realization that everything is designed by God with a distinct purpose.

He sees me as a precious jewel, and I am extremely valuable to Him. He refines my soul, renews my mind, renovates my spirit and teaches me to see the positive and trust Him "to work all things together for the good of those who love Him." If we could just comprehend the measure to which God loves us and shares His love, it would change the world around us.

Prayer: In humility and with a heart full of thanks, I offer my praise and worship to you for your continued presence and the overwhelming sensation of your unfailing love. I am never alone for thou art always with me. Stir my heart to realize that you are all I need or could ever want for life's protection and my soul's refinement. My heart beats with exhilaration as it is comforted with your unfailing love that will not let me go. Amen.

Tidbits:

> "Let them give thanks to the LORD for his unfailing love and his wonderful deeds for mankind." – Psalm 107:21, NIV

> "By the cross we know the gravity of sin and the greatness of God's love toward us." – John Chrysostom

> "One of the greatest evidences of God's love to those that love him is, to send them afflictions, with grace to bear them." – John Wesley

> "The cross is the lightning rod of grace that short-circuits God's wrath to Christ so that only the light of His love remains for believers." – A.W. Tozer

> "The LORD delights in those who fear him, who put their hope in his unfailing love." – Psalm 147:11, NIV

Song Suggestion: Unfailing Love – written by Ed Cash, Chris Tomlin, Cary Pierce

WE ARE MORE
THAN CONQUERORS

"And everyone assembled here will know that the LORD rescues His people, but not with sword and spear. This is the LORD'S battle and He will give you to us!" – 1 Samuel 17:47, NLT

O ur society is currently suffering from an economic recession, political uncertainty and war that rages on in several areas around the world. Similar to the early 60s, we are facing a potential threat of nuclear war as North Korea's new young leader arrogantly threatens South Korea as well as the United States. Even with the magnitude of these adversities, the one you might be personally facing appears larger and insurmountable. Marital hardships, bankruptcy, unemployment, teenage rebellion and addiction, or a terminal health issue may be occupying the forefront of your mind. Yet, as stressful as the former list may seem, there are others whose trials are minor in comparison, but they are facing a giant just the same. They have no heat for furnaces, no power to keep their freezer operational, no consistent meals to ease hunger pains, no consumable drinking water, no injections to ward off disease, and the list is endless. We can examine the world over and there is no absence of difficulty or hardship.

Where is the victory God promised when He says "we are more than conquerors through Him who loved us" (Romans 8:37) Do we find victory in the absence of difficulty and anxiety? We desire success and long to be conquerors but seldom surrender our battles to the Lord. While there are sometimes workable solutions, like cutting a cord of wood to stoke the furnace or seeking a counselor for the betterment of our marriage, these alone are not the victory that God desires for us to find. Victory is not found in the absence of hardship but is found in experiencing the peace of God despite the mountain or giant you are facing. Peace is not found in our personal control of circumstances but in having complete assurance of God's love and that He is in complete control of our challenges and also the immense ones of the world.

God's Word does not fail, and He has provided hundreds of promises of His love and assurance and also instructs us in preparation for battle. Are you wearing your armour? In Ephesians 6:14-18, we are instructed to wear 'truth' tightly belted around our waist; 'righteousness' as a protective breastplate; 'good news' to be our walking shoes; 'faith' as our shield against fiery arrows aimed by the evil one; 'salvation' as our helmet; and the final adornment of the 'Word' as our sword. Despite being fully 'geared-up' for protection, He further instructs us to pray always, as the Spirit leads, and never giving up. We need not fear what battles rage but to stand firm and know that God sees everything and that He is in control.

David, a sheltered and simple shepherd boy, fought the massive giant, Goliath, not because he was cocky and determined to advance himself in stature, but because he had faith that God was with him. He lived a day-to-day reality that God loved and cared for him and he was being used to accomplish God's will. David's insurmountable peace in the most ominous of circumstances was obtained by maintaining a close relationship with God and surrendering to His will.

You won't find any such peace comparable in this world. Surrender to Him, body, soul, and spirit, and be a conqueror.

Prayer: Heavenly Father, I bring praise and rejoice that you are my victory and you are always near. Whether I find myself in the desert of despair, or the fiery furnace of pain and weakness, you are there and worth more than gold. Even in the fever of a battle, I can rest assured that triumph is on the way. No weapon formed against me shall stand. You alone will be victorious. Amen.

Tidbits:

> "I count him braver who overcomes his desires than him who conquers his enemies; for the hardest victory is over self."
> – Aristotle

> "Sometimes standing against evil is more important than defeating it. The greatest heroes stand because it is right to do so, not because they believe they will walk away with their lives. Such selfless courage is a victory in itself." – N.D. Wilson

> "Pay attention. . .This is what the LORD says to you: Don't be frightened or terrified by this large crowd. The battle isn't yours. It's God's." – 2 Chronicles 20:15, GW

Song Suggestion: Desert Song – written by Brooke Ligertwood

A FAITHFUL FRIEND

"One who has unreliable friends soon comes to ruin, but there is
a friend who sticks closer than a brother." – Proverbs 18:24, NIV

I am sure you have heard the quote by Ralph Waldo Emerson, "The only way
to have a friend is to be one." True friends are worth cherishing and can
always be found nearby in your time of need. But, if you are like me, there have
been times in your life where you have felt outright lonely and didn't feel that
you had anyone you could call on.

Though there were always friends available, there still came times where I
felt completely alone. Most of my true friends would have come in an instant
if they knew I was in need, but they were unaware of my desperation. I was
a master deceiver when it came to 'putting on a happy face.' Possibly you can
identify with my facade, or maybe one of the following may strike a chord within
you. Perhaps you are lacking friends because of a recent relocation, or you have
pulled away due to being offended by loose words. Maybe you were excluded
from a special celebration and took it personally, or perchance you have chosen
people outside of your moral circle who really don't have the capacity to be a
friend in the first place. Regardless the reasons, nothing changes the fact that
the state of loneliness is outright painful.

The old adage is still applicable, 'to have a friend, be a friend.' So make the
attempt to step out of your comfort zone and build a friendship. You might
just be rescuing someone else who is suffering from loneliness. Whether you
are already a true friend to someone or looking for a new friend, the following
characteristics of a friend can be positively exercised to everyone's benefit.

> Be available, be kind and careful to listen instead of being
> opinionated and always be supportive.
> Be truthful, loyal, maintain confidence, accept their individu-
> ality and ready to cheer a saddened heart.
> Be sensitive, don't hold grudges and don't let selfish prefer-
> ences get in the way of comfort.
> Be honest without being critical and provide encouragement
> that will help one grow in Christ.

Often our closest of friends live in close proximity. However, finding a
friend whose loyalty knows no distance and does not rely upon frequent conversations can be a challenge. If you can find someone who can understand,
appreciate and support you without keeping track of when your last call was or

who initiated it, that is a treasured friendship to never let go of. But, no one can match the loyalty of a friendship with Christ, who will never let go.

God determined from the very beginning that it was not good for man to be alone and so He created Eve for Adam. God intended for us to reach up for a friendship with Him, and then reach out to establish relationships with one another. The best human friend to have is one who cultivates and builds your personal friendship with Christ. A friendship with Jesus brings eternal benefits. He has promised to always be your friend regardless of your failures or short-comings. Jesus brings us salvation, joy, eternal life, and answered prayers. Being a friend with Jesus calms wicked storms (like cancer), dries salty tears, provides comfort in sorrow and He is that friend that sticks closer than a brother. Jesus is the ultimate best friend; He truly is the only unsinkable-ship and the only one who can save you from drowning.

Prayer: Lord, you bear my grief, my burdens, and shield me from harm. You comfort me in trials and share my sorrows. You listen and answer my deepest prayers. There is no friend like you. Thank you for being my friend. Amen.

Tidbits:

"Wounds from a sincere friend are better than many kisses from an enemy." – Proverbs 27:6, NLT

"A friend is one who walks in when others walk out." – Walter Winchell

"The godly give good advice to their friends; the wicked lead them astray." – Proverbs 12:26, NLT

"My best friend is the one who brings out the best in me." – Henry Ford

"A friend is always loyal, and a brother is born to help in time of need." – Proverbs 17:17, NLT

"True friendship comes when silence between two people is comfortable." – Dave Tyson Gentry

"The heartfelt counsel of a friend is as sweet as perfume and incense." – Proverbs 27:9, NLT

Song Suggestion: Friend of God – written by Michael Gungor, Israel Houghton

A WIN-WIN ATTITUDE

"For to me, to live is Christ and to die is gain." – Philippians 1:21, NIV

As a parent I have often encouraged my children that the goal in participating in sport competitions was not whether you win or lose but to perform to the best of your ability and enjoy the game. My admonition is not much comfort to the deflated soul of someone who has been on the losing team all season, but I do believe that consistent encouragement and showing them unconditional love wins the battle in the long run.

It was a few weeks following the news of my esophageal cancer after hours spent in prayer that I actually realized that I was not in a win-lose situation but a win-win situation. Regardless of the cancer outcome, I would either be blessed by healing and rewarded precious time with my beloved family or blessed "to be away from the body and at home with the Lord" (2 Corinthians 5:8, NIV)

Do you see the win-win? I remember the afternoon lunch when I shared my exciting new revelation with my daughter. As her eyes welled with tears she expressed her unrest with my enthusiasm and informed me that it put her in a win-lose situation as she would be losing her mom. Thankfully, my children are strong in their faith and they have a full understanding of my win-win attitude, and so I know that the joyous attitude that God has given me during my journey has helped them deal with their own momentary fears. Believe me, it isn't easy to contemplate departing this earth and leaving a family behind to grieve their loss, but God has been ever faithful to constantly provide me with moments of his assurance that he loves them more than I do and will always watch over them.

Having a win-win frame of mind means we see life situations as being cooperative and not competitive. A win-win attitude attempts to find solutions to problems beneficial to all participants. This is a difficult concept for us to master since we are surrounded by such competitive spirits in business, sports and those fighting for financial gain. Families find themselves caught up in a competitive format from the very beginning as they compare child to child, accomplishment with accomplishment, and often unknowingly demonstrate conditional love based on their child's performance. A child is moulded, shaped and programmed for life by a win-win or a win-lose attitude, so we need to be constantly aware how we are emotionally supporting our child. Do not withhold your love. I am so very thankful that God does not see one, no not one of His children, better than another.

Despite facing many dismal situations, the Apostle Paul managed to stay heavenly minded and approached every situation with a win-win attitude. When facing his trial in the court of Caesar, he exclaimed that either he is going to let me live, or he's going to put me to death. That's a win-win situation? Paul knew that being in prison allowed him the opportunity to witness to Caesar's bodyguards, and the trial before Caesar would be an opportunity to magnify Christ. While facing physical death, not only did he gain reward with God's stamp of approval to his life, but there was also deliverance to his heavenly mansion and a lifetime with Christ. Christ was everything to Paul. Christ was his life, his passion, his eternity and when we, like Paul, realize how wonderful heaven is, who wouldn't want to go?

It's been a yo-yo struggle to imitate the heart of the Apostle Paul and get to the point of where I can say I am happy to die and be with Christ, or just as happy to stay here on earth and serve His purposes. As a mother, my heart wavers constantly, but my mind knows His truth: "For to me, to live is Christ and to die is gain." It is great to be in a win-win situation, where no matter which way it goes, I come out ahead.

Prayer: Heavenly Father, I praise you that when I take my last earthly breath, I will breathe in the magnificent air of heaven. I look forward to the amazing countless days that I will spend with you throughout eternity. As for now I continue to rely on your strength and mercy. May you give me the courage to declare your love to my friends, family and community. Humbly your servant, until my wings take flight. Amen.

Tidbits:

> "For God so loved the world that he gave his one and only Son, that whoever believes in him shall not perish but have eternal life." – John 3:16, NIV

> "If you want to get warm you must stand near the fire: . . .If you want joy, power, peace, eternal life, you must get close to, or even into, the thing that has them." – C. S. Lewis

> "I write these things to you who believe in the name of the Son of God so that you may know that you have eternal life." – 1 John 5:13, NIV

> "And when my days run out, I will have lived just a blink of time and the rest will be eternal joy." – Abby Danielle Burlbaugh

Song Suggestion: We'll Soon Be Done With Troubles and Trials – written by Cleavant Derricks

ALL FOR HIS GLORY

"Bring all who claim me as their God, for I have made them
for my glory. It was I who created them." – Isaiah 43:7, NLT

I can recall several personal experiences where I have been privileged to view
the glory of God in nature. Waiting in anticipation, perched atop the inactive
volcano of Mount Haleakala in Maui, we marvel at the spectacular glistening
golden sunrise fashioned by His hand. On another trip, while nervously
approaching the edge of the Grand Canyon, in the U.S., we spend endless time
absorbing the majesty of every crevice, rock and valley that span far beyond
what the eye can see. In the dark of night, nestled on the southern coastal sands
of Australia, on another occasion, gazing through night goggles, holding our
breath, we gawk in awe at the incoming fairy penguins retrieving food for their
young. The glory of God's handiwork is indisputable in creation but what does
it mean when He says that we have been created for His glory?

A dictionary refers to glory as being something of honour, praise, or a
height of achievement, enjoyment or prosperity. It can also mean something of
majestic beauty and splendour. While creation displays these attributes, God did
not create us so that His beauty or excellence would be increased, because He
is already absolutely perfect and completely glorious. Isaiah 43:7 gives insight
to the reason for our existence. ". . . every one that is called by my name: for I
have created him for my glory." Also in Isaiah, ". . .the people whom I formed
for myself and so that they may speak my praise." Today God–centredness is
obscured even in our churches. It is extremely important for those of us who
claim Jesus Christ as our Saviour, to intentionally represent Him in magnificence.
Salvation is not for our sake, but for God's sake. He created us so that we would
display His glory and declare His praise. (Isaiah 43:7, 21, KJV)

How do we achieve an alliance with God's goal to glorify Himself? It should
go without saying that you cannot be an example of something or someone
you do not know. So unless you have spent quality and quantity time with
God, you will not begin to know Him or to decipher His will for your life.
God has designed everyone with extraordinary abilities that enable us to glorify
Him in whatever capacity we are gifted. Sometimes, we tend to think the most
dedicated Christians are pastors or missionaries in full time service. God does
not call according to qualifications but according to His purpose. We are not
required to be educated or to be a biblical theologian but only to we know His
Son personally. No matter what our occupation or position of recognition, we
are divinely gifted, and there is no excuse for us not to be glorifying God in all
that we do. We can glorify Him as a serviceman, nurse, sports athlete or lawyer.

In fact, today you are set apart if you are diligent, truthful, and a person who values integrity. These honourable qualities are hard to find. Whatever you do, you can do it for the glory of God, and your labour of love is an act of worship and praise.

When our ambitions are self-centred, and we seek to accomplish our own goals, the results are usually empty and unrewarded. Yet if we are determined to glorify God, to honour Him and to bring Him pleasure, our lives will be filled with abundant joy and purpose. Joy does not come from seeking for joy itself but from sincerely and truly seeking Christ. Let us not lose sight of the reason we are created. All for His glory!

Prayer: Thank you, Jesus for creating me uniquely and for assigning specific gifts in my life that are for the purpose of showing your all surpassing power and to shine for your glory. Help me daily to pursue things of heavenly value and to worship you with a lifestyle that is God honouring. Help my life to be all about you and not about me. Guide me so that my steps are not selfishly patterned. May I constantly be mindful to use my talents or skills to serve others and help them to know you. Amen.

Tidbits:

> "So whether you eat or drink or whatever you do, do it all for the glory of God." – 1 Corinthians 10:31, NLT

> "We are all gifted, but we have to discover the gift, uncover the gift, nurture and develop the gift and use it for the Glory of God and for the liberation struggle of our people." – Louis Farrakhand

> "Whatever you do, whether in word or deed, do it all in the name of the Lord Jesus, giving thanks to God the Father through him." – Colossians 3:17, NIV

> "You are a child of God. Your playing small does not serve the world. There is nothing enlightened about shrinking so that other people won't feel insecure about you. We were born to manifest the glory of God that is within us." – Marianne Williamson

Song Suggestion: Jesus, Lover of My Soul – written by Paul Oakley

BLESS THE LORD

"Bless the Lord, O my soul, and all that is within me, bless his holy name! Bless the Lord, O my soul, and forget not all his benefits, who forgives all your iniquity, who heals all your diseases, who redeems your life from the pit, who crowns you with steadfast love and mercy, who satisfies you with good so that your youth is renewed like the eagles." – Psalm 103:1-5, ESV

Do you ever get alone with God and review your life? Occasionally, I have taken the time to reflect, and it is absolutely amazing to recall instances where you 'just know' that God has synchronized the miraculous. While it is in wider picture that I can see how He made all the pieces fit, there are some specific recollections and instances where His divine fingerprints were definitely evident. There was the time when my feelings had been severely seared by hurtful words, and God provided the grace to forgive, resulting in a godly transformation of my attitude towards that individual.

How about those Nascar squeezes where we narrowly escaped a 'should have been' accident, and God delivered us safely through the keyhole. Several times, He changed my direction in Christian service that provided growth and maturity so that I could be of further spiritual influence in others' lives.

God provided two definite miracles of 'prime real estate,' at unbelievably low prices that fit our budget without strain. It is humbling and profitable to reflect on how God has been my guide through every step of my faith journey. "Bless the Lord, Bless the Lord, O my soul and forget not all His benefits."

We show concern about making spiritual progress when we assess if there has been a pattern of growth. The Psalms indicate that David paused several times to reflect, and despite his numerous failures, chose to "Bless the Lord." He lists five specific benefits the Lord bestowed upon us, as believers.

"He forgives all our iniquity." There would be no fellowship with the Most High God if it were not for His Son, Jesus Christ, providing redemption for our sins. God is merciful to forgive, but salvation is but the first step of our faith.

"He heals all our diseases." If you have never beseeched God for healing, then count your blessings. Many have desired instantaneous healing from a physical or emotional challenge, yet God sometimes delays His answer so we are moulded and nurtured to greater maturity and so that He is glorified in the results.

"He redeems our life from the pit." David was rescued from many near death experiences, thanks to God, and God has the power to protect his children from harm as well, according to His will. Most often momentary misfortune has purpose in bringing us back into the centre of His will.

"He crowns you with steadfast love and mercy." God is steadfast, unchanging and has a limitless supply of love and mercy. He supplies for us spiritually and will never let us down or abandon us.

"He satisfies you with good so that your youth is renewed like the eagles." He knows our daily needs and supplies abundantly. He gives constant renewed strength for our faith journey and shelters us with His wings.

It seems impossible that God would desire a sinful, inadequate, wretched and despicable creature like me to praise Him. Who am I that I can offer or bless a holy, righteous and infinite God? Nothing in and of myself! But, in Christ, I am unique and have been created with divine gifts that are meant to be used for His glory. So with the Psalmist, I will say, "I will bless the Lord at all times, His praise shall continually be in my mouth" (Psalm 34:1, KJV).

Prayer: Heavenly Father, in humility I praise your Holy name and my soul boasts of your limitless love and mercy. I exalt and magnify your name. May your praise be continually on my lips. Amen.

Tidbits:

"The sweetest of all sounds is praise." – Unknown

"And it is impossible to please God without faith. Anyone who wants to come to Him must believe that God exists and that He rewards those who sincerely seek Him." – Hebrews 11:6, NLT

"No matter what looms ahead, if you can eat today, enjoy today, mix good cheer with friends today, enjoy it and bless God for it." – Henry Ward Beecher

"For the LORD is great, and greatly to be praised: He is to be feared above all gods." – Psalm 96:4, ESV

"God is concerned with nations, but nations also need to be concerned with God. No nation can have a monopoly on God, but God will bless any nation whose people seek and honour His will as revealed by Christ and declared through the Holy Spirit." – John Hagee

Song Suggestion: 10,000 Reasons (Bless the Lord) – written by Matt Redman, Jonas Myrin

CHILDREN'S PRAYERS

"Jesus said, "Let the little children come to me and do not hinder them, for to such belongs the kingdom of heaven." – Matthew 19:13-15, ESV

I think one of the most concerning issues about facing my cancer diagnosis was how we would break the news to our children and grandchildren. We planned a family barbecue and invited a close friend of the family to attend, one who wouldn't raise red flags because they frequently kept company with us. She and her children came prepared with age appropriate outdoor activities to capture the attention of the grandchildren while we shared the dismal news with our adult children. After a time of tears and prayer, it was agreed that each family would address the issue with their own children and help them to understand what circumstances might lay ahead. God is always faithful and parental reports indicated that each of the grandchildren handled the news with grace and a pledge to pray. At Christmas, I gave each of them an individual 'Nana Prayer' sock monkey to place near their pillow to remind them of my love and appreciation for their nighttime prayers. Hopefully a nightly representation of my love brings them comfort as they pray and support me in the months ahead.

Many times, as adults, we need to have the humorous outlook and simple faith of a child. The following quips demonstrate the joy and laughter they can shed in a dark situation: (Some shared by other cancer patients).

My preschool granddaughter's petite hands clasped over her shocked five-year-old cherub face, "Nana, where did all your hair go? Now you look just like Papa!"

My fifteen-year-old grandson remarks on the removal of my esophagus and the stomach being attached near the throat. "That's cool! So now when you ride a roller coaster where will your stomach go?"

Seven-year-old niece about lumpectomy, "Have them both taken off Auntie; your kids are done with them anyway!"

Ten-year-old boy's view of mastectomy, "No sweat, Mom, I didn't pay much attention to your boobs anyhow."

Six-year-old's concern over cancer being contagious, "Nana, you just drank from my cup, and you have cancer?!"

As much as we seek to protect those we love from the hardships of life, especially facing the potential loss of a loved one, it is most important that we keep the lines of communication open. If needed, seek advice from your pastor, doctor or another cancer survivor on ways you can help your children (grandchildren) to comprehend and handle future possibilities. Let your child express their feelings and fears; listen calmly and carefully be aware of hidden feelings of uncertainty that they might not be expressing. Realize that everyone processes distressing news in their own way and that each child will progress at a different rate of acceptance and understanding. Honestly answer their questions and address their fears with age appropriate responses, reassuring them of their importance to you. Allow them to be emotionally dependent on you and reassure them of not only your love but also the love and faithfulness of God, especially in times of trouble.

Personal footnote: I realize that this devotional has not focused on spiritual progress, but I hope this information is beneficial in helping you share your own cancer diagnosis with your loved ones. "Casting all your care upon Him; for He careth for you" (1 Peter 5:7, AKJV).

Prayer: Lord, thank you for the love and prayers of my grandchildren, and children. Comfort them beyond measure during this time as they stress over my health. Let the simple prayer of a child, "Dear God, please heal my Nana!" be the prayer of my heart. I love you, My Saviour, Lord and King! Amen.

Tidbits:

> "Grandchildren are the crowning glory of the aged; parents are the pride of their children." – Proverbs 17:6, NLT

> "Children really brighten up a household - they never turn the lights off." – Ralph Bus

> "Direct your children onto the right path, and when they are older, they will not leave it." – Proverbs 22:6, NLT

> "Pretty much all the honest truth telling there is in the world is done by children." – Oliver Wendell Holmes

> "Whatever they grow up to be, they are still our children, and the one most important of all the things we can give to them is unconditional love. Not a love that depends on anything at all except that they are our children." – Rosaleen Dickson

Song Suggestion: Heavenly Sunshine – written by Henry J. Zelley, Charles E. Fuller

CHRIST, MY CARABINER

"Truly, I say to you, whoever says to this mountain, 'Be taken up and thrown into the sea,' and does not doubt in his heart, but believes that what he says will come to pass, it will be done for him." – Mark 11:23, ESV

If your knowledge of sports is challenged, as mine is, you have already reached for a dictionary or 'googled' carabiner and asked, "What in the world is a carabiner." It is a metal loop with a sprung gate, somewhat similar to a looped earrings but much larger. They are made from steel, aluminum and are widely used in rope intensive activities such as mountain climbing, exploring caves, sailing, construction, rope rescue and high-rise window cleaning.

In the scaling of mountains, the carabiner is used to connect a series of ropes to safety pegs as well as a couple of connectors to the climber's safety belt; they are critical to execute a safe climb. Carabiner-styled key rings are currently popular but are stamped with a "Not for Climbing" warning. Unknowingly, I had a couple of carabiners in my junk drawer, left behind by my 'monkey' of a grandson. He is a typical boy and loves tying ropes and climbing anything scalable. He actually packed ropes and several carabiners on one of our road trips in hopes that they would lift him to heights beyond our reach, and he was successful in some smaller scale trees.

In life we all face mountains such as debt, divorce, drugs, delinquent teens, disabilities, declining health and more, and we perhaps wish we could scale our mountains and reach the summit of success. When I am facing my mountain, I choose to visualize myself attached to Christ, with a carabiner, and depend on Him to securely hold the rope. With each crevice of doubt or failure, He is lifting me to His side, the summit of safety.

Throughout the Bible, mountains are used to represent our problems, and we need to realize that they are not permanent. Your mountain may seem insurmountable, and you may have been praying for several years, and yet your crevices do not seem less dangerous or deep. Relax and remember that God is your guide and the perfect mountaineer. Your climb to victory may not happen overnight, and you may not survive the climb without some skinned knees or scraped elbows, but you can be certain that Christ will not let the rope slip. You may not see a stretch-by- stretch triumph, but be assured that He is working behind the scenes and desires nothing but victory for you.

Consider David and how everyone around him was talking about how 'this mountain' was unconquerable. In 1 Samuel, "Goliath is so big, there's no way we can defeat him." David did not focus on the mountain but put the seemingly hopeless situation in God's hands and said, "Goliath, this day the Lord will deliver you into my hands." David was actually saying, "You may be big, but my God is bigger." God can turn your mountains into molehills, but do not forget to trust Him in not only the big events but also in the trivial. Sometimes it is the trivial that cause us the most irritation. These minor annoyances God may be using to teach us godly virtues and mature us into better examples of His character.

Regardless of the speed of your climb over the mountain, remember that Jesus is the only secure and steadfast rope to hang onto. Hold onto the One who has promised to hold onto you. "The LORD Himself goes before you and will be with you; He will never leave you nor forsake you. Do not be afraid; do not be discouraged" (Deuteronomy 31:8, NIV).

Tidbits:

> "And we know that in all things God works for the good of those who love Him, who have been called according to His purpose." – Romans 8:28, NIV

> "Only if you have been in the deepest valley, can you ever know how magnificent it is to be on the highest mountain." – Richard M. Nixon

> "Trust in the LORD with all your heart and lean not on your own understanding; in all your ways submit to Him, and He will make your paths straight." – Proverbs 3:5-6, NIV

> "How you climb a mountain is more important than reaching the top." – Yvon Chouinard

> "Over every mountain there is a path, although it may not be seen from the valley." – Theodore Roethke

> "Don't tell God how big your mountain is. Tell the mountain how big your God is." – Unknown

Song Suggestion: Only a Mountain – written by Jason Castro, Mia Fields, Seth Mosley

CRUISING IN GOD'S CHARIOT

"The chariots of God are tens of thousands and thousands of thousands; the Lord has come from Sinai into his sanctuary."
– Psalm 68:17, NIV

We have a tendency to underestimate the power of God. David was using this verse to awaken our unbelieving hearts to the myriads of angels at His command to do His bidding by saying, "The chariots of God are tens of thousands, and thousands of thousands." This is not an exaggeration, nor is it an exact count but it was recorded to impress on us the innumerable resources available to God to protect His people. To further impress us, he added, "The Lord God is among them." God, the Commander-in-chief, is prepared to face your enemy by protecting the front line.

I recall the physical appearance of a chariot from movies like Ben Hur, Spartacus, Troy and Gladiator. Chariots were most often used for sport but were not a safe way to travel for the driver, and the horse frequently suffered injury and even death. Chariots of war were significantly different as they were usually manned by a crew of two or three men and the sides were mounted with three foot scythes that could easily plow through infantry lines, providing excellent infiltration to destroy the enemy. I want to envision my chariot battle against Satan with massive scythes that can 'rip him to shreds.'

All around us, waiting on every side, we are surrounded by God's chariots and horses waiting to carry us to victory. We are too often expecting a ride in a luxurious cart pulled by a pure white stallion, surrounded by crowds of cheering spectators and parading the flag of triumph, but our chariot is not necessarily always gilded with gold. Some of our less attractive chariots are trials, suffering, disappointment, and challenges that God determines we ride on our path to victory. This is the chariot race where we have a choice whether we allow our enemy to roll over and crush us or mount up in God's chariot and ride a sometimes bumpy road, but with the promise that we ride triumphantly to the finish line. "Some trust in chariots and some in horses, but we trust in the name of the Lord our God" (Psalm 20:7, NIV).

A repeated blunder we make is placing our trust in the 'chariots of Egypt' where the focus is not on the power of God. "What sorrow awaits those who look to Egypt for help, trusting their horses, chariots, and charioteers and depending on the strength of human armies instead of looking to the Lord, the Holy One of Israel?" (Isaiah 31:1, NLT)

We look for solutions that are easy, fleshly and detectable by relying on our friends, counsellors, pastors, our own resources and internet research to guide us through trials instead of looking for God to rescue us. It is often necessary for God to destroy our own prideful chariots so He can force us to a point of climbing into His. "Open my eyes so that I will observe amazing things from your instruction" (Psalm 119:18, ISV). God's chariots may be difficult to see or to determine, but they are there; don't doubt it.

When we choose to run the race in God's chariot, there are no obstacles that can hinder our journey to victory. I can picture myself being lifted to the heights of heaven in the arms of His angels, not because of physical death, but simply because He has brought a victory for me in an existing battle.

Open your spiritual eyes and view each challenge in your life as roaming in God's chariot of success, a continual victorious race to a 'heavenly place' of triumph. Accept each challenge as His will and know that your inner self will find spiritual growth and indestructible peace as you let Him carry you.

Tidbits:

> "Lord, open my eyes that I may see, not the visible enemy, but thy unseen chariots of deliverance." – Hannah Whitall Smith

> "You are not going to get peace with millions of armed men. The chariot of peace cannot advance over a road littered with cannon." – David Lloyd

> "Bring me my bow of burning gold! Bring me my arrows of desire! Bring me my spear! O clouds, unfold! Bring me my chariot of fire!" – William Blake

Song Suggestion: We Trust in the Name (Of the Lord Our God) – written by Steve Curtis Chapman

DOUBT DEFEATER

"Your steadfast love, O Lord, extends to the heavens, your faithfulness to the clouds. Your righteousness is like the highest mountains of God, your judgments are great and deep. . . . How precious is your steadfast love, O God! The children of mankind take refuge in the shadow of your wings." – Psalm 36:5-7, ESV

A cancer patient suffers many reoccurrences of doubt. Will the chemotherapy actually kill those wretched cells? Will radiation cause more harm to my other inward organs than it will the tumour? Will I ever survive these constant pangs of nausea and or the bone-weary tiredness? Will my family be able to endure suffering along this journey with me? How can I possibly be a positive witness to Christ with so much pain and tears?

The questions are endless and doubt continually attempts to creep in and steal our confidence in God's control. The devil is not quiet, nor will he ever stop sabotaging our Christian testimony and to squash our faith. "Be alert and of sober mind. Your enemy the devil prowls around like a roaring lion looking for someone to devour. Resist him, standing firm in the faith. . . And the God of all grace, who called you to his eternal glory in Christ, after you have suffered a little while, will himself restore you and make you strong, firm and steadfast" (1 Peter 5:8-10, NIV).

You are not alone! Not at all. In fact, several biblical characters doubted God; here are three specific doubting heroes. Abraham, despite being mentioned as a pillar of faith, couldn't bring himself to believe that God would provide them with an innumerable nation when Sarah was beyond child bearing years. They both laughed at the prospect and took matters into their own hands by choosing a 'surrogate' to bear an offspring. Gideon doubted God's ability to use him to conquer Israel's persecutors. He tested God, not only once but twice, requesting that the woolen fleece be the only thing dew dampened in the morning, and the next test he reversed by asking the fleece to be dry and the ground wet with dew. Then there is Thomas, known as the doubting apostle. He doubted Jesus had been raised from the dead and said, "Unless I see the nail marks in his hands and put my finger where the nails were, and put my hand into his side, I will not believe" (John 20:25, NIV). Doubt is unavoidable and part of our human condition, but that does not mean that it cannot be overcome.

Doubt is conquered by faith, but the problem is that faith is not a natural part of us. The reason we doubt is because we fear God will fail us, and our difficulties appear much beyond anyone's control. Like Abraham, we take control ourselves, denying God the opportunity to prove His promises to be true. The consequence for us is a faith that does not mature. Fight your fears, discard your doubt and ask the Spirit to give you strength to believe: ". . .blessed are those who have not seen and yet have believed" (John 20:29, NIV). Hide God's Word in your heart for 'faith comes by hearing, and hearing by the word of God" (Romans 10:17, AKJV). Your heart cannot be comforted or freed from doubt when it does not know what God has promised.

Remember that God is always faithful and daily remind yourself that He has a faultless track record. He never changes, He is the same today, yesterday and tomorrow, and His mercies will never come to an end. Stay focused on God, not on your own trying circumstances, and be sure to surround yourself with friends who encourage your faith in God. No matter how much your pain is clouding your mind, and regardless of how you feel, your faith cannot be stolen, crushed or deleted, because your faith in and of itself is from God, and God does not fail. So cast away your doubts, tell the devil to flee, and believe in God's unfailing love for you.

Tidbits:

> "I desire therefore that the men in every place pray, lifting up holy hands without anger and doubting." – 1 Timothy 2:8, WEB

> "Doubts are the ants in the pants of faith. They keep it awake and moving." – Frederick Buechner

> "All the people of Israel should know beyond a doubt that God made Jesus, whom you crucified, both Lord and Christ." – Acts 2:36, GW

> "The only limit to our realization of tomorrow will be our doubts of today. Let us move forward with strong and active faith." – Franklin D. Roosevelt

> "Yet He did not waver through unbelief regarding the promise of God, but was strengthened in his faith, and gave glory to God." – Romans 4:20, NB

Song Suggestion: Your Love, Oh Lord - by Mac Powell, Mark D. Lee, Brad Avery, David Carr, Tai Anderson

KEEP IT SIMPLE

"Do not neglect to show hospitality to strangers, for thereby some have entertained angels unawares." – Hebrew 13:2, ESV

I was facing my most challenging day, as I had finished my first full infusion of aggressive chemo drugs, in a second attempt to bring my esophageal cancer under control, and the nausea was overwhelming. You would think with having previous chemo experience that I would have known better than to eat a full supper following my infusion, despite feeling like almost a million bucks, or at least as close as cancer patients come to feeling amazing. Unfortunately, that meal chose to make several repeat appearances the following day. God was faithful to meet my needs through three unexpected caregiving visitors to my door who ministered to me during a time when I didn't much care if they were there, but certainly no less appreciated for their acts of kindness and love. I couldn't help but notice the frustration they felt when they really could not do anything to help my condition but to simply offer to fetch a drink, a cool cloth, or some comfort food—ah, maybe not so much any food thanks—blankets, and a loving touch, and so on. It was during these moments of helplessness that they demonstrated their sincere love for me and their desire to bring some kind of comfort to my suffering. It was these seemingly minuscule gestures that were exactly the kind of simplicity of love that I held onto like precious jewels in those difficult moments. I sensed their love and deep desire to 'change things' and appreciate how absolutely frustrating it must be for family, children and my spouse who can do nothing to eradicate the pain and suffering except to offer simple acts of love.

The first response of a caregiver is helplessness, so they desperately search out ways to change the situation. Many well-meaning friends have sent numerous articles of miraculous cures from dandelion root to Chinese herbs, to peroxide drops, and so on, and I have dutifully read most material at length, but God has provided complete peace within the medical field at this point.

Others have encouraged healthy eating, exercise, meditation and visualization of disease control, and while they all have a place in promoting a healthier body, not all of them are possible to put into action. Only the one suffering can know their true limitations, and yet the loving encouragement to live beyond the limitations that cancer places on the suffering is of significant importance physically, emotionally and spiritually. If you are looking for ways to minister to the patient or the primary caregiver, remember that most precious gifts come in small packages such as phone calls, emails, cards, bowls of soup, meals for the caregiver, coffee, short visits and a simple listening ear. Keep it simple and show random acts of kindness.

Some caregivers exhaust all their energy, time and financial resources to make sure their loved ones are cared for properly. This is exactly how God provides for us through His Son Jesus. He never tires from helping us. He is long-suffering and offers supernatural care for us daily.

Regardless of our mood, attitude or emotions, God is loyal and showers us with His mercy and love, especially when we least deserve it. When the patient or the caregiver finds themselves out of control, God is there to pick up and minister to our every need, and wants to be our strength as well. In the middle of chaos, vomiting and rolling moans of discomfort, He is still the Good Shepherd who gave His life for His sheep. We can only see God's actions from the limited vantage point of our humanness, and often His purposes are hidden from us until His plans come to fruition. While we may wonder at the terrifying trails our lives take, we can be certain that God is sovereign over all the earth and our lives. His presence guarantees us abundant life, and I am thankful that I don't have to live a miserable life, even in the face of cancer, as it tries to deflate any potential of having a life full of blessing. My days to experience no pain, tears or discomfort will come; no matter the outcome, for me as well as my caregivers and Lord, thank you for the angels that you are sending to me unaware.

Tidbits:

> "For God did not appoint us to suffer wrath but to receive salvation through our Lord Jesus Christ. Encourage one another and build each other up, just as in fact you are doing." – 1 Thessalonians 5:9-11, NIV

> "One person caring about another represents life's greatest value." – Jim Rohn

> "Whatever you did for one of the least of these brothers and sisters of mine, you did it for me." – Matthew 25:40, NIV

> "We make a living by what we get, but we make a life by what we give." – Sir Winston Churchill

> "Give, and it will be given to you. A good measure, pressed down, shaken together and running over, will be poured into your lap. For with the measure you use, it will be measured to you." – Luke 6:38, NIV

Song Suggestion: Your Great Name – written by Michael Neale, Krissy Nordhoff; performed by Natalie Grant

GOD'S GUARANTEE

"He who has prepared us for this very thing is God, who has given us the Spirit as a guarantee." – 2 Corinthians 5:5, ESV

It is almost unbelievable how many places offer extended warranties on products that you purchase. It wasn't long ago that I purchased a simple movie at a local store for around $25.00 and the clerk inquired if I wanted to purchase an extended three-year warranty on it for $8.00. You've got to be kidding. Within the year I can probably replace the movie for $10.00 or less. And no doubt, as Murphy's Law usually goes, the purchased item will most likely break within a day, week or month after the warranty has expired. Am I not right? There are some things in life that come with expected guarantees; if you cut yourself, you'll bleed; if you spend extended periods in the sunlight, your skin will burn; if you fall into a swimming pool, you'll get wet; if you touch an electrical socket with wet hands, you'll get a shock, and so on. These examples of guarantees show negative results, and at the moment I can't think of any positives.

There is one warranty that I am certain that will not result in disappointment, and that is God's guarantee as mentioned in the scripture verse above. God gave us the Holy Spirit as a pledge, a promise, a deposit, which is a guarantee of "what is to come."

A deposit on significantly priced products demonstrates a pledge of future intentions to follow through and complete the intended purchase; such is the down payment on a car, or a home, and so on. The Holy Spirit is God's deposit and the initial investment in our spiritual lives. All future investments are already paid in full by Christ's death on the cross and His resurrection from the grave. Interest began accumulating the very day we accepted the plan of salvation and the Holy Spirit is a guarantee that "He who began a good work will carry it on to completion." (Philippians 1:6, NIV) This one-time irreplaceable down payment provides for us countless elements: intercession, guidance, comfort, peace, hope, forgiveness, grace, mercy, love, patience, and so on. We know that God will not renege on His contract. Consider just a few of His promises:

"For I know the plans I have for you. . . plans for good and not for disaster, to give you a future and a hope" (Jeremiah 29:11, NLT).

"Come to me, all you who are weary and burdened, and I will give you rest" (Matthew 11:28, NIV).

"But all who listen to me will live in peace, untroubled by fear of harm" (Proverbs 1:33, NLT).

"And this same God who takes care of me will supply all your needs from His glorious riches. . ." (Philippians 4:19, NLT).

"So be strong and courageous! Do not be afraid and do not panic before them. For the LORD your God will personally go ahead of you. He will neither fail you nor abandon you" (Deuteronomy 31:6, NLT).

God has an awesome plan for each of us and we need not be fearful of challenging circumstances for His promises are sure. He is with us in difficult times to exchange hope for despair, comfort for pain, peace for anxiety and to bring "joy in the morning." Even if we are facing the valley of death, we have no fear, for physical death does not bring finality, rather our very next breath begins eternity. One day, I have no doubt, His divine work of redemption in me will be perfectly complete and that will result in a promise kept.

Prayer: Lord, oh what comfort it is to my soul that I have a Saviour on whom I can depend. You are all powerful and in control of everything, the noble and the corrupt, the positive and the negative, the cheerful and the gloomy. Thank you for your guarantee of eternal life and the blessings that you bestow during this difficult cancer journey. You have a divine design for my life, and I have no need to fear foreboding circumstances because I know that you love me and will work out all things for my good and your glory.

Tidbits:

"A promise is only as good as the person who makes it. The character of the promisor is what gives the promise its value." – Jennifer K Dean

"God never made a promise that was too good to be true." – Dwight L. Moody

"A promise means nothing until it's delivered." – Unknown

Song Suggestion: He'll Bring You Through – written by Kim Collingsworth

GOD'S SYMPHONY

"Praise the Lord with the harp; make music to him on the ten-stringed lyre. Sing to Him a new song; play skillfully, and shout for joy." – Psalm 33:2-3, NIV

Protocol is strict adherence to precisely correct procedure and doing the 'right thing in the right way.' I am a self-proclaimed perfectionist who certainly understands doing things the correct way, but for the preservation of my sanity, I have made a sincere conscious effort to curb that obsession. By lowering my perfectionist standard, I have created much more harmony with my family, allowing them their slight imperfections and their own individuality. However, I have found plenty of frustration with the term of 'protocol' used repeatedly with regards to my months of jumbled medical timetables. Believe me, I certainly hold the highest respect for the compassionate hands that have lovingly ministered chemo, radiation and apologized for several hour wait times for appointments, yet all the while being given the excuse of 'there is protocol we have to follow.'

I am aware that 'protocol' is necessary for the medical system to run precisely and without error as much as possible, but I don't believe that the term being used is a justifiable excuse to keep me waiting, and waiting, without reasonable explanation for the long delays between appointments. Thankfully, God is my comforter and the master conductor who is in complete control of orchestrating the entire melodic composition of recovery so I comfortably relax in His arms and release my burden of frustration to Him.

A more positive look at 'protocol' is realizing that God adheres to precise procedure and commands us to do the 'right things in the right way.' All Christians are members of God's symphony, but not all play their instruments in harmony. Each instrumentalist is responsible to study the musical score (God's Word), and to practise diligently and to be obedient, so that the entire ensemble (the Church), is much stronger in an orchestrated unity, rather than as a solo performance. Should you find your instrument is suffering periods of discord, perhaps you are a spectator in the audience and, instead, you need to join the ensemble. God is prepared to take your sharps (strengths) and flats (weaknesses) and compose them into a harmonious arrangement but you need to realize His protocol.

God is the master composer, and He alone has transcribed the masterpiece of your life well before you sang your first musical note.

Christ is the master conductor who conducts the entire ensemble with His wand of forgiveness and sacrifice.

The Holy Spirit is our mentor who provides effective communication between us, the instrumentalist, and God, who is the master composer. The Holy Spirit is also our teacher and coaches us to develop our talents to near perfection so they can be used to glorify God.

God expects us to join the symphony, progress in our musical ability, and not just to be a satisfied listener, easily swayed to an alternate beat. He has provided a redeemable eternal life asset for you joining the ensemble and taking part in delivering a masterpiece of music. God rewards the artists who have been outstanding musicians, committed, faithful and diligent, and whose melody honours Him.

I hope that by using a musical analogy to describe God's protocol, you have not lost sight of His divine plan. God, in His grace, has given detailed directives for us to mature in our spiritual life. Our progress is seen in our ability to do the 'right things in the right way,' and being steadfast in the divine path of protocol results in the multiplication of our trust in God and His plan for our life. God's entire purpose for His plan is to glorify His Son, Jesus Christ. My fellow believers, be assured that His course of action for dealing with disharmony is always grace.

Prayer: Heavenly Father, thank you for orchestrating my life and multiplying the trust I have in you. I desire that my life be an ever-improving musical score that brings glory to your Son, Jesus Christ. Amen.

Tidbits:

> "My heart is steadfast, O God; I will sing and make music with all my soul." – Psalm 108:1, NIV

> "How good it is to sing praises to our God, how pleasant and fitting to praise Him." – Psalm 147:1, NIV

> "We get nearer to the Lord through music than perhaps through any other thing except prayer." – J. Reuben Clark, Jr.

> "Inspiring music may fill the soul with heavenly thoughts, move one to righteous action, or speak peace to the soul." – Ezra Taft Benson

Song Suggestion: Praise the Father, Praise the Son – written by Ed Cash, Chris Tomlin

GREATLY BLESSED, HIGHLY FAVOURED

❧

"The Lord God is like the sun that gives us light. He is like a shield that keeps us safe. The Lord blesses us with favour and honour. He doesn't hold back anything good from those whose lives are without blame." – Psalm 84:11, NIRV

My salvation experience dates back to the early 70s when 'all night sings' featuring southern gospel music were bursting at the seams. 'All night sing' is a bit misleading, as we really didn't spend the entire night singing. Some of the great groups that come to mind are: The Speer family, The Blackwood Brothers, Cathedral Quartet, The Kingsmen, The Stamps Quartet and several others whose names have faded from my memory bank. Being a newly born-again Christian, the songs were not familiar and before long my taste in music transferred to that of Michael W. Smith and Amy Grant. Then, even further in my walk with Christ, I enjoyed the music of Third Day, Casting Crowns, Hillsong, Matt Redman, Mercy Me, and more. Now, as seniors, we have come full circle and we've returned to the Southern Gospel roots and some favourites include The Isaacs, Booth Brothers and The Gaither Vocal Band. The Gaithers perform "Greatly Blessed, Highly Favoured" and the words are a wonderful affirmation of my position in Christ. As a result of His sacrifice, I am "Greatly blessed, highly favoured" and an imperfect but forgiven child of God.

Sometimes, as Christians, in our eagerness to share the grace and love of God with others, we fail to communicate love and acceptance and, instead, portray superiority and smugness. I know only too well some individuals whose character emits a 'holier than thou' attitude and before even a word is spoken, the line of communication is severed. Christ was forever an example of humility and we should remember John Bradford's words, that "there but for the grace of God go I."

Maintaining a humble spirit is very important in order to bridge the gap between ourselves and the unsaved. We are still sinners but have been 'greatly blessed' to have our sins forgiven because of repenting and accepting Christ's sacrifice. This is something that we have done nothing to deserve.

173

In today's world, where disasters of all kinds are widespread and negativity rules the airwaves, there has been no greater need for people to know they are loved, accepted and can be greatly blessed and highly favoured.

God does not require us to rid of sinful habits, to clean up one's speech, to strive for holiness, or even love one's neighbours, but simply asks us to repent, and accept Him with the simple faith of a child. It is a message of forgiveness that is so simple that many people find it unbelievable and reject it.

Prayer: Your compassions fail not and your mercies are new every morning. I offer my praise, thanksgiving and worship you for I am highly favoured, deeply loved and greatly, greatly blessed. With all my imperfections, I am humbled to think that you, a Holy God, loves me. God, please help me to lead others to you with a spirit of humility throughout my journey. Thank you, Jesus! Amen.

Tidbits:

> "This is love: not that we have loved God, but that He loved us and sent His Son to be the payment for our sins." – 1 John 4: 10, GW

> "Blessed are they who see beautiful things in humble places. . ." – C. Pissarro

> "Praise the God . . . Through Christ, God has blessed us with every spiritual blessing that heaven has to offer." – Ephesians 1:3, GW

> "Considering that the blessed life we so long for consists in an intimate and true love of God Our Creator and Lord, which binds and obliges us all to a sincere love." – Ignatius Loyola

> "Blessed are the people who have these blessings! Blessed are the people whose God is the LORD!" – Psalm 144:15, GW

Song Suggestion: Greatly Blessed Highly Favoured – written by Larry Gatlin, William J. Gaither

HIDE AND SEEK

"As my glorious presence passes by, I will hide you in the crevice of the rock and cover you with my hand until I have passed by." – Exodus 33:22, NLT

I fondly remember my childhood as we used the neighbour's yards as well as our own when we would feverishly hunt for obscure hiding places in which to take shelter from the person who was "It." It was especially challenging and the most fun when we played at dusk on into darkness. Sometimes we would wait for what would seem like an hour and finally give up and reveal ourselves in a mad dash for 'home,' hoping we wouldn't be caught before tagging 'safe.' Today as a grandmother, I marvel at the innocence of a young child who sneakily hides behind a pillow or flattens himself on the floor covered with a blanket thinking that because he cannot see you that he is invisible.

Our spiritual life can sometimes be like a game of hide and seek. In times of turmoil we run for "home," not afraid of being caught; instead, we are seeking for God and shouting all the way, "Lord, help me!" On the opposite spectrum, when we have done something for which we are totally ashamed, we run away and hide, more than willing to remain unfound for hours, days or longer.

This kind of reminds me of a humorous story. At a potluck luncheon, the hostess noticed that they were low on desserts and, with intention of assuring each a portion of dessert, she placed a note on the cookies that read, "Take only one, please, God is watching." Just further down the table a jokester posted another, "Take all the cherries you want, God is watching the cookies."

Humour aside, this story is far from the truth, for we know that God is quite capable of seeing, hearing, and knowing everything, so it is hopeless to try and hide anything from Him.

". . .for He knows the secrets of every heart" (Psalm 44:21, NLT)

"The eyes of the Lord are in every place." (Proverb 15:3, ESV)

". . .and He knows everything." (1 John 3:20, NIV)

"My eyes are on all their ways; they are not hidden from me, nor is their sin concealed from my eyes." (Jeremiah 16:17, NIV)

God never has a foggy chemo brain or a senior moment. God knows all things, He sees all things and He is everywhere all of the time. God is the Creator of all and through His power, He holds all things together. He plays many roles in the lives of His children; He is our Comforter, our Saviour, our Redeemer and our Friend. He is our Father who renews our strength and our spirit. Nothing is hidden from Him and nothing is beyond His power.

If you are spending time nurturing your relationship with God, then you are divinely comforted knowing He is near, He never moves and He is already working on a solution to your dilemma. However, if you have kept your distance and ignored His Word, then you are extremely uncomfortable with His omniscience (all-knowing), omnipotence (all-powerful), omnipresence (all-around, everywhere).

Despite an earthly population over seven billion people, God still knows the thoughts, problems and sins of everyone. There's no place to hide from God and there is absolutely nothing you can do that will cause Him to hide from you.

Prayer: Thank you that your response to me is devotion, protection and forgiveness. You know my innermost thoughts and failures and still love and restore me. In my troubles you hide me in the shelter of a rock and keep me safe. Your hand is always ready to deliver me. You are amazing, God. Amen.

Tidbits:

> Omniscience - "O LORD, you have searched me and you know me. . . when I sit. . . when I rise; . . .my thoughts from afar. . . my going out. . . my lying down . . . all my ways." – Psalm 139:7-11, NIV

> "The wise still seek Him." – Unknown

> Omnipotence - "Do you not know? Have you not heard? . . . He sits enthroned above the circle of the earth, and its people are like grasshoppers. He stretches out the heavens like a canopy . . . He brings princes to naught and reduces the rulers of this world to nothing. . . To whom will you compare me? Or who is my equal?" says the Holy One." – Isaiah 40:21-26, NIV

> "God rewards those who seek Him. . . . What awaits those who seek Jesus? Nothing short of the heart of Jesus." – Max Lucado

> Omnipresence - "Where can I go from your Spirit? Where can I flee from your presence? If I go up to the heavens, you are there; . . . If I rise on the wings of the dawn, if I settle on the far side of the sea, even there Your hand will guide me . . . even the darkness will not be dark to You; the night will shine like the day, for darkness is as light to You." – Psalm 139:7-12, NIV

Song Suggestion: Indescribable – written by Laura Story, Jesse Reeves

JESUS, OUR CORNERSTONE

"For in Scripture it says: 'See, I lay a stone in Zion, a chosen and precious cornerstone, and the one who trusts in him will never be put to shame.'" – 1 Peter 2:6, NIV

In ancient building practices, the cornerstone was the principal stone placed at the corner of an erected structure and usually one of the largest, most solid stones in the foundation. The entire structure, regardless of its size, was totally dependent upon this single stone being properly positioned.

We are living with a first-hand example of a misplaced cornerstone. Ten years ago, we contracted to have a three- season sunroom added to our home, and there were many 'too many cooks in the kitchen.' A slight miscalculation in the foundational footings made its presence known at the roof level. This error was not noticeable to the naked eye and the wall erection, primarily 90 percent windows, did not present a challenge. However, when workers got to the roof, it became very evident. Every single piece required exact weird dimensions, and a 1– inch error became a 4–inch headache. Individual measurements and puzzle piecing were time consuming and frustrating, but to the naked eye, our completed sunroom is beautiful.

When you are touring a city, you will often notice cornerstones in a prominent position on a building that are displayed for a ceremonial purpose. They are usually not foundationally set but include the name of the architect, business or a memorial that is inscribed with the date, purpose or origin reason for the building's presence. Many early 1800s buildings that were once post offices or government fronts still have their original inscribed cornerstone, yet an entirely different business exists within its structure today. It is heartening to see that some of this architectural history still remains on a prominent structure hundreds of years later.

In Isaiah 28, a spiritual cornerstone was prophesied, and it was a firm and tested foundation on which nothing could be shaken. "Therefore, this is what the Sovereign LORD says: "Look! I am placing a foundation stone in Jerusalem, a firm and tested stone. It is a precious cornerstone that is safe to build on. Whoever believes need never be shaken" (Isaiah 28:16, NLT).

The New Testament has several references to the same cornerstone having once been rejected, and yet He would remain the cornerstone on which the Church would be built. That cornerstone is Jesus Christ. "For Jesus is the one referred to in the Scriptures, where it says, 'The stone that you builders rejected has now become the cornerstone" (Acts 4:11, NLT).

God provided for us a sure foundation in His only son, Jesus Christ. The crucified one is our chief cornerstone for eternity, providing us forgiveness, salvation, righteousness and justice. This does not mean that as Christians we are shielded from disappointment, but we can, through faith, find hope. Hope in knowing that our daunting diagnosis of ill health, wayward faith, or other trials can be surrendered, allowing us to look forward to an improved future. Jesus, our cornerstone, was designed before the beginning of time with our redemption in mind. He is the heart and daily focus of Christian life, the alpha and omega for all of our peace, our faith and our hope.

I have not rejected Christ as my cornerstone, have you?

Prayer: Heavenly Father, I lift my life to you and pray that I would grasp the significance of Jesus being the cornerstone and the cost of His sacrifice. Thank you for the atonement for my sins and a shield of righteousness. You are the source of hope, when things seem hopeless, and the light in the darkest path. Through all my storms, may I rest in you. Amen.

Tidbits:

> "There is only one secure foundation: a genuine, deep relationship with Jesus Christ, which will carry you through any and all turmoil. No matter what storms are raging all around, you'll stand firm if you stand on His love." – Charles Stanley

> "For no one can lay any foundation other than the one already laid, which is Jesus Christ." – 1 Corinthians 3:11, NLT

> "Anyone who trusts in him will never be disgraced." – Romans 10:11, NLT

Song Suggestion: Cornerstone – written by Reuben Morgan, Edward Mote, Jonas Myrin, Eric Liljero, William Batchelder Bradbury; performed by Hillsong

ME, BE STILL?

"He says, Be still, and know that I am God; I will be exalted among the nations, I will be exalted in the earth." – Psalm 46:10, NIV

Whether I look at myself as a child, an adolescent, or an adult, seldom do the words "be still" fit into my vocabulary. Being a type "A" personality, I have always taken charge and preferred to remain active in a variety of ways. There was plenty to investigate and various games to organize during childhood days spent on our family farm, and I certainly cannot lay claim to them always being well thought out. Let's suffice it to say that riding a blackboard down a flight of twenty plus stairs doesn't quite flow as smoothly as a toboggan down a hill, and neither does attempting to drive a tractor at the age of eight with my five-year-old brother hugging the trailer hitch signify any great intelligence. That was definitely an instance where God extended grace and miraculously granted us safety.

My teenage years had their share of dumb ideas, but my extra-curricular activities fortunately involved a variety of sports that kept me busy in a more productive way. Adulthood brought a different kind of busyness, especially being a parent of four children, but I still found plenty of activity for my "not be still" personality. Between kids, taxi service, church activities and responsibilities—which were numerous—and trying my hand at every craft possible, there was little time for God, for I was productively busy.

Don't get me wrong, I knew the Lord personally and spent marginal time reading His word and in prayer, but nothing that I would boast about. As with many servant 'type A' personalities, we find great satisfaction in our accomplishments and often justify not spending quality 'be still' time with the Lord because we are busy serving Him. Despite the head knowledge of knowing that building an intimate relationship with Christ required regular times of solitude, which included meditation, listening and digesting the scriptures, the time I spent with Christ never mushroomed to the level that I have most recently experienced.

This importance of "being still" was never more apparent than when my life seemed to be spiralling out of control with an unexpected cancer diagnosis. For those who share my "A" personality type, know that lacking personal control was quite likely more devastating than the cancer news. There were still seemingly mundane decisions in the everyday life functions, such as meals, domestic chores and so forth that remained normal, and within my control, but the proposed chemo and radiation treatments, the timing process of each and the final outcome of cancer were not. While it was somewhat difficult for me to relinquish control and be dependent upon others, it was in many ways much easier to abandon the anxiety and fears to God. At a time such as this, we are forced to realize that we are incapable of controlling life or its circumstances. Nothing in my life is or ever has been a surprise to God.

The act of being still and getting quiet, especially to spend quality and quantity time with the Lord, is a real challenge in today's hectic world. My gratefulness to God overflows that He has provided this season of cancer, because it has forced me to finally be still in His presence. The relationship that I have built with Him over the past year has been truly amazing, and I feel very privileged to have experienced His love to this degree. I only pray that it continues to grow stronger. God alone knows the plans He has for me, and because I can trust him, I can be still for He alone is sovereign, all knowing, all powerful, holy, faithful and His love is beyond measure.

Instead of always approaching Him with requests and petitions, why not try finding a place of silence and spend it worshiping and listening.

Tidbits:

> "Be still and rest in the Lord; wait for Him and patiently lean yourself upon Him." – Psalm 37:7a, AMP

> "Know that even in the midst of your worst circumstances, you can be still and calm and at peace. . . .because God's got you." – Unknown

> "Be still, all flesh, before the Lord, for He is aroused and risen from His holy habitation." – Zechariah 2:13, AMP

> "I believe people are afraid to be still because we're used to being stimulated." – Michael W. Smith

> "The LORD himself will fight for you. Just stay calm." – Exodus 14:14, NLT

Song Suggestion: Still – written by Reuben Morgan; performed by Hillsong

MORNING'S NEW MERCIES

"Because of the LORD's great love we are not consumed, for his compassions never fail. They are new every morning; great is your faithfulness." – Lamentations 3:22-23, NIV

Parents, I am sure that many of you can identify with me. There were many restless nights that I lay my head on my pillow and drenched the pillowcase with tears and beating heaven's gates with prayer, I ached for a change in direction for my adult child. The situation my made motherly heart heavy with worry, and in the darkness of the night, my imagination would run away with troublesome thoughts. All too often, that worry was borrowed or multiplied due to my own physical weariness, but as time passed, I recognized God's pattern of morning renewal, and so I began a process of releasing my nighttime afflictions as I closed my eyes, knowing that with proper rest the problem would seem much smaller.

A lack of sleep can produce many complications physically, emotionally and spiritually. We find ourselves short tempered and snap at the least offence, frequently saying something that causes irreparable harm to another. Perhaps you are a person with delicate emotions, and the sleeplessness brings a torrent of tears at the slightest demonstration of disappointment or compassion. Today, studies have shown that most of the workplace stress and its health complications are caused by a lack of a restful night's sleep.

Isn't it wonderful that God doesn't need eight hours of sleep before He fulfills His promise of 'new morning mercies?' I treasure the truth in scripture that tells us that His mercies are new every morning. I remember well the many nighttime worries that seemed to melt away or, at the very least, appeared less monstrous as I faced a new day with physical refreshment and renewed strength from God. I am sure He is just as delighted to see our refreshed countenance much like we, as parents, enjoy the beautiful smiles of our awakened toddler who had been put down for a night of sleep in the grumpiest of moods.

While the scripture refers to His mercies being new every morning—and I have applied it to the need of a good night sleep—don't limit God for His mercies are available minute by minute, moment by moment, hour by hour, and day by day. We can never bankrupt His mercies nor does He grow weary in coming to our rescue. God is never depleted, worn out or absent. He has a plentiful supply of mercy and is always ready at your beck and call. He is always present and prepared to shower you with new mercies, and a revitalized outlook at yesterday's problems.

Prayer: Lord, thank you for your miraculous design in the creation of man and for instilling the need of rest for our souls to be refreshed. Your mercies, new with each morning, can brighten the day and lead us in your way. Great is your faithfulness. Amen.

Tidbits:

Life is just totally awesome when God is on the throne.
Hours, days and weeks pass by, yet I am never alone.
His loving mercies are new each day that I rise up and take breath.
His word reveals everlasting promises with more amazing depth.
My prayer for you this very day and throughout the year to come. . .
To realize life is peaceful and fulfilling, when you know His Son.
– Faye Dewhurst

"I am in deep distress. Let us fall into the hands of the LORD, for his mercy is great. . ." – 2 Samuel 24:14a, NIV

"God's mercy and grace give me hope - for myself, and for our world." – Billy Graham

"Do not withhold your mercy from me, LORD; may your love and faithfulness always protect me." – Psalm 40:11, NIV

"I have always found that mercy bears richer fruits than strict justice." – Abraham Lincoln

"Surround me with your tender mercies so I may live, for your instructions are my delight." – Psalm 119:77, NLT

Song Suggestion: New Mercy – written by Dennis J. Matkosky, Denise Phillips, Randy Phillips

ORGANIZING VS PURGING

"O LORD, You have searched me and known me. You know my sitting down and my rising up; You understand my thought afar off." – Psalm 139:1-2, NKJV

S pring and Fall are typically seasons when households take time to organize and purge. Yard sales abound and display some of the most bizarre items that no longer bear any need or use by the original owner.

During most of my adult years, I have been an avid organizer and have been known to frequently express my dismay when a family member hasn't put an item back where it belongs. My husband is actually most notorious for just putting things where he deems them to be convenient and refers to me as a compulsive neat freak. There are actually a few of us around, just ask my brother.

Organizing is the act of arranging or rearranging elements following one or more rules. Compulsive is defined as performing an act persistently and repetitively. The word "obsessive" refers to repetitive behaviour or pursuing an activity to the absolute, or nearly absolute, exclusion of all others and usually associated with anxiety. Purging is the removal of an undesired product. So, my husband would couple those definitions and name me a 'compulsive organizer and obsessive purger.' I know one thing for certain, I am not a hoarder. Hardly a week goes by that my husband isn't asking me where a certain item is, and while I have learned over the years not to purge his things, I still organize them, so they have a place, or in some cases are hidden from view. We have had our fair share of yard sales over the years, but as I age, and to my husband's delight, my obsession with organizing and purging are less practised and the leftovers from my purging just don't seem to warrant a yard sale so we either donate or give them away. Might I add, that without a brood at home to disturb my organization, things actually stay in place for months.

No matter how long we live, or how organized we are, there are always spiritual closets that require cleaning or organizing, and in some cases, habits that require purging. God is using this cancer season to display the dust on my spiritual shelves, dead insects in some corners, and even some mould under the beds. The first dusty items exposed were the dust of busyness and pride, both of them being frequent flyers that require me to be continually dusting to keep them under control. Together we are looking at other things that don't fit and finding some buried bugs like prejudice and intolerance. So we've done some serious sweeping and, prayerfully, have permanently discarded them and have installed an alarm system so they don't return. Lastly, we searched for items that required permanent purging. Not just a simple dusting, or sweeping, but a 'toss them out in the garbage' reaction. I must admit these are a little more difficult to determine. To some they might be bad habits, foul language or idols that have taken God's place as being first in our lives, but I am still meeting with the Lord regularly on what He would have me purge. Thankfully, the cleaning of our souls can be practised on a day-to-day basis and are not just seasonal duties. Let us join David who understood the necessity of being purged and cleansed daily by our Creator. Thankfully, there will be no need to post a yard sale sign for discarded sins—they are not for sale.

Prayer: O Lord, you know everything about me and have forgiven me completely, even when I fail and cling to things that I shouldn't. I praise you for exposing the condition of my closets through this trial and am grateful that you care more for the condition of my heart than the activities or ministry I can do. It's not easy being refined through fire, but I am thankful for the promise of an end result that brings you glory. Amen.

Tidbits:

> "The trouble with organizing a thing is that pretty soon folks get to paying more attention to the organization than to what they're organized for." – Laura Ingalls Wilder

> "Search me, God, and know my heart; test me and know my anxious thoughts. See if there is any offensive way in me, and lead me in the way everlasting." – Psalm 139:23-24, NIV

> "Even an organized person has days that aren't efficient and well-managed." – Deniece Schofield

> "Then the Lord said to him, "Now then, you Pharisees clean the outside of the cup and dish, but inside you are full of greed and wickedness. You foolish people! Did not the one who made the outside make the inside also? But now as for what is inside you-be generous to the poor, and everything will be clean for you." – Luke 11: 39-41, NIV

> "I am somebody cause God don't make no junk" – Ethel Waters

Song Suggestion: Amazing Grace (My Chains are Gone) – written by John Newton, Louie Giglio, Chris Tomlin

PEACE, PEACE,
WONDERFUL PEACE

"And the peace of God, which surpasses all understanding, will guard your hearts and your minds in Christ Jesus." – Philippians 4:7, ESV

As with the majority of persons who are surprised with a diagnosis of cancer, my first source of information was 'Google.' Then days later, without hesitation, my thoracic surgeon asked, "Have you been on the Internet?" Knowing full well the unlimited amount of perplexing information would have me flabbergasted and questioning survival of this wretched disease, he cautioned me.

I was guilty. I had partially reflected on some of the bottomless resources but was very quick to realize that educating myself via 'Google' was not a productive process, and that cancer is as individualistic as we are. Not everything researched could be applied to my particular situation. Consequently, at the doctor's request, I discarded Google and chose instead to look to the scriptures for my comfort and have not looked back. Jesus was and is the answer to every question or situation.

The life-altering devotional during those questionable first weeks was that of Hezekiah when the Lord spoke through Isaiah and told him he was going to die. "In those days Hezekiah was sick and near death. And Isaiah the prophet, the son of Amoz, went to him and said to him, "Thus says the Lord: 'Set your house in order, for you shall die and not live.'" Then Hezekiah turned his face toward the wall, and prayed to the Lord, and said, "Remember now, O Lord, I pray, how I have walked before You in truth and with a loyal heart, and have done what is good in Your sight." And Hezekiah wept bitterly. (Isaiah 38:1-3, NKJV)

Hezekiah wrote a song during this disheartening period, expressing sorrow over his impending death and lamented about perishing in the prime of his life.

(I may be past my prime but I identified with Hezekiah in not being ready to die.)

The Lord was so stirred by Hezekiah's heartfelt pleading that He sent word through Isaiah, "Go and tell Hezekiah, 'Thus says the Lord, the God of David your father: "I have heard your prayer, I have seen your tears; surely I will add to your days fifteen years" (Isaiah 38:5, NKJV).

Upon reading this story and the Lord's change of mind in granting Hezekiah an additional 15 years, I was overcome with an indescribable sense of peace. I prayed and cried and likewise proclaimed a desire to live for the Lord and begged for 15 additional years. No matter what the Lord's allowance is, with regards to the length of my life, I have been completely overwhelmed with the undeniable peace He has provided during my journey.

As I peruse other devotionals written by people about cancer experiences, I can no longer relate to their days of despair, tears, fear and anxiety. They give me reason to marvel at my mindset and this peace I have known. Is there something that I am not facing and refusing to be realistic about? Have I adopted a spirit of denial regarding cancer's potential consequences? Why am I not experiencing bouts of hopelessness? A friend helped me to realize that God has provided me with an aptitude of realism and that my acceptance of death being a reality for all us, and confirming that my days are not numbered by cancer but by God Himself. ". . .all the days ordained for me were written in your book before one of them came to be" (Psalm 139:16, NIV). Regardless of my chemo, radiation treatments and the impending surgery, God knows exactly the hour He has destined for my eternal promotion and that absolute truth has produced "And the peace of God, which transcends all understanding, will guard your hearts and mind in Christ Jesus" (Philippians 4:7, NIV). Thank you, Jesus!

Tidbits:

> "Peace I leave with you; my peace I give to you. Not as the world gives do I give to you. Let not your hearts be troubled, neither let them be afraid." – John 14:27, ESV

> "Peace begins with a smile." – Mother Teresa

> "Peace is a journey of a thousand miles and it must be taken one step at a time." – Lyndon B. Johnson

> "For to set the mind on the flesh is death, but to set the mind on the Spirit is life and peace" – Romans 8:6, ESV

Song Suggestion: Wonderful Peace – written by Warren D. Cornell, Liz Wagley

POWERFUL WORDS

"For the word of God is alive and active. Sharper than any double-edged sword, it penetrates even to dividing soul and spirit, joints and marrow; it judges the thoughts and attitudes of the heart." – Hebrews 4:12, NIV

There is not much beyond the comfort of reciting scriptures that can calm the pulse of a claustrophobic person when entering the CT scan, PET scan or radiation machine. Despite fear of undergoing double intensity radiation treatments for my esophageal cancer, I remained calm by closing my eyes and focusing on the power of God's Word. There was no power within the radiation machine that would render harm outside of God's control, and what calming assurance the comforting scripture brought to my racing mind with each treatment.

Prior to each treatment, there is a precise positioning of the body so the machine can accurately pinpoint the exact location for the strongest dosage of radiation. The entire positional process amazed me so much so, that there was seldom a person with whom I came in contact during those three weeks to whom I didn't explain the whole procedure. First there was the necessary accuracy of both vertical and horizontal laser beams pointing to dots that had been tattooed on my body, and then the alignment of the x-rays taken that day with the same position as during the mapping process completed weeks prior. After aligning the laser beams and the x-rays with the previous computer data, the information was synced and the computer shifted the radiation bed beneath me to an exact position. Once the machine reached the exact scientifically mapped location, the machine began to noisily spin around my entire prone body two times. By the time I was done fifteen treatments I could almost totally self-align my body vertically with a dot on the ceiling. Each treatment was about twenty minutes in length, but the alignment process was by far lengthier than the radiation itself. I am extremely thankful that God was with me, and I can hardly remember the buzzing noises for His peace that helped me to maintain a spiritual focus.

I am seldom able to recite scripture verbatim, nor do I usually know the exact references, but I know there is extreme power when using God's Word, and I am thankful that He doesn't expect recitation perfection but looks on my heart and encourages my faith to grow. I know the "Word of God is living, active and shaper than any two- edged sword." It has the power to unveil our secrets, motives and weaknesses, and through the Holy Spirit, stirs our souls to recognize our spiritual needs and make corrections. God's Word is so powerful that it will remain long past the scientific concepts of evolution and its words will never return to us void or become obsolete. His Word is so powerful that it unlocks the hardened heart, purifies the fornicator, tames a foul tongue, comforts the lonely, and brings hope to the hopeless. It completely changes lives! I am a life that was changed, praise the Lord. Through moments of loneliness in this journey, Jesus has been my companion and kept me company when no one else did, nor could they meet my needs like He can. Jesus is the living Word of God and He is my everything.

Prayer: Heavenly Father, thank you for providing the Bible, your infallible Word, a 'road map' to show me the way. I am thankful for its teaching, rebuking, correcting and training me in righteousness. Your unfailing love is fully exposed between its covers and I am grateful for the power of your Word. How it cuts precisely where it should to mould me into the person you desire me to become. Your word is a lamp unto my feet and a light unto my path. Praise your Holy Name. Amen.

Tidbits:

> "For I am not ashamed of the gospel, for it is the power of God for salvation to everyone who believes, to the Jew first and also to the Greek." – Romans 1:16, ESV

> "Giving in to fear alters God's best plan for your life. So use the power of God's Word to do what He wants you to do. . .even if you have to do it afraid! The rewards are great." – Joyce Meyer

> "All Scripture is God-breathed and is useful for teaching, rebuking, correcting and training in righteousness, so that the servant of God may be thoroughly equipped for every good work." – 2 Timothy 3:16-17, NIV

> "Heaven and earth will pass away, but my words will never pass away." – Matthew 24: 35, NIV

> "Contained within its frail pages is found the eternal message of the One who has existed before time began. Holding the wealth of sixty-six books man is able to explore his beginning, his reason for living and his hope beyond the grave. The Bible is a most remarkable book. A light shining in darkness the words of God open for man the revelation of grace, mercy and saving love." – Kent Heaton

Song Suggestion: Word Is Alive – written by Steven Curtis Chapman, Mark Hall

SOVEREIGN OVER US

"Remember the former things of old; for I am God, and there is no other; I am God, and there is none like me, declaring the end from the beginning and from ancient times things not yet done, saying, 'My counsel shall stand, and I will accomplish all my purpose." – Isaiah 46:9-10, ESV

"There is strength within the sorrow." No one really knows just how they will handle suffering until it happens to them – death of a loved one, health crisis, a community tragedy. The Apostle Paul encourages us to stay true to the Lord during times of suffering, and when you are ready to quit, remember Him and His multiple sufferings. There is a mystery to suffering, but we know God understands suffering and pain as He sacrificed His one and only Son on the cross for our sins. With every time we suffer for the cause of Christ, we are becoming more like Jesus and divine strength is provided for our journey of suffering.

"There is beauty in our tears." When we journey through difficult trials, physical challenges or critical finances, tears are a common expression of emotion. David said "You keep track of all my sorrows. You have collected all my tears in your bottle. You have recorded each one in your book" (Psalm 56:8, NLT). What a comfort it is to know that God understands the tears we shed and that He grieves right along with us. Tears are a language that God understands, and what beauty to know that our collected tears fall onto His hands and He, in return, comforts us.

"You meet us in our mourning." Despite having a heart that will be obliterated by death, scattered by searing words, or devastated by a physical crisis, God is prepared to meet us in our mourning. There will be times that our pain will make us question everything we believe in, but instead of clinging to pain, we must grasp onto the unfailing love that God has for us. When our hearts are broken, and we feel that God isn't near, the truth tells us that He is. "The LORD is near the brokenhearted; He delivers those who are discouraged" (Psalm 34:8, NB). He knows all the places where the pieces of your heart are scattered and is prepared to mend them.

God is faithful in supplying us with an unending love, peace that casts out fear, and He is working while we are waiting for answers. Through our suffering He is sanctifying us, and when all that is happening around us is beyond our understanding, He is simply teaching us to trust. Many persons of the world race to fortunetellers, soothsayers, crystal balls or horoscopes in hopes of being prepared for the future. But the only one who knows the future is the Almighty one who planned it before the beginning of time. When we are faced with overwhelming circumstances, will we turn and praise God for His power and grace and bow in submission to His sovereignty or resist Him and remain in pain and agony? Our only hope in all of life, good or bad, is God! For God, and God alone is sovereign over us.

Prayer: Oh Sovereign God, how I praise you for your wondrous works in my life and for your continued loving presence. During this cancer crisis, please give me the strength to be everything you have planned for me, and show me the way to demonstrate your love despite my pain. Help me to stand when I am weak and to lean on you for all my needs, physical, emotional and, in particular, spiritual. And if it be your will, please heal me. Amen.

Tidbits:

> "Our God is in the heavens; he does all that he pleases." – Psalm 115:3, ESV

> "God is unchanging in His love. He loves you. He has a plan for your life. Don't let the newspaper headlines frighten you. God is still sovereign; He's still on the throne." – Billy Graham

> "Yours, O Lord, is the greatness and the power and the glory and the victory and the majesty, for all that is in the heavens and in the earth is yours. . . Both riches and honour come from you, and you rule over all. In your hand are power and might, and in your hand it is to make great and to give strength to all." – 1 Chronicles 29:11-12, ESV

> "Many are the plans in the mind of a man, but it is the purpose of the Lord that will stand." – Proverbs 19:21 ESV

> "Cheer up, Christian! Things are not left to chance: no blind fate rules the world. God hath purposes, and those purposes are fulfilled. God hath plans, and those plans are wise, and never can be dislocated." – Charles H. Spurgeon

Song Suggestion: Sovereign over Us – written by Aaron Keyes, Jack Mooring, Bryan Brown

SUFFERING WITH CHRIST

"For it has been granted to you on behalf of Christ not only to believe in him, but also to suffer for him. . ." – Philippians 1:29, NIV

S uffering is an experience of unpleasantness or pain which can affect us both physically and mentally. There are varying degrees of intensity or frequency and the level of tolerance varies with each individual. As Christians we are pleased to share in the glories of Christ but seldom delight in suffering, yet in the Bible we are told that if we are to share in Christ's glory we must endure times of trial. The severe examples of suffering felt by his disciples and the early Christians are far from any suffering experience in the Western world or in this decade. From beheading, stoning, crucifixion, thrusting of swords, flogging, torture, being burned with fire, and scourging, these are only some of the descriptions of how pain was inflicted, sometimes even leading to one's death.

Some preachers have taught that suffering is a result of sin in our lives, and while that is true to an extent, where our poor decisions produce consequences of pain, the Bible teaches that beyond the suffering, the consequences of our own decisions, if we desire to share in the glories of Christ, we can also expect to share in His suffering. The degree of anguish will vary from situation to situation, and the level to which we endure varies from individual to individual. Whether we are being tried in the struggles of a ministry, the demise of our marriage, a body ravaged by cancer, or if we are being attacked for our position and proclamation of faith in Christ, the purpose of suffering is the same. "Will I trust Him? Will I hold on to Him or not?"

Many of us express that if our circumstances were changed, we would be more likely to honour God with our lives, but God wants us to depend on Him and demonstrate godly virtues even when our circumstances are unfavourable. We are expected to exercise a greater level of faith and trust in Him when we are in our season of suffering.

Some of our suffering is as a result of straying from living the life that God desires for us as revealed in the Bible. We show little regard for reading His Word and seek a bounty of carnal knowledge instead. We also tend to be as disobedient as Jonah when he refused to speak to the people of Nineveh and procrastinate or deliberately walk in the opposite direction that God has given to us. Too often we marvel at our spiritual deliverance from sin and blessings of delight that we overlook the gifts He has given in His strengthening and staying power during a trial. When we exercise trust in God, we will experience His abundant mercies.

Since I can be counted with the few cancer patients who have suffered very few side effects from chemo and radiation, I have yet to be physically tested where I can identify with Paul's statement in Romans. "For I consider that the sufferings of this present time are not worth comparing with the glory that is to be revealed to us" (Romans 8:18, ESV). Though I have no doubt that the peace that passes all understanding is mine mentally, because God has delivered it, and my belief in the sufferings here on earth will not compare with heaven's glory is also a gift of faith from Him.

Prayer: Father as I face different seasons of suffering, help me not to be rebellious or selfish but to put myself totally in your hands. Purify my faith so that I have a heart of compassion and words of encouragement for others. If I am persecuted for my faith, please help me to be faithful through all my trials, even death, that the crown of life will be given to me to cast at the feet of Jesus. Amen.

Tidbits:

> "Count it all joy, my brothers, when you meet trials of various kinds, for you know that the testing of your faith produces steadfastness. And let steadfastness have its full effect, that you may be perfect and complete, lacking in nothing." – James 1:2-4, ESV (A favourite verse of mine)

> "Without pain, how could we know joy?" – John Green

> "I have said these things to you, that in me you may have peace. In the world you will have tribulation. But take heart; I have overcome the world." – John 16:33, ESV

> "The wound is the place where the Light enters you." – Rumi

> "Suffering has been stronger than all other teaching, and has taught me to understand what your heart used to be. I have been bent and broken, but - I hope - into a better shape." – Charles Dickens

Song Suggestion: Strong Enough – written by Matthew West

THY WORD

"Thy Word have I hid in mine heart, that I might not sin against thee." – Psalm 119:11, KJV

Throughout my life as a parent, there were countless times that God would bring a verse to memory when a trying situation or grateful occasion warranted it to be remembered, recited and renewed. Even though I seldom remembered the exact wording, context or biblical reference, the familiar recollection always brought a spirit of comfort or thanksgiving to my soul. His Word never fails to minister to us in countless ways.

As a mom, I was very persistent in coaching my children to learn multiple Bible verses, especially during the Awana years, but I must plead guilty to having an improper motive. As a young Christian, I didn't understand the superior significance of 'hiding God's Word in our hearts' and pushed for their achievements so that we, as wonderful parents, could beam with pride and be congratulated. God knows we failed miserably at being wonderful at much of anything and, thankfully, God forgave us for that attitude of pride. The children didn't fail to make us proud though, as each finished nine years of the program with a "Timothy" award, which requires the memorization of 836 verses. Ultimately though, it is the faithfulness of God's Word, for which we are eternally grateful and how those heart-hidden verses are ongoing comfort through difficult seasons.

My four children, being raised in the faith from the cradle, are familiar with all the cute Bible stories: how Adam and Eve were created, how God sent a rainbow to save Noah from the flood, how a huge whale swallowed Jonah, how Daniel was safe in the lion's den, how Shadrach, Meshach and Abednego survived the fiery furnace, and more. To multiply the cuteness of those lessons, they also learned many action packed Sunday-School songs; God told Noah to build an arky, arky, or Only a Boy Named David, the B.I.B.L.E and others. Despite being cute and childish, these stories and songs were foundational in building assurance and dependence on the solidity of His Word. Every song or story conveyed the height, depth and width of God's love for His children and that He could be wholly depended on. God used their child-like faith and that early groundwork to be their godly foundation as they face deeper adult challenges today.

There are feelings of sadness and joy that I recall the afternoon when our adult gathering was planned, and arrangements were made to occupy my eleven grandchildren, so that I could reveal my cancer diagnosis to our four children. There was sadness in delivering shocking news, yet joy in the seeing the ultimate results. Each individual responded differently, some expressing tears, others shock and many with delayed reactions; but after processing the diagnosis, pondering various possible outcomes, praying and releasing our heavy concerns to the Lord, each person found peace. Everyone realized that even my cancer was under His control. I cannot emphasize enough that their strong faith is a direct result of having been grounded in the Word at a very young age. Never underestimate how much 'hiding God's word in your heart' benefits every situation that arises.

Families having a strong faith can experience the miracle of facing adversity with hope and then to discover a deeper understanding of 'why' God allows bad things to happen to good people. We may not have all our questions answered and may never know why, but God has proved faithful and He will never fail to teach us through the trials. Our pain is never wasted.

We are extremely blessed to have our adult children raising our precious eleven grandchildren in the faith. Thank you, Jesus for the longevity of your Word and its immeasurable ministry to our souls.

Tidbits:

> "That your faith should not stand in the wisdom of men, but in the power of God." – 1 Corinthians 2:5, KJV

> "Jesus said, "Let the little children come to me and do not hinder them, for to such belongs the kingdom of heaven." – Matthew 19:13-15, ESV

> "It is the same with my word. I send it out, and it always produces fruit. It will accomplish all I want it to, and it will prosper everywhere I send it." – Isaiah 55:11, NLT

Song Suggestion: Thy Word – written by Michael W. Smith, Amy Grant

TRADING MY SORROWS

"We are hard pressed on every side, but not crushed; perplexed, but not in despair; persecuted, but not abandoned; struck down, but not destroyed." – 2 Corinthians 4:8-9, NIV

When my boys were younger, they collected sports cards. They would trade their cards with intention of making a profit. They proudly carried them about in plastic sleeves displaying them openly. One still owns a Wayne Gretsky rookie card which he didn't even have to trade for but was a gift. I believe that many other boys were into trading other commodities such as marbles, hot wheels, micro machines, G.I. Joes and so on, but there was nothing more important to my boys than their cards. A few years ago, my grandson had a fixation with collecting 'YuGiOh' trading cards and sadly was willing to trade hard earned dollars for this temporary phase, underlining the fact that not all trades are wise ones.

Even as we age we are not immune to making poor trades. I am saddened to witness how easily teens will trade an honest promising friendship for a poor less favourable one because the later brings more peer popularity than another. As adults, we have likely made 'poor trades' in matters of business, reaping financial loss or perhaps a damaged reputation. How about those times we have attempted to trade with God himself? "Lord, in exchange for my tithe will you give me ____? The 'blank' can be filled in with tons of different things we think we desire. There is nothing, absolutely nothing, that we have to trade that profits God, yet He allows us to trade and benefit. God welcomes us to exchange all the rubbish in our lives for the wealth found in Him. For our pride, He will replace with humility; for our anger, peace; anxiety for trust; bitterness for forgiveness; complaining for gratitude; pessimism for faith; sorrow for joy; shame for grace; pain for praise, and so on.

I know that my body which is battling the ravages of cancer is crucial to my survival here on earth, but it is not the essence of who I am. I came from God and I will return to Him when my time on earth is done. Cancer does not and will not have a grip on my innermost being, for my soul has been bought by the blood of Calvary. There will be days of suffering when I will lean hard on Jesus for comfort and know that those days are only temporary for He has provided a painless existence for me in heaven for eternity. Though I may feel pressed beneath the weight of pain, He will not allow me to be crushed, for He cares. Even if I am confused about the purpose of my trial, I will not despair for He will provide clarity in His time. The trauma ahead may seem like persecution, but I know He is beside me for He has promised never to abandon me. I am sure there will be plenty of moments where my faith may seem struck down, but it will not be destroyed for God has promised that no one would ever pluck me from His hand. I can be forever comforted by the Holy Spirit, and because of Christ, I can trade all my sorrows, shame, sickness, and pain for the joy of the Lord.

Prayer: Thank you Lord, for choosing me and sending the Holy Spirit to live within my body, your temple. I may feel hard pressed but I will not be crushed, and I may have days of despair but you will never abandon me. There may be days that I may feel like quitting, but I will not lose hope because while you did not promise an easy life, you have promised to be with me when challenges come. I will trade my sorrows and remember that these momentary troubles are achieving an eternal glory. Praise your Name! Amen.

Tidbits:

> "Do you not know that you are the temple of God and that the Spirit of God dwells in you?" – 1 Corinthians 3:16, NKJV

> "Joy isn't tested when things are great, joy is tested and strength is tested when things are difficult. Where are you going to run when things get hard and you don't understand? I'm going to run to you, God. I don't get it, but I'm going to trade this in for joy and just know that walking with You is more than enough to carry me through." – Darrell Evans

> "Do not sorrow, for the joy of the Lord is your strength." – Nehemiah 8:10, NKJV

> "Joy flows right on through trouble; joy flows on through the dark; joy flows in the night as well as in the day; joy flows all through persecution and opposition. It is an unceasing fountain bubbling up in the heart; a secret spring the world can't see and doesn't know anything about. The Lord gives His people perpetual joy when they walk in obedience to Him." – D.L. Moody

> "He will wipe every tear from their eyes, and death shall be no more, neither shall there be mourning, nor crying, nor pain anymore, for the former things have passed away." – Revelation 21:4, ESV

Song Suggestion: Trading My Sorrows – written by Darrell Evans

TRUST IN THE LORD

"Behold, God is my salvation; I will trust, and will not be afraid; for the Lord God is my strength and my song, and he has become my salvation." – Isaiah 12:2, ESV

Do you know someone who is completely trustworthy? Someone you would trust with your bank account or who you would allow residence in your home during a vacation. If you have a person in your life like that, it is a very special relationship that has been built on a track record of honesty and integrity. Trust is only as good as the one you place that trust in. God is trustworthy. We are told in Psalms 118:9, KJV, that "It is better to trust in the LORD than to put confidence in princes." Authentic trust is an invaluable security when it is placed in the One True God.

We trudge through our life, attempting to make our way reasonably safe and void of pitfalls. We seek dependable employment that enables us to support a family and a home. We reluctantly invest in various types of insurance to avoid unforeseen calamity that would deprive us of what stability we have acquired. We half-heartedly keep regular appointments with the doctor in the hope of preventing health complications that would render us helpless or even threaten our life. Unfortunately, some of us make feeble attempts at attending church a few times each year, hoping we are pleasing God enough to bless us. None of our human attempts assure a safe or smooth journey. You can be certain that many times during the course of a lifetime, your trust will be put to the test.

You have probably already encountered some tough pot holes in the past and, highly likely, will meet countless bumps in the road ahead. Your company may downsize and you will be the first let go. Your spouse may decide the other side of the grass is greener and leave. An unexpected accident may take a loved one too early, or a critical health matter may not only threaten your life but also rob you of your entire life's savings. The potential pitfalls are plentiful but I am certain of this: the false gods of world religions or the material gods of money, possessions and power cannot help. Trust placed in the Almighty God doesn't eliminate all of life's pot holes, but God promises to guide and comfort you through them. Only trust placed in God will satisfy and produce positive results unimaginable. This kind of trust comes from believing that the Bible is the infallible, inerrant Word of God and that the directives and promises written within are completely dependable and upright.

What do you trust in? Your trust and faith is only as strong as what, who and where you put it. Trusting in the values of this world, such as money and success, will fail you. Trust in God, and in Him alone, in all things, and you will find Him to be faithful, protective and accompanying you and even carrying you through life's storms.

Prayer: Heavenly Father, the road I am travelling is foggy because the outcome of my cancer battle is yet unknown. I am uncertain of the road directions ahead but know I surrender the route to you, the bumps will be smoothed out. Forgive me when I have allowed my fears to laden the pathway with rocks, and help me to rely on you to remove them and redirect my paths. Increase my trust, carry me when necessary, and escort me through this storm. I will not fear the road ahead for you are with me, thy rod and staff they comfort me. Amen.

Tidbits:

> "All I have seen teaches me to trust the creator for all I have not seen." – Ralph Waldo Emerson

> "When we continually worry we believe more in our problems than we do in God's promises." – Unknown

> "Never be afraid to trust an unknown future to a known God." – Corrie Ten Boom

> "He who dwells in the shelter of the Most High will abide in the shadow of the Almighty." – Psalm 91:1, NASB

Song Suggestion: Dwell – written by Aaron Keyes, Jess Cates

UNBELIEF OR DOUBT

"What then? If some did not believe, will their unbelief cancel God's faithfulness? Absolutely not! God must be true, even if everyone is a liar. . ." – Romans 3:3-4, HCSB

As I read this morning's scripture verse, I was confused as a father was asking Jesus "help me overcome my unbelief" thinking doubt the same as unbelief. It is not. There is a difference: "Doubt is can't believe. Unbelief is won't believe. Doubt is honesty. Unbelief is obstinacy. Doubt is looking for light; unbelief is content with darkness. Doubt asks honest questions, but unbelief refuses to hear the answers." (Henry Drummond)

The line drawn between the two is very fine and the best I can determine is that doubt is a natural emotion that produces honest questions that may or may not be answered directly, but the doubter still has a heart of faith, weak perhaps, but unshakeable. Unbelief is the product of a hardened heart that allows seeds of doubt to wildly grow so they refuse to believe; they don't want any answers and rebel against the truth. Doubt is natural within faith. It comes because of our human weakness and frailty. Unbelief is the decision to live your life as if there is no God. It is a deliberate decision to reject Jesus Christ and all that He stands for. Doubt arises within the context of faith. It is a wistful longing to be sure of the things in which we trust. But it is not and need not be a problem.

Life today is overloaded with sicknesses for which we desire healing, yet various speed bumps threatened to destroy our belief. We believe that Jesus is the Son of God, but we allow doubt to cloud our faith when road blocks seem impossible. Recently our news headlines were ablaze with the senseless slaughter of twenty school children and six adults at Sandy Hook Elementary School in Newtown, Connecticut. The grief was immeasurable, but the difference between doubt and unbelief in this situation would be those who knew, regardless of the unexplainable evil, that God was still a loving God and in control and that He would take what is meant for evil and turn it to good. The unbelief would be demonstrated in allowing the evil to change their weakened faith, if they had any, to bitterness and a hardened heart, with an unwillingness to accept God.

Just because we have doubts does not mean that God cannot be trusted. Our faith is never perfect and is mixed with doubt and belief. Our faith is tried so that we will depend on His faithfulness. In our unbelief we refuse to trust God for an answer, but in our doubt we still trust God for an answer, regardless of the time it takes for questions to be answered.

As I have struggled with cancer for nearly a year and await the medical system to find space for my surgery, the line between doubt and unbelief is still very fine. The unbelief is not in God but in our health care system being efficient enough that I am not overlooked in the mass of needs. My thoughts and my ways are not the Lord's. I am imperfect and I struggle daily and my question is not whether Jesus will help, but when. I daily remind myself that God is in control and that even this long wait is a part of His plan, but the imperfections of the world still surround me, doubt still sprouts but I pray, "Lord, I believe but help me overcome my doubt."

Prayer: Lord, I pray simply that you will continue to grow my faith and diminish my doubts so that your faithfulness is demonstrated through me for your glory. Amen.

Tidbits:

> "I believe that the happiest of all Christians and the truest of Christians are those who never dare to doubt God, but take His Word simply as it stands, and believe it, and ask no questions, just feeling assured that if God has said it, it will be so." – Charles H. Spurgeon

> "Yes, but remember those branches were broken off because they didn't believe in Christ, and you are there because you do believe." – Romans 11:20a, NLT

> "The curse, of this age especially, is unbelief, frittering the real meaning of God's word away, and making it all figure and fiction." – Catherine Booth

> "Yet he did not waver through unbelief regarding the promise of God, but was strengthened in his faith and gave glory to God." – Romans 4:20, NIV

> "There are no sins God's people re more subject to than unbelief and impatience. They are ready either to faint through unbelief, or to fret through impatience." – Thomas Watson

Song Suggestion: Today Is the Day – written by Paul Baloche, Lincoln Brewster

UNCONDITIONAL LOVE

"Your unfailing love is better than life itself. I will praise you."
– Psalm 63:3, NLT

God's love is unconditional, eternal and constant. He will never leave you, forsake you or let you down. He is always present, day after day, year after year. He will always provide comfort and sanctuary. There is nothing you can do or say that will change His love. He loves without measure and without hesitation. There are no restrictions, no strings attached, just a pure and simple unconditional love. We have not earned it and neither do we deserve it, but God loves us simply because He is love.

The story of Hosea is a representation of God's unconditional love. God commanded Hosea to take a prostitute for a wife and present her before his people. Even after she returned to her previous lovers, he was commanded to buy her back again and make a contract that she would never leave again. This was to show the Israelites that even after they had turned to other gods that God would renew His covenant with them. God offered them unconditional love and eternal redemption.

Why does God put no condition on his love? Because the scriptures tell us that God is love. The life, death, burial and resurrection of our Lord Jesus Christ exemplified that love given to us even though we were yet sinners.

In our human understanding, we cannot fathom that gift; it goes way beyond what we experience here on earth. The only earthly love that is slightly close to is the love a parent has for their children. We endeavour to protect, comfort, and defend them even when they have disappointed or exasperated us. Yet as much as we strive to love unconditionally, if we are honest, our actions are appalling next to God's. Only God can offer unconditional love.

"When dark clouds settle in "Give thanks to the God of heaven, for His steadfast love endures forever" (Psalm 135:26, ESV).

Prayer: Heavenly Father, there are no words that will ever adequately express my gratitude for your unconditional love. You have always been there and protected me even well before I came to know that you existed. You oversee every detail of my life, and it is of great comfort to know that you walk with me in this cancer journey; every laboured breath, every wince, every difficult swallow, and every precious heartbeat. You will not abandon me and you have already planned for my healing. I give sincere thanks to you for your steadfast love. Amen.

Tidbits:

"The faithful love of the Lord never ends! His mercies never cease. Great is his faithfulness; his mercies begin afresh each morning." – Lamentations 3:22-23, ESV

"Love is an unconditional commitment to an imperfect person. To love somebody isn't just a strong feeling. It's a decision, a judgment, and a promise." – Unknown

"Learn to love with all your heart and accept the unlovable side of others. For anyone can love a rose, but it takes a great heart to love the thorns." – Unknown

"Love only serves and does not calculate." – Bryant McGill

"I believe that unarmed truth and unconditional love will have the final word in reality." – Martin Luther King, Jr.

"Give thanks to the Lord, for he is good, for his steadfast love endures forever. Give thanks to the God of gods, for his steadfast love endures forever. Give thanks to the Lord of lords, for his steadfast love endures forever;" – Psalm 136:1-3, ESV

Song Suggestion: Your Unfailing Love – written by Reuben Morgan; performed by Hillsong

WHERE DOES MY HELP COME FROM?

"I lift up my eyes to the mountains-where does my help come from? My help comes from the LORD, the Maker of heaven and earth. He will not let your foot slip, he who watches over you will not slumber; indeed, he who watches over Israel will neither slumber nor sleep." – Psalm 121:1-4, NIV

In one way or another, there is seldom a day, week or month that we are not faced with challenges and trials, and within my family nucleus, there seems to be a torrential rainfall. Just when we think we have enough to handle, another rain barrel dumps. Unemployment, business closure, emergency, sicknesses, teenage struggles, employment rejection, work overload, and more have brought temporary clouds of concern but, thankfully, we absolutely know where our help comes from. Do you?

Despite challenges arising almost daily, our "help comes from the Lord." When you are in need of help, who is your ark for the flood? I am mindful to focus and to thank Him for the smallest of details of everyday life that help us to see Him in control.

My mother recently took ill and needed hospitalization. The timing was perfectly orchestrated by God so that I was capable of being a helping hand prior to my own upcoming surgery. He provided a willing family member to give her a temporary place to recover until she regained her strength to return to her own home. The doctor, nurses, physiotherapist and oxygen technician have been very efficient at their jobs, making need of my intervention or follow-up minimal. God provided a free parking spot during hospital visits and provided sufficient energy so that I was able keep up with visits to the hospital and to tend to domestic chores such as laundry, cooking, baking a strawberry-rhubarb pie and paint stripping a worn-out cradle.

Every day there are extra-ordinary crises that require more strength than people find themselves able to endure, but God does not ask us to do it alone. He wants to be our anchor in the storm, the light at the end of the tunnel, and to offer peace that passes all understanding.

King David experienced several extraordinary challenges, too, where he discovered that the only dependable help came from God. He remembered how, with God's help, he had used a sling and four small stones to kill the giant, Goliath, and how he was provided with strength to tear a lion into pieces with his bare hands.

A successful outcome through difficult situations depends on our focus. Where does your help come from? Do you stumble about attempting to solve your problems with money, status, or possessions? Do you not realize that these devices will fail you? An attitude of hopefulness and faith determines how we ride out the storm and often determines the outcome of our crisis. Why not take a step with David and say, "My help comes from the Lord!"

Here is my personal interpretation of Psalm 121:1-8: I lift my eyes to the heavens and know for certain where my help comes from! It is from the Lord, my Saviour, my Redeemer, the Maker of heaven and earth. He will not let cancer cells rule, and He cares about me as much as He cares for Israel, because He promises not to sleep during my crisis. He forever watches over me. He is the light during my difficult days, and chemotherapy, radiation treatment or the surgery are not intended to harm me. He will guide the hands of those that care for me here on earth and He watches over every aspect of my life, both coming and going, both now and forevermore for He is where my help comes from!

Tidbits:

> "The LORD is my light and my salvation—whom shall I fear? The LORD is the stronghold of my life—of whom shall I be afraid?" – Psalm 27:1, NIV

> "We shall steer safely through every storm, so long as our heart is right, our intention fervent, our courage steadfast, and our trust fixed on God." – St. Francis De Sales

> "Surely God is my salvation; I will trust and not be afraid. The LORD, the LORD himself, is my strength and my defense; he has become my salvation." – Isaiah 12:2, NIV

> "Being strong doesn't mean that you can handle every difficult situation on your own, it means that you have the sense to ask God and others for help." Nishan Panwar

> "Peace I leave with you; my peace I give you. I do not give to you as the world gives. Do not let your hearts be troubled and do not be afraid." – John 14:27, NIV

Song Suggestion: My Help Comes from the Lord – written by Jon Abel, Barry Weeks, Bryan Brown, Tony Wood

WHY ME, LORD?

"Now to him who is able to do immeasurably more than all we ask or imagine, according to His power that is at work within us, to him be glory in the church and in Christ Jesus throughout all generations, for ever and ever! Amen." – Ephesians 3:20, NIV

When your life seems to be overloaded with tragedy or trouble, what are your thoughts toward God? Do you ask "Why" or do you think to ask "How?" Most people will ask why and give very little thought to "Why not me?" Why did you take my loved one away from me? Why have you allowed me to have this terminal disease? Why did you abandon me?

Is it a sin to ask God why? David, the Psalmist, asked why. Job, suffering terrible torments, asked why. Even Jesus, just before His crucifixion, asked why, so it seems that asking the question is not sin but allowing the question to grow into resentment is. When our trust in God is fragile, and if we doubt how much He really loves us, then those 'why' questions arise.

In the beginning of my walk with Christ, I did ask 'why.' Why am I not under attack from the devil? Our pastor had cautioned us, if our life was easy and we were not doing enough to advance the gospel, then perhaps we should question the authenticity of our faith, implying the devil attacks only those making progress for God. Did I have reason to question my faith? We really didn't have any overwhelming trials or huge challenges in life at the time, and I took that to mean we were not a threat to Satan. We did have small challenges, but nothing insurmountable and certainly nothing that I deemed were a ploy from the devil to trip us up. But that questionable teaching had me troubled about the validity of my faith. Thankfully, the Lord impressed upon my heart that "the rain falls on the just and the unjust" and not all trials are a ploy of Satan but permitted by God to mature us.

In Isaiah, God cautions us about asking why. "How horrible it will be for the one who quarrels with his maker. He is pottery among other earthenware pots. Does the clay ask the one who shapes it, "What are you making?" Does your work say to you, "There are no handles?" (Isaiah 45:9, GW). Do we dare to question God and give Him instructions on how to mould us?

Despite my early doubts, I now can state with confidence that my faith and salvation are authentic, and having grown in my faith, the questions are no longer 'Why" but "How." Even with the diagnosis of cancer, when most people would question, "Why me?" I have responded with "How." How, Lord, how do you want me to grow or change through this experience? God knows exactly what He is doing, after all, He is the potter and I am the clay. God allows the difficult times for our betterment, and they help us to focus on Him. In Romans, He tells us that one of the reasons for suffering is so we would grow in grace. Don't be tempted to ask God to remove your dilemma, for He has a divine purpose for it! Just ask Him how He wants you to grow, and how He plans to use you for His glory. We don't have to understand His reasoning but simply trust in His sacrificial eternal love.

Prayer: Lord, how grateful I am that my perseverance is not up to me, for in my weakness you provide the strength and grace to move forward. I praise you because you have a plan that is far greater than I can imagine, and I can thank you for placing me here so I can experience your provision and love. I stand in awe of you and your love for me and look forward to being able to see the works of your mighty hand come to fruition. Amen.

Tidbits:

> "A potter has the right to do what he wants to with his clay, doesn't He? He can make something for a special occasion or something for ordinary use from the same lump of clay." – Romans 9:21, ISV

> "For whatever is happening in your life, don't preoccupy yourself with the question why; ponder where this event will bring you. God is leading you to somewhere beautiful beyond the harsh realities of life. . . once you get to where God wants you to be, and then you'll know why. Never lose hope, keep goin'. . ." – Unknown

> "See how the precious children of Jerusalem, worth their weight in fine gold, are now treated like pots of clay made by a common potter." – Lamentations 4:2, NLT

> "He is the potter; we are the clay. He is the shepherd; we are the sheep. He is the Master; we are the servant. No matter how educated we are, no matter how much power and influence we may think we possess, no matter how long we have walked with Him, no matter how significant we may imagine ourselves to be in His plans, none of that qualifies us to grasp why He does what He does. . ." – Joseph Rodgers

Song Suggestion: Why Me, Lord? – written by Kris Kristofferson

STORM PREPARATIONS

"Save us, Lord; we are perishing." And he said to them, "Why are you afraid, O you of little faith?" Then he rose and rebuked the winds and the sea, and there was a great calm." – Matthew 8:25-27 ESV

I f you want to see the sunrise, you have to get up early in the morning. If you want to see a koala bear, you are going to have to travel to Australia. If you want to want to hunt buffalo, you will need to relocate to the western prairies of North America. How about taking a magnificent bicycle ride down Mount Haleakala? For that you'll need to visit Maui in the Pacific Ocean.

There are various items that one might place on a bucket list, but most visions require us to change our geographical location in order to fulfill them; thankfully, we can find God anywhere and everywhere. He doesn't require that we change anything on the outside or geographically, simply that we change our heart and mind with regard to sin. With simple faith—that of a child—God meets us just where we are.

Many of us have bought into the false assumption that the best place to meet God is in church, a worship service, or a prayer meeting, and while He is there and everywhere, the sweetest place to meet God is in the midst of a trial. Of course, that is not the only way to get to know more of God, but, commonly, it is when we are brought to the end of our own resources and facing the storms of life that we draw near to God begging Him to calm the seas. The disciples became quickly aware of their need for Jesus when they were part way across the Sea of Galilee, and a violent squall appeared. They found themselves being tossed about in the boat by the giant waves, and yet their Saviour, Jesus, was sleeping. Despite having crossed this body of water numerous times, they found themselves straining on the oars to avoid capsizing, trying to avoid death. Finally, they abandoned their own attempts and woke Jesus who, shortly there afterwards, calmed the sea. He was there all the time.

Not all storms appear suddenly, such as a dreaded midnight phone call or unexpected diagnosis of cancer; some storms take their time to creep in. The first appearance is usually a thunderhead taking form on the horizon; a barbed verbal attack, unexpected pink slip or nagging physical symptom that is hardly noticeable. Some time passes and you hear the thunder roar from a distance, providing an early warning, and you may take a moment or two to ponder the potential danger, unaware that the testing can be 'nipped in the bud.' We carry on in our own flesh, awaiting a stronger approach. The once-white clouds turned to thunderheads are now darkening the sky overhead, and the thunderous pounding is deafening, yet we still only take a momentary pause in our busyness or selfish ways. Perhaps contemplate the need for safety, a need for Jesus, even express a superficial prayer but continue in foolishness without God's strength and rescue. As with the disciples, it is usually when the flashes of lightning are consistent, the violent waves threaten to capsize our life or normal existence, our strength is gone, and the tunnel dark that we realize our safe deliverance requires more than solutions from our own hand.

When our trials are too monstrous for us to struggle through, in desperation we come to God requesting His presence, even though He has been with you all along, and beg for His hand to provide a miracle of escape.

Before setting sail from the dock, enlist Jesus as your shipmate and let Him man the helm. He is right beside you, waiting for you to request His presence.

Prayer: Heavenly Father, thank you for the storms that you bring into my life. They make me very aware of my need for you. I even thank you for the daily preparations that are needed so that my lifeboats are ready for the rough waters. I know I can count on you to calm the waves and take me on a smooth ride. Amen.

Tidbits:

> "When the righteous cry for help, the Lord hears and delivers them out of all their troubles. . ." – Psalm 34:17, ESV

> "Life isn't about waiting for the storm to pass. . .It's about learning to dance in the rain." – Vivian Greene

> "The LORD is good, a stronghold in the day of trouble; he knows those who take refuge in him." – Nahum 1:7, ESV

> "Sometimes God calms the storm; sometimes He lets the storm rage and calms His child." – Unknown

> "He made the storm be still, and the waves of the sea were hushed." – Psalm 107:29, ESV

> "When you come out of the storm, you won't be the same person who walked in. That's what this storm's all about." – H. Murakami

Song Suggestion: You Never Let Go – written by Matt & Beth Redman

SURRENDER

"Surrender yourself to the LORD, and wait patiently for him."
– Psalm 37:7 GW

It happened on September 21, 1971, the day of surrender. I was admiring the skill of my sister-in-law as she professionally practised an upcoming choir selection called "But Still He Loved Me." A line of the lyrics read, "I scourged the back of Jesus," and I didn't know what the word 'scourged' meant. She briefly explained it and took me to her friend who would then lead me in a prayer to accept Jesus Christ into my heart.

This first simple step of 'surrender' will provide the blessing of an eternity in heaven and an unlimited flowing of His love forever and ever. Surrender means to yield the power and control, of ourselves and our possessions, to that of another. In our humanity, this can be a very difficult action to totally surrender to Jesus' control.

Are you willing to follow God when you are not certain where He is leading? Are you waiting patiently for His timing in answer to your prayers? Do you have an unwavering trust in God's ability to lead you through your trial, without having to understand the circumstances? It is far easier to 'talk the talk' instead of 'walking the walk.' Even mature Christians are caught up in today's 'me, my and mine' culture. When God is not first in our lives, how can we expect Him to pour out His blessings on us? In complete surrender, we let God be the divine controller of our past, present and future.

The past is probably the easiest to surrender, because upon receiving His forgiveness and knowing Jesus paid the debt for all our sins, He gives us a clean slate and unbelievably frees us up from the burden we've been shouldering. Sometimes the biggest difficulty is forgiving ourselves and putting our forgiven sins behind us. I encourage you to step out in faith and put those ugly sins under the blood of Jesus and leave them there.

My grand-daughter's favorite verse can be found in Matthew where we are encouraged to take one day at a time. How wise is she to take this on as her favorite. . . "So don't worry about tomorrow, for tomorrow will bring its own worries. Today's trouble is enough for today" (Matthew 6:34, NLT). When we don't borrow trouble from tomorrow, God provides the strength to surrender our future to Him.

The most difficult to surrender is probably your todays—the present. When we are encompassed with our pain, our troubles, and face to face with growing anxiety, we desire to repair our problems immediately so we can be rid of our worries. We defeat ourselves when we attempt to apply our resolutions without God's help, for His wisdom is far beyond ours. He does not need our help to provide us with divine deliverance. You are totally surrendered to God when you rely on Him to work things out instead of trying to manipulate things yourself.

Jesus was our supreme example of surrender, when just before His crucifixion on the cross, He surrendered to God's plan. "Father, everything is possible for You. Please take this cup of suffering away from me. Yet I want Your will, not mine" (Mark 14:36, NLT).

Can you identify with Jesus and release your pain, sickness and trials to God, praying for His will and not your own? Total surrender is impossible without God's power to declare war on our self-centred nature. Make a deliberate choice to 'let go and let God' work for you and then you, too, can say, "Father, everything is possible for You!"

Prayer: Dear Lord, I am so deeply grateful for every breath of life that you provide, and for loving me beyond all measure. You will continue to calm my anxiety and provide your peace and assurance that you are in control. Grow me up this day so that my desires and my will are moulded into yours. Amen.

Tidbits:

> ". . .your kingdom come, your will be done, on earth as it is in heaven." – Matthew 6:10, NIV

> "You cannot fulfill God's purposes for your life while focusing on your own plans." – Rick Warren

> "Submit yourselves, then, to God. Resist the devil, and he will flee from you." – James 4:7, NIV

> "Often times, the greatest peace comes of surrender." – Richard Paul Evans

> "Submit yourselves for the Lord's sake to every human authority: whether to the emperor, as the supreme authority." – 1 Peter 2:13, NIV

> "Few souls understand what God would accomplish in them if they were to abandon themselves unreservedly to Him and if they were to allow His grace to mold them accordingly." – St. Ignatius of Loyola

> "Do not be stiff-necked, as your ancestors were; submit to the LORD." – 2 Chronicles 30:8a, NIV

Song Suggestion: Surrender – written by Marc James

FROM THE INSIDE OUT

"Don't you know that you are God's temple and that God's Spirit lives in you? . . . You are that holy temple! Don't deceive yourselves. If any of you think you are wise in the ways of this world, you should give up that wisdom . . . The wisdom of this world is nonsense in God's sight." – 1 Corinthians 3:16-19, GW

My first memory with regards to "what goes in is what comes out" is from my early days as a Christian, being a Junior Church song leader attempting to impress on young children to take extreme caution in what they allow to enter their minds. The song "Input, Output" was one of the songs we sang. As much as I knew the truth of this song and the crucial lesson taught, I failed to practise what we were singing. During that early period of growing in Christ, I had not yet surrendered my interest in reading risqué romantic novels. Thankfully, there was a point the Holy Spirit worked in my heart because the romanticized input was affecting the expectations I placed on my husband and creating discontentment in me. So the novels were 'outputted' (trashed) and I gained a valuable 'input' lesson and the learning did not stop there.

We currently live nearby several large ponds that serve as a good object lesson to 'input – output." They take in extra rain runoff and accumulate so much throughout the spring and summer season that they reach the brim. When the pond water is allowed to stand for months without pumping portions into the nearby ditch and recirculating the remaining contents, the water becomes stagnant, green, slimy and raunchy-smelling. As Christians, we cannot continue throughout our lives to 'input' God's truths for season after season and not 'output' them, for we too become stagnant and stale. We are intended to be vessels for God's message, and if we don't output the contents, we leave no room for new information, and when we fail to realize the benefits to ourselves and others. There is very little growth, and we lack appreciation for how we can be used for God's glory when we remain stagnant.

You can relate this principle through imagining that your body is a computer and you are storing God data as well as world data on your hard drive, your mind. Hard drives require cleaning, defragging and deleting of information so that they continue in fine working order. We need to keep our minds defragged and virus free from the detrimental information of the world and intentionally input 'holy' data and 'output' unholy data. Better yet, don't input evil data at all. Our culture has no shortage of worldly filth to fill our minds and influence our behaviour, and so we cannot expect to be transformed and maintain undefiled temples with only Sunday portions of 'input' from our clergy persons. Our bodies will not survive on one meal a week. Aim to filter your 'input' and do not become overly comfortable with the things of this world. Focus on God and be mindful of "what goes in is what comes out" and God will change you from the inside out.

Prayer: Heavenly Father, I admit that being comfortable living here below is easy, and there is far too much worldly input in my life. Help me to filter the input so my mind focuses on things that are true, honourable, pure, lovely and of good report. Also that I would purpose to 'output' the same to those you wish to bring into my life to receive your message of love. Amen.

Tidbits:

> "Do not be conformed to this world, but be transformed by the renewal of your mind, that by testing you may discern what is the will of God, what is good and acceptable and perfect." – Romans 12:2, ESV

> "You change your life by changing your heart." – Unknown

> "Fix your thoughts on what is true, and honourable, and right, and pure, and lovely, and admirable. Think about things that are excellent and worthy of praise." – Philippians 4:8, NLT

> "Then let us all do what is right, strive with all our might toward the unattainable, develop as fully as we can the gifts God has given us, and never stop learning." – Ludwig van Beethoven

> "Keep your eyes focused on what is right, and look straight ahead to what is good. Be careful what you do, and always do what is right. Don't turn off the road of goodness; keep away from evil paths." – Proverbs 4:25-27, NCV

Song Suggestion: From the Inside Out – written by Joel Houston

STEP BY STEP

"Since we live by the Spirit, let us keep in step with the Spirit."
– Galatians 5:25 NIV

What do you think about when someone uses the phrase "step by step?" My first thought is that of a baby transitioning into the toddler phase, and how they have to learn how to run by first accomplishing baby step by baby step until their balance is more secure. Then before you know it, they are running. Secondly, my home economics course in high school required me to learn how to construct a garment suitable for wearing by following step-by-step instructions, laying out a pattern, pinning, cutting and sewing with a proper seam allowance, then praying that the finished product might get a decent grade. Another image that comes to mind is that of a step ladder and how reaching any height to paint, pick apples, or repair a roof requires climbing the rungs one at a time to do the job. Almost every goal you design, whether it is parenting or being a mechanic, graduate, lawyer, teacher. Living a Christian life surely requires this process.

The absolute first step is called salvation, which is coming to the realization that you are unworthy and sinful to be accepted by a Holy God and, consequently, repent from your sin and accept Christ as a personal Saviour. You learn that because He paid the penalty for your sins on the cross, securing redemption and worthiness, you can be called a child of God.

The following verses remind us of this gift of redemption:

> Romans 3:23, NIV: "This righteousness is given through faith in Jesus Christ to all who believe. . . for all have sinned and fall short of the glory of God."

> John 14:6, NIV: "Jesus answered; I am the way and the truth and the life. No one comes to the Father except through me."

> Ephesians 2:8-9, NIV: "For it is by grace you have been saved, through faith, and this is not from yourselves, it is the gift of God. Not by works, so that no one can boast."

The secondary step is obedience in baptism, which is a public declaration of your faith in Christ, however, your salvation or your eternal destiny in heaven is not dependent on this step, but your Christian growth very well may be. A step-by-step process of growing in Christ is also known as 'Walking with Christ.'

Your effectiveness of sharing the love, grace and hope of Christ will only be as successful as your personal walk with Him.

Alexander the Great, a magnificent military leader, made a commendable point with a guard who had fallen asleep while on duty (punishable by death), but Alexander inquired, "What is your name?" The answer from the guard, "Alexander, sir." The general asked the question three times in succession then he instructed the guard to either change his name or change his conduct.

When we call ourselves Christians, we are associating our life with Christ and we should be mindful at all times to walk worthy of our declaration. Our paths will not always be straight, our decisions not always right and we will never be found consistently obedient, but we are called to always strive to become more Christ-like with each day that passes.

A children's song I am particularly fond of and have listened to repeatedly with my grandchildren is based on Micah 6:8 and states very simply to "do justly, to love mercy, and to walk humbly. . ."

Prayer: Father, help me to act justly, love mercy and walk humbly with you. Amen.

Tidbits:

> "He has shown you, O man, what is good; and what does the LORD require of you? But to do justly, to love mercy, and to walk humbly with your God!" – Micah 6:8, NKJV

> "Take the first step in faith. You don't have to see the whole staircase, just take the first step." – Martin Luther King, Jr.

> "A gullible person believes anything, but a sensible person watches his step." – Proverbs 14:15, GW

> "Take steps each day to be sure your life expresses commitment to Jesus." – Charles Stanley

> "For what is our lot from God above, our heritage from the Almighty on high? Does He not see my ways and count my every step?" – Job 31:2, 4, NIV

> "One step at a time is all that's possible - even when those steps are taken on the run." – Anne W. Schaef

Song Suggestion: Step by Step – written by David Beaker Strasser

THERE IS NONE LIKE YOU

"Among the gods there is none like you, Lord; no deeds can compare with yours." – Psalm 86:8, NIV

Have you ever given much thought to the uniqueness of creation? I remember when I was young I was told that no two snowflakes were alike, and as an adult when I consider the massive countless number of flakes that have fallen since creation, and that not one is alike another, it seems totally impossible, yet nothing is impossible with God.

Thankfully, humans have also been uniquely and individually created, for it would be quite boring if we were all clones. Science has even proven that identical twins are not truly identical for they do not share the same fingerprints. Another amazing fact is that no two people in the nearly seven billion people on earth have the same fingerprint, and that fact holds true for the countless humans who existed since creation. It goes without saying that God created everything with uniqueness, individuality, distinctiveness, and with Him nothing is impossible. God himself is unique for in Psalms 86:8, NIV David declares, ". . .among the gods there is none like you, Lord." There is no one like our God!

Because society has so easily accepted the philosophy that people can believe whatever they want to believe, and that is a right belief for them, we have numerous sects and religions that claim they have the right way, and yet scripture states: "There is a way that seems right to a man but its end is the way of death" (Proverbs 14:12, NKJV). There are bits of truth to each of the false religions, and in this way the devil is able to deceive many, but they are eternally lost for there is only one truth, only one God.

Judaism and Islam follow whom they consider to be the same God, the God of Abraham, yet they do not recognize Jesus Christ as God's Son. The Jews are still waiting for their Messiah to come, and the Muslims refer to their God as Allah and regard Jesus only as a great prophet. No matter what other religion you list, Buddhism, Mormonism, Scientology, and so on, they all fail to recognize the need of a Saviour to redeem them from their sin, as they believe in the idea that their human personal acts or works will provide atonement. For it is by grace you have been saved, through faith—and this is not from yourselves, it is the gift of God—not by works, so that no one can boast" (Ephesians 2:8-9, NIV).

In Isaiah 46:5, NIV, God himself invites us to compare, "With whom will you compare me or count me equal? To whom will you liken me that we may be compared?" I personally answer that question with, "There is no God like our God!" Our God desires a personal relationship with us and makes that possible through His Son. Because of His earthly experience, Jesus understands our emotions, pain and doubts. Our God is not dead but is a living God, unreservedly available for us every second of every day. Our God is a God of endless love, grace and mercy for He does not encourage us to have hatred towards the unbeliever or the fallen but to love them. No matter how sinful our past, or no matter how ugly our sinfulness is, God loves us. There is no one like our God!"

Prayer: Heavenly Father, each day your blessings and your mercy exclaims your uniqueness and the fact that there is none like you. Thank you for opening my eyes to your plan of redemption, provision of strength and wisdom and especially for loving me just as I am. Amen.

Tidbits:

> "LORD, the God of Israel, there is no God like you in heaven above or on earth below." – 1 Kings 8:23a, NIV

> "I love to think of nature as an unlimited broadcasting station, through which God speaks to us every hour, if we will only tune in." – George Washington Carver

> "No one is like you, LORD; you are great, and your name is mighty in power." – Jeremiah 10:6, NIV

> "Darkness cannot drive out darkness; only light can do that. Hate cannot drive out hate; only love can do that." – Martin Luther King Jr.

Song Suggestion: There is None Like You – written by Lenny LeBlanc

OVERCOMING FEAR

"So do not fear, for I am with you; do not be dismayed, for I am your God. I will strengthen you and help you; I will uphold you with my righteous right hand." – Isaiah 41:10, NIV

Fear is an emotion experienced in anticipation of some impending pain or danger. Fear is to be afraid, scared, frightened, uneasy or apprehensive about something. Have you ever seen someone gripped by fear? Their body language will convey their desperation as they may be cowering in a corner, shivering with fright or stalled in complete silence or shock. I have some memories of being fearful, such as being crushed by a train or falling off the side of a cliff, but these fears were unnecessary concerns as I didn't face any of them in reality, and most of our worries are just that, a waste of time and energy. However, there was one situation that I had sincere fear for the safety of my family.

Several years ago, we were moved to minister to a new young family. Through church and other extra-curricular activities, we became quite close to them. Time passed and the husband made some unwise choices and found himself involved in an armed robbery. He pleaded innocence, claiming to be in a drug-induced sleep during the entire crime and was subpoenaed to be a crown witness. Unbeknownst to us, he was guilty, and in an effort to throw suspicions off his track, he convinced his wife to endure a fake violent stabbing attack that resulted in her being hospitalized. Still unaware of his evil, we offered to watch their young children during her recovery. During those weeks of caring for the children, we were fearful and suspicious of every unknown visitor and every automobile that slowly cruised past our home, fearing the same thugs may take violent recourse against their children or ours. Considerably later in life, we learned that our fear and uneasiness was quite unnecessary as the husband himself was the 'thug.' Unfortunately, that didn't minimize the emotional scars the imagined danger had taken on our teenager. Nothing was evident at the time, but following the September 2011 terrorist attacks on the Twin Towers and the Pentagon, years of buried anxiety surfaced, some of which could be traced back to that time when that child felt unsafe in our very own home.

Thankfully, as Christians, we don't have to live in a spirit of fear. Our teenager, having a personal relationship with Christ, was able to relinquish the fear of planes, terrorists, and other fears of threats, to Christ. Fear did not enslave or cripple our teen, for with each step taken in faith, there was freedom. The devil uses fear as a net to entrap us in his clutches and to knock us down.

In Psalm 91:4-6, NIV, we read: "He will cover you with his feathers, and under his wings you will find refuge. . .You will not fear the terror of night, nor the arrow that flies by day, nor the pestilence that stalks in the darkness, nor the plague that destroys at midday." This does not mean we are not to exercise caution in the presence of danger, but we are not to fear the imagined or the unknown, and even when fear is authentic, we need to lean on Christ and trust in His strength to carry us through. Fear has the power to cripple, make life miserable, warp personality and suffocate our trust in God. Surrender each moment of fright to our omnipotent God. Pray and release your fears to God, the one who can do anything and everything, and He will give you the strength to overcome them.

Prayer: Heavenly Father, when fear knocks at my heart, please help my faith to grow and continue to move me by your Spirit to lean and trust in you. I need not fear for I am your precious child, and you are on my side. Amen.

Tidbits:

> "Fear knocked at the door. Faith answered. No one was there." – Unknown

> "Be strong and courageous. Do not fear or be in dread of them, for it is the LORD your God who goes with you. He will not leave you or forsake you." – Deuteronomy 31:6, ESV

> "Fear can keep us up all night long, but faith makes one fine pillow." – Unknown

> "The Lord is on my side; I will not fear. What can man do to me?" – Psalm 118:6, ESV

> "No God, know fear. Know God, no fear." – Unknown

Song Suggestion: Take Heart – written by Joel Houston

ALL IS WELL

"So do not fear, for I am with you; do not be dismayed, for I am your God. I will strengthen you and help you; I will uphold you with my righteous right hand." – Isaiah 41:10, NIV

With today's devotional, I am going to stray from the usual format and address two songs instead of one, each having a similar theme. Just this past week during the Sunday service, our Pastor shared the story behind "It Is Well" by Horatio Spafford, and while I previously knew its background, God used the song and its story to stir new emotions in me and several others.

After having suffered the loss of his only son, the destruction of his business investments in the Chicago fire of 1871 and shortly thereafter losing all four of his daughters in a boating incident when they were crossing the Atlantic to visit England, Spafford penned the words to "It Is Well" on route to meet his grieving wife in England. For more than a century, his strength, courage and faith in the face of adversity has given hope to thousands.

In the composition of his song, "All Is Well," Michael W. Smith writes, "Let there be peace on earth, Christ is come, go and tell." We can sing this song with as much enthusiasm as "It Is Well" for both songs confirm the presence of Christ. Yet I can't imagine that all seemed well to Mary and Joseph when they delivered Jesus to the world. Young, unmarried, and pregnant with child, Mary had already suffered the glares and stares of many for what appeared to be the ultimate indiscretion. Despite her delicate condition they were required to travel a great distance to partake in the census, and if that wasn't enough with travelling, delivering the child far from home, Herod issued a decree to kill all the babies of Jerusalem, in hopes of eliminating the King rumoured to take his place.

Difficult times then, now, and in the future, yet God is working out His plan. From the very beginning of time, God had a plan and He will continue to bring it to fruition despite the hardships and interferences of man. Despite disease destroying Africa, Islam extremists spreading hatred, narcotics, and materialism destroying America, cancer and heart disease taking the lives of thousands across the globe we can still echo, "All is well!" Even with nation rising against nation, politicians rampant dishonesty, and sin abounding`, God is still on the throne and working out His purposes. We might wonder, but the song writers say, "All is well."

The day for my surgery is quickly approaching. In just two days a surgeon will be removing 80 percent of my esophagus and any associated lymph glands, as well as my thyroid and four infected glands nearby. My stomach will be loosened from its mid-chest position and stretched to meet the remaining three inches of my esophagus left for swallowing purposes. Yet in facing all of this, and because of Jesus and His answers to prayers, I can say, "All is Well" and "It Is Well." For you see, even with me, from the beginning of time, God had a plan, and His plan for me will not end until He says it will. The storm may be raging, but my heart is calm for the captain of my ship is God. "Sometimes God calms the storm, but sometimes God lets the storm rage and calms His child."—Leslie Gould

Prayer: Heavenly Father, as I pen this devotional, your peace still fills my heart and I step forward, expecting great things from your loving hand. Thank you for providing refuge in your arms and for calming my seas. Please continue to fill me with your strength and peace in the coming days as I face this surgery and the recovery that follows. Help me to share your amazing love with others in the midst. Amen.

Tidbits:

> "He who dwells in the shelter of the Most High will abide in the shadow of the Almighty. I will say to the LORD, "My refuge and my fortress, My God, in whom I trust!" – Psalm 91:1-2, NASB

> "Before me, even as behind, God is, and all is well." – J. Whittier

> "For the eyes of the LORD run to and fro throughout the whole earth, to show Himself strong on behalf of those whose heart is loyal to Him." – 2 Chronicles 16:9a, NKJV

> "All is well! What's a rainy day? Never mind that cloud . . .behind that cloud you'll find a golden ray!" – Unknown

Song Suggestion: All Is Well – by Michael W. Smith

Song Suggestion: It Is Well – written by Horatio Gates Spafford, Philip Paul Bliss

THE MIRACLE OF MUSIC

"I waited patiently for the LORD to help me, and he turned to me and heard my cry. He lifted me out of the pit of despair, out of the mud and the mire. He set my feet on solid ground and steadied me as I walked along. He has given me a new song to sing, a hymn of praise to our God." – Psalm 40:1-3a, NLT

I have been privileged to experience the miracle of music for my entire life, and it never fails to minister to the very heart of my being when I need it most. I am very thankful to have developed modest piano skills and to have a voice capable of staying on key during times of worship, and those times when I am low in spirit and spend time at the piano or listening to music that lifts me up.

King David's love for music is apparent in many of his recorded Psalms. As a shepherd, he played his harp in the fields as well as for the delight of King Saul to lift him out of his depression. In today's verse, he speaks of God giving him a 'new song to sing' after a season of trouble, yet he prefaces it by describing his being in a pit of despair.

When I was a teenager and dating John—now my husband—his family farm neighboured a gravel pit where venturous young men would race their motocross bikes and rusty decaying old jalopies. Locally, there was also a natural swimming hole that was popular for the area teens to cool off during the hot summer days, after the farm chores, of course. It was a pit of enjoyment, but neither of these types of pits was like the one that David was describing. His was a pit of turmoil. David was experiencing leadership difficulties as well as political opposition; he speaks indirectly of having lost his 'song.' We are no different when we are faced with our own problems, whether it's a pit of hopelessness, vulnerability, depression, uselessness or despair, we too mislay our ability to sing from our heart. David describes his season of desperation as a watery pit, a struggle in slimy mud, but he manages to struggle out of the pit with God's help and finds himself once again stable, with secure footing on the rock. The rock, His sure foundation is God.

There are numerous seasons throughout life and, in particular, the battle of cancer that bring moments of desperation. Only after we acknowledge that we have slid into a watery, slimy pit of despair and need God to help us escape, and wait on Him, does He gives us a new song to sing. He becomes our reason for singing. I cannot count the times that singing and rejoicing, whether I be in the shower, travelling on the road, quietly as I fall asleep, in a church service, or while at work that music has been the avenue in which God has ministered to my soul. Sometimes it is even in the simple chirping of the birds as I awake in the morning, or the bullfrogs croaking in the ponds next door, in what used to be the 'ole gravel pit' we swam in many years ago.

The Israelites sang a song of rescue when Moses lead them out of slavery, and David, too, sang many songs of deliverance from his many trials. We, who know the Lord personally, can sing a song of redemption. So whatever you are facing, whatever is troubling your soul choose to apply God's miracle of music and sing a new song.

Prayer: Lord, thank you for the gift of music and how you miraculously use it to minister to my innermost being. Use our songs of worship and praise to magnify your name, and as a miracle to soften the hearts of those who don't know you. Thank you for each new song you bring for me to sing. Amen.

Tidbits:

"Sing unto him a new song: play skillfully with a loud noise."
– Psalm 33:3, KJV

"If everyone started off the day singing, just think how happy they'd be." – Lauren Myracle

"Sing to the LORD a new song; sing to the LORD, all the earth." – Psalm 96:1, NIV

"I don't sing because I'm happy; I'm happy because I sing."
– William James

"I will sing a new song to you, O God! I will sing your praises with a ten-stringed harp." – Psalm 144:9, NLT

"Words make you think. Music makes you feel. A song makes you feel a thought." – Yip Harburg

"O sing unto the LORD a new song; for he hath done marvelous things!" – Psalm 98:1, ESV

"I only sing in the shower. I would join a choir, but I don't think my bathtub can hold that many people." – Jarod Kintz

Song Suggestion: Everlasting God – written by Brenton Brown, Ken Riley

THE POWER OF HOPE

"You will be confident, because there is hope. You will look carefully about and lie down in safety. You will lie down without fear. . ." – Job 11:18-19a, HCSB

When we step outside of our own box, attempt to escape from our troubles and take a look at the wars, depravity, crime, immorality and countless horrors happening on a day-to-day basis around the world, we may conclude that all hope is lost. The truth is, for those without Christ it is, but Jeremiah assures the Christian, "Blessed is the man that trusteth in the LORD, and whose hope the LORD is" (Jeremiah 17: 7, KJV). The absence of hope is nothing new; the church of Corinth was overrun with problems such as false doctrine, worldly lusts, and the denial of the resurrection. Paul was firm and yet compassionate in his rebuke with the intent of laying a solid foundation of hope. Hope is a powerful thing.

"There is no medicine like hope, no incentive so great, and no tonic so powerful as expectation of something better tomorrow," wrote GK Chesterton. And Martin Luther said, "Everything that is done in the world is done by hope."

Hope, from the world's viewpoint, is to wish for something to happen, yet the scriptures teach us that hope is a deep settled confidence in God and that He will keep His promises.

As I inch closer to the date of my scheduled cancer surgery, I am somewhat anxious, but know that a calm spirit will only come as I release my fears to Christ. I am determined to 'lie down in safety' and to 'lie down without fear,' because my confidence and hope are placed in Him. I envision His angels in flight over my stretcher as they wheel me into the sterile operating room. The hands that lovingly administer the sedative, skillfully and carefully use the scalpel and with perfect precision so the sutures will be guided by the hands of my Lord. As I am in complete darkness from anesthesia, may God fill my silence with the music of His angels and the illumination of His presence.

I might seem off my rocker, but I asked permission to place 'hearing buds' into my ears so I could listen to uplifting gospel music during the nine hours of surgery, but my brother said that anesthesia puts the brain completely to sleep and I wouldn't even know that the music was playing. I choose to believe that God has the power to encourage us through our subconscious, despite the human ability to turn it off. Even as the battle against cancer rages around within my body, I desire to be safely tucked in my Saviour's arms until He awakes me to a new future. Whatever happens, my life is in His capable compassionate hands.

Hope in Christ provides stability, steadfastness, persistence and strength, not because of who I am, but because of who He is. I have battles to face, but I have the power of hope. I have a deep settled confidence that God is in control. God has already provided countless blessings throughout my journey and in the power of hope, I know that there will be more.

Prayer: Heavenly Father, I have no doubt that the devil will seek to bury the hope and confidence I have in you. The valleys we walk through do not come without having to tread through muddy puddles and so I ask you to shelter me from harm and despair. You have moved mountains in my life before, and I do not doubt that you will either move this one or help me to climb it. Fill me with your peace and loving presence and keep me close always, empowering me with continual hope, powerful hope, in you. Amen.

Tidbits:

> "The eyes of the LORD are on those who fear him, on those whose hope is in his unfailing love. . . We wait in hope for the LORD; He is our help and our shield." – Psalm 33:18-22, NIV

> "Rejoice in hope, be patient in tribulation, be constant in prayer." – Romans 12:12, ESV

> "In all things it is better to hope than to despair." – Johann Goethe

> "For I know the plans I have for you, declares the LORD, plans for welfare and not for evil, to give you a future and a hope." – Jeremiah 29:11, ESV

> "What oxygen is to the lungs, such is hope to the meaning of life." – E. Brunner

Song Suggestion: I Am Not Alone – written by Mia Fields, Marty Sampson, Kari Jobe, Grant Pittman, Ben Davis, Austin Davis, Dustin Sauder

WHILE I'M WAITING

"Be still in the presence of the LORD, and wait patiently for him to act. Don't worry about evil people who prosper or fret about their wicked schemes. Stop being angry! Turn from your rage! Do not lose your temper-it only leads to harm. For the wicked will be destroyed, but those who trust in the LORD will possess the land." – Psalm 37:7-9, NLT

I am usually very patient when waiting for something, whether it be waiting for traffic lights to turn green, for lines in the grocery store or bank to move, and most times I am even patient in a doctor's office, though I must admit when it reaches the three hour mark, I find my patience to be well tested. My impatience rises when waiting for someone who says they are coming but are notoriously late for everything, showing a lack of respect for my time. I don't like to unnecessarily waste time. In relevance to waiting and lateness, I can't help but think about those who narrowly escaped death during the September 11th terrorist attacks simply because they had to wait or were running late. One stayed up late to finish a Master's thesis; another had two personal phones calls at home that made her late for work. A secretary found herself late after waiting in a line for a muffin and coffee; an exhausted jet-setting businessman hit the snooze button several times; a father stopped to tie his toddler's shoes and deliver him to daycare; and yet another had responsibility that day to pick up the routine donuts and coffee for the staff. Whether the survivors deem it luck or divine intervention, there are many very thankful to still be alive.

Since I have been diagnosed with cancer, I have experienced much waiting, the hardest being the wait for doctors to decide on a plan of action, and secondly, waiting for a date for surgery to be scheduled, which is now only three days away. Why do you suppose God make us wait? I believe sometimes it is divine intervention to keep us from a tragic accident or an unfavorable result in our decision making. However, mostly He intervenes to get our attention, to slow us down during busyness and to force quietness so we will listen to what He has to say. To wait, be still, be silent, listen, and let God do what it is that He must do. My cancer journey has been a slow down period and I am thankful to God for orchestrating this quietness so I can build my relationship with Him.

The Bible is full of examples of heroes that waited for God, some for hundreds of years. Caleb wandered in the wilderness for forty years with steadfast commitment to God before he was allowed to cross over into the Promised Land. The Apostle Paul waited in prison numerous times for God's deliverance. Job waited while in mourning and pain for God's restoration. Noah waited 100 years, while building the ark, for the flood to come. David waited for God's timing in to rebuild the temple, and yet it was his son Solomon who built it. Despite the wait, each one continued in faith serving God and allowing God to lead.

If God has you in a holding pattern, don't despair, for though you may have no idea why, you can be confident that He is going to do something. What are you going to do while you are waiting? Will you whine, beg, negotiate and manipulate so the wait time is shortened? Or will you follow the examples of the biblical heroes who practised obedience, continued in service, were faithful in fellowship and persistent in prayer? Our attitude during our waiting is as important as the wait itself.

Prayer: Heavenly Father, despite being fairly patient, I do need to learn how to wait on you in a period of stillness and with an open heart and listening ears. Thank you for this quiet year where you have forced me, in my sickness, to seek your will, your heart and to claim your promises. Amen.

Tidbits:

> "Our soul waits for the LORD; he is our help and our shield. For our heart is glad in him, because we trust in his holy name."
> – Psalm 33:20-22, ESV

> "Stand still" – keep the posture of an upright man, ready for action, expecting further orders, cheerfully and patiently awaiting the directing voice; and it will not be long ere God shall say to you, as distinctly as Moses said it to the people of Israel, "Go forward." – Charles H. Spurgeon

> "Therefore the LORD waits to be gracious to you, and therefore he exalts himself to show mercy to you. For the LORD is a God of justice; blessed are all those who wait for him."
> – Isaiah 30:18, ESV

Song Suggestion: While I Am Waiting – written by John Waller

THE BATTLE BELONGS
TO THE LORD

"Finally, be strong in the Lord and in the strength of his might. Put on the full armor of God, so that you will be able to stand firm against the schemes of the devil. . . . . For our struggle is not against flesh and blood, but against the rulers, against the powers, against the world forces of this darkness, against the spiritual forces of wickedness in the heavenly places." – Ephesians 6:10-12, NIV

During my years as worship coordinator, the song "The Battle Belongs to the Lord" was a congregational favourite, but never did the words mean more to me than while I was facing my days, weeks, months and now a full year of cancer. "In heavenly armor we'll enter the land." In Ephesians 6 our heavenly armour that is necessary for battle is listed: "Stand your ground, putting on the belt of truth and the body armor of God's righteousness" (6:14). Truth is, our spiritual belt of protection indicating we are His, made in His image and always to be under His divine protection. Satan hates truth and flees from the presence of truth and by wearing God's breastplate, inscribed with His Holy crest, we are protected.

"For shoes, put on the peace that comes from the Good News so that you will be fully prepared" (6:15). There is no better stability to withstand chaotic challenges that surround us than to be walking with the peace of God in our hearts and spirit. Without God's peace, we are extremely vulnerable to Satan's attacks.

"In addition to all of these, hold up the shield of faith to stop the fiery arrows of the devil" (6:16). One never goes into battle without a shield; our protection is faith. With faith as our shield, the spears or darts aimed at us will fall short and will not harm us.

"Put on salvation as your helmet, and take the sword of the Spirit, which is the word of God" (6:17). The most important part of the body, one that you cannot battle without is the head, so the helmet is the strongest protection we have; that is our salvation. This is foundational to our encountering war and experiencing victory, for Jesus alone is the victor over death and evil.

The last article of armour mentioned is the sword, representing the Word of God. The sword is our only offensive weapon with which to fight. The Bible is our empowerment and supernatural weapon that drives deep and penetrates the soul. "No weapon that's fashioned against us shall stand." There is absolutely no challenge or tribulation that can overcome us when we are clothed in the heavenly armour of God.

"The power of darkness comes in like a flood." Dark days were few, but they did appear during those first few days when we attempted to digest the shocking cancer news and the following discouraging report that survival rates for esophageal cancer are quite low. "He's raised up a standard, the power of His blood." The truth in this statement was unveiled in the weeks to come as God blessed my steps of faith, while devouring His Word and His precious promises, by providing divine strength through the power of His blood and an optimistic attitude with which to press on.

"When your enemy presses in hard do not fear." Thankfully, there were very few moments where I felt the enemy attacking, and I know that this was also a blessing bestowed by God, in particular the 'no fear' portion. The peace that He has given me is totally indescribable and in no way can be attributed to anything or anyone but Him and the petitions of the prayers of others on my behalf. I have only hours left before I face the most challenging portion of my cancer battle—surgery—and yet I have no fear for my redemption is near.

"Take courage my friend, your redemption is near." I do not know what God has planned for me beyond surgery, but I know that He is my redeemer, my victory and the battle belongs to Him.

We all face trials and battles in life against temptation, against thoughts of worry and depression, and mental or physical health. The battle belongs to the Lord and we need to fight with the Lord's weapon, His Word.

Tidbits:

> "For the battle is the LORD's, and he will give you into our hand." – 1 Samuel 17:47 ESV

> "To effectively combat the devil, you need to pray. If you do not pray, you easily become a prey!" – Pedro Okoro

> "The horse is made ready for the day of battle, but the victory belongs to the LORD." – Proverbs 21:31, ESV

> "When we turn away from the battle we've been assigned to, we face a battle we're not equipped for." – Bill Johnson

> "O LORD, God of our ancestors, you alone are the God who is in heaven. You are ruler of all the kingdoms of the earth. You are powerful and mighty; no one can stand against you!" – 2 Chronicles 20:6, NLT

> "The triumphant Christian does not fight for victory; he celebrates a victory already won." – Captain Reginald Wallis

Song Suggestion: The Battle Belongs to the Lord – written by Jamie Owens-Collins

BOW THE KNEE

"For this reason I bow my knees before the Father." – Ephesians 3:14, ESV

What comes to mind when you read the phrase, "Bow the Knee?" As Christians we know that it is referring to a physical position we take when praying, but that is not the first image that comes to my mind, probably because there is so little kneeling in prayer today. My first depiction is that of a commoner kneeling before an emperor and being granted a honourary position of service known as knighthood. A second image would be of an ordinary citizen showing respect or honour to the monarch by kneeling or curtsying in their presence. Something unearthed during my research on bowing is that unless you are a citizen of Great Britain, you are not expected to curtsy or bow before the Queen of England. In both of these instances, the "bowing of the knee" is an outward physical expression of honour, respect or humility. The only one truly deserving of our 'bowing the knee' and displaying honour is God, for He is the most holy Sovereign.

The apostle Paul is a great example of coming before the Lord, kneeling in prayer, but interestingly enough this was an inappropriate response. According to the Jewish custom, people did not kneel but stood during their prayers. I can just imagine the horror on the faces of the Jewish leaders and Pharisees when they witnessed Paul in prayer. Of course, it is not our physical position that is important, but that we have a heartfelt attitude of repentance, humility and dependence before our King; after all He is the Creator of the Universe. Personally, kneeling in prayer has been somewhat awkward to practise, primarily because is it not customary, but also because I have erroneously viewed it as a means of drawing attention to oneself. While it is not my place to pass judgment, and this is an attitude that I need to change, it has been my experience that many who approach an altar and kneel in prayer have not displayed a position of humility but desire to be noticed.

Paul was continually overwhelmed with God and His plan to redeem His people. He was astounded by God's provision of love and grace and moved by the awesomeness of God. Paul was careful to bow the knee and offer praise and adoration instead of filling his prayers with selfish petitions. In fact, Paul asked for a refreshing of the Holy Spirit, for more strength and power, and for a heart that would see increased faith, all for the purpose of being a more effectual and faithful servant for Christ.

Oh, that we would bow the knee and invite the Holy Spirit to fill us and to mature our faith so that we are shaped to be more like Christ on a daily basis. It may not be customary or familiar to bow the knee in prayer, but we can be mindful to 'bow the heart' and come before the throne of grace with an honourable attitude and honest motives. Our lives are the only testimony of God's love the world may ever see, depraved or favourable, and they care not if we bow the knee, but they are most certainly watching how we live. We need to realize the purpose of our existence is to honour God. We can accomplish this in our everyday life by being honest and responsible in our vocations and jobs, by taming our tongues and refraining from gossip or foul language, and by esteeming others above ourselves. So may we bow the knee and ask for God's strength that we would become a greater witness of His divine attributes.

Prayer: Heavenly Father, as I come before you, find my heart bent in adoration and appreciation for who you are and what you have done for me. I confess my wrongful attitude towards the bowing of the knee; please, help me to refrain from judging others when they chose to honour you in their own ways. You are deserving of all that we have and all that we are and so much more. Amen.

Tidbits:

> "To get nations back on their feet, we must first get down on our knees." – Billy Graham

> "As surely as I live," says the Lord, "every knee will bow before me; every tongue will acknowledge God." – Romans 14:11, NIV

> "Do not pray for easy lives. Pray to be stronger men. Do not pray for tasks equal to your powers, pray for powers equal to your task." – Phillip Brooks

> ". . .at the name of Jesus every knee should bow, in heaven and on earth and under the earth. . ." – Philippians 2:10, NIV

Song Suggestion: Bow the Knee – written by Christopher Machen, Mike Harland

A RAGGED TENT

"For we know that if the tent that is our earthly home is destroyed, we have a building from God, a house not made with hands, eternal in the heavens." – 2 Corinthians 5:1, ESV

I am sure as this earthly tent, being my aging body, progresses through what breaths remain, I will have many times that I'll wish I could exchange it for a younger and healthier tent. My husband, a licensed mechanic, and I have had several visionary talks where we took flight with our imaginations and swapped a worn-out or diseased body part for that of a new one just as simply as spare parts are replaced on old jalopies. While medical science has advanced to the degree that they are able to remove various diseased organs and exchange them with healthy ones, increasing a person's quality and quantity of life, no surgery or miracle cream can stop the aging process. I continue in the wait for a surgical date to remove the cancerous thyroid and esophagus, making the journey thus far fairly uneventful. However, the past two weeks have brought a significant change. Throughout the chemo infusions, radiation therapy, and the past two months of recovery, I had been functioning quite well. Suddenly, after several weeks of feeling great, I am now experiencing weakened limbs, painful joints, bowel issues, memory loss, and significantly increased difficulty with swallowing. I find myself wishing with all my heart that I could cash in this earthly tent for a new one. This elderly failing shelter has, over the years, been cut, sewn, and repaired for minor ailments such as a tonsillectomy, hearing disabilities and being patched up after three pregnancies. It has definitely seen better days.

In Philippians 1:21-23, NIV, the writer Paul spoke of the struggle with his own earthly tent's destruction, and yet even he expressed a compelling desire to remain here on Earth to gain spiritual successes for the glory of the Lord. "For to me, to live is Christ and to die is gain. . . . Yet what shall I choose? I do not know! I am torn between the two: I desire to depart and be with Christ, which is better by far. . ." Paul was a tentmaker by trade and he knew well that "to dwell" translated in Greek means to "strike one's tent."

As a family we spent many vacations camping in canvas tents, though hard-top campers were by far my preferred shelter. Tenting required a ton of work with staking, erecting, water-proofing, and re-erecting after a storm, not to mention the necessary skill of perfection packing for six to fit in a K-car. A tent was definitely not an abode that I would desire to live in permanently. A parallel to this analogy should be our attitude towards our earthly tent. As Paul assures us in Philippians, it is temporary, and while we live here on earth, the maintenance of our 'earthy tent' requires work and spiritual sustenance. As mentioned in several of my devotions, reading the word, praying, meditation and spending quiet time with God helps sustain you spiritually despite the aging process that brings certain decay to your earthly tent. (Philippians 1:21-23, NIV)

James warned us of our tent's brevity and that we should not put our trust in its future. "You who say, "Today or tomorrow we will go into such a town and spend a year there and trade. . . yet you do not know what tomorrow will bring. What is your life? For you, are a mist that appears for a little time and then vanishes." (James 4:13-14, NIV) On average, our lives have the potential of reaching the grand old age of 75. For some of you that might seem to be eons away, and to others seem a bit too soon, but our mortal lives come with no guarantee. Regardless of their span of years or decades are, when compared with eternity, they are short, fleeting, the wink of an eye, brief, momentary, or a beat of the heart, so we would do well to use our time wisely. "Preach the word; be prepared in season and out of season; correct, rebuke and encourage-with great patience and careful instruction" (2 Timothy 4:2, NIV).

Prayer: Lord, I praise you for holding this earthly body in your hands and guiding all that touches it, the poison chemo chemicals, burning radiation rays and the surgeon's scalpel. You alone are able to do exceedingly and abundantly beyond all I ask or imagine according to your power that is at work in me. I look expectantly to the day when this earthly tent is exchanged for a heavenly one. Amen.

Tidbits:

> "Enlarge the place of your tent, and let the curtains of your habitations be stretched out; do not hold back; lengthen your cords and strengthen your stakes." – Isaiah 54:2, ESV

> "This earthly body is slow and heavy in all its motions, listless and soon tired with action. But our heavenly bodies shall be as fire; as active and as nimble as our thoughts are." – John Wesley

> "Our earthly bodies are planted in the ground when we die, but they will be raised to live forever. . . buried in brokenness . . . raised in glory. . . buried in weakness . . . raised in strength . . . buried as natural human bodies . . . raised as spiritual bodies." – 1 Corinthians 15:42-45, NIV

Song Suggestion: He's With You – written by Cindy Morgan, Ronnie Freeman

A SURE FOUNDATION

"He will be the sure foundation for your times, a rich store of salvation and wisdom and knowledge; the fear of the LORD is the key to this treasure." – Isaiah 33:6, NIV

About five years ago I spent several weeks laying a flagstone walkway around the complete circumference of our home to alleviate the need of continual weeding and grass trimming. I studied several different ways to begin the project, all of which gave instructions to lay a 4-inch layer of gravel and pea stone as a foundation, and that gravel had to be levelled. In my own distorted wisdom, I was sure as we already lived on gravel land that I could skip that step and begin laying the flagstone. Painstakingly, I arranged hundreds of shapes and sizes to artistically piece the walkway together to my own level of perfection. Merely a few years later, I discovered that it was a mistake to have skipped that vital step. As a result of my neglect to establish a sure foundation, the stones have heaved and shifted because of frost and heat, and now there remain very few sections on which one can safely walk. A sure foundation for any type of construction is absolutely necessary, since every single project must come to a successful completion.

Whether it be pottery, homes, corporations, roadways, or marriages, each needs an unshakeable foundation. In the book of Matthew, we are warned by Jesus not to build our house upon the sand, but upon the rock. "He is like a man building a house, who dug deep and laid the foundation on the rock. And when a flood arose, the stream broke against that house and could not shake it, because it had been well built. But the one who hears and does not do them is like a man who built a house on the ground without a foundation. When the stream broke against it, immediately it fell, and the ruin of that house was great" (Luke 6:47-49, ESV).

Today relationships are crumbling, businesses face liquidation, churches are fractured and often the entire world seems to be in disarray. Millions experience seasons of desperation, and some are destined for eternal destruction. The human culprit for all of the unnecessary disaster today is that we fail to build our lives, morals, families, schools, and so on, upon a sure foundation. The sure foundation for life is Jesus Christ. "For no one can lay any foundation other than the one already laid, which is Jesus Christ" (1 Corinthians 3:11, NIV).

But note that the wind, rain and floods will threaten your foundation whether you are a Christian or not. If we were guaranteed absolutely safety when facing the storms of life by accepting Him, then people by the millions would flock to receive Jesus as their Saviour. Jesus does not want our allegiance, because we seek pleasure, prosperity or protection but wants us to love and accept Him because of who He is. The hope and peace that I have facing my current cancer journey and other adversities is there because I have chosen to build my sure foundation in Him. The reason I can sing praises in the darkness comes because of His provision of grace. If you compliment my faith, my positive outlook and my fortitude, it is simply a testament to the fact that I have allowed Jesus to be my sure foundation, and may the glory and praise be His. "Look! I am placing a foundation stone in Jerusalem, a firm and tested stone. It is a precious cornerstone that is safe to build on. Whoever believes need never be shaken" (Isaiah 28:16, NLT).

Prayer: Thank you, Jesus, for providing a sure foundation for my past, my present and my eternal future. You are a treasure above all treasures and I find comfort in your loving arms. When the storms come, my foundation will not be shaken. Amen.

Tidbits:

> "If we would build on a sure foundation in friendship, we must love friends for their sake rather than for our own." – Charlotte Bronte

> "God's firm foundation stands, bearing this seal: "The Lord knows those who are his," and, "Let everyone who names the name of the Lord depart from iniquity." – 2 Timothy 2:19, ESV

> "If the biblical creation account is in any degree unreliable, the rest of Scripture stands on a shaky foundation." – John MacArthur

> "They are to do good, to be rich in good works, to be generous and ready to share, thus storing up treasure for themselves as a good foundation for the future, so that they may take hold of that which is truly life." – 1 Timothy 6:19, ESV

> "Living life is like building a house, you have to have a solid foundation before you begin to build or your whole structure will come tumbling down." – Rashida Rowe

Song Suggestion: Sure Foundation – written by Don Harris

AMAZING GRACE

"But he said to me, "My grace is sufficient for you, for my power is made perfect in weakness." – 2 Corinthians 12:9, ESV

G race focuses on the forgiveness of sins, the gift of eternal life and the spirit of peace, all given by God, not because of anything we have done, but because God desires us to have it. It is amazing that an all sovereign God would choose to sacrifice His only Son for contemptible sinners. Grace is different from mercy in that the gift of mercy is extended when we deserve punishment, yet God withholds judgment and wrath and chooses to show compassion instead. His grace is amazing!

There was a time when people were amazed by things that we now take for granted: television, automobiles, microwaves, air conditioning, and even eight track stereos but nothing, absolutely nothing, is more amazing than the grace of God. Despite the fact that we are undeserving of God's grace, He chooses unworthy, poor, unsuccessful and unimportant people to express His love and grace to the world. Unfortunately, we look with prejudice at others and take it upon ourselves to determine if they are qualified to serve, but God calls the unqualified. He calls the scraggly bearded leather-clad biker, who we might deem as a Hell's Angel member, to stand strong and bring His word to 'undesirables.' He called an unknown, poor, yet faithful young Nazarene girl to bear His son and to mother Him through childhood. He calls a recovering alcoholic or a rescued prostitute to declare His amazing measure of grace. He called an aged barren Sarah to give birth to Abraham's son as the beginning of millions of descendants that God promised. God does not choose the obvious or necessarily the capable, but according to His will, He selects His messengers and enables them to serve. He delivers to them amazing grace.

What does God's grace provide?

Salvation: "For it is by grace that you have been saved through faith. . ." (Ephesians 2:8, NASB)

Direction: "And He will make your paths straight." (Proverbs 3:6b, NIV)

Victory: "whatever is born of God overcomes the world." (1 John 5:4a, NASB)

Restoration: "God of all grace. . .will himself restore, confirm, strengthen, and establish you." (1 Peter 5:10, ESV)

Deliverance: "For sin will have no dominion over you, since

you are not under law but under grace." (Romans 6:14, ESV)

Provision: "God is able to bless you abundantly. . . having all that you need; you will abound in every good work." (2 Corinthians 9:8, NIV)

Fellowship: "I will never leave you nor forsake you." (Hebrews 13:5, ESV)

When we truly grasp God's grace, the absolutely amazing gift that has been given to us, our service to Him will be motivated by a grateful and loving response and the fear of being good enough will vanish. In Christ, we already measure up. This sacrificial gift of grace never ceases to amaze me.

Prayer: Lord, I stand in awe of your love for me. Your mercies are new every morning. Thank you for your immeasurable grace that enables me to walk this cancer journey. As I depend on you, please help me to be a testimony of your amazing grace. I have no unsatisfied needs because your grace amazes me. Amen.

Tidbits:

"And the Word became flesh and dwelt among us, and we have seen his glory, glory as of the only Son from the Father, full of grace and truth." – John 1:14, ESV

"For the victorious Christian, the one who lives as more than a conqueror, grace is more than a theological term. Grace is a reality, a fact of life. It is by grace that one becomes a Christian, and it is by grace that one lives the Christian life." – Kay Arthur

"Let us then with confidence draw near to the throne of grace, that we may receive mercy and find grace to help in time of need." – Hebrews 4:16, ESV

G.R.A.C.E – God's Riches at Christ's Expense (source unknown)

"For from his fullness we have all received, grace upon grace. For the law was given through Moses; grace and truth came through Jesus Christ." – John 1:16-17, ESV

"Give us grace and strength to forbear and to persevere. Give us courage and gaiety and the quiet mind, spare to us our friends, and soften to us our enemies." – Robert Louis Stevenson

Song Suggestion: Your Grace Still Amazes Me – written by Shawn Craig, Connie Harrington

GOD, RAISE ME UP

"The Spirit of God, who raised Jesus from the dead, lives in you. And just as God raised Christ Jesus from the dead, he will give life to your mortal bodies by this same Spirit living within you." – Romans 8:11, NLT

I don't know that any year is without challenges, but this past year has had more than its share and our family is still facing many tests including my upcoming surgery for esophageal and thyroid cancer. The long-awaited call from the hospital, following four months of investigation, three months of chemotherapy, two months of radiation treatments and a two month recovery period, came yesterday and we've got two weeks of anxious waiting left. The future is uncertain, and I long for a season of normalcy for our entire family where we can sail some crystal clear calm waters without anxiety and the fear of the unknown. I know that we are not alone in wishing for a day of smooth sailing, but our pre-set course through life, at the moment, doesn't consist of steady straight winds with an unmanned helm.

Reaching our destination comes with 'tacking' through stormy gales, wind-crested water, and mechanical breakdowns, all of which are steered through by the masterful hand of God. I have no doubt that the most challenging days of my battle with cancer still lie ahead for which I expect there will be days when the waters will seek to capsize my craft, my boat (body) will be racked with pain and ache for miraculous repair, and my helm (mind) will be challenged to stay the course but "God (who) raised up the Lord, and will also raise us (me) up by His power" (1 Corinthians 6:14, ESV).

The longer I sojourn this world of cancer and witness the ever-growing number of warriors, survivors and victims, the big "C" word becomes less alarming. It somewhat disturbs me that my heart, along with many others, is becoming too accustomed to its frequent diagnosis, seemingly almost as often as a common cold, that we have desensitized ourselves. Sincere well-intended responses such as "I'll pray for you", "You're strong, you'll make it" and "Oh, you'll be alright" are welcomed, yet for the 'sailor' the horizon is as far as the east is from the west. Many are fortunate to see the shoreline in the distance, yet can still be capsized before they reach the dock. I sincerely hope that accepting the horrible, almost ordinary cancer occurrences, is not numbing us from facing reality or blocking us from falling to our knees. We still need to accept our course with a ferocious intent for battle. Of course we pray to be cured of cancer, saved from the times of pain, and sidestep its consequences, but each journey of 'tacking the storm' is different, yet similar in that God cries with us when we cry. God isn't unaware of our suffering. In the rustling of the sails, listen for His comforting voice and know that He is at the helm. He will bring the calm seas once again. As in the popular song, You Raise Me Up, by Rolf U. Lovland, Brendan Graham and Amy Sand, God will enable us to stand on mountains, and walk on stormy seas.

Prayer: Jesus, raise me up to stay the course, fight the fight, and win the battle for your glory. Enable me to be an honest representation of your love, mercy and compassion. Thank you for the mountains and the valleys and the storms you have brought me through. You are the Master at the helm and my sails will continue because of your refreshing breath in my life. Amen.

Tidbits:

> "And God raised us up with Christ and seated us with him in the heavenly realms in Christ Jesus." – Ephesians 2:6, NIV

> "We have great needs, but we have a great Christ for our needs" – Charles H. Spurgeon

> "But may you have mercy on me, LORD; raise me up. . ." – Psalm 41:10a, NIV

> "I know I'm not perfect, I know I make mistakes, but still You lift me up when I am weak." – Unknown

Song Suggestion: You Raise Me Up – written by Rolf Lovland, Brendan Graham

"I AM WHO I AM"

"So do not fear, for I am with you; do not be dismayed, for I
am your God; I will strengthen you and help you; I will uphold
you with my righteous right hand." – Isaiah 41:10, NIV

Have you ever thought of the profound and immense significance of the
smallest of declarations by God—"I AM" and "I Am Who I Am!" It
takes my breath away just to repeat it audibly and prompts me to contemplate
just how many 'God' names are revealed in the scriptures. Depending on
different theologian's interpretations the count varies and my search results
revealed almost a hundred names used thousands of times: Yahweh 6,800;
Elohim 2,600; Adonai 439; El 238, and that doesn't begin to exhaust the list.
God is also called Jehovah, Almighty, Consuming Fire, Counselor, Deliverer,
Emmanuel, Fortress, Good Shepherd, Holy One, Intercessor, King of Glory,
Living Water, Messiah, Omega, Prince of Peace, Redeemer, Strong Tower,
Truth, Wonderful, and this just scratches the surface, yet the simple declaration
of "I Am Who I Am" just causes my heart to pound.

Where did we first meet God when he announced that this was the way he
was to be known? The Israelites had lived for years as slaves in Egypt and when
the time of their deliverance was near, God appeared to Moses in a burning bush.
He was chosen to be God's servant of deliverance and he reluctantly obeyed but
wanted to know what 'name' he should give to the people to describe who sent
him. "God said to Moses, "I am Who I Am." This is what you are to say to the
Israelites: "'I AM' has sent me to you'" (Exodus 3:14, NIV). God is absolute.

Absolute, as defined in the Canadian Oxford Dictionary, means complete,
utter, and perfect. It can also mean someone in sole control; possessing supreme
power; independent; unconstrained authority; perfect in quality; not to be
doubted; complete. Each of these definitions for the word 'absolute' describes
God. He never had a beginning and neither will He come to an end. God is
constant, the same yesterday, today and forever. God is perfect, the absolute
standard of truth, and He is everything. What a privilege to have Him as my
God! God is my God, and in Him I have a safe harbour. In Him I find peace
and hope. These days, when morals shift as often as the sands are swept by the
tide and the consequences of sin abound in our families, communities, and
even our churches, it is very reassuring to know I Am, my God, is rock solid.

I recall a past sermon where the speaker highlighted the repetition used
in Isaiah where it is stated "Holy, Holy, Holy is the Lord God Almighty." To
encourage my heart through these challenging cancer days I choose to triple

emphasis and repeat. . . Do not fear, Do not fear, Do not fear. . . for I Am with you, for I Am with you, for I Am with you.

Can we really fathom the awesome daily presence of the "I Am?" Jehovah-Sabaoth will protect us, and Jehovah-Shammah stays right beside us all of the way. Jehovah-Rapha answers, "for I am the LORD, who heals you." Jehovah-Jireh is our provider. Jehovah-Ezer is our helper. Jehovah-Shalom is our peace. If we get it, if we embrace it and really get it deep down into our hearts that He truly is God with us, that He is the "I Am Who I Am" in every trial, every shift, every change, we will never fear even if walking through the valley of the shadow of death. Fear thou not, for I am with thee!

Prayer: Father, thank you for each and every one of your great names, each of them represents the breadth of your divinity and characteristics. I stand in awe of your presence and absoluteness. My protector, healer, provider, you are my everything and I will trust in you. Amen.

Tidbits:

"Listen to me, O Jacob, and Israel, whom I called! I am he; I am the first, and I am the last." – Isaiah 48:12, ESV

"You can't analyze God. He is too awesome, too big, and too mysterious. I know now, Lord, why you utter no answer. You are the answer." – C.S. Lewis

"Jesus told him, "I am the way, the truth, and the life. No one can come to the Father except through me." – John 14:6, NLT

"The universe is centered on neither the earth nor the sun. It is centered on God." – Alfred Noyes

"As long as I am in the world, I am the light of the world." – John 9:5, ESV

"To fall in love with God is the greatest of all romances; to seek him, the greatest adventure; to find him, the greatest human achievement." – Raphael Simon

"You are not here by accident. You have been chosen by the Creator of the universe. Your destiny is not determined by external circumstances. Your destiny is determined by Almighty God. God has already laid out a life of victory for you." – Jefroy Hanson

Suggested Song: I Am – written by Frank P. Dyck

INSEPARABLE LOVE

"And I am convinced that nothing can ever separate us from God's love. Neither death nor life, neither angels nor demons, neither our fears for today nor our worries about tomorrow—not even the powers of hell can separate us from God's love. No power in the sky above or in the earth below—indeed, nothing in all creation will ever be able to separate us from the love of God that is revealed in Christ Jesus our Lord." – Romans 8:38-39, NLT

If you have ever been in love, you realize the magnetic bond one human can have with another; many would refer to a clingy couple as being inseparable. In fact, the secondary definition describes them as seemingly always together and very intimate. I have witnessed such love between married couples where one spouse is seldom ever found without the other, and they almost literally live and breathe hip to hip. However, despite their intimate relationship, they can be separated, as with some of our notions of inseparable things, such as peanut butter and jelly or diapers and babies. This thought of 'inseparable' challenged me to think of some items that are non-functioning without the other: Fire/heat; tree/roots; heart/blood; light bulb/electricity. Yet the most important thing that is totally inseparable is our relationship with Christ.

Do you doubt His love? Do you think anyone or anything can drive a wedge between you and Christ? Do you have doubts about your security in Christ? You are not alone, for the devil manages over the course of everyone's Christian lifetime to instill doubts in us. Satan's goal is to create doubt and detach us from our Saviour and His love. Don't doubt, trust in Christ for He alone has power over Satan. Even when you feel like the love of Christ is gone because you are facing tribulation, distress, persecution, famine, sickness, hatred, tragedy, suffering, and guilt from sin, He is still there covering everything with His love. We may experience extreme loss of love when a spouse, a parent, or a child expresses hatred toward us, and we suffer heartbreak and pain, but Christ's love is not conditional like that of humans. He loves us and His love is unconditional.

Consider the magnitude of His love. He, the Son of the divine, eternal and supreme God who is exalted to His right hand, who also has all the power in heaven and earth, loves us. He was willing to suffer an extreme sacrifice in order to demonstrate His Father's love for you. He was beaten and crucified because of our sins, yet He does not hesitate for one second to embrace our sinful condition. This one act provides us with the forgiveness of all our sins, past, present and future, and even now prepares a place for us for all in eternity.

No one else loves us this much. Even death cannot separate us from the love of God. There is absolutely nothing in the whole universe that can diminish God's love for you nor separate you from Him. Nothing at all! His love knows no end.

Prayer: Heavenly Father, in my human understanding, it is difficult to comprehend the magnitude of your immense love for me, yet I believe it's true. You are faithful to express that love and fill my heart with your peace, despite my failures, and for that I am eternally grateful. Amen.

Tidbits:

> "I give them eternal life, and they will never perish, and no one will snatch them out of my hand." – John 10:28, ESV

> "There is nothing we could ever do to make God love us more; there is nothing we can do to make Him love us less." – Dillon Burroughs

> "For God so loved the world that he gave his one and only Son, that whoever believes in him shall not perish but have eternal life." – John 3:16, NIV

> "The only way love can last a lifetime is if it's unconditional. The truth is this: love is not determined by the one being loved but rather by the one choosing to love." – Stephen Kendrick

> "Can anything ever separate us from Christ's love? Does it mean he no longer loves us if we have trouble or calamity, or are persecuted, or hungry, or destitute, or in danger, or threatened with death? . . . No, despite all these things, overwhelming victory is ours through Christ, who loved us." – Romans 8:35-37, NLT

Song Suggestion: Love Knows No End – written by Reuben Morgan, Harrison Wood, Ben Fielding; performed by Hillsong

JOY IN THE JOURNEY

"But let all who take refuge in you rejoice; let them sing joyful praises forever. Spread your protection over them, that all who love your name may be filled with joy." – Psalm 5:11, NLT

Never in my wildest imagination did I ever expect to find joy in my cancer journey. During the six weeks between my initial diagnosis, until a determined plan of treatment was orchestrated, my mind rolled with dreadful anticipation. Thoughts that my cancer-wracked body stirred incessantly throughout the night while I tried to sleep, then my lack of sleep resulted in hours of snoozing during daylight hours, recovering from a restless night. I suffered bouts of loneliness throughout the months of forced confinement—to avoid contracting viruses that would threaten my weakened immune system—plus awkwardly stumbling and crawling through daily domestic chores because of a deteriorated physical body. Praise God that, despite an imagination running wild, I could be assured that His faithfulness, mercy and grace; it overflowed beyond my expectations, and he spared me many of those disheartening side-effects. Please know that I don't want to minimize these potential side effects as many cancer patients do endure debilitating symptoms. I want to encourage you, because even in the darkest hours, when you seek God's face you will find joy in the journey.

Now you are probably asking how can I praise Him and be thankful when I am uncertain of what lies ahead. Believe me when I tell you that I am familiar with that crippling thought. Even though my journey, currently in the third phase (of chemo, radiation, surgery) of a minimum of three, has been nearly free of side effects, I still had unnerving images with each new phase of treatment. But I made a choice, and elected to focus on God and find an answer. What was His purpose for designing this journey for me. He never failed to meet each daily need and lifted up and bathed me with His peace. I knew that no matter where I was, mentally, in my journey, that He was in control. I also chose to practice the "JOY" acronym that I had heard preached about throughout my years in church, and so that is where we put Jesus first, others second, and yourself last. This is certainly not easy to do when your body is constantly reminding you otherwise, but I can testify to the fact that when one modifies their focus from inward to outward, the perspective becomes brighter. Practise this during your journey, even if it includes cancer (or any journey that life takes you on) and you will be amazed how the Lord will bless you. You will see your own joy blossom when another is encouraged by your smile, your words of compassion, or when you are able, the work of your serving hands. Make it you purpose to steer away from pity parties, and don't let the negativity of some people influence your spirit. Refrain from complaining and replace a cantankerous spirit by reading and taking to heart encouraging scriptures. "Finally, brethren, whatsoever things are true, whatsoever things are honest, whatsoever things are just, whatsoever things are pure, whatsoever things are lovely, whatsoever things are of good report; if there be any virtue, and if there be any praise, think on these things" (Philippians 4:8, KJV).

Choose to look for God's blessing in each day for I guarantee you, pessimism kills joy.

Prayer: Lord, I can never praise you enough nor can I stop rejoicing in all that you have done for me. I have an endless list of blessings that I am unable to count but know that you love me beyond all measure. You have brought wonder and freedom to my life and a spirit of hopefulness. As I continue to walk in the valley of cancer, I depend on your unchanging and infinite grace to carry me. Help me to continually seek your face and delight in the path you have designed for me. Amen.

Tidbits:

> "We could never learn to be brave and patient if there were only joy in the world." – Helen Keller

> "The secret to joy is to keep seeking God where we doubt He is." – Ann Voskamp

> "The Lord is my strength and my shield; my heart trusts in him, and he helps me. My heart leaps for joy, and with my song I praise him." – Psalm 28:7, NIV

> "Do everything readily and cheerfully – no bickering, no second-guessing allowed! Go out into the world uncorrupted, a breath of fresh air in this squalid and polluted society. Provide people with a glimpse of good living and of the living God." – Philippians 2:14, MSG

Song Suggestion: Joy in the Journey – written by Michael Card

POWER SURGES

"Now unto him that is able to do exceedingly abundantly above all that we ask or think, according to the power at work in us. . . ." – Ephesians 3:20, KJV

Every day five thousand join the booming majority into the Big "M" Club. The qualifications for membership are unstoppable tears, non-patterned insomnia, achy muscles, pulsating heart rhythms and foggy forgetfulness. It's a gender specific club otherwise known as menopause, the change of life, or a season of power surges. Somewhere between the ages of 40 and 60, the menses may gradually cease or end sharply, and years of perplexing symptoms crash into our lives like a train wreck. A time in our lives when we are referred to as middle-aged or seniors, possibly shouldering wrinkled parents, arduous adult children and grandchildren who may have come to roost again, and amalgamating with emotions fluctuating more than the rising tides. "Are we having fun yet?"

As women, we are major participants in making the world go 'round' especially in our families. Recent statistics reveal that 50 percent of the world's population is women, and that we perform 75 percent of the world's work, yet only recompensed with.01 percent of the world's salaries. Now simmer down that instant power surge, for there is no reason to reboot a woman's lib revolution. To our praise, our primary reason for serving is for the satisfaction of meeting other people's needs, feeling responsible, and not for monetary gain. If I haven't depressed you enough, this wonderful 'middle stage' of life finds us suffering hair loss, a need for three pairs of glasses for driving, reading and the computer; a muffin top indicating we have probably had one too many muffins; and a necessity to 'nightlight' a path to the bathroom. The change of life has just mushroomed with more changes then we ever wanted to face.

Perhaps this is a great time in our lives to cultivate positive changes to counterbalance what we consider to be negative changes. Few of us look forward to the aging process, and the world is greatly threatened by the prospect of death, yet Jesus came with the message that this life is temporary, and that change is unavoidable. We are to set our sights on heavenly treasures and not temporal gains. "Store your treasures in heaven, where moths and rust cannot destroy, and thieves do not break in and steal" (Matthew 6:20, NLT).

God loves to see change, because change means growth, and growth means we are making efforts to blossom in our faith and trust in God. After middle age, the world expects us to retire and coast towards the finish line, but not God—He is in the revitalization business. There are several tests through our phases of life—puberty, marriage, work, parenting middle age and beyond—each designed by God to help us grow. Several Big "M" members have had amazing transformations taken place during their season of change and made use of their power surges to reignite their lives. Will you settle in and resign yourself to a coasting speed, or make use of your surges and seek renewal? I guarantee that God is the revitalization King, one whom you should join forces with.

Prayer: Lord, I am so thankful that I am fearfully and wonderfully made, and each season of my life from cradle to the grave in under your total control. I appreciate the moments you have made yourself so very real to me, and with each new trial, may I continue to turn toward you alone, and know the immeasurable peace that only you can give. Amen.

Tidbits:

> "Since you have been raised to new life with Christ, set your sights on the realities of heaven, where Christ sits in the place of honour at God's right hand." – Colossians 3:1, NLT

> "Some changes look negative on the surface but you will soon realize that space is being created in your life for something new to emerge." – Eckhart Tolle

> Restore us, O LORD, and bring us back to you again! Give us back the joys we once had!" – Lamentations 5:21, NLT

> "You are changing, getting ready to be initiated into the third stage of your life. Are you ready for the ride of your life?" – Susun Weed

> "He will renew your life and sustain you in your old age." – Ruth 4:15a, NIV

> "What you believe can change your experience." □ Staness Jonekos

Song Suggestion: Consuming Fire – written by Tim Hughes

RISE UP ON EAGLES WINGS

"But they who wait for the Lord shall renew their strength; they shall mount up with wings like eagles; they shall run and not be weary; they shall walk and not faint." – Isaiah 40:31, ESV

God has used numerous comparisons of things to His people: sheep, branches in a vine, soldiers, runners, and lights on a hill. One of the most significant and powerful comparisons is that of the mighty and graceful eagle which is considered king of the bird species and recognized as a symbol of strength. When eaglets are born, both parents work together to provide food and protection. Their nest is built in the highest of trees or mountains to provide them with the ultimate shelter from predators. When danger does appear, the parents are always quick protect by covering the eaglets with their wings and attacking the predator with their strong beaks, if necessary. Eaglets are not eager to leave their comfort zone, therefore requiring of the parents a task of stirring them up and out of the nest so that they can begin the process of learning to fly. The mother tears the nest to pieces and then teaches them to imitate her wing flapping motion, and then after practising repetitive 'drop and rescue' sessions the eaglets begin to soar on their own.

Just like the parent eagles, God wants us to learn how to fly. In the early days of our Christian journey, we are like the little eaglets, desiring and requiring comfort, food provisions and nurturing. If we are fortunate, we are mentored by more mature Christians and encouraged to feed on the Word of God to grow and become stronger in our faith. As time passes we become too comfortable and passive in our Christian walk, and God finds it necessary to 'push us out of our comfy nest.' There are countless ways to get us to try flying again, and they are usually trials that awaken us to our need to draw closer to Him, but remember even when we are shoved out of the nest, He is always hovering around to 'swoop in' and protect us by the 'drop and rescue.'

Sometimes we have become so comfortable that without noticing, we have become arrogant, prideful and self-sufficient, and we progress through daily life without a need for God. This requires God to enforce a plan of action to bring humility. Just as an eagle has a molting season, that is a time of pain, a shedding of feathers, beak and talons, God designs for us whatever he deems necessary to obtain renewed feathers and wings for flight, new and stronger beaks, and new sharpened talons for our defense, so that forthcoming threats are fought with capable force, enabling victory. Other times we are encouraged through our trials to slow down and rest, and that is what is apparent to me in my cancer journey. God designed this season for me to provide rest for renewal. Whether we are at battle or at rest, God wants us to succeed and win our battles, to be a fine representation of Christ so that He receives the glory. God wants us to learn to fly, to maintain our flight, and to bear His insignia on our wings. As the eagle avoids the storms by flying high above them, so, too, God will help us to soar like an eagle above our storms of life.

So whether you are at battle, in flight, or nesting, depend on God's majestic and mighty wings and fly, fly, fly.

Prayer: Father, there is much to learn within the lesson of the eagle. Help me to rely on the Holy Spirit to leap up and take flight and not stay in a comfortable nest. Help me to rely on your strength during gale force winds and to enjoy soaring on the winds of rest while they last. I thank you for this restful interlude, despite its challenges, and help me to find joy and peace until I am renewed and rise up on eagle's wings. Amen.

Tidbits:

> "If we never had the courage to take a leap of faith, we'd be cheating God out of a chance to mount us up with wings like eagles and watch us soar." – Jen Stephens

> "You know how I carried you on eagles' wings and brought you to myself." – Exodus 19:4b, NLT

> "Grace is what picks me up and lifts my wings high above and I fly! Grace always conquers!" – C. JoyBell C.

> "Rise up and help us; rescue us because of your unfailing love." – Psalm 44:26, NIV

Song Suggestion: I Will Rise – written by Chris Tomlin, Jesse Reeves, Matt Maher, Louie Giglio

ROOTED IN CHRIST

"So then, just as you received Christ Jesus as Lord, continue
to live in him, rooted and built up in him, strengthened in the
faith as you were taught, and overflowing with thankfulness."
– Colossians 2:6-7, NIV

I don't know if you have ever given much thought to the root system of any
plant, and in particular a tree, but I can remember being amazed when we
strolled the family farm several years ago taking note of the many injured trees
and their ability to survive, despite what appeared to be irreparable injuries they
received during their youth. In particular, there were several beautiful white
birches that John's grandfather had planted on the southern perimeter of the
farm long before John was born and now at a mature height. You could see
the chains and barbed wire fence that were completely encased in the trunk
of the tree. In one case, a tree had nearly enveloped a four- foot-tall cement
fence post that was created as a farm property marker near the turn of the
century. Despite the opposition of that imposing rusty fence, a solid cement
fence post, distorted, ragged and scarred through battering storms, the trees
remained strongly rooted and swayed with dignity. Unfortunately, today, as we
walk that same farm perimeter, none of the lovely white birches sway in the
wind, spreading their glorious shady branches for they have reached the end
of their lifespan. Their days were numbered, but God designed them with a
prosperous root system that enabled them to grow to maturity despite great
opposition. This imagery is reflected in our own lives, if we are rooted in Christ.

As proper roots are absolutely vital to the birch tree's health, and the other
millions of living things in God's creation, they are just as important for our lives
as Christians. A deep root system provides stability and guarantees the existence
of an entire tree, the trunk, branches, leaves and fruit. With Christ as our root
system, we, too, are provided with stability throughout our years of growing
in Him, and to produce fruit in ministry, whether it is in the area of mercy,
teaching, hospitality, administration, exhortation, serving, or giving. Another
responsibility of the root system is to soak up water and minerals from the soils
to ensure continued growth and so that the roots tap as deep as the tree is tall
to survive seasons of drought. We, undoubtedly, will have seasons where our
spiritual growth is a slow, but if we remain deeply rooted in the written Word
and tapped into the Holy Spirit, our deeply rooted nutrient system and growth
will continue despite extreme hardships.

Healthy growth and long term survival during all of life's tests are totally
dependent upon your root system. Ask yourself if you are producing fruit or if

you are just a leafy show with pretty foliage because you are not firmly rooted in Christ. "But blessed is the one who trusts in the Lord, whose confidence is in Him. They will be like a tree planted by the water that sends out its roots by the stream. It does not fear when heat comes; its leaves are always green. It has no worries in a year of drought and never fails to bear fruit" (Jeremiah 17:7-9, NIV).

Prayer: Heavenly Father, I am grateful that you have supplied a deep, unshakeable root system in Christ and that you look beyond my scars and imperfections and still choose to use my limbs to provide shade and bear fruit. Even through the battle against cancer, you have provided nourishments of grace and mercy to thrive and survive. You alone have made me strong, like a tree planted by the waters, and I shall not be moved. Amen.

Tidbits:

> "The creation of a thousand forests is in one acorn" – Ralph Waldo Emerson

> "They are like trees planted along the riverbank, bearing fruit each season. Their leaves never wither, and they prosper in all they do." – Psalm 1:3, NLT

> "God has cared for these trees, saved them from drought, disease, avalanches, and a thousand tempests and floods. But he cannot save them from fools." – John Muir

> "The righteous will flourish like a palm tree, they will grow like a cedar of Lebanon; planted in the house of the LORD, they will flourish in the courts of our God." – Psalm 92:12-13, NIV

> "The trees are God's great alphabet: With them He writes in shining green across the world His thoughts serene." – Leonora Speyer

> "But I am like an olive tree flourishing in the house of God; I trust in God's unfailing love forever and ever." – Psalm 52:8 NIV

Song Suggestion: I Shall Not Be Moved – written by V. O. Fossett

STEADY MY HEART

"My heart, O God, is steadfast, my heart is steadfast; I will sing and make music." – Psalm 57:7, NIV

To echo the words of songwriter Matt Bronleewe, "Why is life so messy?" When we are confronted with trials beyond our control, unpredictable emotions sweep over us, and it seems as if the world may end, or at the very least, we are convinced that no good is in it. We are overwhelmed and filled with uncertainty, despair, anxiety, and confusion.

Just this morning, we had another challenge heaped upon the growing pile our family was already facing. My husband writhed in pain from the slow and excruciating passage of another kidney stone. This along with the things already clouding our ability to be steadfast—cancer, bankruptcy, unemployment, an adult child's in-law parent's heart attack, divorce and intestinal sickness found me shouting, "Really, Lord, there's more? When will the light begin to shine at the end of our tunnels? Do you really know what you are doing? Do you really have plans for our good?

In difficult circumstances, we tend to lose our equilibrium and we need to find a pillar of steadiness. Being 'steady" is to be fixed in a firm position, unfaltering, unwavering with a purpose that is steadfast, reliable and dependable. Remember the old adage of "slow and steady wins the race?"

If you have experience with cross-country racing, you know that the runner doesn't 'push the pedal to the metal' and speed to the finish line but runs the distance at a practised pace with balanced discipline and controlled breathing. He does not panic when the 'hare' passes him to the left or the right but takes on the adage of the 'turtle' and knows that previous performances have revealed techniques that work the best for him. The Christian life is not to be lived in reckless speeds, jerky jumps, sudden stops and starts, but is to be lived like the turtle striding to the finish line, constant and steady. Having Christ Jesus as our pillar changes how we react to moments of stress.

As Christians we know that the Lord allows affliction for our benefit. God may push us to the edge and wait for us to plummet and fall into His arms, but He knows exactly where our limit is and will not push us beyond it. The enemy wants us to take our eyes off the prize and settle for temporary happiness, so we will not only quit running but abandon the race altogether. Your action or reaction to suffering and distress will always reveal the real you and the spiritual strength you have gained. Are you a quitter? Is the stride you are tracking that of Jesus, or are you letting the devil be the detour to your faith and slow down your pace?

Our human capacity for running well or finishing is deficient, and to win the race we must rely on Jesus. He will provide the fortitude that enables us to be steadfast, dependable and reliable. When we claim His promises, we find assurance, pleasure, courage, wisdom, joy, hope, tranquility, and clarity. Jesus is my forerunner and coach, and He alone will steady my heart.

Prayer: I will sing praise unto you, O God, for you are the creator of my soul and the keeper of my heart. Help me to relax in the palm of your hand and fill my very being with your peace as I stride the race you have designed for me. May I come forth as gold singing your praises. Amen,

Tidbits:

> "Do you not know that in a race all the runners run, but only one receives the prize? So run that you may obtain it." – 1 Corinthians 9:24, ESV

> "God does not die on the day when we cease to believe in a personal deity, but we die on the day when our lives cease to be illumined by the steady radiance, renewed daily, of a wonder, the source of which is beyond all reason." – Dag Hammarskjold

> "Therefore, since we are surrounded by so great a cloud of witnesses, let us also lay aside every weight, and sin which clings so closely, and let us run with endurance the race that is set before us." – Hebrews 12:1, ESV

> "The steady discipline of intimate friendship with Jesus results in men becoming like Him." – Harry Emerson Fosdick

> "But one thing I do: forgetting what lies behind and straining forward to what lies ahead, I press on toward the goal for the prize of the upward call of God in Christ Jesus." – Philippians 3:13b-14, ESV

Song Suggestion: Steady My Heart – written by Ben Glover, Kari Jobe, Matt Bronleewe

WHISPER MY NAME

"The Lord said, 'Go out and stand on the mountain in the presence of the Lord'. . . Then a great and powerful wind tore the mountains apart. . . but the Lord was not in the wind. . . there was an earthquake, but the Lord was not in the earthquake. . . a fire, but the Lord was not in the fire. And after the fire came a gentle whisper." – 1 Kings 19:11-12, NIV

W hy do people whisper? Primarily, they are attempting to communicate to a nearby companion without disturbing others around them—a disconcerting behaviour apparent during Sunday sermons. However, I prefer that they whisper quietly rather than showing complete disrespect by speaking in a nearly normal tone of voice. Another reason may be because of sharing information that is secret or confidential. Whispering can be very effective as a calming influence or of getting one's attention. Remember when you cradled a crying infant and your soothing whisper of 'shhh' would calm them? As a grandmother I have learned to coax a naughty child closer to me and whispered in their ear quiet reprimand or words of encouragement instead of resorting to 'being heard above the crowd,' otherwise known as yelling. Though, humbly, I must say there are times when the hullabaloo is so deafening that I still must raise my voice to get their attention. God uses many different ways to communicate to us, but in the case of Elijah He chose to whisper. God is a whisperer.

Elijah was a prophet during the era of Israel's wicked King Ahab and his evil wife Jezebel. Elijah's life was being threatened by Jezebel, and he was quite exasperated with his ministry, since none of the Israelites seemed to give his warning any attention. He was feeling isolated, unwelcomed, and in peril. He was looking for something really big from God so the Israelite's might heed the message, but eventually in total frustration, he found seclusion in a cave. Instead of continuing in prayer for the Israelites' eyes to be opened to the truth, he wanted God to take his life.

I can visualize Elijah standing at the mouth of the cave waiting to find God in the broken rocks of the fallen mountain that were a result of the mighty and terrible wind. God was not in the wind. Then there was an earthquake strong enough to shake the foundation of any weakened soul, but God was not in the quake. Still there was fire and God was not in the fire. Elijah remained protected from harm despite these disasters and finally God came. God was in the whisper. Not the wind, nor the earthquake and fire, but in the whisper. When Elijah realized that God was in it, he hid his face.

We are so familiar with God working in spectacular ways, such as appearing to Moses in a burning bush, knocking down the walls of Jericho with a simple walk and trumpet song, violent winds and tongues of fire at Pentecost, and Paul's dramatic conversion on the road to Damascus, that we tend to be deaf to His whispers. God speaks to the very place that we need comfort, usually by whispering.

In order to hear a whisper, it is necessary to be close and the surroundings to be very quiet. God is a whisperer and He speaks with a whisper that reminds you of Christ's love, mercy, forgiveness and compassion. You may be in a state of defeat or in the midst of a storm, but it is necessary to be still and listen to God's small voice. If you are frustrated, seeking solitude in your 'cave of choice' and feeling abandoned, be assured that God is still working in your life to provide hope and comfort. Look beyond the wind, past the earthquake, and disregard the fire, and in quiet stillness, listen for His whisper.

Prayer: Heavenly Father, thank you for the times that you have made yourself very clear in a loud voice and also for the precious quiet times that you choose to whisper. Help me to remain close by so I can hear your whisper of hope and encouragement over the noise of the wind and the rubble of earthquakes. You calmed the sea for the disciples so I have no doubt when your time is perfect, you will calm the waters of my life. Amen.

Tidbits:

>"He stilled the storm to a whisper; the waves of the sea were hushed." – Psalm 107:29, NIV

>"Keep listening for the "still small voice" if you are weary on life's road; The Lord will make your heart rejoice if you will let Him take your load." – Hans Ernst Hess

>"Be still, and know that I am God; I will be exalted among the nations, I will be exalted in the earth." – Psalm 46:10, NIV

>"To tune in to God's voice we must tune out this world's noise." – Albert Lee

Song Suggestion: Whisper My Name – written by Deirdre Neely Close, John Hartley

YOU ARE LOVE

"But because of his great love for us, God, who is rich in mercy, made us alive with Christ even when we were dead in transgressions—it is by grace you have been saved." – Ephesians 2:4-5, NIV

One of my prayer warriors sent a Youtube link to Laura Story's "You are Love" and it totally blessed the socks off me, so I decided to concentrate on the vastness of Christ's love for me. Of course any investigation of His love is endless because there are no boundaries, and the enormous love that Christ has for us is immeasurable. We are always the focus of His divine love. Incomprehensible! Unfathomable! If we could but grasp how much He loves us, our faith would grow in leaps and bounds. Even with there being billions of people in the world today, He still thinks of you and me exclusively and gives each of us His undivided attention. The greatest expression of God's love is "For God so loved the world that he gave his one and only Son, that whoever believes in him shall not perish but have eternal life" (John 3:16, NIV).

God's love is sacrificial and unconditional, not based on feelings or "intense affection" as defined in the dictionary. It is very difficult for humans to comprehend unconditional love and nearly impossible to believe that He loves us especially when we are most unlovable. In my limited understanding of His amazing love, I was weak in believing that He would bother to provide astonishing things in my life, and yet He has, He does and He will continue to do so. God is love.

The Bible describes love in this way: "Love is patient, love is kind. It does not envy, it does not boast, it is not proud. It does not dishonour others, it is not self-seeking, it is not easily angered, it keeps no record of wrongs. Love does not delight in evil but rejoices with the truth. It always protects, always trusts, always hopes, and always perseveres. Love never fails" (1 Corinthians 13:4-8a, NIV).

God is patient in waiting for us to come to Him and waiting for us to grow in Him. God is kind and does not show partiality, regardless of behaviour, colour or creed. God need not boast of His works of creation or the sacrifice paid, for His creative earthy and human artwork and actions speak of His love. There are no records kept of our wrong doings, for our sins are as far as the east is from the west. God is forever and always ready to provide hope, protection, and loves us with a love that never fails. God is love.

Love is not just a characteristic of God, but it is the very core of God. I continually stand in awe of His love for me. God need not work miracles or visibly write in the sky of His love, because His book of love, the Bible, has been written for us to read and believe. His demonstration of sacrificial love through Christ is complete. Because of God's unchangeable character and His endless love, my faith is secure and I expect great things because "Jesus Loves Me, this I know." If you want to know this immeasurable, unconditional love, come to God for He is ready to pour out His endless love on you.

Prayer: Heavenly Father, thank you for your immeasurable sacrifice of love through your only Son, Jesus Christ. May my understanding of the vastness of your love for me and for your people continue to grow and flow freely, so that others may see and know that you love them. Amen.

Tidbits:

> "You are loved more than you will ever know, by someone who died to know you." – Unknown

> "Give thanks to the God of heaven. His love endures forever." – Psalm 136:26, NIV

> "Though our feelings come and go, God's love for us does not." – C. S. Lewis

> "See how great a love the Father has bestowed upon us, that we should be called children of God; and such we are." – 1 John 3:1a, NASB

> "By the cross we know the gravity of sin and the greatness of God's love toward us." – John Chrysostom

> "And so we know and rely on the love God has for us. God is love. Whoever lives in love lives in God, and God in them." – 1 John 4:16, NIV

Song Suggestion: You Are Love – written by Carl Cartree, Jonathan Lee, Laura Story

NOT FORSAKEN

"Do not forsake me, O LORD! O my God, be not far from me!" – Psalm 38:21, ESV

As I have spent the past couple of days striving to wade out of a flood of darkness and disappointment, as I am given the information that my cancer is spreading rather than shrinking, I have been barely able to rise above the water for breath. I am overcome with wild imaginations and abruptly brought to the realization that I don't want to die. I know all the spiritual clichés and verses, and hundreds continue in prayer before the throne on my behalf, but despite the encouragement and spiritual head knowledge, my heart was capsized, and I was left floating about anxiously searching for a life raft. A song from the earlier years of my walk with the Lord came to mind, called "Part the Waters." It speaks of God's care for us wherever we go and whatever we do, providing assurance that God will be with us along the way.

This is a time when I can identify and sincerely understand the feelings Peter had when the raging storm was threatening their fishing boat, as he was torn between his faith and his fear. Just as the devil immediately planted thoughts of fear in Peter when he focused on the stormy waves instead of Christ, he had also deterred my focus from the power of Christ to the power of my growing cancer. My reaction of fear is a direct opposite of walking in faith and believing what God has said, and it proved to me just how fine the line is between faith and fear. No matter how much I mature in my faith, the devil will always have a fear tactic to attempt to drown me. How long I allowed myself to wallow in the fear verses, retreating back to a spirit of faith, is a testament to my recent growth in relying on Christ. I have to choose to believe in my heart that God's plans for my life are for good and choose to walk in obedience, in faith, regardless of my feelings. It is a moment- by- moment process to overcome fear of physical death, but I will continue to pray, read and meditate on His marvelous promises, and I will once again feel completely sheltered by His love and filled with divine peace. If we are to have a successful maturing spiritual life, we cannot afford to rely on our flesh. It is very comforting that, through every raging storm, dark trial, weary battle, and problematic cancer, God is always beside us, never leaving us to fight the battles alone. No one and nothing can defeat us; no enemy formed against us shall prevail. Christ was forsaken on the cross and because of this truth the righteous will never be forsaken. He paid a very high price for our redemption, and not for a moment is He about to forsake us.

Tidbits:

> "Be strong and courageous. Do not fear or be in dread of them, for it is the LORD your God who goes with you. He will not leave you or forsake you." – Deuteronomy 31:6, ESV

> "It is the Lord who goes before you. He will be with you; He will not leave you or forsake you. Do not fear or be dismayed." – Deuteronomy 31:8, ESV

> "If you live for any joy on earth, you may be forsaken; but, oh, live for Jesus, and He will never forsake you!" – Matthew Simpson

> "No man shall be able to stand before you all the days of your life. Just as I was with Moses, so I will be with you. I will not leave you or forsake you." – Joshua 1:5, ESV

Song Suggestion: Not for a Moment (After All) - written by Jacob Sooter, Meredith Andrews, Mia Fieldes

WORN AND DISCOURAGED

"We are hard pressed on every side, but not crushed; perplexed, but not in despair; persecuted, but not abandoned; struck down, but not destroyed." – 2 Corinthians 4:8-9, NIV

D o God's children ever become discouraged and feel like giving up? Yes! I am there today. I am discouraged, frustrated, confused, and frightened. I have exercised patience for over a year with our Canadian medical system and do not have any complaints with the quality of care I have received, but I am completely frustrated with its slow motion. It's been fourteen months, and this past week I was scheduled to have surgery to remove my esophageal and thyroid cancer as well as infected tumours only to have the time line redrawn. My husband and children, who were nervously awaiting news, were surprised when the surgeon entered the waiting room three hours earlier than expected with news that the cancer had spread and they cancelled the surgery. Was this a crisis?

Upon my departure from the hospital the following day, we were informed that a chest x-ray would be forthcoming, but not until three weeks later. Three weeks. . . and I wanted the cancer eradicated yesterday. I know that we are to count it all joy when we fall into various trials and temptations, but I am becoming weary and worn from all the disappointments. I need divine intervention to utter so much as a thank you or to count it all joy. Despite how I feel emotionally, I know that praising God and thanking Him is appropriate, and I believe when I coast past my weariness, that God has allowed this difficulty for my good.

The recent results of cancelled surgery have hard pressed me on every side and caused some concern about surviving cancer, but I am not crushed. I have not given up hope for I believe God has promised me more. The biggest difficulty in receiving this blow was the muddle that surfaced in me, my family, and the surgeon alike. Where do we go after catching this curve ball? We are worn out and perplexed, but we are not in despair, for we belong to an Almighty God and know that this is not a surprise to Him. He is not confused and He is already working out future details for my benefit and His glory. When we are at our wits' end, we can count on God to do His best work.

This temporary persecution will not deter us for we are not abandoned; we will rise up in the Lord's strength and begin this journey to the unknown once again and take each step in a step of faith. We will have more opposition, but we have a God bigger than the adversities. God's got our back always, so we will not be destroyed or overcome by trials.

Everyone can smile when the sun is shining, but can we smile when it's raining, or when the rain becomes a thunderstorm. How about when the thunderstorm becomes a tornado? As Christians we will be perplexed, pressured, confused, persecuted, and struck down, but by abiding in Christ, we will not be crushed, abandoned, destroyed or left in despair. As I am worn and my heart is heavy, I will lift my eyes to the heavens. As my soul feels pressed by frustration and I am in need of rest, I will offer my weary bones for Him to carry. Let me see redemption win, let me know the struggle ends, and that you, Lord Jesus, will bring peace, comfort and healing.

Prayer: Holy Spirit, I simply bare my heart of frustration today and ask that you will intercede before the throne on my behalf. I am worn and weary and need to just rest in the promise that your utterings before the Father will bring me the peace that passes all understanding, once again. Amen.

Tidbits:

> "Let us then approach God's throne of grace with confidence, so that we may receive mercy and find grace to help us in our time of need." – Hebrews 4:16, NIV

> "Saints are sinners who kept on going." – Robert Louis Stevenson

> "Cast your cares on the LORD and He will sustain you; He will never let the righteous fall." – Psalm 55:22, NIV

> "Problems are not stop signs, they are guidelines." – Robert Schuller

> "Consider Him who endured such opposition from sinners, so that you will not grow weary and lose heart." – Hebrews 12:3, NIV

> "To wait on God means to pause and soberly consider our own inadequacy and the Lord's all-sufficiency, and to seek counsel and help from the Lord, and to hope in Him. The folly of not waiting for God is that we forfeit the blessing of having God work for us. The evil of not waiting on God is that we oppose God's will to exalt Himself in mercy." – John Piper

Song Suggestion: Worn – written by Jason Ingram, Jeff Owen, Mike Donehey; performed by Tenth Avenue North

GOD, I LOOK TO YOU

"In the multitude of my anxieties within me, Your comforts
delight my soul." – Psalm 94:19, NKJV

I t has been four days since we received the news that my cancer was still
spreading, despite the chemo and radiation treatments, and I am discouraged
and confused about the next direction to take. I have been attempting to focus
on God's Word, His promises and the knowledge that He has not moved, He
has not failed, and I continue to be His beloved, but my mind keeps wandering
and losing concentration. There is a nagging subtle pain in my right side to keep
reminding me that I am not well, despite my feeling good and considering the
cancer is dusting my liver, stomach, and taking residence in several glands as
well as growing within the esophageal tumour.

I must admit that I began to feel in the later part of this drizzly day, the
hundreds and perhaps thousands of prayers being delivered to God's ears from
my super support system, as my spirits have lifted, and I have made my purpose
not to wallow in self-pity. It might be a short-lived determination, but God will
keep me close and keep nudging me back on track. Knowing that self-pity is
a sin and that I am to "throw off everything that hinders and the sin that so
easily entangles, and run the race with perseverance," I will attempt to do just
that all the while trusting and walking with God each minute and depending on
His strength and not mine.

Nothing good comes from being overwhelmed, and I can vouch for that
fact in a mere unbearably long four days the negative results of allowing Satan
to dominate and fill me with fear has produced poor eating habits, anger, lack
of positive vision and withdrawal. I chose to live in a spirit of fear instead of
trust, with anxiety instead of peace, and with doubt instead of faith. God will
help me during this valley of darkness but I must do my part and walk with Him
with every step. "They will have no fear of bad news; their hearts are steadfast,
trusting in the LORD" (Psalm 112:7, NIV).

I may be overwhelmed but God is not and never is. God is not even tired of
the repetition of my prayers, as they seem to be nothing but the same requests
over and over. I may be overwhelmed by my current circumstances, but He is
my help. My world may seem to be totally falling apart, but God provides my
hope. And when I feel alone in my suffering, I know He remains faithfully
forever by my side. As I pour out my heart and soul before God and honestly
share my fears and weaknesses, I know I am not the first, the last, nor do I stand
alone in my pain.

In Chronicles the servants of King Jehoshaphat brought dismal news that his kingdom was surrounded by a multitude of enemies. The king was terrified and overwhelmed but he didn't run, break down, or have a temporary pity-party. He "set his face to seek the Lord" and reminded himself of all the ways God had delivered him before. "We do not know what to do, but our eyes are on you" (2 Chronicles 20:12b, NIV). Slightly paraphrased, I echo the same petition, "Lord I know not what to do, but please help me to keep my eyes focused on You." I am so blessed to have God on my side, no matter what I face.

Prayer: Thank you, Father, that I can bring all my fears to you and that nothing overwhelms you. Help me to keep trusting in your faithfulness to see me and my family through whatever lies ahead. Amen.

Tidbits:

> "When my heart is overwhelmed; lead me to the rock that is higher than I." – Psalm 61:2b, KJB

> "The strong hands of God twisted the crown of thorns into a crown of glory; and in such hands we are safe." – Charles Williams

> "When my spirit was overwhelmed within me, You knew my path." – Psalm 142:3, NASB

> "We are not necessarily doubting that God will do the best for us; we are wondering how painful the best will turn out to be." – C. S. Lewis

> "Yet those who wait for the LORD will gain new strength; they will mount up with wings like eagles, they will run and not get tired, they will walk and not become weary." – Isaiah 40:31, NASB

Song Suggestion: God, I Look to You – written by Jenn Johnson, Ian Mcintosh

HEALING IS IN YOUR HANDS

"So do not fear, for I am with you; do not be dismayed, for I am your God. I will strengthen you and help you; I will uphold you with my righteous right hand." – Isaiah 41:10, NIV

I have reached a crisis in my illness where the cancer is not shrinking but growing. Thousands are praying for a miracle of healing. This is a spiritual subject that I have struggled with for several decades and not because that my faith is too small. With all my heart I believe God is the Great Physician and has the power to heal. I have had the privilege of witnessing the raising up of a crippled polio victim who was wheelchair bound for years, and then to the amazement of all, she walked into a Sunday morning service. God deserved all the glory. On the other hand, we were personally affected when a young six- year -old bravely battled kidney cancer for a few years, and all the well-intentioned prayers for a miraculous cure were not answered.

Sometimes healing happens and sometimes it doesn't. Neither is easy to understand 'why some' and 'why not others' except to realize that God is sovereign and His perspective on each crisis is divine and has purpose. I believe, regarding the thousands of prayers for my miraculous healing, that God will either choose to heal through a miracle, perhaps through further treatment, but He may choose not to heal me from cancer at all. He decides!

The difficulty I have surrounding the subject of healing is the two complete opposite spectrums that exist in the Christian community where some do not believe that Jesus heals at all today and the opposites who claim that if healing is non-evident, then it is a lack of one's own faith. With the first argument, there is enough evidence that Jesus does heal today, but let me caution you not to believe everything that you see. I am one of the toughest skeptics when it comes to self-promoting healers because scripture does not convince me that secondary persons are required to bring healing. Many self-promoting healers are deceiving you for their own gain. However, God has given the gift of healing and may use a preacher, layman or another to bring healing, but they are not a requirement, for of our own accord, we can request healing. "You may ask me for anything in my name, and I will do it." (John 14:14, NIV) Anything means anything. Anything is not limited. God's own written exception is that we ask in accordance with His will.

Secondly, the argument that healing is unavailable to those who have little faith is also a two- sided debate. I do believe that if one does not know Jesus Christ personally, that they cannot expect to have their prayers answered, because without Christ they have no faith. No faith to even be measured, large or small. Yet, for believers, Jesus tells us that even faith the size of a mustard seed is capable of moving mountains, and I don't know about you, but I haven't seen too many mountains moved into a sea. Apparently, not God's will! If our healing depended on the measure of our faith, it would not totally be from God but would have an existing human element and then not a divine working. God does not need anything from us in order to perform a miracle of His choosing. He will do what He pleases, with or without our help. Consider Paul, Timothy in biblical times, or Billy Graham, in our time, who have all health complications and yet God did not heal the ailments for these great men of faith. Was that because their faith was too small? No way, God did not intervene in their illnesses for He knew that His provision of grace was enough for them to continue in ministry, and He also had designed them purposely for their own personal growth.

Healing is in God's hands and I continue in prayer that it may be His will for me, but I am prepared to meet Him if it is not.

Prayer: Thank you, Father, for your healing power and that you allow us to approach your throne, in the name of Jesus, to request healing. Help me to accept whatever you have designed for me through the cancer journey, pain, sickness or discomfort and help me to bear it with your grace to bring honour and glory to your name. Amen.

Tidbits:

> "Christianity doesn't in any way lessen suffering. It enables you to take it, to face it, to work through it, and eventually convert it." – Robert Kellemen

> "The eyes of the Lord are toward the righteous, and His ears are open to their cry." – Psalm 34:15, NASB

> "He's the best physician who knows the worthlessness of most medicines." – Benjamin Franklin

> "For I will restore health to you, and your wounds I will heal, declares the LORD." – Jeremiah 30:17a, ESV

Song Suggestion: Healing Is in Your Hands – written by Daniel Carson, Chris Tomlin, Christy Nockels, Matt Redman, Nathan Nockels

ONE THING REMAINS

"Who shall separate us from the love of Christ? Shall trouble
or hardship or persecution or famine or nakedness or danger
or sword? . . . For I am convinced that neither death nor life,
neither angels nor demons, neither the present nor the future,
nor any powers, neither height nor depth, nor anything else in
all creation, will be able to separate us from the love of God
that is in Christ Jesus our Lord." – Romans 8:35, 38, 39 NIV

Failure is inevitable. It's even guaranteed. You have probably been the victim of the "one day too late" warranty policy. Your appliance decides to bite the dust, and you frantically search for the warranty paperwork only to find out that it expired just last week. You bought a new car and purchased the extra coverage for maintenance, with the intentions of avoiding outrageously priced repairs, only to find out the part that 'conked out' is not covered by the policy. I guess we should have read the fine print. How about that dream vacation package you have saved for years to enjoy, and once you've been stowed away in the outdated decorated space the size of a tin can with the majestic scenery of blue garbage bins from the neighbouring resort, you realize the photo-shopped brochures did not do your new abode fair representation. Epic failure. Whatever you encounter in life, some things will 'make the grade,' but most often you don't quite get what you paid for—what was promised, what was insured—and warranties will always be full of limitations and restrictions.

Failure isn't just represented in material possessions and dreams but also in relationships. People, no matter how long they have known each other or how deep a relationship grows, will always fail at one time or another. When I was attending Grade 3 in a one-room school house in the late 1950s, it was customary for the boys and girls to have designated play areas and entrance doors. Quite happily at play, while I laid out the blueprint framework of my playhouse with firewood stacked at the rear of the schoolhouse, a boy interrupted my play by tossing a large tobacco worm into my house. After a short season of his teasing, I objected to his behaviour and tossed the worm back in his direction. Guess who was looking out the window? Of course the young boy lied, and I took the punishment for the entire fiasco. This example may be simplistic, but it was one of the earlier times I remembered how a friend failed me when it was important to tell the truth. There have been several other relationship disappointments over the years which only serve to prove that failure is guaranteed. Our failures, their failures, parents' failures, pastoral failures, and so on, prove that failure is inevitable except in God. God's love never fails.

If we practised the love described in 1 Corinthians 13, we would be less likely to fail at relationships. This kind of love is to be the symbol of proof that we are God's children and the exact love we are to share with a hurting world, but as much as we try, we will still fail at some point. But not God! God is perfect love. God always loves. He demonstrated an eternal love in what He gave away. He gave Himself away for the likes of us. That's love! True love. And the absolute best attribute of God's love is that it never fails. Nothing can separate me from the love of God. His abundant, unconditional, eternal love is the one thing that remains when all else fails in this world.

Prayer: Heavenly Father, thank you for the eternal assurance of your unfailing love, no matter what shortages exist in our mundane lives. Each day may I grow deeper in my relationship with you and not only understand the vastness of your love but share it with others too. Amen.

Tidbits:

> "But because of His great love for us, God, who is rich in mercy, made us alive with Christ even when we were dead in transgressions – it is by grace you have been saved." – Ephesians 2:4-5, NIV

> "God loves each of us as if there were only one of us." – St. Augustine

> "But you, Lord, are a compassionate and gracious God, slow to anger, abounding in love and faithfulness." – Psalm 86:15, NIV

> "God is love. He didn't need us. But He wanted us. And that is the most amazing thing." – Rick Warren

Song Suggestion: One Thing Remains (Your Love Never Fails) – written by Brian Johnson, Christa Black-Gifford, Jeremy Riddle

SEIZE THE DAY

"Be very careful, then, how you live - not as unwise but as wise, making the most of every opportunity, because the days are evil." – Ephesians 5:15-16, NIV

I am sure if you have spent any time wondering, you have asked yourself, "What is my purpose in life?" If we asked that same question to the masses, the answers would be as broad as the oceans are wide and as far-reaching as the mountains are high. As there are many different seasons in the year, each with different purposes, there are varied seasons in our lives that have diverse purposes. As a child or young teen, our life is more carefree and hopefully not burdened with specific achievements, but as we mature, it becomes clearer that our lives need to have a purpose. Perhaps it is to be an excellent student, a productive worker, a successful lawyer, a masterful artist, or a perfect parent; whatever the goal, it is seldom that any individual just wants to be average, and most often the desire is to succeed and to be effective. Unfortunately, we get so caught up in striving, achieving and dealing with the details of successful living that we don't take time to 'stop and smell the roses'– 'wake up and smell the coffee' – or 'seize the day.'

Redeeming time never seems very important when we are young and our days of 'gray' feel eons away, but as years swiftly fly by and we find ourselves experiencing middle age—hopefully graying gracefully—we realize how much time we have wasted focusing on things that never really mattered. For example, you never hear a grandfather say, "I sincerely regret focusing so much time on my children; because of them I now live in poverty," but quite the opposite. It is unfortunate that we seldom realize how much we have allowed work commitments, publishing deadlines, excessive sport participation, and confused priorities to crowd our lives until it is almost too late to make each day count. However, if you are still breathing, it is never too late to 'seize the day.'

God wants us to live everyday with purpose, but He also wants us to prioritize, so that every day earthly purposes become secondary to that of our primary purpose. We are created by God for a primary purpose: to be like Jesus. Even while we are living our day-to-day lives in achieving our secondary purposes, it is possible to be prosperous at those while focusing on our primary goal, to become more Christ-like. In fact, God says you are more likely to reach your secondary goals successfully if you first seek the kingdom of God. "But seek first the kingdom of God and his righteousness, and all these things will be added to you" (Matthew 6:33, ESV).

Do you want to live life to the fullest? Then make the most of those days. Whether you are at work, at play or at rest, make every tick of the clock count. Regardless of your age, and no matter whether your life has been a roller coaster trip or a leisurely carousel ride, the only way to live life to the fullest is under God's divine hand.

Prayer: Lord, I am guilty of having wasted precious time pursuing goals that I deemed important at the expense of nurturing a relationship with you and witnessing to others about your plan of redemption. Help me to prioritize and redeem my time. For my days are numbered, and people need the Lord. Amen.

Tidbits:

"Lost time is never found again." – Benjamin Franklin

"I once thought all these things were so very important, but now I consider them worthless because of what Christ has done." – Philippians 3:7, NLT

"Redeem thy misspent time that's past, and live this day as if thy last." – Thomas Ken

"Therefore, as we have opportunity, let us do good to all people, especially to those who belong to the family of believers." – Galatians 6:10, NIV

"Get action. Seize the moment. Man was never intended to become an oyster." – Theodore Roosevelt

"Walk in wisdom toward outsiders, making the best use of the time." – Colossians 4:5, ESV

"I held a moment in my hand, brilliant as a star, fragile as a flower, a tiny sliver of one hour. I dripped it carelessly, I didn't know, I held opportunity." – Hazel Lee

Song Suggestion: Seize the Day – written by Carolyn Arends

I'LL CARRY YOU

"He will tend his flock like a shepherd; He will gather the lambs in his arms; He will carry them in his bosom, and gently lead those that are with young." – Isaiah 40:11, ESV

When one is struggling through the ravages of cancer this song "I'll Carry You" contains several of the questions contained in the confused heart of the patient. We wonder if our painful existence has a reason, when even the very thought of taking another breath actually takes our breath away. And the nights, oh, the long dark nights we spend wrestling with unanswered questions and feelings of abandonment, wondering if we will have the strength to make it through another day. But as the song so adequately informs us, we were never meant to walk this road alone, for God has promised to walk it with us.

I am yet to begin my second attempt with a newly devised chemo cocktail. We have hopes that it will bring my cancer growth under control and fervently pray that it will bring a miracle within those small ounces of poison or one that doesn't require medical intervention. So the next few months of anticipated discomfort and loneliness are just that, anticipated, but I know that God has promised to supply the strength, the breath, and the stamina to endure each day as I lean on Him. He will carry me and be my strength to pull me through each long treatment. He will reach for me, take my hand, and pray with me through each season of nausea and constipation. We will stand together and be strong to demonstrate a peace that the world is crying out to experience. The famous poem, "Footprints," written by Margaret Fishback Powers expresses it best:

> He whispered, "My precious child,
> I love you and will never leave you
> never, ever, during your trials and testing.
> When you saw only one set of footprints
> it was then that I carried you.

These dismal expectations may not be mine as yet, and may not be, since God so blessed me with a pleasant journey through my first chemo treatment, but I do know that there are many cancer patients who do experience the most undesirable effects from treatment that they question whether death would not be the easier option. Whatever encumbrances weigh us down and cause our minds to welcome death—God will provide the strength. "No temptation has overtaken you except what is common to mankind. And God is faithful; He will not let you be tempted beyond what you can bear. But when you are tempted, He will also provide a way out so that you can endure it" (1 Corinthians 10:13, NIV).

When our first born infant son was hospitalized for several weeks with no medical answers, for his inability thrive and keep his feedings down, we were not alone. God carried us. When my husband lost control in the passing lane, hit a cement structure which sent him into a cartwheel- type momentum with the truck, he landed alive but in pain from gravel imbedded in his skull and shoulders. It was God who carried us through the weeks of healing. When our newly started business was barely up and running, and a critical economic recession threatened to close the doors, it was God who carried us through. And now, with entering my second year of battling cancer, it will be God whom I can count on to carry me through. Without fail. The song also indicates that God alone is not the only compassionate one lifting and carrying the weary, but that there are fellow brethren helping. Praise the Lord for those who serve me, to hold my hand, pray, listen. Just the presence of a concerned friend can lift the spirits of a struggling soul, so let us not leave the entire compassionate process to God, but be one who God uses to administer His grace and love.

Prayer: Heavenly Father, thank you for being our burden bearer, and help us to obey your command to love others and to carry one another's burdens by doing so we are being obedient to you. Amen.

Tidbits:

> "Let your faith be in the quiet confidence that God will every day and every moment keep you as the apple of His eyes." – Andrew Murray

> "Bear one another's burdens, and so fulfill the law of Christ." – Galatians 6:2, NIV

> "The measure of a life, after all, is not its duration, but its donation." – C.S. Lewis

> "Cast your burden on the LORD, and he will sustain you; he will never permit the righteous to be moved." – Psalm 55:22, ESV

> "Caring words, friendship, affectionate touch—all of these have a healing quality. Why? Because we were all created by God to give and receive love." – Jack Frost

Song Suggestion: I Will Carry You – written by Eric Laughlin, Michael W. Smith

LORD, LEAD ME ON

"The Lord is my shepherd; I shall not want. He makes me lie down in green pastures. He leads me beside still waters. He restores my soul . . .Surely goodness and mercy shall follow me all the days of my life, and I shall dwell in the house of the Lord forever." – Psalm 23:1-3, 6, ESV

Today's song "Lord, Lead Me On," begins with "when the way seems dark and long," which is so appropriate for my current position. I am weary of the battle, and yet another dark journey looms ahead. It has been a year of battling cancer with chemo, radiation and prayer, and it appears to the human eye to be unsuccessful. With another season of stronger chemotherapy ahead, I wrestle with whether the cancer battle is worth another attempt. Selfishly, I am not ready to leave my precious family. Sometimes I just wish God still spoke audibly so that His directions for us could be clearer than spring water. I know that a deeper desire to remain here is just priorities gone awry, so I am purposely focusing on things that are worthy and of good report: to be thankful for daily blessings, praise Him in everything, persevering, focused on Him, and willing to walk this path designed for me, and apply all His wonderful promises to my heart. But the journey is still difficult. I know what I know, and I know that He loves me. I am His, and nothing will separate me from His love. Even though my desire is to be in the center of His will, my flesh aches to stay here on Earth, which creates a struggle against my spiritual knowledge that Heaven is a better place. Each day requires that I die to myself and trust God for His guidance over this pathway, but it still remains rocky and not easy to navigate smoothly.

The Lord is my shepherd and He cares for me personally in so many ways, and because of this I should not be afraid. He makes me to lie down in green pastures for nourishment and leads me beside still, quiet waters—a place of peaceful rest where I can slow down and focus on His guidance. These specific caring aspects are with purpose to provide restoration. So, now I say to myself, heed the Word, listen and trust the Shepherd who lovingly cares for you. Cast away fear, feed adequately, rest peacefully and be fully restored with strength to continue the journey. Like me, most of us know the right road we should take, but selfishness and sinfulness often lead us astray. Being like dumb sheep, we stray, disregarding the shepherd's guidance.

Now for the hardest portion, there is no need to fear death. "Even though I walk through the valley of the shadow of death, I will fear no evil. . ." With today's sarcasm I say, "Ya right, easier said than done!" I don't believe I have ever met a person who doesn't fear death. Well, maybe not the destination after death, or death itself, but the process of dying is everyone's greatest fear, mine included. Pain and I are not good friends, but the scripture refers to "the shadow of death." It cannot harm us if we stay close to the shepherd. Again I must trust Him.

There is no need to fear evil, no need to fear enemies, no need to fear any problem. When we know the Shepherd personally, and stay close to Him, we should want to follow Him wherever He leads and trust that he has the path already planned. I continue to apply what I know in my mind to my heart, and find that it is a continual yielding to Him.

Prayer: In my life, Lord, lead the way. In my family, Lord, lead the way. With my children, Lord, lead the way. I'll wait on you. Lord, I'll trust in you though the journey may seem dark and long, and I ask that you never let go of my hand even when my grasp is weak, and then provide me strength to endure. Amen.

Tidbits:

> "The steps of a man are established by the LORD." – Psalm 37:23, NASB

> "Never be afraid to trust an unknown future to a known God."
> – Corrie ten Boom

> "The Lord will guide you continually, giving you water when you are dry and restoring your strength." – Isaiah 58:11, NLT

> "Go to God Himself. . . for as certainly as He has a plan or calling for you, He will somehow guide you into it." – Unknown

> "Teach me thy way, O LORD, and lead me in a plain path." – Psalm 27:11, KJV

> "We shall steer safely through every storm, so long as our heart is right, our intention fervent, our courage steadfast, and our trust fixed on God." – St. Francis De Sales

Song Suggestion: Lord, Lead Me On – written by Bill Monroe & His Bluegrass Boys

I WILL LIFT MY EYES

"I lift up my eyes to the hills; where does my help come from? My help comes from the LORD, the Maker of heaven and earth." – Psalm 121:1-2, NIV

What are you currently focusing on? Are your eyes turned heavenward and focusing on Christ and what is yet to come in relation to His promises? Perhaps you are not focused at all but drifting from day to day without any purpose of maturing spirituality in Christ.

A potential life sentence was issued to me with regards to my fight against esophageal cancer, and it has shifted my focus onto the chemo miseries and has brought fear and a lack of peace. Shortly afterwards a dear friend inquired as to what 'bucket list' items I might wish to accomplish. I could think of nothing. The Lord has blessed me with a wonderful husband who has provided adequately for our comfort and pleasure. I am blessed with four God-fearing adult children and likeminded spouses who love and serve the Lord, and whose chief purpose is to raise up yet another generation to do the same. I have enjoyed spoiling eleven healthy grandchildren and had the opportunity to watch several of them mature into fine responsible young teens and treasure the child-like antics of the younger set. It was a wise diversion to help me focus on my lifetime of blessings.

Her inquisitions didn't stop there, and she asked, "Do you have any regrets?" Hmm. . . Thinking. . . I am sure I have many regrets regarding poor choices, wrong directions, or angry words, but those are covered under the blood and I thank God for His eternal gift of salvation that encompasses forgiveness. The one regret I have was not more avidly pursuing my love of photography.

As a young teen—more like a teenybopper—I began clicking the Brownie Kodak camera buttons feverishly, shooting anything and everything without purpose, and all my hard-earned babysitting funds went to pay for film developing. If we'd had digital options then, my shelves would not be currently bending beneath the weight of countless albums holding thousands of faded and unprofessional shots of anything and everything, including a Beatle-wannabe jam session on popcorn tins.

My love of photography has provided many memories and recently progressed into a love of scrapbooking and the organization of those aging photos into more appropriate collections for my children to enjoy.

In both the skill of photography and scrapbooking, it is all about the focus. Where do you want to draw the eyes of the beholder? Lighting and embellishments make an immense difference in the overall portrayal of the subject. With each individual shot, there is a careful viewing of the eye to zoom in on whatever you wish to highlight.

Whatever the subject—a non-intimate object, a bird in flight, or a simple dew drop on a glistening leaf—each photo requires the photographer to determine where to draw one's focus. With this lesson in mind, I must chastise myself for my lack of focus on God, and draw my eyes away from what causes me fear and robs me of my peace. I must, in faith, focus on His promises and His ability to overcome.

When Moses and the Israelites were cornered at the Red Sea, Moses did not panic or run, but instead he focused on God. When Joshua was challenged by the walls of Jericho, he did not search for ways to physically destroy them, but focused on God. When Daniel was in the den with the lions, the King expected he would be destroyed by the lions, but Daniel focused on God's ability to deliver him. When Peter feared for his life in a sinking boat, and then again when walking on the water, he had to make the choice to focus on God, through his son, Jesus, the Giver of Life. Staying focused on God is not easy, especially when death looms overhead, but instead of focusing on the darkness, I must choose to lift my eyes and focus on my Maker. He will help me to climb the mountains that I cannot climb and rid me of problems I cannot solve. When I find that the raging seas are rising up inside of me, I will lift my eyes and focus on the calmer, because only God can calm the storm.

Tidbits:

> "For we live by faith, not by sight." – 2 Corinthians 5:7, NIV

> "Don't focus on your problems, there is no solution. Focus on God, He is the solution." – Unknown

> "Don't be afraid! Stand still, and see what the LORD will do to save you today." – Exodus 14:13, GW

> "Focus on giants, you stumble. Focus on God, giants tumble." – Max Lucado

> "My flesh and my heart may fail, but God is the strength of my heart and my portion forever." – Psalm 73:26, NIV

> "You cannot fulfill God's purposes for your life while focusing on your own plans." – Rick Warren

Song Suggestion: I Will Lift My Eyes – written by Bebo Norman, Jason Ingram

MOUNTAINS TO CLIMB

"Carry each other's burdens, and in this way, you will fulfill the law of Christ." – Galatians 6:2, NIV

Today's devotional was a difficult one to compose for I am struggling with depression and the painful disappointment surrounding several aspects of having cancer and now facing the reality that my story may not have a fairytale ending here on Earth. Whether it is with regards to compassionate support, medical intervention or solutions, or the reality that I don't understand God's intention with this designed journey, it is a tireless struggle.

My daughter and I were talking about our heartache and the platitudes that are commonly used, and how, despite the truth encompassed in well-meaning statements, they just don't lessen the anguish we are feeling. "Everything happens for a reason" is a commonly used statement; though we know it as truth, reasons are not evident in the moment and the words lack comfort. Or, "God won't give you more than you can handle." Yes, but often things are overwhelming. "God will be with us every step of the way." I have no doubt that He is right beside me, but that doesn't mean I always feel His presence. "Everything will be all right." Only God knows the outcome, and though His way is perfect, everything may not be alright according to our own wishes. "I'll be praying for you." This is the most important cliché. All too often, this is simply a phrase with good intentions, but can sometimes be just a futile verbal statement rather than a commitment to pray.

Don't misunderstand or take offense of my truthfulness here, for I am not saying I don't appreciate the compassion expressed in words, deeds, cards, and so on, but unfortunately, sometimes they just don't bring comfort or relief. That is not necessarily because the comforter has failed or that God has failed. God does not fail, but I have failed. Though I know I am not alone in experiencing teeter-tottering emotions, it is a constant battle to remain focused; to continue to climb the mountain instead of roaming in the desolate valley; to be steadfast in focusing on the divine and eternal when daily physical struggles remind me of my temporal home here on earth.

What do we do when the miracle we hoped for, prayed for, and desperately wait for hasn't happened? Do we quit praying or hoping? Absolutely not, but we pray with even more passion than before. What do we do when we know the path that God has allowed leads us to a valley deeper than anything we have ever known? Do we lose faith in God and misplace our trust elsewhere? Absolutely not, but we turn to His Word, plead and pray that He will strengthen us to endure. The simple truth is that sometimes in this world the reality of disappointment, grief and pain gets 'right in our face' and the answers we pray for don't happen.

In the accidental death of his daughter, Steven Curtis Chapman suffered unbearable grief, and I'm sure they struggled with questions. In the tragic death of Rick Warren's son, we also witnessed the deep, deep pain that only another grieving parent can begin to understand. All to prove, though, that distress falls on all of us. In seasons of disappointment and desperation, we must force ourselves to look upward, rely on Christ, and look forward to better days. I know that this current existence is not forever, and this Earth is neither my 'home' nor my final resting place. Spiritually, I anxiously look forward to being united with my Saviour and worshiping Him endlessly, but unfortunately that does not make contemplating a temporal departure from my family any easier. Yet it does help to understand the unimaginable sorrow that God suffered had when He send His Son to die for my sins.

This life will never be free of disappointment, and the struggles to remain focused on Christ will be a regular tussle, as we are at war between the flesh and the spiritual. In the meantime, I depend on God for hope and strength to fight both my physical cancer and the spiritual battles.

Prayer: Heavenly Father, forgive me when I have offered the glib response of "I'll pray for you," and not taken serious the responsibility of praying faithfully. I humbly come before you and pray for the strength to rise and stand strong in my faith. Of course, I desire a miracle of healing, but foremost I desire to be an honourable testimony of your love and grace. Amen.

Tidbits:

> "But if anyone has the world's goods and sees his brother in need, yet closes his heart against him, how does God's love abide in him?" – 1 John 3:17, ESV

> "No one is useless in this world who lightens the burdens of another." – Charles Dickens

> "We who are strong have an obligation to bear with the failings of the weak, and not to please ourselves." – Romans 15:1, ESV

> "Good works is giving to the poor and the helpless, but divine works is showing them their worth to the One who matters." – Criss Jami

> "Let each of you look not only to his own interests, but also to the interests of others." – Philippians 2:4, ESV

Song Suggestion: Mountains Wait – written by Eric Hochhalter

HE RESTORES MY SOUL

"The Lord is my shepherd; I shall not want. He makes me to
lie down in green pastures; He leads me beside the still waters.
He restores my soul." – Psalm 23:1-2, NKJV

David's Psalm is a popular passage for memorization and commonly recited
by hundreds who think that when they have repeated these sacred words
they have done enough to solicit the grace of God. While the shepherd's psalm
may comfort a distressed mind by repetition, the first line of the psalm states
that one must claim the Lord as his or her personal shepherd (otherwise as your
personal Saviour). God responds to His own people, "My sheep hear my voice,
and I know them, and they follow me" (John 10:27, ESV).

David was very familiar with the duties of a shepherd and paralleled those
with the benefits of personally knowing God. A shepherd cares for his flock,
providing fertile areas for nourishment and green pastures for rest, as well as
leading them besides water. He offers safety from predators and other hazards
that would cause them harm. They have want for nothing because the shepherd
provides for all their needs. Our soul is restored to a place of joy, representing
a sheep that once was lost but then is found. When we are questioning our
direction, God guides us in the path of righteousness.

The journey of cancer is very difficult and we often allow the shadow
of death to cloud our mind, but the Lord is with us and for this reason we
should fear no evil. The shepherd carries a rod and a staff to guide and protect
his sheep, and the Lord also prods or pushes us at times for our own good,
to keep us on the narrow path or to prod us along a more difficult path for
necessary growth. Even in the presence of our enemies, depression, sickness,
chemotherapy, radiation, disease, and so on, God prepares our way. Anointing
one's head with oil is to indicate a person of honour; we are extraordinary
because of our position in Christ. Our cup runs over with abundant blessings
of the Lord who provides beyond our needs. God loves us and His goodness
and mercy are ours for all the days of our life.

David spent what seemed like endless days hiding from his enemies yet he
still had a heart that sought after God. He found a quiet place to experience
God's joy and peace instead of wallowing in self-pity.

While you walk through the valley of the shadow of death, keep your focus
on the renewal that lies ahead. God's restoration will bring you back to a state of
new strength, stamina and revitalized eternal perspectives. Don't question your
challenges, but come near to God and believe that He will heal your brokenness
and bring your frustrations to an end, in His time. The closer you get to God,

the more you realize that only He can offer you true security. Only He can give rest to your weary soul. Don't let anyone or anything steal you of your peace. Jesus paid a high price to set you free.

Tidbits:

> "Restore to me the joy of your salvation, and uphold me with a willing spirit." – Psalm 51:12, ESV

> "Jesus specializes in restoration." – Unknown

> "For I will restore you to health and I will heal you of your wounds,' declares the LORD." – Jeremiah 30:17, NAS

> "I've learned that trust isn't something that you put in people, it is something that you put in God. While people will fail you time and time again, God never will." – Sashauni Aaeliyae

> "Restore us, O LORD God of hosts! Let your face shine, that we may be saved!" – Psalm 80:19, ESV

> "Restore us to You, O Lord, that we may be restored." – Lamentations 5:21, NASB

Song Suggestion: He Restoreth My Soul – written by Dottie Rambo

BEAUTIFUL SAVIOUR

"One thing I ask from the LORD. . . to gaze on the beauty of the LORD. . ." – Psalm 27:4, NIV

How do you experience the beauty of God? Do you see, hear, feel or inhale the beauty? Do you see Him in the setting of the summer sun, the cresting and crashing of cresting waves, or in the majestic grandeur of a purple mountain range? Maybe you hear the beauty in the melodious chirping of the whippoorwill, the restless rustling of autumn leaves, or the soft whimpering of a newborn baby? Do you smell the beauty in the drifting odour of climbing honeysuckle, the freshness of spring after a cleansing rain, or the all-encompassing odour of cedar in a newly constructed closet? How about touching the beauty, where do you feel it? Is it in the gentle caressing of toddler's back as you rock the child to sleep, the wiping away of joyful or grieving tears of a precious friend, or in the simple pleasure of plucking the petals of a daisy with a "He loves me, He loves me not?" God has provided many ways for us to experience His beauty, but one thing is certain, we all need to have the beauty of God, His Son, living inside of us.

We have been so blessed to have experienced the beauty of God in creation through our many vacationing excursions. We have gazed in amazement upon the majestic snow-capped peaks of Mount McKinney in Alaska and the glazing bronzed outback rock of Uluru in Australia. We swam and snorkeled in the crystal blue waters of the Great Barrier Reef, the eye of an underwater volcano in Maui, and the cherished coral reef of Cozumel. We explored the heights of the rainforest of Cairns, the mountainside of the Rockies and zip-lined a trail of Mexico's luscious forestry. A refreshing cascading mist of Yosemite's Bridal Falls has kissed our faces whereas the sweat-drenching heat of Death Valley soaked the back of our necks. And though we have been witnesses to many stunning visions of God's creation, we have been blessed with an abundance of God's simplistic beauty right in our own backyard. A grandchild's smile, a dewdrop on burgundy clematis, a bright black and orange oriole perched in our cherry tree, or a squirrel busy gathering walnuts for the winter. God's beauty is everywhere and each one of us has different experiences that speak to us, so that we might share with others how God is personally present to us.

What I find most amazing and incomprehensible is that God's beauty, when we see Him face to face, is still far beyond the beauty that He has displayed for us to see here on earth. His beauty will completely overfill the longing of our souls. His is a beauty that shines from the inside out, and neither outshines the other. He is the culmination of all of earth's beauty and more. Can we even begin to comprehend the immeasurable beauty of God? I don't believe we can, but as we have been created in His image and live in such a way that we imitate Christ, there is a portion of divine beauty to be seen in each of us. Illuminate this dreary world and shine for Christ, worship the Creator with praise and thanksgiving always, and know that the ultimate perfection of God's beauty is represented in the sacrificial death of Christ on the cross for our sins. God's beauty is overflowing with love on a daily basis and with my lips I will continually praise Him, along with creation.

Prayer: Heavenly Father, I cannot begin to comprehend your beauty, yet through your majestic and beautiful handiwork displayed in nature and the miracle of physical and spiritual birth, my heart is filled with praise and worship. You are an awesome most beautiful God, and I want to experience your beauty with all of the senses you have created in me. Amen.

Tidbits:

> "Splendour and majesty are before him; strength and beauty are in his sanctuary." – Psalm 96:6, ESV

> "Never lose an opportunity of seeing anything beautiful, for beauty is God's handwriting." – Ralph Waldo Emerson

> "Out of Zion, the perfection of beauty, God shines forth." – Psalm 50:2, ESV

> "A Christian's God-focused enjoyment of creation makes it taste better, look better, feel better, smell better, and sound better." – Steve DeWitt

> "For God is sheer beauty, all-generous in love, loyal always and ever." – Psalm 100:5, MSG

> "There is not one blade of grass, there is no colour in this world that is not intended to make us rejoice." – Jean Calvin

Song Suggestion: Beautiful Saviour – written by Henry Seeley

DAY BY DAY

"Trust in him at all times, O people; pour out your heart before him; God is a refuge for us." – Psalm 62:8, ESV

The hymn, "Day By Day," by Lina Sandell, is one of my all-time favourite hymns, and it's sad to think that many generations to follow will not experience its truth and harmonic beauty, because hymns are not the norm for worship these days. Not only does the content of this hymn resonate truth to the very centre of the soul, but the composition of music lends itself to the freedom of harmonious embellishment by this amateur pianist. I love to sing the alto harmony in the soprano key while allowing the melody to ring out amidst the outstretched thumb and pinky fingers. When I was researching some information with regards to this hymn, I was sad to read the account of its beginnings.

Karolina Wilhelmina Sandell-Berg, known to her Swedish kinsman as Lina Sandell, and also tagged as the 'Fanny Crosby of Sweden" scribed most of her psalms and poetry anonymously as "L.S." It was a fellow countryman, Oskar Ahnfelt, who made her hymns popular and secured public appeal when he was singing them, simply accompanied by guitar throughout Scandanavia. Lina, at 29, and her father were crossing a lake in a boat when her father was catapulted overboard and drowned before her eyes. Undoubtedly, this tragic and dramatic accident greatly impacted the rest her life, and at the age of 33 she penned the words "Day by Day." While she wrote 650 hymns and most were popular due to the simple, beautiful melodies composed to accompany them, the inspired words of "Day by Day" (1865) most definitely found higher popularity, thus the song is treasured by millions of pianists, vocalists and choirs alike.

> Day by day, and with each passing moment,
> Strength I find, to meet my trials here;
> Trusting in my Father's wise bestowment,
> I've no cause for worry or for fear.
> He Whose heart is kind beyond all measure
> Gives unto each day what He deems best—
> Lovingly, it's part of pain and pleasure,
> Mingling toil with peace and rest.

Further research into other songs that Lina composed drew me to the conclusion that most of her compositions were penned during times of adversity and sorrow. There was not one other song that was familiar to me, though the words of many of them still have power to soften and turn the heart towards Christ. She was obviously very close and leaned on Him throughout her trials.

As with the tragic death of Lina's father, there is no guarantee for any of us as to how many days one has to live here on earth. They are divinely numbered and we know not when our end will come. My own father died suddenly in a farming accident in the 1980s when he was taking a corner at a country intersection on route to harvest soya beans. The attached plow swung wide and hooked the raised edge along the creek and, consequently, the tractor somersaulted, and he perished, crushed beneath the weight of the tractor. Unbelievably, we passed the emergency vehicles and flashing lights on our way out of town and had no knowledge that the accident involved my father. The most concerning part of his death is that I do not know his personal position with the Lord at the time. As Lina wrote, "Help me Lord when trial and trouble meeting. . . E'er to take as from a Father's hand. . .till we reach the Promised Land." it is understood that to enter heaven, one needs to have a personal relationship with the Father. He will take our hand and lead us to the Promised Land. The Bible makes it very clear that only those who know Christ will see heaven. So only God knows, whether my earthly father and I will meet again.

Prayer: Heavenly Father, you give us but one day at a time, and we are told not to trouble ourselves about tomorrow. Help me to treasure each day as a gift and to make the most of each day sharing precious time with loved ones and witnessing to those who need to find a personal relationship with you. Amen.

Tidbits:

> Jesus said to him, "I am the way, and the truth, and the life. No one comes to the Father except through me." – John 14:6, ESV

> "Our lives begin to end the day we become silent about things that matter." – Martin Luther King Jr.

> "So we do not lose heart. Though our outer self is wasting away, our inner self is being renewed day by day." – 2 Corinthians 4:16, ESV

> "When we take our eyes off the whirl of day-to-day activity and concentrate on honouring Him and following in His way, we find a consistent peace that carries us through both plenty and poverty." – Charles Stanley

> "This is the day that the LORD has made; let us rejoice and be glad in it." – Psalm 118:24, ESV

> "The best thing about the future is that it comes only one day at a time." – Abraham Lincoln

Song Suggestion: Day by Day – written by Karolina Wilhelmina Sandell-Berg, Oskar Ahnfelt, Andrew L. Skoog

JUST TO BE WITH YOU

"Father, I desire that they also, whom you have given me, may be with me where I am, to see my glory that you have given me because you loved me before the foundation of the world." – John 17:24, ESV

If you have had the privilege of falling in love, finding your soul mate and marrying him or her then you understand the phrase, "just to be with you." I remember when John and I first crossed paths in the school hallway and then shortly there afterwards again at the dance hall. I had already set my heart on him, yet he had not even noticed me. I convinced him to give me a ride home from the dance and then some rides to school, before long we were an 'item.' We spent two years of those moments before we married in 1969 and have since been blessed with 44 years together. We are thankful to God for the sometimes wavy, but mostly smooth, ride together. That's not to say that we didn't learn to allow our union to be represented by our own individuality, but that in most things we desire to spend our time together. Even when fishing wasn't my choice of things to do, I would gather my book and pillow and prop the fishing pole between my toes, relaxing, reading and waiting for the tug between my toes before frantically attempting to draw in the odd nibble, all for the sake of sharing time together. I can recall each of my four children experiencing their courtships and how they were nearly inseparable because of their love for one another. That's what love is, it desires a companion and a relationship.

Jesus is no different in wanting a relationship with us. He spoke of his disciples in a prayer at his last meal with them, "Father, I desire that they also, whom you have given me, may be with me where I am . . ."

Can you imagine the heartbreak He feels when we show no interest in spending time with Him? It would be so much deeper than our being absent from those we love on earth, for Jesus gave so much more love to secure our position with Him. You may know some of that type of pain if you have suffered the death of a loved one, the loss of a wayward child, or maybe a marriage that ended in divorce. Jesus' desire is to spend time with those who have placed their faith in Him, for He wants to know them, grow them, love them, and build the strongest of relationship with each of his children. We are part of His eternal plan, and He desires to build a strong love foundation long before we cross over into the eternal place called heaven.

There are many types of Christians with a variety of masks of spirituality, and sometimes as we watch their behaviours, we are easily convinced that we don't want our mansion built anywhere near theirs. What we need to remember, though, is that the cross is big enough and "His arms" are wide enough to embrace even someone like me, so none of us is in a position to cast judgment on those He calls His friends. Jesus desires our company, not because He is lonely, but because He loves us and wants us beside Him. He does not need us, for He lacks nothing, but He desires to be in companionship with us. God's love gave Jesus the courage to hang on the cross and suffer the cost of our sin. It is a love so deep, so wide, so high and so incomprehensible that we cannot measure or understand the love He gave to save us. He desires to build a relationship with us while we remain on earth, yet His deepest desire is to have us with Him eternally. "They are not of the world, even as I am not of the world." We, as humans, remain focused on our life here and strive to make Him present in our homes, our business, our amusements and in our hearts, but Jesus desires that, foremost, we want to be with Him in paradise. He spoke to the disciples about the Father's house having many dwelling places and that He would be going there to pr DEWHURST_HopeLives_6x9_P epare a place for them, and that He will come again and receive them to Himself. As difficult as approaching death is for any of us, the ultimate love relationship will be complete when we stand before Jesus, the lover of our soul, witnessing the glory of His presence.

Tidbits:

> "In my Father's house are many rooms. If it were not so, would I have told you that I go to prepare a place fo DEWHURST_HopeLives_6x9_P r you? And if I go and prepare a place for you, I will come again and will take you to myself, that where I am you may be also." – John 14:2-3, ESV

> "We talk about heaven being so far away. It is within speaking distance to those who belong there. Heaven is a prepared place for a prepared people." – Dwight L Moody

> "And God shall wipe away all tears from their eyes; and there shall be no more death, neither sorrow, nor crying, neither shall there be any more pain: for the former things are passed away." – Revelation 21:4, ESV

> "But according to his promise we are waiting for new heavens and a new earth in which righteousness dwells." – 2 Peter 3:13, ESV

Song Suggestion: Love Song – written by Brad Avery, David Carr, Mac Powell, Mark D. Lee, Tai Anderson; performed by Third Day

FACING MY GIANT

"Do not withhold your mercy from me, LORD; may your love and faithfulness always protect me." – Psalm 40:11, NIV

I don't know what 'giant' you might be facing today, whether it is unemployment, divorce, abuse, addiction or financial disaster but my giant is cancer. And what an enormous giant it claims to be. In the story of David and Goliath, God helped David to defeat the giant so that we can have the confidence that he is able to strike ours down as well. If you are fortunate enough to be one who can already raise your voice and declare victory, to God be the glory. At this time, I am not yet able to declare victory over the mutated cells that desire to conquer my body, but I will continue to pray for God's mercy and wait in hope that he will deliver a mighty miracle to conquer this giant.

I don't believe that this giant that we call cancer carries any more weight than the giant Goliath carried when He faced David, for in actuality the giant faced God himself. No matter what giant we are facing, it only matters where we are focusing. When David approached Goliath, he was the only one who was focused on God. "The Lord, who delivered me from the paw of the lion and from the paw of the bear will deliver me from the hand of the Philistine" (1 Sam 17:37, ESV). David chose to believe that His God was much bigger than the giant that stood before Him, and he ran with confidence to slay Goliath.

God said that "David was a man after God's own heart," and I dare not to even presume that I can be counted with the likes of David, but I do desire to live as God wants me to and to face my giant with His strength. David's life was not one of honour in all accounts, for he failed God several times and, as giants strive to tear our Christian testimony to pieces, we, too, will find ourselves in times of failure, rejection and remorse. God does not expect us to face our giants alone, but He does expect us to divert our focus from the giant and the threats the giant poses and focus on Him. I hope and pray and wait for God, who delivered David from his giant, to deliver me from mine. May my ears and my very soul be ever listening to the voice of truth that tells me "Do not be afraid" and "This is for My glory." Above all, may the voices that will call out to me attempting to discourage and destroy my hope, peace and faith be drowned by the 'voice of truth.'

Prayer: Heavenly Father, have mercy on me and provide for me immeasurable hope as I face this raging giant. No matter what claims cancer attempts to make on my life and my faith, please continue to provide me shelter in your arms and give me the strength to overcome. Please, provide for me a miraculous victory for your glory. Amen.

Tidbits:

> "Let us then with confidence draw near to the throne of grace, that we may receive mercy and find grace to help in time of need." – Hebrews 4:16, ESV

> "Courage doesn't always roar. Sometimes courage is the quiet voice at the end of the day saying, 'I will try again tomorrow.'" – Mary Anne Radmacher

> "My grace is sufficient for you, for my power is made perfect in weakness. Therefore I will boast all the more gladly of my weaknesses, so that the power of Christ may rest upon me." – 2 Corinthians 12:9, ESV

> "A person who wholly follows the Lord is one who believes that the promises of God are trustworthy, that He is with His people, and that they are well able to overcome." – Watchman Nee

Song Suggestion: The Voice of Truth – written by Mark Hall, Steven Curtis Chapman

YOU ARE FOR ME

"If God is for us, who can be against us?" – Romans 8:31b, NIV

Are you a team player? I fondly remember the seemingly endless early Saturday mornings that our three boys were actively involved in house league hockey. They were not always proud to call me 'mom' as I made them 'tow the mark' and play the game fairly without violent checking and vicious high sticking antics that were readily displayed by other players and accepted by coaches and parents alike. You may think me to be eccentric, but I expected the Christian character to be displayed not only in life but also on the ice. Of course, the greatest detriment to any team is the 'puck hog' who is determined to grasp all the glory for himself, which usually backfires, because games are not usually won with solo showoffs, but by a team that plays as a team. Despite my sons being annoyed with my hounding them about 'fair play' and other sportsmanship admonitions, they knew that I was always in their corner cheering them on. Today I enjoy watching my various grandchildren display their athletic skills and they, too, know that they have enthusiastic support in their corner. No matter what we are attempting to achieve in life, nothing matters more than having devotees in our corner.

My journey with cancer has proven to me, on both counts, that I have a team that plays as a team, represented by the hundreds of prayer warriors, exhorters, devotees and comforters in my corner. Not only do I have a supportive team, but I also have the perfect team captain. "If God is for us (me), who can be against us (me)?"

Do we truly comprehend who we have in our corner? The ultimate general fights battles with us and for us, yet that does not mean all our earthly battles will be won. The Apostle Paul faced numerous trials and tribulations that included flogging, beatings, betrayal, shipwrecks, jail time, just to name a few, and he experienced miraculous delivery from many, but he was yet left to suffer the 'thorn in his flesh' he often referred to, and of which we are not given specifics. Many biblical characters experienced both the agony of defeat and the thrill of victory through Christ, and in the context of the opposites, we acknowledge God's hand, for He will conquer all regardless of how we tend to view the battle. "I've told you all this so that trusting me, you will be unshakable and assured, deeply at peace. In this godless world you will continue to experience difficulties. But take heart! I've conquered the world" (John 16:33, MSG).

Regardless of my hardships and sufferings, I am confident that God loves me. He is on my side and in my corner. God's Word does not change, and His promises never fail. Christ has overcome the world and, step by step, He will help me overcome earthly obstacles until He promotes me to glory. Through my highs and lows, droughts and floods, hills and valleys, God is always my team captain and my warring general. He has a purpose for me and has already prepared a victory for this battle. God is greater than the adversary, and He that is in me is greater than he that is in the world. The power of God's love provides me strength to endure. The brilliance of His love shines a light during my darkest moments and there is nothing that can separate me from His love.

Prayer: Heavenly Father, how do I even comprehend the magnitude of having you as my battle general and divine deliverer. Though I cannot fathom the immeasurable capacity of your love for me, I stand by faith on your Word and promises and wait for your perfect will to be accomplished in my life. During the lows of agony and the heights of victory, may I be careful to give you all the glory, honour and praise. Amen.

Tidbits:

> "And we know that for those who love God all things work together for good, for those who are called to his purpose."
> – Romans 8:28, ESV

> "He will keep you strong until the end, so that you will be blameless on the Day of our Lord Jesus the Messiah. Faithful is the God by whom you were called into fellowship with his Son Jesus the Messiah our Lord." – 1 Corinthians 1:8-9, ISV

> "If God sends us on strong paths, we are provided strong shoes." – Corrie ten Boom

Song Suggestion: You Are for Me – written by Kari Jobe

HE WILL CARRY ME

"Thanks be to the Lord, who daily carries our burdens for us.
God is our salvation." – Psalm 68:19, GW

My faith has not wavered, for I remain confident that God is in control and that He has a divine purpose for my suffering, but it is a daily struggle now to find a position of comfort. I must rely more and more on the strength of the Lord and acknowledge my weakness to endure, and so I pray to feel Him physically carrying me as He is carrying me spiritually. I can't help but think of the poem "Footprints in the Sand" by Margaret Fishback Powers, which speaks of there being one set of footprints in that sand and making reference to that being the time in which the Lord was doing the carrying. Another mental image is that of a toddler who is weary from walking, and he stretches his hands upward towards his father and pleads for a piggyback ride. The father lovingly hoists him high in the air and perches his son proudly on his shoulders and gives rest to the young lad's weary legs. I feel like that toddler for I am weary, and I am stretching my arms heavenward and pleading with my Heavenly Father to carry me. I have no doubt that He will. He will reach down in love when He deems it is time, and He will give me rest. "Come to me, all you who are weary and burdened, and I will give you rest" (Matthew 11:28, NIV).

I heard the story of a young wife who related her extreme suffering when her husband was killed during a tour of duty. Facing each day was an over-whelming burden for her. Many times through her grieving process, she was at the point of breaking and just wanted life to stop so she didn't have to feel the pain. With each mundane task required of her as a mother to maintain some normalcy of routine, there were painful reminders of the emptiness inside and the absence of the friend she would always call upon for assistance yet was no longer there. Despite having friends that would offer comfort and walk through the grieving process with her, the pain she felt was hers alone, and often she would find herself saying, "I can't do this!"

I surely cannot understand her grief and loneliness, but I do understand, to a degree, her despair in the midst of pain, and her desperation to feel Jesus physically carrying her. There are moments for me that I, too, doubt my ability to walk this road designed for me, and again I turn to my comforter, Jesus. There is no one but Jesus who can bring the perfect rest. "I will be your God throughout your lifetime—until your hair is white with age. I made you, and I will care for you. I will carry you along and save you" (Isaiah 46:4, NLT).

I know that I am on a difficult journey where I have more questions than answers, and my heart is weary, and my strength fades daily, but it is times like these when I do not understand, that I depend on God to carry me. The Lord has carried me this far and He is not going to drop me now. Even when I think I can't make it and I'm too weak or weary, the Lord says, "We'll make it!" It is a moment-by- moment process to remind myself that my burdens are not too great, because He bears them, and He will carry me as well. He wants nothing more than to be my all in all.

Prayer: Heavenly Father, this has been a difficult day, and my mind is confused and with unclear direction because of my physical discomfort. Help me please to focus on you and your purposes for this journey and to find strength again, but for now I need you to carry me for a stretch. Give me rest, Lord, and comfort my discomfort. Amen.

Tidbits:

> "I'm nothing without my faith. Life is hard, I sometimes struggle, I feel the pain but I know God will bring me through it all." – Unknown

> "The Lord is close to the brokenhearted and saves those who are crushed in spirit." – Psalm 34:18, NIV

> "Sometimes God will leave us in troubled waters; Not for us to drown, but only for us to learn how to swim." – Unknown

> "My grace is sufficient for you, for my power is made perfect in weakness." – 2 Corinthians 12:9a, NIV

> "Never never give up, have faith in God and He will see you through no matter what you are going through. The Most High God sees." – Unknown

> "Casting all your anxieties on him, because he cares for you." – 1 Peter 5:7, ESV

> "God will guide you through thick and thin, no matter how many problems, big or small. He will help you see who and what truly matters. He has my trust and faith." – Unknown

Song Suggestion: He Will Carry Me– written by Mark Schultz, Dennis Kurttila, Sampson Brueher

DEATH IS VICTORY?

"Then, when our dying bodies have been transformed into bodies that will never die, this Scripture will be fulfilled: "Death is swallowed up in victory." – 1 Corinthians 15:54, NLT

The devotional writings are not coming as easy these days, probably for two reasons; one, I feel like I have covered the main topics of trust, hope, peace, love and faith adequately enough that more emphasis would be vain repetition, and two, I'm dealing with a roller coaster of emotions and not always sure what to write as I desire my writings to be an encouragement to others.

Picture a fist full of lovely white daisies, which happens to be my favourite flower, and there is a continual plucking of each petal with: "He loves me! He loves me not." I wish the verbal sentiments that I am echoing in my mind were that simplistic, but they are not, for I am questioning: "Will He heal me? Will He not? There has never been a single doubt in my mind and spiritual being that Jesus, my Lord and Saviour loves me. He loves me unconditionally and there is nothing, absolutely nothing, will ever separate me from that love. "And I am convinced that nothing can ever separate us from God's love. Neither death nor life, neither angels nor demons, neither our fears for today nor our worries about tomorrow—not even the powers of hell can separate us from God's love" (Romans 8:38, NLT).

My struggles lay in the conflict of facing death. How does one approach death gracefully and remain an honourable testimony of the love of Christ, while at the same time trying to maintain hope for a God-given miracle. I also struggled with the spiritual issue of how we are supposed to be looking forward to being united with Christ in heaven, all the while desiring to remain here on earth so I can continue to enjoy my family and life, as I expected it would be. We all struggle between the powers of darkness and light, with some conflicts being miniscule in the measurement of our earthly minds and others of mountainous proportions. I am facing the mountain. I am facing a giant. Is my God bigger than any mountain? Yes! Can my God handle this giant called cancer? Yes! There is also no doubt in my mind that He is the Great I Am, and He can conquer anything and everything. My question has never been can He, but will He? You see, we cannot always know the will of God concerning our future, with the exception that He provided an eternal one through His son, Jesus. "My thoughts are nothing like your thoughts," says the LORD. "And my ways are far beyond anything you could imagine" (Isaiah 55:8, NLT).

I believe in God's power to heal, by miracle and by medicine, and while I walk on and wait for the Lord's intentions to be revealled in my ongoing journey with cancer, I foremost want to be found faithful to Him and willing to learn and grow closer to Him with each passing day. It is difficult to view cancer as a gift from God, especially when there is suffering involved, and yet in relation to the fact that it has drawn me closer to God than I have ever before experienced it is, if nothing else, a blessing. Satan desires to destroy my love for Christ through cancer, but God has designed it to deepen my love for Him. Our culture is terrified of facing death, and I believe that even for the Christian, there is a constant struggle between earthly desires and heavenly focus, for we have not arrived. While on earth, there is a constant struggle between good and evil, but hopefully by communicating honestly, I am able to convey how very important it is to have the assurance of eternal salvation and that only then is 'death is swallowed up in victory.' It is so difficult for our human mind to comprehend, but death is not the end, but rather the beginning.

Prayer: Heavenly Father, as I struggle with my emotions of wanting to remain with my family, and knowing that it is better to be absent from this diseased body and be present with you, please strengthen me and fill me with a longing that only you can bestow. Help me to be an honourable testimony of your love and to endure this time of suffering that you have designed, with dignity. Amen.

Tidbits:

> "Think of how powerless death actually is! Rather than rid us of our health, it introduces us to "riches eternal." Death might temporarily take our friends from us, but only to introduce us to that land in which there are no good-byes." – Erwin Lutzer

> "He will wipe away every tear from their eyes, and death shall be no more, neither shall there be mourning, nor crying, nor pain anymore, for the former things have passed away." – Revelation 21:4, ESV

> "Has this world been so kind to you that you should leave it with regret? There are better things ahead than any we leave behind." – C.S. Lewis

Song Suggestion: God of Ages – written by Ben Fielding

CHAIN, CHAIN, CHAINS

"In my distress I prayed to the LORD, and the LORD answered me and set me free." – Psalm 118:5, NLT

"Chain, chain . . . chain of fools," a Motown favourite performed by Aretha Franklin in the 60s has very little reference to today's blog, except that it is ringing through my ears. Chains come in various sizes and purposes. They are found in feminine adornment for necklaces, earrings and anklets and usually have a 'fob' feature to which the chain is attached. A slightly larger chain might hang from your ceiling fan or connect your pet to his leash, and even larger still, would be the lead weight solid links that attach your delinquent automobile to a Good Samaritan's car, willing to tow it to a garage. Some people even jokingly refer to their marriage or relationship being that of a ball-and-chain imprisonment.

The chains of imprisonment, for propagating the gospel, were literal chains that Paul and Peter were bound in. In Acts 12, an angel appeared to Peter. The angel told him to move and follow, and his chains fell off, and at first Peter thought he just imagining it in a vision. Despite the fact that the people had been praying, when Peter arrived at the home, those same people were more than surprised that he was free. They were encompassed by the 'chain' of no expectancy.' I am quite familiar with the 'chain' of no expectancy. When I pray, I believe He can work a miracle and know that He wants to work a miracle on my behalf, but I am not so sure that I have the confidence that He "will" work a miracle and rid me of cancer. While we pray, we don't always pray with expectancy, and then we are surprised when God decides to answer our requests, but we shouldn't be, because He cares for us.

Our chains that keep us bound from living life to the fullest may not be literal, but they might as well be, as we are imprisoned by multiple challenges and stressful diversions. Another chain among us is the 'chain of tradition' that limits us in experiencing a meaningful, powerful and purposeful service each Sunday. So many people have preconceived ideas or traditional preferences of what a worship service should entail that when it strays outside their 'box' they will even go so far as avoiding the music, the drama, the sermon or the entire service. Many are so enchained to tradition that any change within the church constitutes a disagreement, but let me remind you that God is not confined to a box, and when we come to worship, it is the focus of our heart that is our primary importance, not our preferences. Focus on worship. Focus on Christ.

Next we have the 'chain of hesitancy' and that is overwhelmingly evident today where churches are struggling to find fully dedicated people to serve.

Sunday Schools are closing, prayer services declining, and the majority of churches today have one service per week. The reasons behind this overall decline are innumerable and would bog down this devotional with debatable content, but it boils down to a 'lack of commitment' or a hesitancy to get involved. The 'unfaithful' majorities are straddling the fence attempting to enjoy the best of both worlds, but scripture instructs us differently. "No one can serve two masters, for either he will hate one and love the other; or he will be devoted to the one and despise the other" (Matthew 6:24a, ESV).

Chains can be broken, and the chains of tradition and hesitancy, at the very least, need to be loosened. There is a mental, spiritual and physical process in facing our chains; first we must accept that we are indeed 'chained' or imprisoned. We have many chains unmentioned and, far too often, we look for a quick fix when it takes time to change our perspective and see things through God's eyes. God wants us to come to a place of acceptance and, in Christ's power, begin to make changes. God may not entirely 'unchain' you, but perhaps expect you to use your situation to help others. Ultimately, the question is, "Do you want your chain to be broken?"

Prayer: Heavenly Father, help me as I struggle with prayers of expectation for I know you can heal me, but the nagging question of "will you?" is always there. Help me to continue to walk close and to identify chains that keep me from being fully devoted to you. Amen.

Tidbits:

> "If you hold to my teaching, you are really my disciples. Then you will know the truth, and the truth will set you free." – John 8:31-32, NIV

> "The chains of habit are too weak to be felt until they are too strong to be broken." – Samuel Johnson

Song Suggestion: I Bless Your Name – written performed by Selah

WHAT'S IN A NAME?

"Therefore God has highly exalted him and bestowed on him the name that is above every name, so that at the name of Jesus every knee should bow, in heaven and on earth and under the earth, and every tongue confess that Jesus Christ is Lord, to the glory of God the Father." – Philippians 2:9-11, ESV

All the hype these days is about George Alexander Louis, the future heir to the throne of England and first born son of Prince William Arthur Philip Louis and the Duchess of Cambridge, Catherine Middleton. George carries the namesake of his great, great grandfather King George VI, Queen Elizabeth's late father, who gained popularity with his decision to remain in London during World War II, in the face of German bombing raids. Alexander is said to more closely represent the Queen's second name, Alexandra, yet there were several kings of Scotland with the same name, not to mention that it was one of Kate's favourites. Simply, Alex suits me. Louis bears reference to a well-esteemed uncle of Prince Philip, the Duke of Edinburgh, and also to his birth father's fourth title. Those who hold respect for traditional name games are probably not passing judgment on their choice of moniker, though millions were hoping to see a swing towards a more common signature as the royal couple so easily displays more normalcy than previous royalty.

My parents followed a 1950s tradition when they chose to honour my paternal grandmother, Mildred Faye Coghill Wigle, whom I never had the pleasure of meeting as she had died from complications of childbirth when my father when only a toddler. My mother had fully intended on filling out the necessary paperwork to read Faye Mildred, but an uncaught error left me with the legal registration of Mildred, hence the reason behind my Facebook blog being named "Millie's Motivational and Medical Posts," that provided repetitive alliteration. As I much preferred being called Faye for all of sixty years, recently during my battle with cancer, my legal name appears on all forms and each verbal declaration at every waiting room, medical tests and prescription line is Mildred, and so you might say that I am getting used to a different moniker. During today's medical ultrasound of 'tapping' or draining of the abdominal fluid that developed in the ongoing war of my internal parts against cancer, I am pleased to report the delivery of 'Fluidity Relief' at a healthy, or perhaps unhealthy, 6 pounds, 6 ounces. I have no doubt that she left a portion of a twin behind, but at this point 'Relief' is most welcomed.

So what's in a name? Even the name of England's future king pales in comparison to that of my Lord and Saviour, Jesus. "Jesus, the mere mention of His Name can calm the storm, heal the broken and raise the dead. At the name of Jesus, hatred and bitterness turn to love and forgiveness and arguments cease. Emperors have tried to destroy it; philosophies have tried to stamp it out, but there will come a final day when every voice that has ever uttered a sound, every voice of Adam's race, shall raise in one great mighty chorus to proclaim the Name of Jesus! Ah, so you see, it was not mere chance that caused the angel one night long ago to say to a virgin maiden, "and you will name him Jesus" (Matthew 1:21, NKJV).

Prayer: Heavenly Father, I stand in awe of your many names that represent you as a Healer, Comforter, Creator, Shepherd, Deliverer, Father, Counselor, Great High Priest, Lamb of God, Messiah, Redeemer and more. There is nothing that soothes our hearts and delights the ears like the name of Jesus. May I continue to esteem your name above all others and never debase or degrade your majestic addresses, but always display respect and honour. Amen.

Tidbits:

> "The name of Jesus is the one lever that lifts the world." – Unknown

> "For to us a child is born, to us a son is given, and the government will be on his shoulders. And he will be called Wonderful Counselor, Mighty God, Everlasting Father, Prince of Peace. Of the greatness of his government and peace there will be no end. . ." – Isaiah 9:6-7, NIV

> "Every character has an inward spring; let Christ be that spring. Every action has a keynote; let Christ be that note, to which your whole life is attuned." – Henry Drummond

> "And it shall come to pass, that whosoever shall call on the name of Jehovah shall be delivered." – Joel 2:32, ASV

> "How sweet the name of Jesus sounds in a believer's ear; it soothes his sorrows, heals his wounds, and drives away his fear." – John Newton

Song Suggestion: He Is Jehovah – written by Betty Jean Robinson

HE IS JEALOUS FOR ME

"For the Lord your God in your midst is a jealous God . . ."
– Deuteronomy 6:15, ESV

In a popular chorus we sing today in worship, the lyrics go like this: "He is jealous for me." It essentially says that God loves us like a tree that's bent toward him. I don't have a problem understanding that I am to be humbled in His presence and to be found 'bending' in appreciation for the magnitude of His love and mercy; at least that's my feeble interpretation of the lyrics, but I must admit that the mention of jealousy is a difficult term to deal with. As humans we don't view jealously as an honourable attribute of affection, but in this instance, that is how it is to be interpreted. Our God jealously desires our love and affection.

From our human perspective, jealousy is recognized as an intolerance of competition such as can be found between two individuals in a relationship. In my teen years, I remember being somewhat jealous of girls who John (now my husband) had friendships with. I can see now that those feelings were unwarranted and immature. Fortunately, in regards to my spousal relationship, he has never given me reason to be jealous, though I remind him in a teasing manner that I have reason to be jealous of the relationship he has with his garden and feline friend, as they get plenty of his attention. Another angle of jealousy is that of the accomplishments of another person that gain them acclamation that we wish for ourselves, and which further causes us to have resentment toward them. This is probably the one that most individuals have difficulty dealing with, as we are so programmed to participate in our 'keeping up with the Joneses in today's society.

Saul is an excellent example of achievement jealousy since he was quite disturbed by the attention that David was receiving over his military victories. Joseph's brothers were so jealous of the favouritism his father showed him that they sold him into slavery.

If you pay attention, in everyday conversation between individuals, family and even grandchildren, you can always pick up on someone attempting to make themselves look better than another by boasting or belittling. Jealousy is a sin when it is a desire for something that does not belong to you, and because of our negative connotations, we struggle to see jealousy in a positive light, yet with God it is.

Our relationship with God is somewhat similar to that of a marriage, for when we confess and receive Jesus as our Lord and Saviour, repenting of our sins, we have exchanged our old sinful life for a new spiritual relationship, one in which God has asked us to put nothing else first. You shall have no other gods before me."

As within a marriage, the relationship matures into a more solid foundation when we determine to "Love the Lord your God with all your heart and with all your soul and with all your mind." God is jealous when we give something to another that rightly belongs to Him. Worship, praise, honour, and adoration belong to God alone, for only He is truly worthy of it. (Exodus 20:3, NIV; Matthew 22:37, NIV)

It is difficult to comprehend that the Creator of the universe, the Almighty God, actually craves and desires to build an intimate relationship with each of us. God wants nothing but the best for us, and that is Him. Jesus paid the sacrificial price for our eternal salvation; that should be simply enough to warrant our devoted love, but we fail miserably, and yet He continues to bless, love and extend grace throughout all our lives. I do not comprehend love of such measure, but I am thankful that He is jealous for me.

Prayer: Heavenly Father, help me to focus on your glory and overlook the temporary afflictions of my cancer battle. Might I daily find myself sinking in the bottomless ocean of the love you have for me. Help me to revel in the idea that you are jealous for me, and give me the strength to put you first above all things in my life. Amen.

Tidbits:

"Do not worship any other god, for the LORD, whose name is Jealous, is a jealous God." – Exodus 34:14, NIV

"Jealousy is central to the fundamental essence of who God is. Jealousy is at the core of God's identity as God. Jealousy is that defining characteristic or personality trait that makes God, God. At the very core of His being, in the center of His personality is an inextinguishable blaze of immeasurable love called jealousy." – Sam Storms

"You shall not bow yourself down to them, nor serve them, for I, Yahweh your God, am a jealous God. . ." – Exodus 20:5, WEB

"Let it be remembered then, that jealousy, like anger, is not evil in itself, or it could never be ascribed to God; His jealousy is ever a pure and holy flame." – C.H. Spurgeon

Song Suggestion: How He Loves – written by John Mark McMillan

FARTHER ALONG

"My grace is sufficient for you, for my power is made perfect in weakness." – 2 Corinthians 12:9b, NIV

Affliction comes in many shapes and sizes and makes itself at home even when uninvited. We are never at home or comfortable with its presence and would probably do almost anything to escort affliction out the front door, march it right over to the sewer well, and dispose of it into the bowels of the earth, hoping to never see it again. Unfortunately, most afflictions are not that easily removed, and some we may have to endure for a lifetime. Paul appealed to the Lord three times that his affliction would leave him, but he was told that God's grace was sufficient and that God's power is made perfect in weakness. Oh, that I could demonstrate complete and total weakness so God's power could be undeniably demonstrated for my family, friends and community to see His mighty and unbelievable power and the immeasurable amount with which He loves all of us. My suffering would be worth it all if His message of love and redemption could be shared and received by the lost and confused.

As a type "A" personality, it's been most difficult to have an affliction and not be able to control it to any degree. Most disorders such as broken ankles, hearing loss, stomach ulcers, and arthritis allow us some type of simple control, but not so with cancer. We try, but as much as science has made great advances with trying to understand that dirty "C" word, it is still broad in destruction and widely unknown. Most everyone these days has been touched by cancer in some way, and we are severely lacking the ability to offer comfort. Doctors wage war on the disease with drugs and therapies that result in side-effects that are hardly tolerable. My own personal affliction has made me realize what a deep sense of powerlessness I now have, though this loss of control has been a gift from God, forcing me to realize how independently I had been living, and how much more I needed to include Him, depend on Him and lean on Him. God has a specific reason for allowing these nasty molecular cells to produce and grow in my body, and I believe that it was His aim to knock me off my feet and cause me to utterly rely on Him. As a natural born 'control freak,' experiencing a total lack of control has been a hard journey, yet it has been most enlightening and has also provided spiritual growth to heights I have never experienced before. I am thankful for the closer relationship I share with Him now.

When I was coming out of the anesthesia from surgery, and the doctor's solemn face peered into mine, with a hand gently waking me in the recovery room, he shared the dismal news of the cancer being present in a new location. I groggily remember saying to him, "So I'm going to die?"

He replied, "We'll, we're all going to die."

Death is an absolute that will be experienced by all of us, short of Jesus Christ returning in this lifetime, but having cancer is like carrying a bomb on your back, not knowing with it will detonate. This is where faith grows and becomes more real than ever before, and you begin to understand what it means to trust in God. I am still seeking out medical intervention, but ultimately I ache and pray for God's total intervention to destroy the cancer cells and heal my body. Despite all medical advances, it is all in His control and a mystery to not be understood. Why He heals some and not others is not known, but we will understand it farther along.

Prayer: Heavenly Father, your ways and thoughts are far above my own, and I may not totally understand why you have allowed me to have this cancerous affliction, but search my heart and help me to conduct myself righteously so that your name is glorified in whatever outcome you bring. Amen.

Tidbits:

> "And my God will supply every need of yours according to his riches in glory in Christ Jesus." – Philippians 4:19, ESV

> "The Lord gets His best soldiers out of the highlands of affliction." – Charles H. Spurgeon

> "Let us then with confidence draw near to the throne of grace, that we may receive mercy and find grace to help in time of need." – Hebrews 4:16, ESV

> "Extraordinary afflictions are not always the punishment of extraordinary sins, but sometimes the trial of extraordinary graces." – Matthew Henry

> "You will keep in perfect peace those whose minds are steadfast, because they trust in you." Trust in the LORD forever, for the LORD, the LORD himself, is the Rock eternal." – Isaiah 26:3-4, NIV

Song Suggestion: Farther Along – attributed to W. B. Stevens

GOD, MY HEALER

"If you will diligently hearken to the voice of the Lord your God and do what is right in His sight, and will listen to and obey His commandments and keep all His statutes, I will put none of the diseases upon you which I brought upon the Egyptians, for I am the Lord, who heals you." – Exodus 15:26, AMP

"For I am the Lord, your healer." This reference to God—Jehovah Rapha, the God who heals and restores, was revealed in Exodus under unusual circumstances. He had provided the Israelites deliverance from Egyptian slavery, and they had also witnessed the miracle in the dividing of the Red Sea, allowing their escape and drowning the Pharaoh's' army. They had only journeyed further by a mere three days in the desert of Shur when they came upon a supply of water in Marah. The water was unpleasant and they were quick to complain to Moses about its bitterness. It wasn't just the water that was bitter, but so, without reason, were His people.

Moses cried out to God and received instructions to toss a piece of wood into the water which inexplicably made the water sweetened and ready to drink. I can hardly believe that after having witnessed God's amazing protection through the plagues in Egypt, being shielded from murder of their first born, having the protection of the pillar of cloud by day and a pillar of fire by night as they travelled through the wilderness, and the dividing of the Red Sea without harm, that it took only three days for their spirit of gratefulness to be overcome with complaining.

God introduced a decree and stated that the people were to listen, pay attention to His commands, keep His statutes, and that they would not suffer the diseases of the Egyptians, and that he would be their healer. Personally, I know that there are tons of reliable documentation of authentic healing, but I am a guarded skeptic when it comes to 'so-called miracles" and probably because of aggressively proclaimed 'miracles' on television. The Bible clearly teaches that God is our healer and I have complete faith that all that is written is absolutely true. Though as Christians, we cannot assume that healing is God's plan for our life. I have seen both answered and unanswered prayers with regards to healing. Life doesn't always work out the way we expect it to, and it leaves us struggling to believe or expect a miracle for ourselves.

A friend prayed with extreme confidence for extraordinary healing of my cancer, and while that is my heart's desire, I don't presume to know the absolute will of God for my life, and so I don't pray with the same confidence. Some may say I have little faith, and that I am allowing my skepticism to overshadow my faith. You are welcome to your own opinion, however, I choose to instead have absolute confidence that God will have His way and He will be my strength, whatever the path, be it healing or remission.

Before we cast judgment on the Israelites' complaints, we might find ourselves paralleling their behaviour. When God doesn't answer our prayers the way we expect, we sometimes develop a spirit of resentment. We may wrongly compare our lives to other Christians and begrudge that they are experiencing God's blessings and yet we are not. Perhaps God has cured their cancer, and yet you still struggle with the disease and side effects that may be nearly unbearable. Don't give up on prayer, or the expectation of an answer. However, be careful not to let the root of bitterness grow and distance you in your relationship with God. Healing is not presented in the same degree, or in the same time frame, from one situation to another. Submit your desires to the will of God and trust that Jesus—Jehovah-Rapha—will heal you according to His time.

Prayer: God, I acknowledge you are the Great Physician and know that you can heal all afflictions, whether they be physical, mental, or emotional, in accordance with you will. My journey forward still has many unknowns and I desire to feel your presence in a very real way. As I await the outcome and trust you for healing, help me to wait on you for my ongoing needs. Oh, Lord, I wait on you, trust in you, and look forward to the healing that lies ahead, be it on Earth or in Heaven. Thank you for loving me, building my faith through this trial and for comforting me with your arms of love. Amen.

Tidbits:

> "Bless the LORD, O my soul, and forget none of His benefits; who pardons all your iniquities, who heals all your diseases," – Psalm 103:2-3, NASB

> "No one heals himself by wounding another." – St. Ambrose

> "O LORD my God, I cried to You for help, and You healed me." – Psalm 30:2, NASB

> "Some people see scars, and it is wounding they remember. To me they are proof of the fact that there is healing." – Linda Hogan

Song Suggestion: Healer – written by Michael Guglielmucci

HELP IS ON THE WAY

"I lift up my eyes to the mountains-where does my help come from? My help comes from the Lord, the Maker of heaven and the earth." – Psalm 121:1-2, NIV

The 2012 hurricane-force winds of Sandy wreaked havoc on Jamaica, Haiti, Cuba, over 24 states of the eastern United States, as well as portions of Canada, leaving record-breaking and unimaginable destruction in its path. It flooded streets, tunnels, subways, bringing down power structures and homes innumerable. Countless areas were declared a 'state of emergency.' No doubt one of the most common phrases the victims of this storm probably heard was "Help is on the way." Just a couple of months later the headlines were ablaze with the tragic unnecessary massacre of 26 innocent victims, mostly young children. As distraught parents, spouses and guardians stood for an eternity outside awaiting what they hoped would be good news, there, too, I am sure they were told, "Help is on the way." Very recently my own country suffered extreme flooding in High River, Calgary as well as surrounding suburbs that was unmatched in destruction. The social pages of Facebook were bombarded with disastrous pictures of destruction and mounds of mud that needed to be removed. I imagine they also heard "Help is on the way."

I know for a fact that even nearly two years later there are still hundreds of Hurricane Sandy victims who are still awaiting help and wondering if there will ever be a 'normal' in their lives again. And no doubt, painfully deep emotional scars involving the loss of their children, parents of students at Sandy Hook school in Connecticut are still reeling in disbelief, grief, with insufficient help to heal their wounds. As I type this devotional, Albertans are still in a flooded mess, and it is yet to be seen if "Help is on the Way" will hold any concrete truth after the passage of time. In all types of disasters and emergencies, and even cancer diagnosis, there are many quick or first responders that come to the rescue offering goods, services, restoration, emotional support, and the appreciation for their comforting services cannot be undervalued. However, as time passes and the first responders have completed their role, there still remain many people in turmoil who are quickly forgotten once the media has swung to another 'front page' phenomenon. The comforting phrase, "Help is on the way," doesn't hold truth for them.

Many old western movies have the white-Stetson hat hero riding into save the day, or there are the many 'caped crusaders' who swing in to rescue the world from the evil plotters. Micah was a prophet when Israel and Judah lived amidst the super powers of the Assyrian army. He instructed the people to stay strong in their faith because, 'Help is on the way.'

Many countries today are gripped with fear of terrorists, neighbourhood thieves, and so they arm themselves with security cameras, guns and locks; some have an extensive stock of armaments. We have been convinced that being big and powerful is the answer so we supply big machines, wads of money, countless armies, and I can't help but think about the Dutch boy who stuck a single finger in the dyke wall and saved his homeland from the flood. Big is not always better and sometimes simple works, but this is not the help that the world is in need of today. The only big and powerful one who can bring sustained comfort and an infallible measurement of help is God. During my current cancer disaster, I choose to "lift my eyes to the hills, where my help comes from," for from God and God alone, my help is on the way!

Prayer: Praise You, O Lord, for you alone are my tower of strength and you alone can rescue me from the current medical crisis that you have allowed in my life. Help me to learn what lessons you intend for me to understand. I pray that your ears and heart are attuned to my plea for life, should it be your will for me. Amen.

Tidbits:

> "Now to Him who is able to do far more abundantly beyond all that we ask or think, according to the power that works within us." – Ephesians 3:20, NASB

> "Do not be afraid to suffer. . . It is from being shaken apart and not being destroyed that we become strong and courageous." – Laura Lewis Lanier

> "Our help is in the name of the LORD, the Maker of heaven and earth." – Psalm 124:8, NIV

> "You can't analyze God. He is too awesome, too big, too mysterious. "I know now, Lord, why you utter no answer. You, Yourself are the answer." – C.S. Lewis

> "I will answer them before they even call to me. While they are still talking about their needs, I will go ahead and answer their prayers!" – Isaiah 65:24, NLT

> "I trust in you, Lord, but keep helping me in my moments of distrust and doubt." – Henry Nouwen

Song Suggestion: Help Is on the Way – written by Israel Houghton, Deborah D. Smith, Michael W. Smith, Christa Black

SPRINT OR MARATHON?

"Therefore, since we are surrounded by so great a cloud of witnesses, let us also lay aside every weight, and sin which clings so closely, and let us run with endurance the race that is set before us, looking to Jesus, the founder and perfecter of our faith. . ." – Hebrew 12:1-2a, ESV

During my later elementary and early high school years, I participated in track and field events, and of all of the sports available in track and field, running was my strength. In particular, the shorter distances from the 100 metre dash to the 400 metre sprint were my preferences. Though I had never participated in a marathon, and the longest race I attempted was actually the mile in my first year of high school, I was coaxed into participating by a friend who didn't want to race alone. She asked if I would accompany her, so I reluctantly I agreed. Ignorantly, and without proper training, I ran along beside her and we kept each other company for three and a half laps, with still the final yards ahead of us. She signalled to me that it was time to increase our speed to the finish line. To my surprise I pulled ahead and won the race. The ribbon award was not the highlight of my memory, as I was too focused on my rubbery legs feeling completely detached. I have no idea how I managed to keep going, stride after stride, to the finish line. It was an indescribable experience that I am sure thousands of racers are familiar with, but it was new to me and never to be experienced again.

While both the sprint and a marathon have start and finish lines, the preparation for each race is entirely different. A sprint requires sudden, strong and short bursts of energy, whereas the marathon runners require participants to pace themselves in order to endure the distance. Each runner is focused on the finish line, with most hoping to win, but a marathoner's goal is to beat his previous time records. All long distance runners will tell you that their body is in agony from the soles of their feet, their rubbery legs, to their bursting lungs each time they race.

The race of faith is a marathon, not a sprint. We are all marathoners running the race of life, living for the Lord, with God setting the pace. Our responsibility is to train and run. As a marathon runner is concerned about making progress beyond that of his previous races, the same should be the measurement of our Christian race. Are we making progress in our Christian growth? Are we more Christ-like today than we were last month, last year, or even five years or more ago? Professional contenders do not focus on those running alongside of them or the spectators in the grandstands; they focus on the goal, the finish line. Are you running the race without comparing yourself with the other racers, and keeping your eye on Jesus Christ? To endure the agony of the race that God has called us to run, we need to be absolutely dependent on Him.

Paul warned the Corinthians, trying to coach them back on track. They were not running like disciplined athletes but had lost focus. In Hebrews we are encouraged to take stock of what is hindering us from running successfully by throwing off the sin that entangles us and slows or delays our growth. We are not instructed to rest but to run with perseverance, to fix our eyes on Jesus, and not grow weary and lose heart. We persevere because Christ has provided hope and deliverance for us from suffering and trials. Can we echo the same words of Paul, "I press on to reach the end of the race and receive the heavenly prize for which God, through Christ Jesus, is calling us" (Philippians 3:14, NLT).

Prayer: Oh God, give me the strength to finish the race. Give me your strength to endure the obstacles that I may finish well for your glory. Amen.

Tidbits:

> "Not only so, but we also glory in our sufferings, because we know that suffering produces perseverance, perseverance, character; and character, hope." – Romans 5:3-4, NIV

> "The readiest way to escape from our sufferings is, to be willing they should endure as long as God pleases." – John Wesley

> "You need to persevere so that when you have done the will of God, you will receive what he has promised." – Hebrews 10:36, NIV

> "Then let us all do what is right, strive with all our might toward the unattainable, develop as fully as we can the gifts God has given us, and never stop learning" – Ludwig van Beethoven

> "Endurance is not just the ability to bear a hard thing, but to turn it into glory." – William Barclay

Song Suggestion: Running – written by Scott Ligertwood, Matt Crocker; performed by Hillsong

SUBMISSION OR HONOUR?

"Submit to one another out of reverence for Christ." – Ephesians 5:21, NIV

The concept of submission sadly conjures up an impression of superiority or domination and is not well received in today's society. Even within the Christian realm, it is misunderstood. The dictionary defines submission as bowing down to, surrendering to, deferring to or to succumbing to the power of another. The world views submission as a weakness and expects one to exercise their rights, strive for superiority, and crush your opponents, proving that all that matters is one's self, 'numero uno.' This selfish concept is far from what the Bible teaches and negative connotations are not what God intended. Even after years of living a Christian faith, many women still struggle with the biblical view of submission. In particular, Ephesians 5:22, NIV, where it says, "Wives submit to your husbands." God did not mean for woman to be dominated by, owned by, or enslaved by a man. Nor when He said, "slaves obey your earthly masters" did He imply for the masters to be slave drivers, or superior tyrants. I believe that submission is related to honour. "Honour one another above yourselves" (Romans 12:10b, NIV).

Submission is always used in the context of authority. God designed an order of authority throughout His entire creation, and He is the highest authority. "We must obey God, rather than men." Personal submission is simply voluntarily yielding to another with an obedient heart and with an attitude of cooperation and support. Scripture does not support us being trampled upon like a doormat. Philippians 2:3, NLT, says, "Don't be selfish; don't try to impress others. Be humble, thinking of others as better than yourselves." This is opposite to the world's view of being 'numero uno!"

At one point in our marriage, when things were a bit difficult, a wise pastor advised me, "If you want to be treated like a Queen, treat your husband like a King." Certainly a difficult principle to consistently practise, especially if you have hardened your heart to the spirit's leading, yet I have proven it to be true, for I now most often live with a King. However, this King and Queen fail repeatedly and often treat each other like paupers. This is where our marriage survives only by the grace of God. Regardless of how we feel, we recall our vows spoken before God, submit to Him and then to each other, forgive one another, and once again honour one another as God commanded. Only because of our commitment to put God first do either of us find the strength and faith to continually recommit to our marriage. In time, with repetition of these steps, to God and to each other, do our cloudy times appear less often and our love for each other and God grows deeper.

Any authentic relationship—you and Christ, you and your spouse, your family and friends—can only deepen with a consistent demonstration of mutual respect and honouring of one another. Submission, to me, is not a dirty word. Selfishness does not bring success, only failure, but honour and respect reap bushels of love.

Prayer: Almighty God, thank you for the gift of my husband and the unselfish ways in which he cares for me. Strengthen him as he supports me through this cancer journey. Thank you for teaching us how to love one another unconditionally and for helping us to put each above ourselves. Thank you for being the example of sacrificial love and forgiving our sins. You do exceedingly abundantly beyond anything we ask. I worship and adore you for you alone are worthy! Amen.

Tidbits:

> "Submission is not about authority and it is not obedience; it is all about relationships of love and respect." – Wm. Paul Young

> "Let every soul be subject unto the higher powers. For there is no power but of God: the powers that be are ordained of God." – Romans 13:1, KJV

> "The reason why many are still troubled, still seeking, still making little forward progress is because they haven't yet come to the end of themselves. We're still trying to give orders, and interfering with God's work within us." – A.W. Tozer

> "Submit yourselves, then, to God. Resist the devil, and he will flee from you." – James 4:7, NIV

> "You cannot fulfill God's purposes for your life while focusing on your own plans." – Rick Warren

> "How you respond to authority over you says a lot about what you claim to believe. When your standard of living is Christ-centered, you invariably live to honour others." - Kevin Thoman

Song Suggestion: The Marriage Prayer – written by John Waller, Patrick Morely

JESUS, MY DELIVERER

"I love you, O LORD, my strength. The LORD is my rock
and my fortress and my deliverer, my God, my rock, in whom
I take refuge, my shield, and the horn of my salvation, my
stronghold." – Psalm 18:1–2, ESV

I have had a recent dry spell in my 'blogging' basically for two reasons: One,
my last chemo infusion was quite intense, and I didn't bounce back or have
the stamina to study, pray or write each day. Thankfully the Holy Spirit provides
intercession when we have only groans to offer. Praise God that He knows our
needs before we even think of them. Secondly, my devotional base has been
largely reliant on the gospel songs that friends on Facebook shared with me
during this year's cancer journey, and the list that remains is quite short and
the themes so repetitive I am somewhat unsure of what I have already written
and fear repeating myself. However, I so missed the daily communion with the
Lord during these personalized study times, I decided that even if my 'blogs'
are repetitive, it is not necessary that I publish them all, and that we as frail
forgetful people can benefit greatly from hearing the Word again, again and
again. If ever there was a week that I needed to recognize God as My Deliverer,
it was this past one. I was totally unprepared for this second chemo protocol
and the upheaval to my body: vomiting, lack of appetite, constipation, diarrhea,
metallic taste in my mouth, lack of stamina, mobility and an unexpected need
for rest. Not only does my body require deliverance, but so does my mind. Being
physically exhausted increased my desire to be delivered from the jaws of this
earth as I became war weary. This is the very time I need to trust God to be
the unshakable rock, mighty fortress, impenetrable shield and my everlasting
stronghold. This is the time to run, not walk—not away from, but towards the
Deliverer. "The righteous cry out and the Lord heard them; He delivers them
from all their troubles. The Lord is close to the brokenhearted and saves those
who are crushed in spirit" (Psalm 34:17-18, NIV).

Deliver means to be rescued, and I plainly see the saving illustration of
Jesus snatching Peter and pulling him out of the waves when he is sinking and
his faith was weak.

Deliver means to be given strength. While Samson pulled away from God,
ditched his morals and took temporary companionship with the enemy, God
provided him with divine strength to be used for His glory, to the point of death.

Deliver means to provide safety. When Saul's army was breathing down
David's very neck for over forty years with purpose of killing him, God provided
divine protection.

Deliver means to be provided with impenetrable hope. Though Job's possessions were destroyed and he suffered innumerable calamities, he remained
steadfast in hope and his worship of God. The Israelites were delivered from

slavery and Jonah found himself with a second chance to be obedient when he was spewed from the stomach of the whale. Daniel was spared from the jaws of the lions, and Shadrach, Meshach and Abednego were spared from even a simple singe of flame from the fiery furnace.

We may not consider ourselves comparable to the biblical heroes God delivered, but God does have a plan for us, just as He did for them. His plan for us is higher than anything we know or understand. That's why He will also deliver.

We may each deal with disobedience, failure and rebellion, yet God loves us unfailingly and offers mercy, forgiveness and deliverance. Jesus, my deliverer, has the power to overcome sin, devilish dangers, worldly influence, deceitful hearts, temptation forces and damnation. Jesus delivers me freely, repeatedly and effectually and always in His perfect time. Jesus has promised to respond whenever I call upon His name and He provides the means to overcome anything that might hinder Him from working things out for His glory. When hardship comes we need to run to Jesus who is our deliverer, for He is the only stabilizing factor that will get us through the pain and trials we face.

Prayer: Heavenly Father, as I struggle through the pain and physical discomfort, help me to focus on my spiritual need to remain steadfast in my faith with unmovable trust and impenetrable hope. All of deliverance is in you! Amen

Tidbits:

> "He is my loving God and my fortress, my stronghold and my deliverer, my shield, in whom I take refuge, who subdues peoples under me." – Psalm 144:2, NIV

> "Never forget that God is far more interested in our getting to know the Deliverer than simply being delivered." – Beth Moore

> "The LORD is my rock, my fortress, and my deliverer." – Psalm18:2a, NIV

> "Out of suffering comes the serious mind; out of salvation, the grateful heart; out of endurance, fortitude; out of deliverance faith." – John Ruskin

> ". . .come quickly to me, O God. You are my help and my deliverer; Lord, do not delay." – Psalm 70:5, NIV

Song Suggestion: My Deliverer – written by Mandisa

I WILL NEVER
LEAVE YOU ALONE

"Never will I leave you; never will I forsake you." – Hebrews 13:5b, NIV

I just shiver with goose bumps when the presence of God is so clearly evident that there is absolutely no denying, 'that was a God moment." Yesterday in my blog, I stated the reason for my recent 'blogger's block' was a result of the list of songs that had been shared with me as means of encouragement was shortening. In response, a dear friend sent a 'comfort' song called, "I Will Never Leave You Alone" by Janet Paschal. This morning's study on loneliness had already commenced when the call of nature summoned and brought a temporary stall to my study. While enthroned on the great white, I picked up the quick devotional and there was my 'God moment' and His loving confirmation. . . "Never will I leave you; Never will I forsake you." Goosebumps! Praise! Charles Spurgeon said, 'It is impossible for English (transcription) to give the full weight of the original Greek, but the verse should read, "I will never, never leave thee; I will never, never, never forsake thee." Repetition intensifies the message, just as when David found victory in the slaying of Goliath, with but one stone, yet it is recorded he picked up five. When the angels declare "Holy, Holy, Holy, the Lord God Almighty," we see how repetition serves a great purpose.

Have you ever felt like you were alone? Loneliness is something that many people struggle with. My mind takes me back to my childhood when I spent darkened long lonely nights in fear of mice. Just why God brought this example to mind shows His sense of humour, but I suppose there is no greater loneliness than that of a child feeling abandoned and alone in the dark, which if you have not experienced personally, maybe you have comforted your own children or a grandchild through 'the ghost' in the closet stage. I remember sharing a large bed with my sister, and for some reason I have a visual recollection of each foot on my poster bed sunk in a bucket of water and a mountainous piling of sheets and blankets on top, so not even an edge would reach the floor with the purpose of keeping the little furry varmints from disturbing our sleep. Literally decades have passed, and I pondered whether my memory served me well, or it was just childhood imagination gone wild when we had the opportunity to visit our 1886 Wigle homestead and view its restoration when I noticed the old wooden door to the third floor attic area, just a room's length away from our childhood bedroom, and the small chewed-out corner that still remained from the mid-1900s, giving confirmation to my childhood fear. While I may have felt very alone, I was not alone. My family was near and God is always nearer.

Childhood memories are very potent, and they have the capacity to shape and form us as we move through into adulthood; they can also form our understanding and experience of God. Despite my temporary 'mice nightmare,' I knew from simple Bible school teaching that I was never truly alone, for God never leaves us no matter what we do or don't do. He is with us always.

While our retirement dreams have been short lived to date, and our lives are in a somewhat temporary holding pattern during my battle with cancer, it is very clear to me that He has not abandoned me. He will never leave or forsake me. There is a comfort zone that is indescribable, satisfying, fulfilling and complete in knowing Jesus and standing on this specific promise. I realize, regardless of my circumstances, that God is good and He loves me. He is in total control, and I am abundantly blessed far beyond what I deserve. And the truest of life's riches is daily in my grasp, because my treasures are in heaven and not worldly wealth or health.

Tidbits:

"A man forsaken of men may still entertain some hope. But let him be forsaken of God and then hope hath failed; the last window is shut; not a ray of light now streams into the thick darkness of his mind." – Charles H. Spurgeon.

"It is the Lord who goes before you. He will be with you; he will not leave you or forsake you. "Do not fear or be dismayed." – Deuteronomy 31:8, ESV

"The most important lesson that I have learned is to trust God in every circumstance. Lots of times we go through different trials and following God's plan seems like it doesn't make any sense at all. God is always in control and he will never leave us." – Allyson Felix

"And behold, I am with you always, to the end of the age." – Matthew 28:20b, ESV

"Just as I was with Moses, so I will be with you. I will not leave you or forsake you" – Joshua 1:5b, ESV

Song Suggestion: I Will Never Leave You Alone – written by Janet Paschal

GRATITUDE ATTITUDE

"This is the day that the LORD has made; let us rejoice and be glad in it." – Psalm 118:24, ESV

I found something very comical today in my study where Martin Luther said: "You cannot stop birds from flying over your head, but you can keep them from making nests in your hair." What's humorous is the fact the my previous cancer treatments have left me with a predominantly gray curly mop-like head of hair very different both in colour and texture from the hair I had before. I can just picture the birds desiring to make a handsome nest, and from there I visualize the ill-dreaded white slime deposit, yes, those yucky ones, sliding down each temple, making my appearance even more hideous. It may be a warped sense of humour, but it is comical all the same. I have always desired to have hair with body and curls, but it certainly wasn't through cancer, nor was I wishing for it to be grey in colour. One has to appreciate God's humour in that. My point being that each and every day the Lord gives us breath, and for that reason alone, we should be filled with a gratitude attitude. Our indebtedness to God is enormous, and yet we rarely offer thanks, especially when things are not going our way.

As a cancer patient, I don't think there is anything more frustrating than when a friend visits and proceeds to complain about their hangnails, stubbed toes and even broken fingers, for those are simple controllable discomforts while cancer chooses to eat away, out of control, in portions of my body.

The disease of the lepers was one where complaint was warranted. They suffered not only physical pain, but also found themselves shut out and cast away from society. Friends didn't even come to visit, and worse yet they pronounced "unclean, unclean" when they passed by a leper on the roadside. They lived exceptionally lonely lives.

The same can be paralleled with a lost sinner who is today not welcome in the church or Christian circles, and who, in our ignorant opinion, is certainly not the person to be found strolling next to Jesus. Yet, why exactly did Jesus come? And who exactly are we? When Jesus passed by, the lepers exclaimed "Master, have mercy on us." Jesus told them to show themselves to the priests and they were cleansed—all ten of them—and though each of them uttered the same prayer for healing, and were granted their request, only one of the ten returned to offer praise and gratitude.

A familiar Baldwin cartoon shows a long line of people at the; 'Complaints' window and none at the 'Gratitude' window. Unfortunately, this is a fairly accurate picture for the majority of us who live in a prosperous land and society where we find more reasons to complain than for which to be thankful. Regardless of life's circumstances, God expects us to show gratitude, and He is certainly deserving of our praise, even when we have been allowed a disease like cancer.

Cancer has forced me to reflect over my life and find an attitude of gratitude for all of it, especially the fact that our family has been extremely blessed with good health and spiritual wellbeing. Cancer has required me to recognize the brevity of life and to be thankful for even the smallest of blessings—the hug of a grandchild or their simple eyes searching mine with concern and asking, "Are you ok, Nana?" Cancer has provided me a broad opportunity to share my faith with hundreds and to proclaim that the reason for authentic Christian living is Jesus Christ and Him alone. Cancer has caused me to cultivate a day-by-day growth in my relationship with Jesus that I would trade not even for restored health. Now don't think that isn't a hard one, to desire a miracle and stay with my family or to have this close walk with Jesus. Honestly, it has been a precious journey with Him and I would love to have both. All the same, I never want to be found, for whatever days my Lord chooses to grant me here to breathe, without an attitude of gratitude. Contentment doesn't come with having it all, but by being thankful in all things and despite all circumstances.

Tidbits:

> "Let the message of Christ dwell among you richly as you teach and admonish one another with all wisdom through psalms, hymns, and songs from the Spirit, singing to God with gratitude in your hearts." – Colossians 3:16, NIV

> "When it comes to life the critical thing is whether you take things for granted or take them with gratitude." – G.K. Chesterton

> "The LORD strengthens and protects me; I trust in him with all my heart. I am rescued and my heart is full of joy; I will sing to him in gratitude." – Psalm 28:7, NBV

> "For today and its blessings, I owe the world an attitude of gratitude." – W. T. Pukiser

> "For everything God created is good, and nothing is to be rejected if it is received with thanksgiving." – 1 Timothy 4:4, NIV

Song Suggestion: Still Feelin' Fine – written by Mosie Lister

OPEN UP THE HEAVENS

"The LORD will open the heavens, the storehouse of his bounty, to send rain on your land in season and to bless all the work of your hands." – Deuteronomy 28:12, NIV

The refrain of the song selection for today starts this way: "Open up the heavens" and continues with lyrics pleading that God would show his love. What exactly does this dialogue mean? I believe it is the hope of experiencing some of heaven here on earth. We can experience the heavens as it rains down blessings and also for the floodgates of God's heart to overflow with love for each of us. But experiencing a taste of heaven on earth requires a commitment on our part to believe in God and his Word, also that the Word of God is complete and infallible. This is the most important step as it is backed up by God himself, and every promise in the book will come to pass if we just believe what it says. If you don't believe the Word then you have no basis to believe that a divine miracle will happen in your life.

Unfortunately, today we tend to want to analyze, dissect and put reasoning behind the blessings and miracles of God instead of just accepting them in simple faith. You are either on the side of belief or the side of unbelief, and unbelief will produce nothing because you expect nothing.

Secondly, to open the floodgates of heaven we need to do something. The lepers didn't sit at the city gate waiting to die, but they pushed forward and begged God for mercy. Abraham didn't wallow in self-pity when sent to sacrifice His son Isaac on the altar, but he stepped forward in obedience, and God provided the appropriate offering to replace his son. The statement, God helps those who help themselves, is not scriptural but it makes a good point about taking action towards the goals desired. That doesn't mean taking total control but to take action.

Your action may not seem logical, but God can work blessings out of the most stressed of circumstances. Maybe you've heard the story about the day a farmer's donkey fell down into a well, cried piteously for hours, and finally the farmer decided the animal was old, hardly worth retrieving, and began to cover him up. He invited all his neighbours to help him and they all grabbed a shovel and began to shovel dirt into the well. At first, the donkey realized what was happening and cried out in horror. Then, to everyone's amazement, he quieted down. A few shovel loads later, the farmer peered down the well and was astonished at what he saw. With every shovel of dirt that hit his back, the donkey was doing something amazing! He would shake it off and take a step up. The farmer's neighbours continued to shovel dirt on top of the animal, and the donkey continued to step up. Pretty soon, everyone was amazed as the donkey stepped up over the edge of the well and trotted off.

In Hebrews 11:6, NLT, we read, "And it is impossible to please God without faith. Anyone who wants to come to him must believe that God exists and that he rewards those who sincerely seek him." He wants to minister to the whole person body, soul and spirit, and God always honours His Word. We can trust what the Word says, but we must take a step of faith and do something if we want the floodgates of blessings pour from the heavens.

I know that I am the daughter of the Most High God. I am loved, redeemed and renewed. God has plans for me that include hope not harm; blessings not banishment. God knows me thoroughly, and even so He loves me completely. I am chosen, blameless and holy through the blood of Christ. I was bought with great price and I belong to Him. In faith I believe that the He has many more floodgates to open on my behalf and I will accept them in faith and with grace.

Prayer: Heavenly Father, might I be so tuned into your Word and you personally, through connection in prayer, that it is impossible for me to miss out on the floodgates of heaven being opening and raining down your abundant blessings. Amen.

Tidbits:

> "Jehovah doth open to thee His good treasure - the heavens - to give the rain of thy land in its season, and to bless all the work of thy hand." – Deuteronomy 28:12, YLT

> "You heavens above rain down my righteousness; let the clouds shower it down. Let the earth open wide, let salvation spring up, let righteousness flourish with it; I, the LORD, have created it." – Isaiah 45:8, ISV

> "All the blessings we enjoy are Divine deposits, committed to our trust on this condition, that they should be dispensed for the benefit of our neighbours." – John Calvin

> "So be truly glad. There is wonderful joy ahead, even though you must endure many trials for a little while." – 1 Peter 1:6, NLT

> "Ask God's blessings on your work but don't ask Him to do it for you." – Dame Flora Robson

Song Suggestion: Open Up the Heavens – written by James Macdonald, Jason Ingram, Stuart Garrard, Andi Rozier, Meredith Andrews

HOW GREAT IS THE LOVE

"See what great love the Father has lavished on us, that we should be called children of God! And that is what we are!" – 1 John 3:1, NIV

The topic of love has been covered several times in my devotionals, and one would think that you would be able to exhaust the topic and yet the love of our Saviour is inexhaustible. Immeasurable! Unfathomable! Unlimited! Boundless! Ceaseless! Eternal! The words to describe the love of God are nearly as inexhaustible as His love itself.

Have you ever felt lavished in love by someone? I can think of several kind gestures where my husband has displayed his love for me, some impressive and others simplistic. Two weeks before the delivery of our twin boys, he decidedly expressed love by purchasing a dishwasher that would eliminate my need for hand washing bottles and everyday dishes. This was one of the most treasured gifts I have received since it really lightened my everyday load of domestic responsibilities. It was a gift of genuine thoughtfulness. Many years later, he gave me a sapphire diamond ring for Christmas. I remember the magnitude of the effort he put into wrapping the gift in one container after another so that it finally fit into the large dishwasher size box. The wrapping ordeal, or should I say unwrapping ordeal, was just as impressive as the actual ring. You have to understand his hatred of wrapping gifts to appreciate the thought, let alone the fact that he detests shopping to any degree. Lately, it has been the simplistic ways in which he is demonstrating his love, such as bringing in a simple cutting of a flower in my garden—which he is now faithfully tending to—and placing the flower in our bay window for me to treasure, or in offering me the first fruits of our trees and bounty from his garden. He loves me and demonstrates that love in the way that suits his character, but I can guarantee that it does not even come close to the love the Saviour has for me.

God has lavished us with love and He didn't have to. When He created Adam, He could have created man in His exact image. Instead he chose to create man in his likeness, but give them a free will. Therefore empowering us with the ability to believe, trust, love, and obey, all on our own accord. He does not command our love, and He is under no obligation to love us in return and yet how great is His love for us that we should be called His children. God is under no obligation to love us or even to save us. He owes us nothing but blesses us continually nonetheless. All of this represents who He is. God is love!

God not only planned our lives far before we were created, but He also designed a plan where we could choose to love and honour Him for eternity.

He sacrificed His only Son, Jesus Christ, on the cross of Calvary and then raised Him to life again, thus laying the groundwork of His salvation plan. By repenting of our sins and accepting, in faith, the sacrifice of Christ as personal payment, we are forgiven and from that day forward "should be called children of God." On that day when the Lord appears, we will see Him as He is and the highly anticipated portion of God's plan is that we shall be like Him. My aging, cancer-ravaged body will be exchanged for a glorious body like His, with no aches, pains, diseases, and even no wrinkles. No need for pills, chemo, radiation, blood tests or injections. The gift of a perfect body and eternal life demonstrates how great is our Saviour's love.

Prayer: Heavenly Father, in the routine of everyday life help me to remember the magnificent price you paid for my redemption. Might I always be ready to be found with a testimony of your great love and possess the courage to share it so that others may come to know you as their own personal friend and Saviour. Amen.

Tidbits:

> "For God so loved the world that he gave his one and only Son, that whoever believes in him shall not perish but have eternal life." – John 3:16, NIV

> "Love means doing all we can, at whatever cost to ourselves, to help people be enthralled with the glory of God. When they are, they are satisfied and God is glorified." – John Piper

> "But because of his great love for us, God, who is rich in mercy, made us alive with Christ even when we were dead in transgressions - it is by grace you have been saved." – Ephesians 2:4-5, NIV

> "The love of God is like the ocean, you can see its beginnings, but you cannot imagine its width and depth. God loves you immensely in a way you can never imagine." – Ritu Ghatourey

Song Suggestion: How Great Is the Love – written by Jacob Sooter, Meredith Andrews, Paul Baloche

PRAISE YOU WITH THE DANCE

"Let them praise his name in the dance: let them sing praises
unto him with the timbrel and harp." – Psalms 149:3, KJB

C oming to faith in the early 70s under the umbrella of a Baptist faith, the
mention of the word "dance" raised many a frowning eyebrow. Primarily
they refrain because of what is associated with dance: bars, dance halls, drinking,
and the fact that much dance is provocative and equated with dirty dancing,
consequently far from conveying a pure spirit before the Lord. Baptists are not
alone with their conviction about refraining from dance, but neither are they
united on the subject. In fact, in many evangelical circles today, there is much
interpretative dance being used in celebration of praise to the Lord. I firmly
believe that this is a controversial subject that lends itself to the studying of
God's Word and personal conviction.

Not having been raised in church, I could not understand why dancing was
bad and found it most confusing when neither did any of my fellow brethren
when they were asked. "You just didn't do it." I danced at two of our four
children's weddings, and would sometimes awkwardly shuffle to the dance floor
at other celebrations, much to the dismay of some. Yet, I don't believe that my
choice of freedom in this area in any way condemns me to hell. I do hold certain
standards, with whom and to what I will dance to, but for the most part, my
convictions to refrain from dancing are simply with the purpose of not being
a stumbling block to others of faith who have different convictions. You may
totally disagree, and you are entitled to your opinion, but I encourage you to
base your conviction on your own personalized study and not the 'because we
just don't' theology. It is unfortunate that dancing is perceived by many in the
Christian world as taboo when scripture gives us biblical basis for dancing. In the
Old Testament, dancing was permitted during a time of victory celebration or in
the presence of God to represent one's own worship, praise and joy in the Lord.

David spoke in the Psalms about a time of mourning having been turned
into a season of gladness and dancing because of answered prayer; he used it as
an expression of his gratitude. The King of Israel and King of Judah sought to
destroy the rebellious King of Moab, and without consulting God, they marched
their fully armed soldiers across the valley. When they were but halfway, they
found themselves and their horses parched and thirsty. Realizing they couldn't
survive for very long, they called on Elisha, who called on a musician, for God
had told them that before He would respond, they must worship, praise, dance,
and rejoice before the Lord and they did as God commanded.

Have you ever stopped from your hectic life long enough to gaze at nature and wonder how it giving praise to its Creator? How about staring at a magnificent tall and strong maple tree with its lush and full green leaves and watch the trunk gently twist and sway in the wind while the outstretched branches continue in circular motion. There's an imagery used in a song that indicates the appearance of the tree clapping its hands in a dance. How about while sitting at the massive ocean shoreline while you are stretched out on the smooth sandy beach gazing at the rapidly forming and reforming clouds. The clouds offer numerous shapes beyond our imagination, all the while you hear the consistent gentle sound of the surf gentling lapping against the shoreline with each wave whispering in perfect rhythm, Jesus, Jesus, Jesus! The ocean is praising the creator and dancing.

God calls us to worship and praise Him whether it is dancing, kneeling, raising our hands, or singing. God's approval of our worship style is worth more than the disapproval of fellow believers. Dance, with the pure spirit and righteous heart, can be used by the Holy Spirit to help us let go of our selfish pride and self-righteous bondage and simply worship Christ. David didn't need a dance instructor, yet was he was moved in a spontaneous moment of emotion and praised God while he danced.

Tidbits:

"Praise God in his sanctuary; praise him in his mighty heavens. Praise him for his acts of power; praise him for his surpassing greatness." – Psalm 150:1-2, NIV

"Life isn't about waiting for the storm to pass. . .It's about learning to dance in the rain." – Vivian Greene

"You turned my wailing into dancing; you removed my sackcloth and clothed me with joy, that my heart may sing your praises and not be silent. Lord my God, I will praise you forever." – Psalm 30: 11-12, NIV

"I see dance being used as communication between body and soul, to express what it too deep to find for words." – Ruth St. Denis

Song Suggestion: Praise You with this Dance – written by Mark Hall, performed by Casting Crowns

HOW GREAT IS OUR GOD

"Now to Him who is able to do far more abundantly than all that we ask or think, according to the power at work within us. . ." – Ephesians 3:20, ESV

It has been a few days now since I have blogged in relation to my list of songs, those shared by many beloved friends and family throughout my cancer battle, for it has slowly decreased to three, and while our praise and worship of God should be endless, I find it difficult to compose new thoughts on subjects already covered. Today's theme, the greatness of God—along with God's other numerous characteristics—is an eternal attribute that my human mind, not having eternal comprehension is limited to, and prayerfully God will give me refreshing words to encourage you, and myself too, on the greatness of Himself. When I attempt to visualize the greatness of God, I am strolling on the banks of an ocean and casting my gaze over crystal clear calm waters; the naked eye scans the horizon which has no end, or perhaps I have been airlifted up above the clouds and the cottony white fluffiness goes on forever in a peaceful protective blanket covering the ugliness of the sin below. Whatever we envision to represent the greatness of God has its limitations, and yet the greatness of God is not limited, and its immeasurable capacity is hard for us to comprehend.

The time we spend in praising God our Father is healthy and beneficial to each and every child of God. Whether we are walking through the valley or flying high in the mountaintops, there is nothing greater than praising God. There is a chorus by Chris Tomlin called, "How Can I Keep From Singing" that reflects on singing in troubled times. My heart just overflows with appreciation and praise when majestic and descriptive songs like this and others declare the greatness of God. The Apostle Paul said, "Rejoice in the Lord always, and again I say rejoice." (Philippians 4:4, NIV) The psalmist said, "Rejoice in the LORD, ye righteous; and give thanks at the remembrance of His holiness" (Psalm 97:12, KJV).

You have probably uncovered some of these catchy phrases about God in your reading, but none of them capture the breadth, the length, the depth and the height of the love of Christ. God is like Ford. . . He's got a better idea. God is like Coke. . . He's the real thing. If you were to look them up, you would find more phrases, but these get the message across. They in no way begin to describe God's greatness for God is above all things. He is a God who deserves praise, He is worthy, and we ought to be a people who spend our days boasting of His greatness. God is love. God is light. He is the God of peace, and greatly to be feared. When was the last time you boasted of God's greatness?

Prayer: Heavenly Father, thank you for your greatness, your kindness, love and mercy, for you are everything to me. Help me to continually find praise for you and to worship you with all that I am until I draw my last breath. Amen.

Tidbits:

"There is none like you, O Lord; you are great and your name is great in might." – Jeremiah 10:6, ESV

"Seek not greatness, but seek truth and you will find both." – Horace Mann

"For great is the Lord, and greatly to be praised; he is to be feared above all gods." – Psalm 96:4, ESV

"It is about the greatness of God, not the significance of man. God made man small and the universe big to say something about Himself." – John Piper

"For the Lord, the Most High, is to be feared, a great king over all the earth." – Psalm 47:2, ESV

"There is greatness in the fear of God, contentment in faith of God, and honour in humility." – Abu Bakr

Song Suggestion: How Great Is Our God – written by Chris Tomlin, Ed Cash, Jesse Reeves

NEED YOU NOW

"You, God, are my God, earnestly I seek you; I thirst for you, my whole being longs for you, in a dry and parched land where there is no water. I have seen you in the sanctuary and beheld your power and your glory. Because your love is better than life, my lips will glorify you." – Psalm 63:1-3, NIV

Today was one of those overloaded days having a full chemo infusion treatment that was time pressured to complete eight bags of chemo cocktail dripping in for over five hours. The time lapse allowed for me to also obtain an outpatient appointment to have my abdominal cavity drained of 9 pounds and 4 ounces of fluid, which required another 2 hours of tubes. God was wonderful and kept the nausea away, and even the pain management had found a happy medium and allowed me to finish the treatments feeling quite well.

We arrived home to find our living room beautifully displaying our new carpet only to be overwhelmed when our vacuum beater bar snagged a straggling thread and tore up about ten feet of the seam. God, I need you now! Somewhat fearful that the carpet company would dispose of all the remnants and there would be no offer to repair it, I called only to find all three managers unavailable. Regrettably, I didn't maintain composure and unfairly cast poor judgment on them, before awaiting their response, and showed an unfavourable aggressive side that may have been triggered by the steroids that I take to ease nausea. Though that may be a valid excuse and justification, it is still not the character of a Christian, and I was brought to tears by my own immediate recognition of sin. I did offer my apologies to the kind receptionist, made my confession to God, and prayed that the outcome of both negatives would be used for His glory. Surely only He can do it.

Are you able to identify with David's words in Psalm 63:3,NIV "You, God, are my God, earnestly I seek you" or paraphrased, "I need you, God!" Travelling through my cancer journey, I cannot even begin to count the hundreds of times that I have echoed those words of despair. "I need you now!"

David had a particular time where one of his sons had turned against him and was trying to take away his kingdom and his very own life, and once again David found himself thrust back in the wilderness. In the face of crisis, there is only one person he desired, and that was God. David knew where to go to get all of his needs met, whether they were physical or spiritual. David held God in awe and had complete faith in Him because God alone had the power; David had already experienced the unfailing love of God.

Unlike us, whose love is so conditional and fickle, God's love is unconditional, unfailing and unwavering. During the course of David's life he often failed God and was unfaithful to God. Despite the fact that he slept with Bathsheba and murdered her husband, Uriah, God still loved him and still considered him to be His child. And like David, I know that God still loves me despite my daily failure to represent Him properly, and misrepresenting His tremendous love and mercy to others.

God made you and me; He knows our physical needs, and because He loves us, He has made arrangements for us to be taken care of. God is also fully aware of the spiritual needs that people have, foremost our need to be reconciled to God, for we are all sinners. As proof of his love and grace, God sent His son, Jesus, to die on the cross, and thereon take upon Himself the punishment for the sin that we deserve, and as a result the door was opened "that whosoever believes in Him will have eternal life." (John 3:16, KJV) Anyone who turns to Jesus in faith and repentance might come to have eternal life and peace with God. Those who truly have recognized their need for God demonstrate this by being active in seeking His forgiveness and accepting the plan of redemption personally. A long time ago, Augustine, being one of the early church fathers said "Our souls are restless till they find their rest in God."

Prayer: Heavenly Father, I am so thankful that your love requires nothing beyond our acceptance of your divine plan. We have nothing within ourselves that can ever endear us to you outside of believing that Christ paid it all. Amen.

Tidbits:

> "If the Spirit of him who raised Jesus from the dead dwells in you, he who raised Christ Jesus from the dead will also give life to your mortal bodies through his Spirit who dwells in you." – Romans 8:11, ESV

> "God is, even though the whole world denies him. Truth stands, even if there be no public support. It is self-sustained." – Mahatma Gandhi

> "Bless the Lord, O my soul, and forget not all his benefits: who forgives all your iniquity, who heals all your diseases." – Psalm 103:2-3, ESV

Song Suggestion: Need You Now – written by Tiffany Arbuckle Lee, Luke Sheets, Christa Wells, performed by Plumb

WE WON'T BE SHAKEN

"Truly He is my rock and my salvation; He is my fortress, I will not be shaken." – Psalm 62:6, NIV

The workplace, church, and even our Christian homes today are so full of drama, turmoil and controversy, leaving many excessively too stressed to provide for themselves and their family. That coupled with the world's growing corruption and immoral decline can lead to much insecurity about one's future. The devil labours and longs to see a Christian shaken from their roots to the point that they find themselves 'eternity insecure.' This often is a result of relying on one's feelings, yet we need to remind ourselves that regardless of how we feel, the Lord works all things for good and His light shines the brightest in the darkness.

Have you ever been frustrated with the humidity gathered in your salt shaker and tried feverishly to season your food when nothing would be shaken loose. We have tried inserting rice and toothpicks and found success to some degree, yet the holes eventually plug again. Our spiritual lives are somewhat like this, for when we stray from standing on the foundation of God's Word, and Satan manages to shake us, seasoning our minds with reoccurring doubt about making heaven. We are and will remain God's children surrounded by His divine protection. We can have confidence that God will keep us from falling. "To Him who is able to keep you from stumbling and to present you before His glorious presence without fault and with great joy" (Jude 1:24, NIV).

People go to great lengths to protect their homes by installing various electronics gadgets to keep evil at bay, but if we compare these actions to our salvation, we find Christ is our ultimate defense. He is our advocate, intercessor, payment for our sin and our righteousness before God, and we will not be 'shaken' because Christ is our foundation. Our faith will be tested and may sometimes falter, but nothing, absolutely nothing, will cause God to disown us or abandon us. Our salvation is a nonnegotiable contract, and while sin may influence some decisions we make, we will not be permanently scarred for the full price for our sin has already been paid.

Believers are not perfect and we will often choose a crooked path and lose a few battles along the way, but the war has been won. Though it does concern me with the inconsistency of some to claim to be Christian while having no interest in worship, biblical teaching, fellowship, Godly virtues, or acts of Christians service for how we live that verifies the authenticity of our faith, the world looks on in judgment of our confession and whether our walk matches our 'talk.' We're like Jerusalem—fortified and secure. We may wander like lost sheep at times, but the Good Shepherd will bring us back to the fold. We may slip and stumble, but God will hold on to us.

Following are some verses regarding this love:

I will not be shaken for I know that God is in control. "In the world you have tribulation. But take heart; I have overcome the world." (John 16:33, ESV)

I will not be shaken for I know that God will provide for my needs no matter what. "Cast all your anxiety on Him because He cares for you." (1 Peter 5:7, NIV)

I will not be shaken for I'm not living for me and my identity is not rooted in my profession or occupation but of who I am in Christ. "See what great love the Father has lavished on us, that we should be called children of God! And that is what we are!" (1 John 3:1, NIV)

Prayer: Heavenly Father, I thank you for the eternal security that you have provided through the sacrifice of your only Son and for the continued promises that fill me with blessed assurance of your unfailing love. Amen.

Tidbits:

> "I keep my eyes always on the LORD. With Him at my right hand, I will not be shaken." – Psalm 16:8, NIV

> "All the plots of hell and commotions on earth have not so much as shaken God's hand to spoil one letter or line He has been drawing." – William Gurnall

> "Surely the righteous will never be shaken; they will be remembered forever. They will have no fear of bad news; their hearts are steadfast, trusting in the LORD." – Psalm 112:6-7, NIV

> "Christians are like the several flowers in a garden that have each of them the dew of heaven, which, being shaken with the wind, they let fall at each other's roots, whereby they are jointly nourished and become nourishers of each other." – John Bunyan

Song Suggestion: We Won't Be Shaken – written by Jason Roy, Jonathan Smith, Casey Brown, Tim Rosenau, performed by Building 429

ALL IN THE FAMILY

"For just as each of us has one body with many members, and
these members do not all have the same function so in Christ
we, though many, form one body, and each member belongs
to all the others." – Romans 12:4-5, NIV

As I was contemplating today's blog based on "Mighty to Save," the lyrics
reflecting the need for compassion, unfailing love, and a Saviour. I
couldn't help but be reminded of the spiritual gifts that God has manifested in
each of His children with which to serve Him. During this year's annual family
vacation, my precious daughter-in-law, and God's naturally gifted administrator,
hung on the wall in the cottage an envelope for each family member with
instructions to write down on cue cards kind thoughts of each other. Then they
were to deposit those notes in the appropriate envelope. Even the youngest ones
were enthusiastic and participated by drawing pictures for all to enjoy. It was
delightful to witness spiritual growth even in the beginning stages of life as well
as with those whom we could call more mature, sometimes.

I marvelled at the work of God's hands and how He not only distributes
these gifts amongst the church body, but that He has placed much diversity of
gifts within our family to enable us to serve in almost all the gifts as well. We find
the gift of teaching, where a researcher of the Word is capable of illuminating
the truth and design it specifically to meet the needs of others.

Prophecy is present in a person who has the eyes of foresight into presence
of sin in the midst and the ability to know how to lovingly deal with it.

Discernment is an attribute found in a couple of our family members and
they have the ability to make detailed judgments about good and evil and give
sound godly advice to another usually having exceptional listening skills.

Ministering or the gift of service is where the servant's heart is motivated
by being the 'doer,' the hands of the body, and is content meeting specific
needs to whomever God brings across their path. These four gifts are strongly
represented in our male counterparts, and while some may have secondary gifts
that overlap with their stronger gifts, their diversity brings much to complete
the ministry possible within the context of each individual, each family unit,
and our family as a whole.

As for the women, their gifts are those of a more nurturing kind with motivational and specific acts of service. Our encourager uses her words carefully
so they are uplifting to the spirit and she motivates others to see the practical
and positive purpose to edify the body. She can usually be always found smiling
and in a friendly mood. Our givers are those with a true servants' heart, which is

very similar to the gift of help where they delight in being the arms of the body but desire to have their deeds done quietly without reward. Our best addition has been compassion which is most evident in a caring heart for everyone. My own primary gift has always been organization or administration and it is a great delight to see that God placed this motivational gift in a couple of others where I can now step aside to take care of my aging cancerous body. Two of the females strongly represent that gift of mercy. A merciful person senses the joy or distress in other people and is very sensitive to their feelings and needs.

What an awesome presentation of all of these various gifts being represented in our family unit. We have a great calling to maintain closeness to God so that the gifts are used with their positive attributes, and not those that produce negativity. I can personally confess to times when my own gifts have had negative results when a hidden agenda was my goal. The key is to stay centred on Christ, His love and compassion, His kindness and mercy, and in keeping the heart of a servant; we ourselves can minister to, and serve one to another.

Tidbits:

> "As each has received a gift, use it to serve one another, as good stewards of God's varied grace." – 1 Peter 4:10 ESV

> "In the New Testament, we don't find our gift through self-examination and introspection and then find ways to express it. Instead, we love one another, serve one another, help one another, and in so doing we see how God has equipped us to do so." – Russell Moore

> "Having gifts that differ according to the grace given to us, let us use them: if prophecy, in proportion to our faith; if service, in our serving; the one who teaches, in his teaching; the one who exhorts, in his exhortation; the one who contributes, in generosity; the one who leads, with zeal; the one who does acts of mercy, with cheerfulness." – Romans 12:6-8, ESV

Song Suggestion: Mighty to Save – written by Reuben Morgan, Ben Fielding, performed by Hillsong

LORD, YOU ARE GOOD

"For the Lord is good; His mercy is everlasting; and His truth endureth to all generations." – Psalm 100:5, KJV

I have just awakened to face another wonderful day, quite possibly one of a mother hen's best days. You see, my family arranged for us to share a condo in Collingwood, Ontario, for four full days under one roof, with nine bedrooms, three bathrooms, three large common rooms, a hot tub, and even an indoor swimming pool. What mother hen does not treasure her brood all in one place to bask in the glory of the nearest thing we have on Earth to unconditional love. I tiptoed across the second level upon my early rising, daring not to wake anyone from slumber at the predawn hours, knowing full well that the four teenagers are sure to sleep until at the very least the food bell or shopping excursion deadline is announced. At times like these, none of us have difficulty announcing to the world that "Lord, You Are Good," yet even when things are not going our way, God is still good. When we have been diagnosed with cancer, lost our job, faced financial collapse, lost all our belongings to fire, or are confronted with a simple but painful ingrown toenail, the Lord is still good. He is perfect, and in Him no evil or darkness can reside.

We all, with our human limitations, need to read and rely on scriptures to reaffirm this truth. Reading the many verses in Psalms that reiterate His absolute goodness, no matter what our circumstances, is a great way for us to plant our feet firmly on that belief.

"Praise you the LORD. Give thanks to the LORD, for he is good; his love endures forever" (Psalm 106:1, NIV) This verse is repeated almost verbatim in Psalm 107:1, Psalm 118:1, 29, and Psalm 136:1. "Praise the LORD; for the LORD is good: sing praises unto His name; for it is pleasant" (Psalm 135:3, NIV). "The LORD is good to all; he has compassion on all he has made." (Psalm 145:9, NIV).

Reading and repeating the several passages, affirming God's goodness, leaves us with worthy, uplifted and joyful feelings. Despite our own attempts to reaffirm that fact, there are thousands who struggle to believe it especially after the attacks of September 11th in New York City. Many have expressed that God allowed this act of terrorism as a vile judgment, or at the very least wonder why He didn't prevent it. We all have a deep desire to understand 'Why' and try to find how any goodness can come out of such tragedies, both large and small. Hundreds of circumstances contradict God's goodness, and though they may temporarily shake our faith, they should not destroy it. We believe because He *is* good, not because we feel He is. Because people are in so much pain and under stress in their lives, the most difficult truth sometimes for them to believe about Christianity is the idea that God is a good God!

The question is not whether God is or is not good, the problem lies in our perception of His goodness, and whether we choose to recognize it even in the midst of tragedies. As Paul said, "Now we see things imperfectly, like puzzling reflections in a mirror, but then we will see everything with perfect clarity." (1 Corinthians 13:12, NLT) Also "We can see and understand only a little about God now." We are often unwilling to accept our limitations and little understanding and, as a result, we stumble in our faith instead of walking with confidence. The problem is not: is God good? The problem is us. We want to set the terms, dictate how, when, and where He is good. We want to define His goodness according to our standards, all the while we are looking through a foggy, distorted mirror that distorted our reality of God's goodness. God is good through you and me. God shows His goodness to others. God is a good God, and He has good people who are full of good works, touching hurting lives in little deeds of kindness in an effort to alleviate pain and suffering. We are His hands extended to show others, that "Lord, You are Good."

Prayer: Heavenly Father, thank you so much that despite my diagnosis with cancer, time after time you have proven that you are good even in the darkest of circumstances. And you have promised to work out everything for our good so that you might be glorified. Amen.

Tidbits:

> "We are not necessarily doubting that God will do the best for us; we are wondering how painful the best will turn out to be." – C.S. Lewis

> "God is good. It is only by His grace that I am able to see a new day, to take another breath, to live this wonderful life. . ." – Unknown

> "I believe God is managing affairs and that He doesn't need any advice from me. With God in charge, I believe everything will work out for the best in the end. So what is there to worry about." – Henry Ford

Song Suggestion: The Lord Our God – written by Kristian Stanfill, Jason Ingram

THE GIFT OF CANCER

"For just as each of us has one body with many members, and
these members do not all have the same function, so in Christ
we, though many, form one body, and each member belongs
to all the others. We have different gifts, according to the grace
given to each of us." – Romans 12:4-6a, NIV

B efore blowing your mind and informing you about my sincere gratitude
for having cancer, though I have probably already blown your mind with
the title alone, I am going to focus on the body and its many members all having
different functions.

At a very early age, before puberty, I was treated for tonsillitis and ear
complications for several years and, ultimately, had to wear a hearing aid—which
I still wear today—to compensate for my hearing disability. Though I let my
vanity take precedence during my high school years and refused to wear the aid,
fortunately, I was able to read lips fairly well and studied hard on my own so my
grades didn't suffer. With my hearing not functioning at a reasonable capacity,
my other senses compensated, and now my extreme sense of smell frustrates
my husband to no end. The scent of a roaming skunk several miles away fills
my nostrils well before he notices, and I am constantly complaining about the
foul odour emanating from our sink or washing machine. Despite using multiple
treatments including vinegar wash to rid the pipes of the smell, it is still a regular
complaint for which he probably wishes we could find an easy solution. Maybe
pinching the nose closed with a clothespin?

The body of Christ functions very similarly to that of our personal bodies
where each member has a specific function to contribute to the entire well-being
of the body. The ear does not see, the eye does not taste, the tongue does not
hear and so forth. Just as God has created our bodies with intricate parts, each
having individual tasks, the body of Christ is comprised of the same. "Christ
gave gifts to men. He gave to some the gift to be missionaries, some to be
preachers, others to be preachers who go from town to town. He gave others
the gift to be church leaders and teachers. These gifts help His people work
well for Him" (Ephesians 4:11-12, NLV). We do not all look the same (that's
a good thing), do not all speak the same nor act the same, and in keeping with
our individuality, God has given each of us different gifts we are to use for the
good of the entire body.

This is where I can blow your mind away in giving thanks for the gift of
cancer. It is not a disease that anyone would choose to have, but I am thankful
to God for this gift primarily for the spiritual growth and the closeness I now

have with my Saviour. This has been a spiritual journey, dare I say, I would not trade because the majesty of Christ has been unveiled such as I have never experienced before. An additional positive is the privilege I have had to witness the different gifts of our church family being shared in ministry (as a gift to me), and others currently battling cancer or ill from other health complications. Some have organized meals, exercised their gift of hospitality; several ministered to me with cards containing words of exhortation, and some special friends showed their love and mercy through personal visits. My husband has probably been the best example of love and patience, and I thank the Lord for him. Each and every member who followed the nudging of the Holy Spirit has been a compassionate contributor to the ease of my journey, and though it is not mentioned in Ephesians, I am thankful for the gift of prayer. Literally hundreds have been praying for my recovery, and many of them I do not even know, but they are exercising the love of Christ in the most important function of all.

Prayer: Thank you, Jesus, for providing so many prayer warriors and those who you sent to me in other gifts of ministry. Bless them. Amen.

Tidbits:

> "There are different kinds of gifts, but the same Spirit distributes them. There are different kinds of service, but the same Lord. There are different kinds of working, but in all of them and in everyone it is the same God at work." – 1 Corinthians 12:4, NIV

> "Spiritual gifts are divine enablement for ministry, characteristics of Jesus Christ that are to be manifested through the body corporate just as they were manifested through the body incarnate." – John Macarthur

> "We never become truly spiritual by sitting down and wishing to become so. You must undertake something so great that you cannot accomplish it unaided." – Phillip Brooks

Song Suggestion: If We Are the Body – written by Mark Hall; performed by Casting Crowns

CHRIST AND CANCER

"For I consider that the sufferings of this present time are not worth comparing with the glory that is to be revealed to us." – Romans 8:18, ESV

I can remember that just a couple of years ago, I made a boasting comment to my husband on how blessed we were for our ideal health and that we were almost the only ones within our family demographics who were not relying on medications for health ailments. As one would say, "pride goes before the fall," it was in the Fall of 2012 that we were confronted with an uncertain future and an anxiety- filled diagnosis of cancer (the little "c"). While I do not believe that every sickness is necessarily a divine judgment on sin, or that failure to be healed is a sign of false faith, I have used this 'down' time to examine my heart and to fervently seek God's purpose in allowing this undesired distress.

In Romans 8:21, NLT we read, ". . .the creation looks forward to the day when it will join God's children in glorious freedom from death and decay," and since our bodies are part of creation, they, too, partake in all the decay and futility to which creation is exposed. As long as we remain on earth, our physical bodies are subject to deterioration and disease, but we can have a season or preview of physical renewal. The gift of eternal forgiveness and physical healing were purchased by Christ when He died for us on the cross, covering all of our sin. He can and does heal the physically oppressed, mentally exhausted and spiritually fragmented in answer to our prayers, but not always, and the hardest challenge you or I may have to face is in the waiting. In whatever way we find ourselves afflicted, in oppression or sickness, all of life's challenges are intended by God to increase our godliness, by reaching the bottom of our own resources and causing us to rely more on Him. His light is more apt to shine through us when ours is dimmed and shattered.

"We know that all things work together for the good of those who love God: those who are called according to His purpose" (Romans 8:28, HCSB). This passage gives us hope and reason to pray for strength to endure and faith to believe. His glory can be manifested in the healing of our disease, in the steadfastness of our faith, and in the peace that passes all understanding while we remain in a season of misery. We should always trust in the power and love of God, especially in our darkest hours of suffering.

Prayer: Heavenly Father, I ask forgiveness for my boasting and praise you as the giver of life. As I cope with this cancer diagnosis, both its realities and unknowns, I desire to lean on you and you alone with all that I am. I seek to discover the magnificent reason you have designed this path for me and desire each day that I be vigilant to share your incomparable love with others. Thank you for the numerous blessings already bestowed on me and for the undeniable peace that is from you. Amen.

Tidbits:

> "I can do all things through Christ who gives me strength." – Philippians 4:13, NIV

> "Every test in our life makes us bitter or better, every problem comes to make us or break us, the choice is ours whether to become victim or victor." – Unknown

> "We all know people who have been made much meaner and more irritable and more intolerable to live with by suffering: it is not right to say that all suffering perfects. It only perfects one type of person – the one who accepts the call of God in Christ Jesus." – Oswald Chambers

Song Suggestion: The Hurt and the Healer – written by Barry Graul, Bart Millard, Jim Bryson, Mike Scheuchzer, Nathan Cochran, Robby Shaffer; performed by Mercy Me

THE SANDMAN COMETH

"When you lie down, you will not be afraid; yes, you will lie down and your sleep will be sweet." – Proverbs 3:24, NKJV

It didn't take a rocket scientist to explain to me the necessity of a good night's sleep during my physical battle with cancer, and since my body's clock tends to be a midnight runner, I opted to use melatonin to help me in falling asleep—with the doctor's permission of course. Staying asleep has never been a problem for me, but getting there has been a struggle for several years. I know my genetic composition predisposed me to this 'counting sheep' dilemma since I have siblings and children who struggle with the same frustration—a brain that doesn't shut off. There were many nights prior to dealing with the depressing news of cancer—which causes any brain to work overtime—that I waited for the 'sandman to come.'

There are several hormones directly affected by sleeplessness, and they lessen our ability to fight cancer. The hormone, Cortisol, helps regulate the immune system, and it peaks at the break of dawn. It's proven that night shift workers have higher rates of breast cancer because their cortisol rhythm is shifted. This hormone is also called a 'stress' hormone and malfunctions during times of anxiety. Sleeplessness also leads to a decrease in our natural melatonin, which explains the wide use of this as a sleep aid in today's society. The lack of sleep is a merry-go-round where stress equals lack of sleep, equals low hormones, equals lack of sleep, equals inability to handle stress, equals stress, equals lack of sleep, and so on. Providing our body adequate time to rest is a key factor in helping people to deal with and fight cancer. It is proven that even taking small naps is greatly beneficial to our body's health. I am not recommending you commence a program of taking pills to help in getting a good night's sleep; that is something that you need to discuss with your doctor, especially when taking other medications. I share only because I want you to realize how very important it is to get proper rest. Might I suggest that you allow God to be your sandman?

King David suffered unimaginable stress when the jealous King Saul plotted his death in order to destroy David's popularity with the people. Absalom, his own son, sought to steal his throne, crown and kingdom from him, and yet David wrote in the Psalms how he could lay himself to sleep with complete peace, because he knew God would protect him. When you are struggling to shut your eyes, concentrate on the Psalms and release your stress to God in prayer. I cannot count the nights I have fallen asleep in the midst of prayer. God will use your restful periods to refresh your spirit, boost your immune system, and manufacture new brain cells for clearer thinking, then you will be ready to face another day head-on with Him. When we don't get enough sleep, our waking life is harder; we become depressed and maintaining healthy relationships, even with Christ, is more difficult. There are several healthy initiatives that can be taken in order to lead to restful sleep, simply search them out and apply the ones that prove to be a success for your own body.

The apostle Paul speaks to us about a different kind of sleep. When we shut our eyes in the sleep of death, we will not sleep forever, but we will be changed. We will be restored, resurrected; our bodies will be new and strong, and brilliantly like Jesus' body after His resurrection (1 Corinthians 15).

If you do not know Christ as your personal Saviour, this is a 'sandman' that you are not ready to meet. As for me, I am ready to be in heaven where there will be no more need for sleep, and I can allow my 'non-stop' brain to continually worship my majestic King, Christ Jesus. Praise God, 'the sandman cometh,' but this is the 'sandman' you must be ready for.

Prayer: Lord, I am so thankful that you never sleep, that when I am sleepless, you hear my prayers. I'm amazed to consider that you watch over me every second of darkness and of light. Thank you for the words of David that encourage us and increase our trust in you, because it worked for him in trials unimaginable. Help me to get the necessary rest each and every day so that my immune system can fight against the cancerous cells in my body. Amen.

Tidbits:

> "At this I awoke and looked, and my sleep was pleasant to me." – Jeremiah 31:26, ESV

> "In peace I will lie down and sleep, for you alone, O LORD, will keep me safe." – Psalms 4:8, NLT

Song Suggestion: Still, Be Still My Soul – written by Keith & Kristen Getty

PRAY

by Dawn Ure

"In the same way, the Spirit helps us in our weakness. We do not know what we ought to pray for, but the Spirit himself intercedes for us through wordless groans. And we know that in all things God works for the good of those who love him, who have been called according to his purpose." – Romans 8:26, 28, NIV

It isn't until one actually experiences the feeling of heart-wrenching pain that they can fully understand what God provided for us in giving us the Spirit that lives within us to intercede for us. At moments as horrific as this, often there isn't the ability to pray, sometimes all we can do is scream, whether that be auditory or just a screaming from the depths of our soul. I recall this feeling on the day of Mom's surgery, I remember sitting with my brother and Dad, anticipating a minimum of 4–6 hours wait. You can imagine the shock when, after just over an hour, the doctor himself walked to the waiting room and called out our name. . . "Dewhurst?" He guided us to a room down the hall from the waiting room, one that was obviously used for this type of conversation. Hearing the "I have cancer" diagnosis from our Mom, in the Fall of 2012, had nowhere near the same agony that the doctor's announcement brought. When she told us, though she was concerned herself, she portrayed it to her children as any godly mother would, with confidence in her Healer, and determination to one day be called a survivor. In those moments, she was more concerned about us than herself. But today. . . today is different. The doctor has no candy coating to offer, no words that could offer any comfort. His words cut like a sword, "The cancer has spread and there is nothing more we can do." Cue internal soul screaming! That was my first raw and desperate encounter with needing the Holy Spirit to that magnitude. The second would follow her death in the Fall of 2013.

God knew that there would be times when we were not able to put our soul screams into words. He knew that nothing in this world would offer any amount of comfort that would be sufficient in times like this. So He left us the Holy Spirit, who would both intercede for us and bring us comfort.

I think of Jesus himself as the time was drawing closer to the day of his crucifixion. Much like us now, with our Mom, He too knew it was coming. "My soul is overwhelmed with sorrow to the point of death" is what Jesus told His friends. So, what did He do? He went off to pray. The Bible states that He fell to the ground and pleaded with God that this "cup" be taken from Him.

Both at the news of the diagnosis and nine months later when the doctor advised us that it was terminal, did I fall to the ground, in a manner of speaking, and plead that God would take this situation away from us. Pleading for mercy. Begging for healing. Hoping for more time—much more time. But just like Jesus, we were willing to follow God's lead wherever it would take us, and her. And just like Jesus, it ended with death. But just like in the case of Jesus, we can say "Where, O death where is your victory? Where, O death is your sting?" (1 Corinthians 15:55, NIV) Just like Jesus, she will rise again.

Before Jesus left this place, He promised that His Father was sending the Holy Spirit. He knew that we would need the comfort that no one else could provide and He knew that our soul screams could only be understood and interpreted for us by the divine. I am thankful that through the journey alongside our mother that we, being believers, had the Holy Spirit with us.

Prayer: God I want to say thank you for giving us a comforter. Thank you that we have Jesus who experienced the same gut-wrenching pain of having to follow a master plan that we can't see or understand. I thank you that you are a God who is okay with our soul screaming, and love us unconditionally, even at those desperate moments when we have no words to say. Thank you, God, for giving us the Holy Spirit. Amen.

Tidbits:

> "And I will ask the Father, and He will give you another advocate to help you and be with you forever." – John 14:16, NIV

> "One cannot get through life without pain. . .What we can do is choose how to use the pain life presents to us." – Bernie S. Siegel

> "Abba, Father," he said, "everything is possible for you. Take this cup from me. Yet not what I will, but what you will." – Mark 14:36, NIV

Song Suggestion: Pray – written by Chris Rohman, Christopher Stevens, Matt Hammitt; performed by Sanctus Real

PERFECT PEACE AND REST

"He will wipe away every tear from their eyes. There will be no more death or mourning or crying or pain, for the old order of things has passed away." – Revelation 21:4, NIV

October 8th, 2013 – (Blog post on Facebook "Millie's Motivational" by daughter Dawn Ure)

In our present culture, aren't we are all longing for rest? While Mom awaits her eternal rest, which is likely just days away, we await rest from physical weariness and heavily laden hearts. The good news is that we can find the rest we desire. Then Jesus said, "Come to me, all who are tired from carrying heavy loads, and I will give you rest" (Matthew 11:28, GW)

Towards the end of last week, we came to the realization that the ravaging war of this disease over Mom's body was no longer one that we were equipped to fight. For her sake and ours, we felt that the next step in her process would be for us to place her in the care of those who are trained in caring for her at this tender stage. We were growing weary physically, and she deserved more care than we were capable of administering. By divine intervention, we received a room at Hospice Windsor, a home that specializes in caring for the dying and helping the family by making the most of the final stage of life with their loved one. As a family, though it is extremely difficult not to have her home, we are very grateful to be able to expend all of our energy on loving her which is what we know best, and want most, and to leave the medical care professionals to do what they do best. We ache to make the most of every minute that passes.

Mom's earthly body is very quickly failing her. She is immensely weak and requires our assistance in every movement. She is no longer walking, has not been able to eat for weeks now, and takes in very little fluid. We are in the final stretch, and so we are soaking up every moment as if each of them were more precious than diamonds. Though the fight has seemed as though it has lasted forever, it now feels as though we are moving faster than the speed of light toward the finish line. We are so very thankful that she remains free of any pain! We are humbled by your continued support, in prayers and otherwise.

May the blessings be poured back onto those who continue to pray, love and support us! We are humbled at your love for us.

October 10th 2013 – (Blog post by daughter Dawn Ure)

With incredible all-consuming sadness, we share the news that today, shortly before 9 a.m., our beloved mother passed away. Literally, just as her favourite hymn "Like a River Glorious" finished playing, she was welcomed into the arms of her Saviour and Healer!

Prayer: Precious Lord, in the midst of our grief "yet will we praise you." We will praise you for the life of our dear mother. We are thankful for the testimony of her life. We are humbled that you chose us to be her children. We know, God, that her life did, and will continue to bring you glory. We take comfort in knowing that every joy and trial falleth from above. Until we meet again, may we be found faithful. Amen.

Tidbits:

"Surely goodness and love will follow me all the days of my life, and I will dwell in the house of the Lord forever." – Psalm 23:6, NIV

"No one ever told me that grief felt so much like fear." – C.S. Lewis

"The Master was full of praise. 'Well done, my good and faithful servant. . . Let's celebrate together!" – Matthew 25:21, NLT

"For the Christian, death is not the end of adventure but a doorway from a world where dreams and adventures shrink, to a world where dreams and adventures forever expand." – Randy Alcorn

"Better is one day in your courts than a thousand elsewhere." – Psalm 84:10a, NIV

Song Suggestion: Like a River Glorious – by Frances R. Havergal

Like a river, glorious
Is God's perfect peace,
Over all victorious
In its bright increase;
Perfect, yet it floweth
Fuller every day,
Perfect, yet it groweth
Deeper all the way.

Stayed upon Jehovah
Hearts are fully blessed
Finding as He promised,
Perfect peace and rest.

Every joy or trial
Falleth from above,
Traced upon our dial
By the Sun of Love.
We may trust Him fully
All for us to do;
They who trust Him wholly
Find Him wholly true.

(1876, in the public domain)

THIS IS NOT WHERE
WE BELONG

"What no eye has seen, what no ear has heard, and what no human mind has conceived, the things God has prepared for those who love Him." – 1 Corinthians 2:9, NIV

November 10th, 2013 – (Blog post by daughter Dawn Ure)

Here we are. . . November 10th, 2013, and the first 30 days without Mum have passed. For all of us it still seems so unreal. Grief is an odd journey. In our immediate family, most of us, having not really experienced loss to this magnitude before, are still wandering somewhat dazed and confused.

Periodically through Mom's journey, people—including us kids—would send her songs that inspired us so that she could pour on them her words of devotion to add to her book and encourage us. This is a song that I had wanted to send to her many times but could never bring myself to do it, because it would make me resign to the idea that God might actually choose to take her, and I wasn't okay with that. Still today I struggle with my selfish wish for her survival, discouraged and disappointed with God's plan for her life, but I know that with my human eyes, it is impossible to see the whole purpose God had for her.

In 1 Corinthians 2:9, NIV, we read, "What no eye has seen, what no ear has heard, and what no human mind has conceived, the things God has prepared for those who love Him," (. . .and oh how she loved Him).

I am comforted that He promises in His precious Word to complete the work in us and so, whatever her purpose was. . . it was fulfilled.

> Philippians 1:6, MSG: "There has never been the slightest doubt in my mind that the God who started this great work in you would keep at it and bring it to a flourishing finish on the very day Christ Jesus appears."

It's hard to imagine that her work here on Earth was done. My hands tremble as I type and my chest heaves in sobs as my soul cries out. . . but we weren't done with her yet!

But for as much as I want her here, even more she wants us there. . .

We're not home yet. . . and home is where my Mom is!

The writer of Hebrews 13:14, NLT, says, "For this world is not our permanent home; we are looking forward to a home yet to come."

God bless everyone who loved her and shared in her journey.

My heart is sad, but my hope is eternal. Not only will I run one day into the arms of my loving Creator, but also to the woman who was used by God to be the birthing vessel of my life on Earth—my Mom.

Song Selection – Where I Belong – written by Jason Roy, Jason Ingram; performed by Building 429

CLOSING

In the preface, we consider the scientific possibility that we are an accident suspended between two accidents—life and death. And that the string that attaches the two is full of trouble. What if, by any chance, life is not an accident? What if a loving Creator made us, loves us, and desires us to really know Him? What if there is a purpose that is far beyond the string of trouble that attaches life to death? What if the hope that drives us to faith is the journey that we all must travel to learn, grow and love our Creator? Does that seem twisted, backwards or even cruel? Might I ask you: Why else would we put our faith in something without experiencing the need for it?

Jesus said, "In this world you will have trouble. But take heart! I have overcome the world." (John 16:33, NIV)

I know when trouble comes in my life, it brings anxiety, stress, insecurities, and fear. Why does a loving God allow fear to percolate among us? Is He not caring enough to know that this hurts us? What do I make of watching hopelessly as a loved one suffers? Why does the hope of healing and expressions of faith in prayer not end in healing? These are the questions my family had when my mother was taken from us by cancer.

It is a rare instance when a human, in the midst of the troubles of life, faces his or her fears and demonstrates true hope and faith.

This hope is found only in Jesus Christ. He is the only hope of saving us from our trouble with sin. If you believe in Him and live a life after Him, you too can experience this hope. My mother lived with this hope in life, and faith in death. She chose to allow the trouble on her journey to bring her closer to the Creator. For me, my mom exemplified having the most admirable faith during the storm of her life that would bring it to an end. My mom was, to me, a hero of faith in Christ.

I miss her, but I have assurance that at the end of my road of hope and faith, that I will see her again.

Fay's son, Wayne

PHOTOS

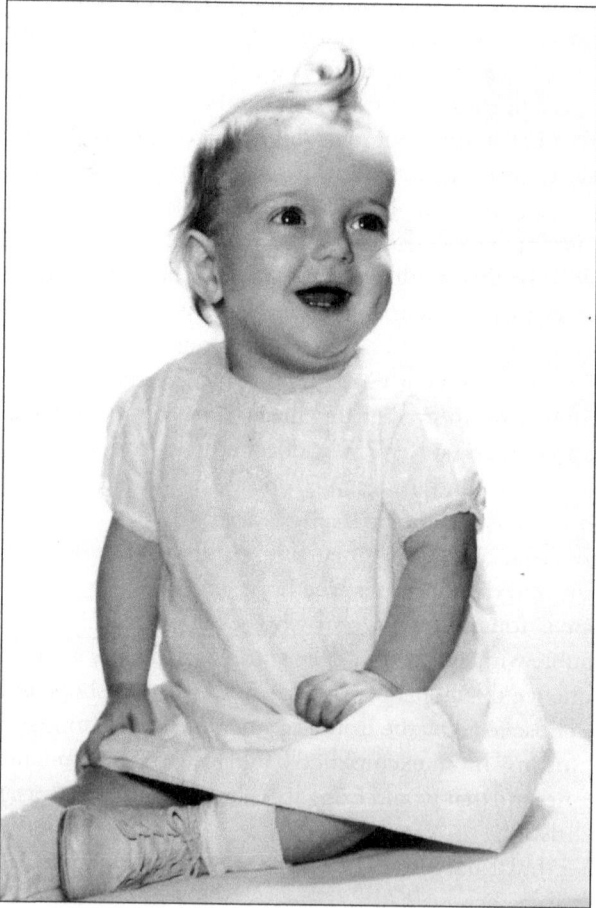

Faye Wigle was born in Kingsville, Ontario, on April 9, 1952.

Faye's mother, Verna Maxine Shaw Wigle Bullee, raised her, primarily as a single mother, along with her siblings, Marilyn, Ron, and Guy

Faye's graduation from Kingsville District High School

Wedding Day – August 23rd 1969 –
Married for 44 years to John Wesley Dewhurst

Family Photo, 1979

John & Faye, 2010

The Grandkids, 2010

John & Faye

The Grandkids, 2012

John & Faye with their 4 children
(right to left): Wayne, Mark, Dawn, Wesley

The Dewhurst Family

The Grandkids 2013

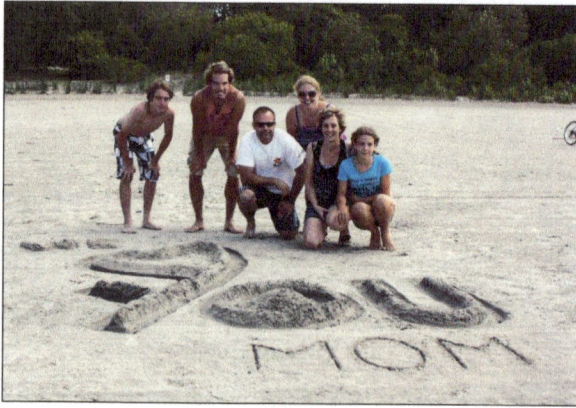

A message in the sand for Mom, August 2013

Her last walk through the yard, October 2013

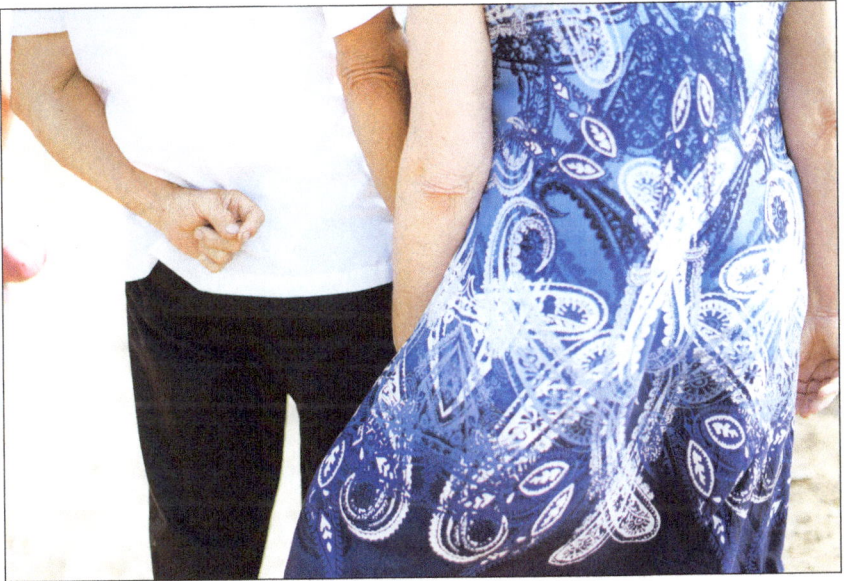

John & Faye - Until we meet again.

EULOGY

✦

October 14ᵗʰ 2013 – Thanksgiving Day
Eulogy for Mildred "Faye" Dewhurst written by her daughter Dawn Ure

***

On April 9ᵗʰ 1951, a firstborn daughter was born to Verna Shaw & Meryl Wigle. Born at just 3lbs., 12oz., her character of strength was required right from the start. Three siblings would follow, Ron, Marilyn and Guy. Following the death of her father at a young age, Faye became the second in command to her hard-working single mom. A one-room school house was where her early learning years began and, of course, she claims to have walked a mile each way (Probably uphill, but she didn't mention that part). Her early childhood memories recall many outdoor activities playing with neighbours, and even walking through manure and loving the feeling of it squishing between her toes.

Through her adolescent years, Faye excelled at both organized school sports, such as baseball, basketball, volleyball and track & field, as well as academics. She attended Kingsville District High School from 1965-1969, where she was the top student in her business class for 4 years in a row, and graduated with honours. As the song goes. . . "In the summer of '69," on August 23ʳᵈ she married her best friend, John. Without a formal proposal, she simply informed him that they were going to get married, claiming that if she waited for him, he would have never asked because he was just too shy. They moved into the family farm and resided in a very small house that was meant for the farm workers.

In the following years, with the leading of Eva Wiens & Sandi Dewhurst-Jamieson, she put her faith in Jesus Christ in the early 1970s, and was mothered with spiritual guidance from Bonnie Dawson for many years to come.

And this is when her own mighty legacy truly begins to unfold.

In the summer of 1972, while John was writing his mechanics exam in Windsor, she gave birth to their firstborn daughter. Dawn was a challenge and was great at polishing Mom's patience. In 1975, Mark was born at a very low birth weight and spent weeks in London Hospital. Mark is a mostly passive character which brought a much needed balance to the house. The twins, Wayne and Wesley were born in 1978 and filled her plate. With a 6-year-old, 3-year old, and twins, her life suddenly became nothing but parenting.

Thoughts of our childhood brings memories of outdoor play, farm wandering, playing with family and friends (which were never of any shortage around our house), amazing themed birthday parties with money cakes, cousins and friends, and well-thought-out family camping trips every year. Even a 3-day drive in the red station wagon to visit our cousins in Alberta, which is a trip with many interesting stories all of its own. Though she had only four biological children, there were many "unofficially" adopted children. Mom and Dad both claim to have wished that they had not allowed their finances to make their decision not to have any more children. Children were what made life worth living. By mothering all of these additional children, I believe that she accomplished what they had wished for.

Whether you were her own child, an "unofficially" adopted child, or a niece or nephew, she gave everyone the things necessary for survival. *Air:* with lots of farm fresh air and backyard fun. *Food:* particularly the cookie sheet full of chocolate chip cookies, and don't forget the refreshing glass of Kool-Aid made with sulfur water. *Shelter:* be it a tent in the backyard, a camper, or a mattress on the floor under a tent of sheets.

Her heart poured out love that knew no boundaries. But, if you fell into any of these categories you were also putting your life at risk for getting "the board." The board was a very well know correction tool that I think almost everyone who visited our home became a victim of. Though it was no fun to be in that line-up, we quickly learned the difference between acceptable and unacceptable behaviour, though not all of us learned quite as quickly as the others. I'm quite sure that Wes and Dawn wore off the veneer coating on it. Mom was never shy about making everyone "toe the line."

On top of performing the many tasks required of a stay-at-home mom, she also spent these years sharing her talents of organization and planning with others. She served in the AWANA ministry at New Testament Church & Calvary Baptist Church for 21 years, planned themed parties of all kinds, car rallies, euchre parties, mother and daughter banquets, Christmas concerts and plays, family reunions, games at every and any event, including murder mystery parties. She organized and participated in choir cantatas, played piano at church, and more. Her love for organizing and planning brought hundreds of people together in fellowship with each other. She created so many opportunities for people to enjoy life, meet others, and simply be in each other's presence. She was a vessel used by God to create community among people.

Over the past decade she and Dad enjoyed travelling and had the opportunity to visit places such as Alaska; Tennessee; Florida; California; Branson, Missouri;

Hawaii; Vancouver; Alberta; Australia; Nova Scotia; New York; Mexico, and many more.

Mom poured out her love and creativity on others like a flood. She was forever mailing birthday and Christmas cards with her famous Christmas letter. Her craftiness has left us with so many gifts which now have eternal value. There were "Faye" dolls, bedspreads, ornaments, sock monkeys, scrapbooks, cross-stich, beaded jewellery, and more.

When I ask the question, what was her favourite thing to do, or what did she love to do the most? I can't come up with anything. I think that it is because, though she may not have consciously known it, she just loved giving to, caring for, and serving others. She lived a very selfless life in which most everything she did was for somebody else's benefit. Right to the end, she was ministering to people through her Facebook daily devotion blog. Yes, its purpose began as a tool for her own personal devotion, but it has ministered to hundreds of people, and publishing those blog posts into a book to share with even more people was one of her final requests.

The institution of marriage was also one that held high value in our home. We were taught that the commitment of marriage was never one to be taken lightly. Mom and Dad were thrilled to have 4 more unofficially adopted children acquired through the marriages of their children. Bob, Leah, Michelle and Lisa are as much children to them as their biological children.

There wasn't anything in the world that our mother would say mattered as much as her 12 grandchildren (Dalton & McKenna), (Brooke, Adam, Lauryn & Austin), (Jordan & Kaden), (Tanner, Brynn & Jesse) . . .and Sarah the grand-daughter she never met until just yesterday, in heaven. She was a fully involved Nana, who was the preschool caregiver for most of them, and the nurse called in for sick days. There were permanently fixed car seats in her van for more than a decade and rarely a time when they weren't occupied. Her love for them was enormous, and they, of all people, are missing out on the wealth of years that they deserved to have with her. I can still hear her telling them "love you bigger than the moon" and "more than all the stars in the sky."

Christ was always placed forefront in our home & heritage. We prayed together, memorized Bible verses, attended church (a lot), and we read the Christmas story before opening presents every year (and still do). We learned that only Jesus can offer unconditional love, a peace in our present lives, true forgiveness, and the hope of life eternal. As a result, she leaves the legacy of a family that is whole-heartedly committed to loving God and serving others.

We have a tradition that Mom started in our home several years ago. Our Thanksgiving dinner table was always adorned with a white tablecloth. Every year we took time to consider what we are thankful for and then wrote those things on the tablecloth. Our year has been riddled with many hard things, and we can look back at this year as an entire immediate family and see heartache and struggles endured at every angle. We were "hard pressed on every side but not crushed" (2. Cor. 4:8). But for all of these things, including the loss of our mom, we are thankful. God has given us a basket full of experiences from which we will now be able to minister to, and bestow love on others. Having a servant heart is a legacy that Mom modelled, and we are committed to carry on.

Our Thanksgiving will never be the same, but we will always be reminded of how blessed we were to have such an amazing woman in our life, and we give thanks to God for the gift of her life to us. We will miss her forever on Earth and will eagerly await being wrapped in her arms again when God calls *us* home.

CPSIA information can be obtained at www.ICGtesting.com
Printed in the USA
LVOW01s0229140315

430405LV00001B/1/P